Dedicated to

my late father Rev Bualkhama, who led me to Christ, and is my hero who shaped me to be what I am today. The completion of my doctoral work comes as a fulfilment of one of his dreams for me.

This is a fine, carefully argued book that restores Hosea to a central place in scholarship on the eighth-century prophets. Ronald Laldinsuah has shed new light on the relational aspects of justice and so shown that the theme of relational justice pervades all parts of the book. It contains a detailed study of the text of Hosea, but its central thesis about relational justice draws out the connections with the other prophets of his time. Justice is not absent from Hosea – he simply deals with justice in a fresh way.

The scholarship is thorough and contemporary, and Laldinsuah is careful not to over-argue his case. The result is a sustained, compelling argument about Hosea's passionate concern for relationships to be ordered and restored in a God-honouring way. It will shift the debate in Hosea studies by the force of the author's ideas.

Lindsay Wilson
Academic Dean, Senior Lecturer in Old Testament,
Ridley College, Melbourne, Australia

Ronald Laldinsuah has written a careful and thorough analysis, convincingly arguing that Hosea is a prophet of relational justice. He demonstrates that the key themes and structure of Hosea reflects the categories of responsibility, chastisement and restoration. He shows that Hosea addresses fundamental issues of justice in Israel before its fall to Assyria. In this, Laldinsuah corrects the commonly held view that Hosea is a prophet of love. This book is highly recommended for all students of Hosea, as well as those interested in eighth century Israel and the period of its destruction.

Paul A. Barker
Visiting Lecturer in Old Testament,
South Asia Institute of Advanced Christian Studies, India
Langham Preaching Coordinator, Asia

Responsibility, Chastisement and Restoration

Relational Justice in the Book of Hosea

Ronald Laldinsuah

MONOGRAPHS

© 2015 by Ronald Laldinsuah

Published 2015 by Langham Monographs
an imprint of Langham Creative Projects

Langham Partnership
PO Box 296, Carlisle, Cumbria CA3 9WZ, UK
www.langham.org

ISBNs:
978-1-78368-902-6 Print
978-1-78368-881-4 Mobi
978-1-78368-882-1 ePub
978-1-78368-880-7 PDF

Ronald Laldinsuah has asserted his right under the Copyright, Designs and Patents Act, 1988 to be identified as the Author of this work.

All rights reserved. No part of this publication may be reproduced, stored in a retrieval system or transmitted, in any form or by any means, electronic, mechanical, photocopying, recording or otherwise, without the prior written permission of the publisher or the Copyright Licensing Agency.

British Library Cataloguing in Publication Data

Laldinsuah, Ronald, author.
　Responsibility, chastisement, and restoration : relational
　justice in the Book of Hosea.
　1. Bible. Hosea--Criticism, interpretation, etc.
　2. Justice--Biblical teaching. 3. Reconciliation--
　Religious aspects--Christianity. 4. Justice. 5. Bible.
　Prophets--Criticism, interpretation, etc.
　I. Title
　224.6'06-dc23

ISBN-13: 9781783689026

Cover & Book Design: projectluz.com

Langham Partnership actively supports theological dialogue and a scholar's right to publish but does not necessarily endorse the views and opinions set forth, and works referenced within this publication or guarantee its technical and grammatical correctness. Langham Partnership does not accept any responsibility or liability to persons or property as a consequence of the reading, use or interpretation of its published content.

Contents

Abstract xi

Acknowledgements xiii

Abbreviations xv

Chapter One 1
Introductory Issues
    Statement of the Problem 1
    Elaboration of Problem 2
    The Scope and Nature of this Study 5
    Thesis Statement 9
    Procedure of this Study 9

Chapter Two 15
Research on the Book of Hosea
    Overview of Research 15
    Major Commentaries on Hosea 17
    Major Studies on Hosea 26
        Redactional, Synchronic, Final Form and Literary Analysis 26
        Feminist Criticism, Metaphorical Studies and Hosea as
            Part of the Twelve 30
        Summary Assessment 38
    Justice Studies in the Hebrew Bible 40
        Summary Assessment 49

Chapter Three 51
In Search of Principles: Toward a Relational Justice
    Justice in the Writings of Classical Philosophy 51
        Summary Assessment 57
    Contemporary Forms of Justice 57
        Commutative Justice 58
        Social Justice 58
        Distributive Justice 59
        Retributive Justice 61
        Restorative Justice 62
        Summary Assessment 64
    Integrating Different Types of Justice in Biblical Contexts 65
        Summary and Conclusion 71

Chapter Four 73
The Biblical Concept of Relational Justice
   Justice in Biblical Perspective 73
      צדק as Relational Faithfulness..74
      חסד as an extra Deed of one Person to another 80
      משפט/שפט as Sustaining Relationship......................................86
   Summary and Conclusion..94

Chapter Five 95
Hosea: The Socio-Political Background and His Message
   The Socio-political Background of Hosea......................................95
      Political Achievement: The Resurgence of Israel's Imperialism....98
      From Stability to Chaos: the Aftermath of Jeroboam II.............99
      Economic Situation: the Zenith of Prosperity 101
      Moral Sickness: The Impact of Political Expansion and
         Economic Growth...103
      Summary Assessment..106
   Hosea's Message 107
      Responsibility..107
      Chastisement 114
      Restoration 118
      Summary Assessment..120

Chapter Six 123
*Relational Justice: Responsibility, Chastisement and Restoration
in Hosea*
      A Structure of Six Cycles...124
      Excursus: Remarks on Metaphor Studies and
         Feminist Readings...126
   Hosea and His Family (1:2–3:5) 128
      Structural Analysis of Hosea 1–3 128
   Responsibility (1:2b–3; 2:4–7 [2–5]; 3:1–2) 132
      Hosea as Relationally Faithful Father/Husband.......................133
      Gomer as Relationally Faithless Mother/Wife 136
      Yahweh as Israel's Covenant Father/Husband..........................143
   Chastisements (1:4–9 [2–5]; 2:8–15 [6–13]; 3:3–4) 148
      Embryonic Names for Chastisement (1:4–9) 149
      Reaction from a Spurned Husband (2:8–15) 150
      Hosea's Stricture to his Wife (3:3–4).......................................152
   Restoration (2:1–3 [1:10–2:1]; 2:16–25 [14–23]; 3:5) 153
      Reversals of Ill-omened Names (2:1–3)...................................153

    Images of Faithful Relationship (2:16–25) 155
    Chastised but Restored (3:5) 159
  Summary Assessment 161

Chapter Seven 163
  Yahweh and His People (4:1–6:3)
  Structural Analysis of Hosea 4–11 163
  Responsibility (4:1–5:7) 167
    Yahweh's Controversy against the People (4:1–3) 168
    The Irresponsible Priests, People and Rulers (4:4–19) 180
  Chastisement (5:8–15) 186
    An Urgent Warning of War (5:8) 188
    The Culpability of Judah and Ephraim (5:10–11) 189
    Yahweh as Illness and Ferocious Lion (5:12–15a) 191
  Restoration (5:15b–6:3) 193
    Exhortation to Return to Yahweh (6:1–2) 195
    A Pathway to Return (6:3) 196
  Summary Assessment 198

Chapter Eight 201
  Yahweh and His People (6:4–11:11)
  Responsibility (6:4–8:14) 201
    The Fleeting Relational Virtues (6:4–6) 202
    Horrible Deeds Encompass the Entire House of Israel
      (6:7–7:2) 204
    Debauchery and Perfidy within the Royal Court (7:3–7) 207
    Ephraim is like an Unturned Cake, a Fooled Dove and
      a Faulty Bow (7:8–16) 210
    Israel is Rebellious, Rejecting what is Relationally Good
      (8:1–14) 213
  Chastisement (9:1–10:15) 218
    From Days of Celebrations to Days of Dispersion (9:1–9) 219
    From Grapes in the Desert to Barrenness (9:10–17) 224
    From Luxuriant Vines to Poisonous Weeds (10:1–8) 227
    A Trained Heifer who Ploughs for Wickedness (10:9–15) 230
  Restoration (11:1–11) 234
    Yahweh's Consistent Unilateral Love (11:1–4) 236
    Corrective Measures for Rebellious Ephraim (11:5–7) 239
    A Compassion that Thwarts Human Logic (11:8–11) 242
  Summary Assessment 246

Chapter Nine 249
 Yahweh and His People (12:1–14:10 [11:12–14:9])
  Structural Analysis of Hosea 12–14..249
  Responsibility (12:1–15 [11:12–12:14]) 250
   Ephraim's Socio-political Irresponsibility (12:1–3, 4–6)...........251
   Ephraim's Socio-economic/Ethical Violations (12:7, 8–10)......255
   Ephraim's Socio-religious Infidelity (12:12, 13–15) 258
  Chastisement (13:1–14:1 [13:1–16]) 260
   Ephraim's Chastisement for Illegitimate Cult (13:1–3) 262
   Ephraim's Chastisement for Moral Decay (13:4–10)................264
   Ephraim's Chastisement for Political Folly
    (13:10–14:1 [13:10–16]) 267
  Restoration (14:2–9 [14:1–8]) 272
   A Final Prophetic Call to Return (14:2–4)................................273
   Yahweh's Express Will to Restore the Nation (14:5) 275
   The Consequences of the Restored Relationship (14:6–9)........276
   The Epilogue of the Book: A Wisdom Poem (14:10) 278
  Summary Assessment..280

Chapter Ten 283
 Conclusions
  Relational Justice and Hosea 283
   Relational Justice in Hosea 1–3...289
   Relational Justice in Hosea 4:1–6:3...293
   Relational Justice in Hosea 6:4–11:11.......................................296
   Relational Justice in Hosea 12:1–14:1.......................................301
  Hosea's Social Critique..305

Bibliography... 313

Abstract

The purpose of this dissertation is to offer an in-depth analysis of Hosea's message on justice. It is argued that the traditional characterisation of the classical prophets (Amos, Micah and Isaiah) as prophets of justice as opposed to Hosea as a prophet of love is a misrepresentation.

In order to establish Hosea's sense of justice, this study analyses the biblical concept of justice and secular notions of justice. In so doing, it has observed that the ultimate concern of justice in both the secular sphere and the biblical understanding is justice in relationship. Its core aim is to perpetuate right and true relationships. Injustice, therefore, is the loss of right relationship. This relational justice assumes an inseparable relationship among humans, and between humans and God. It entails three constituting realities: responsibility, correction and restoration.

An exegetical study of the text reveals that these components form the three structural mechanisms of Hosea's prophetic words. His prophecy always begins with the call for responsibility on the part on Israel to maintain right relationship. This is always followed by the message of chastisement with a view to recreate the lost right relationship and is eventually culminated by the message of divine reconciliation even when Israel does not call for a right relationship. Based on this theoretical framework, this study argues for six cycles of responsibility-chastisement-restoration in the book.

This study confirms the general trend of Hosean studies that Hosea is a prophet of God's love. It also confirms that the two dominant themes are judgment and restoration. However, this thesis argues that Hosea is not merely a prophetic figure who addresses only religious problems. It observes that the bulk of his prophetic collection includes accusations of irresponsibility, dealing with social issues. Moreover, Hosea does not preach justice that retaliates or annihilates. His called-for and hoped-for message is for right and true relationships among humans, and between humans and God. Hosea's sense of justice goes deeper than that of other prophets. Thus, he is indeed a prophet of God's love as well as a prophet of justice *par excellence*.

Acknowledgements

All serious academic endeavours like this require a lot of support from families, friends and colleagues. A few lines of acknowledgement like this barely do justice to those who have assisted my research in various ways during my three and half years in Australia. Yet I am deeply indebted to the following people:

1. First and foremost, I should express my thanks to my family. Without my wife (Mary), my sons (Jed and Bruce) and my daughter (Rodi), my research would not have been accomplished. I thank them all for their blissful patience with my obsession and busyness for my work. Their constant support, love and patience have enabled me to do this dissertation. What a joy to have them in life!

2. I should like to express my sincere thanks to Rev Dr Lindsay Wilson, my supervisor, for his careful and thoughtful supervision. This thesis came into formation as a result of his warm encouragement, thought-provoking comments and meticulous supervision. Writing a research paper in one's fourth language is an enormous challenge, but his guidance and assistance in myriad ways have helped me persevere and complete this thesis.

3. My special thanks go to Langham Partnership Australia, the Executive Director Wendy Toulmin (and Dr Graham Toulmin for his personal care and fellowship) and all the Langham team members, for their enormous financial support for our family needs while in Australia.

4. My sincere thanks also go to my friend Rev Dr Paul Barker, who has been a true friend along the way. I acknowledge that he was

the one who initiated and facilitated the possibility of my studies in Australia.

5. I am grateful to Ridley Melbourne for awarding me the Raggatt Family Scholarship, covering my full fees at the college. I am deeply indebted to the Raggatts for their generous assistance.
6. A debt is also owed to many friends at Holy Trinity Anglican Church, Doncaster and the Lead Pastor, Rev Dr Andrew Reid. I am deeply grateful to them all for their pastoral support and financial assistance. A special thank also goes to Anne Willett for sparing her valuable time for reading my manuscripts and making necessary English corrections.
7. I must express my heartfelt gratitude to Ken and Jan Budin who first welcomed me to their home and hosted me and my family subsequently in their granny flat for almost two years. I delight to thank them for their warm welcome and generosity.
8. I thank my mom, my brothers and sisters and all my church members at Hlainthyar Community Church, Yangon, for their unceasing prayers for me and my family. I cannot even put into words how much I am thankful to them.
9. Thank you also to Melbourne Mizo Church, which I helped found, for the privilege of ministering at the church during our stay in Melbourne. Their prayers, friendship and financial assistance mean a lot to us.
10. Finally, I thank all my colleagues at MEGST (Myanmar Evangelical Graduate School of Theology), Yangon, for sending me here to Ridley Melbourne for my doctoral studies. Their prayers, expectation and encouragement have generated the power to do my research work.

Abbreviations

I. Miscellaneous Abbreviations and Symbols

BC	before Christ
cf.	compare
ed(s).	editor(s); edited by; edition
e.g.	for example
et al.	*et alii* (and others)
lit.	literally
LXX	Septuagint
MT	Masoretic Text
OT	Old Testament
repr.	reprint(ed)
rev. ed.	revised edition
trans.	translator(s); translated by
v(v).	verse(s)
vol.	volume

II. Publications

ÄAT	Ägypten und Altes Testament
AB	Anchor Bible
ABD	*Anchor Bible Dictionary.* Edited by D. N. Freedman. 6 vols. New York: Doubleday, 1992.
AcBib	Academia Biblica
AJBI	*Annual of the Japanese Biblical Institute*

ANET	*Ancient Near Eastern Texts Relating to the Old Testament.* Edited by James B. Pritchard. Translated by W. F. Albright et al. 2nd revised and enlarged edition. Princeton: Princeton University Press, 1955.
ANE	Ancient Near East
AnOr	Analecta orientalia
AOAT	Alter Orient und Altes Testament
AOTC	Abingdon Old Testament Commentary
ATD	Das Alte Testament Deutsch
AUS	American University Studies
BA	*Biblical Archaeologist*
BASOR	*Bulletin of the American Schools of Oriental Research*
BBB	Bonner biblische Beiträge
BCOT	Biblical Commentary on the Old Testament
BDB	Brown, F., S. R. Driver & C. A. Briggs, eds. *Hebrew English Lexicon of the Old Testament.* Peabody: Hendrickson Publishers, 1979.
Berit Olam	Berit Olam: Studies in Hebrew Narrative & Poetry
BETL	Bibliotheca Ephemeridum Theologicarum Lovaniensium
BHS	*Biblia Hebraica Stuttgartensia.* Edited by K. Elliger and W. Rudolph. Stuttgart: Deutsche Bibelstiftung, 1977.
BHT	Beiträge zur Historischen Theologie
Bib	*Biblica*
BibOr	Biblica et Orientalia
BKAT	Biblischer Kommentar, Altes Testament. Edited by M. Noth and H. W. Wolff
BLS	Bible and Literature Series
BR	*Biblical Research*
BSac	*Bibliotheca sacra*
BT	*The Bible Translator*
BTB	*Biblical Theology Bulletin*
BWANT	Beiträge zur Wissenschaft vom Alten (und Neuen) Testament
BZAW	Beihefte zur Zeitschrift für die alttestamentliche Wissenschaft
CAT	Commentaire de l'Ancien Testament
CBQ	*Catholic Biblical Quarterly*

CBR	*Currents in Biblical Research*
CC	*Cross Currents*
CJR	*The Contemporary Justice Review*
ConBOT	Coniectanea biblica: Old Testament Series
CTJ	*Calvin Theological Journal*
EDT	*Evangelical Dictionary of Theology*. Edited by Walter A. Elwell. 2nd ed. Grand Rapids: Baker Academic, 2001.
ER	*Ecumenical Review*
ERT	*Evangelical Review of Theology*
ETL	*Ephemerides Theologicae Lovanienses*
EvT	*Evangelische Theologie*
ExpTim	*Expository Times*
FAT	Forschungen zum Alten Testament
FB	Forschung zur Bibel
FOTL	Forms of the Old Testament Literature
FRLANT	Forschungen zur Religion und Literatur des Alten und Neuen Testaments
HBM	Hebrew Bible Monographs
HBS	Herders Biblische Studien
HBT	*Horizons in Biblical Theology*
HTR	*Harvard Theological Review*
HUCA	*Hebrew Union College Annual*
ICC	International Critical Commentary
IDB	*The Interpreters Dictionary of the Bible*. Edited by George Buttrick. 4 vols. New York: Abingdon Press, 1962
Int	*Interpretation*
JAOS	*Journal of the American Oriental Society*
JBL	*Journal of Biblical Literature*
JBQ	*Jewish Bible Quarterly*
JBPR	*Journal of Biblical and Pneumatological Research*
JBTh	*Jahrbücher für Deutsche Theologie*
JCS	*Journal of Cuneiform Studies*
JCTS	*Journal of the Colombo Theological Seminary*
JDTh	*Jahrbücher für deutsche Theologie*

JES	*Journal of Ecumenical Studies*
JETS	*Journal of the Evangelical Theological Society*
JNES	*Journal of Near Eastern Studies*
JNSL	*Journal of Northwest Semitic Languages*
JSCE	*Journal of the Society of Christian Ethics*
JSOT	*Journal for the Study of the Old Testament*
JSOTSup	Journal for the Study of the Old Testament, Supplement Series
KD	*Kerygma und Dogma*
LM	*Liturgical Ministry*
LXX	Septuagint
MBPS	Mellin Biblical Press Series
MQR	*Michigan Quarterly Review*
MT	Masoretic Text
NAC	New American Commentary
NCBC	The New Century Bible Commentary
NIBC	New International Biblical Commentary
NIDNTT	*The New International Dictionary of New Testament Theology.* Edited by Colin Brown et. al. 4 vols. Nashville: Abingdon Press, 1978.
NICOT	New International Commentary on the Old Testament
NIDOTTE	*New International Dictionary of Old Testament Theology & Exegesis.* Edited by Willem A. VanGemeren. 5 vols. Grand Rapids, 1997
NSBT	New Studies in Biblical Theology
OBO	Orbis Biblicus et orientalis
OTE	*Old Testament Essays*
OTG	Old Testament Guides
OTL	Old Testament Library
OTM	Oxford Theological Monographs
OtSt	Oudtestamentische Studiën
PBM	Paternoster Biblical Monographs
PPer	*Pittsburgh Perspectives*
RB	*Revue biblique*
RevExp	*Review and Expositor*

SBL	Society of Biblical Literature
SBLAB	SBL Academica Biblica
SBLDS	SBL Dissertation Series
SBLSymS	SBL Symposium Series
SBS	Stuttgarter Bibelstudien
SCJ	*Stone-Campbell Journal*
SEÅ	*Svensk exegetisk årsbok*
SJLA	Studies in Judaism in Late Antiquity
SJOT	*Scandinavian Journal of the Old Testament*
SNTSMS	Society for New Testament Studies Monograph Series
SSN	Studia Semitica Neerlandica
SwJT	*Southwestern Journal of Theology*
TB	*Tyndale Bulletin*
TBC	Torch Bible Commentaries
TDNT	*Theological Dictionary of the New Testament*. Edited by G. Kittel and G. Friedrich. Translated by G. W. Bromiley. 10 vols. Grand Rapids, 1964–1976.
TDOT	*Theological Dictionary of the Old Testament*. Edited by G. J. Botterweck – H. Ringgren. Translated by J. T. Willis, G. W. Bromiley and D. E. Green. So far 15 vols. Grand Rapids, 1972ff.
THAT	*Theologisches Handwörterbuch zum Alten Testament*. Edited by E. Jenni and C. Westermann. 2 vols. München, 1971–1976.
TLOT	*Theological Lexicon of the Old Testament*. Edited by E. Jenni and C. Westermann. Translated by M. E. Biddle. 3 vols. Peabody, 1997.
TOTC	Tyndale Old Testament Commentaries
TQ	*Theologische Quartalschrift*
TR	Theology and Religion
TTS	Thelogische Texte und Studien
TZ	*Theologische Zeitschrift*
VT	*Vetus Testamentum*
VTSup	Supplements to Vetus Testamentum
WBC	Word Biblical Commentary

WMANT	Wissenschaftliche Monographien zum Alten und Neuen Testament
WW	*Word & World*
ZAW	*Zeitschrift für die alttestamentliche Wissenschaft*
ZTK	*Zeitschrift für Theologie und Kirche*

CHAPTER ONE

Introductory Issues

Statement of the Problem

Despite a good number of studies on the eighth-century BC prophets and their quests for justice, there is no study which has thoroughly examined Hosea's teaching on justice. Such a lack apparently arises from the fact that many have characterised Amos, Micah and Isaiah as prophets of justice as opposed to Hosea as a prophet of love.[1] Even those who consider that Hosea contains matters of justice have explored it only in passing. In other words, existing studies on Hosea have largely failed to examine adequately the content of Hosea's social critique of the eighth-century Israel. The goal of this study is to address this deficiency in Hosea studies and to offer an in-depth analysis of Hosea's message on justice.

---

1. For example, Joseph Blenkinsopp, *A History of Prophecy in Israel* (rev. and enl. ed.; 1983; repr., Louisville: John Knox Press, 1996), 90, argues that unlike Amos, Hosea has relatively little to say about social justice and the civil rights of the disadvantaged. He appears to be correct in stating that "if justice and righteousness (משפט, צדקה) are key words for Amos (5:24), Hosea prefers to speak of fidelity (חסד) and the knowledge of God (דעת אלהים)." However, Blenkinsopp fails to explain the meaning of the latter two concepts in Hosea's own terms.

Elaboration of Problem

Kelle's wide-ranging survey of Hosea studies has not found any single piece of work devoted to an in-depth assessment of justice.[2] Moreover, the customary representation of the eighth-century prophets as prophets of justice as opposed to Hosea as a prophet of love has continued to appear until recent times.[3] Though there are major scholarly discussions on justice in Amos, Isaiah and Micah, scholars have neglected to explore Hosea. Those who do mention it often only do so in passing. In other words, even if scholars do not dismiss the issue of justice in the book, it takes only a secondary position to other concerns and themes. This indicates that a substantial study of justice in the book of Hosea is needed.

Second, there have been differing opinions regarding the interpretation of Hosea's marriage metaphor. Some major commentaries view the book's primary concern as Israel's apostasy to the Baal cult, while other scholars challenge this view and deny the very existence of the fertility rites in ancient Israel. For instance, Wolff considers that the aim of Hosea's marriage metaphor is to "expose the guilt of contemporary Israel, who had succumbed to the Canaanite fertility rites."[4] Yet Keefe does not see any evidence of syncretistic fertility cult based on any firm textual or extra-textual support.[5] Abma dismisses the sacred sexual ritual by establishing that the evidence for the existence of such sexual rituals is scanty, even in Mesopotamia, Sumeria and Ugarit.[6] Similarly, Yee categorically maintains that Hosea's metaphor is to demonstrate the actual historical and economic

---

2. Brad E. Kelle, "Hosea 1–3 in Twentieth-Century Scholarship," *CBR* 7 (2009): 179–216; "Hosea 4–14 in Twentieth-Century Scholarship," *CBR* 8 (2010): 314–375.
3. One title which depicts this trend is Gert Kwakkel, "Hosea, Prophet of God's Love," in *The Lion Has Roared: Theological Themes in the Prophetic Literature of the Old Testament*, eds. H. G. L. Peels and S. D. Snyman (Eugene: Pickwick Publications, 2012), 27–39.
4. Hans W. Wolff, *Hosea*, trans. Gary Stansell (Hermenia; BKAT 14.1: Neukirchner-Verlag: Neukirchen-Vluyn, 1965; repr., Philadelphia: Fortress, 1974), xxii.
5. Alice A. Keefe, *Woman's Body and the Social Body in Hosea* (JSOTSup 10; Sheffield: Sheffield Academic Press, 2001), 11.
6. Richtsje Abma, *Bonds of Love: Methodic Studies of Prophetic Texts with Marriage Imagery, Isaiah 50:1–3 and 54:1–10, Hosea 1–3, Jeremiah 2–3* (SSN 40; Assen: Van Gorcum, 1999), 14–15.

crisis.⁷ Conceivably, both these seemingly contradictory opinions have merits in helping us to understand the overall message of Hosea. At the same time, they also indicate that no attempt has been made to accommodate these differing views. Our argument is that this tension can be resolved through viewing it from the perspective of relational justice. Hosea's metaphorical indictments are aimed at the entire corporate life of Israel, calling for right relationships, whether in the context of religious or social spheres.

The importance of relationships in the book of Hosea has been noticed by many scholars and yet surprisingly little work has been done on using this vital thread as a means of tracing the message behind Hosea's metaphors and other discourses. For example, Wolff asserts that Israel's sin above all else is the termination of her personal relationship with her God.⁸ Eichrodt also recognises that the mutuality of the process of knowing entails involvement in a relationship of love and trust.⁹ Similarly, McComiskey identifies the positive terms intentionally employed by Hosea to show the lack of those qualities in social relationships,¹⁰ and Garrett notes that 'knowing God' implies the deepest relationship with Yahweh.¹¹ Although these scholars recognise the significance of relationship between Yahweh and Israel, they fail to stress the prominent social relationship between people, especially in the context of Ancient Near Eastern corporate responsibility. Hosea points to the total brokenness of relationships affecting all walks of life, which includes both cultic and socio-economic aspects. Accordingly, we need a substantial study that will elucidate the biblical concepts in Hosea's metaphorical critique of the eighth-century Israelites.

There is also a need to address the restorative function of justice in the book. While there has been investigation into the themes of judgment

---

7. Gale A. Yee, *Poor Banished Children of Eve: Woman as Evil in the Hebrew Bible* (Minneapolis: Fortress Press, 2003), 137.

8. Wolff, *Hosea*, xviii.

9. Walther Eichrodt, '"The Holy One in Your Midst": The Theology of Hosea,' *Int* 15 (1961): 259–273 (264).

10. Thomas E. McComiskey, "Hosea," in *The Minor Prophets: An Exegetical and Expository Commentary, Vol. 1*, ed. Thomas E. McComiskey (Grand Rapids: Baker Academic, 1992), 93.

11. Duane A. Garrett, *Hosea, Joel* (NAC 19A; Nashville: Broadman and Holman, 1997), 39.

and restoration within Hosea, there is still a lack of attention to the link between Yahweh's destructive judgment and his eventual aim of restoration. My preliminary contention in this matter is that judgment in Hosea is far from being annihilation. Rather, it is a part of a process where the goal is restoration. Most scholars recognise the presence of Yahweh's punitive justice in the book. For Wolff, Yahweh's decision to bring judgment upon Israel results from her apostasy to the Baal cult.[12] Mays notes that the judgment which Yahweh brings, namely, the loss of state and cult, are a means to win the people back.[13] Nevertheless, Mays fails to explore the relational aspect of judgment in his dealing with Hosea's message as a whole. Eichrodt also overlooks judgment as a part of God's relational aspect with his people.[14] Sweeney pays good attention to the thematic condemnation and restoration of Israel/Judah. However, owing to his attempt to see a programmatic theme of central issues addressed throughout the Book of the Twelve, he too, fails to stress the restorative aspect of judgment.[15] It is the purpose of this study to ascertain the motives behind Yahweh's judgment of Israel and to see whether the intention of judgment is to pave the way to restoration. If so, the theme of judgment in Hosea is positive and thus must be understood as "chastisement." This issue deserves fresh investigation.

Finally, God's relational and restorative justice impinges upon one of the main themes in Hosea studies, that is, covenant. Various Hosean scholars have stressed this central theme in the book. For instance, Eichrodt rightly emphasises that the breaking of the covenant of love and trust can result in immense harm.[16] The question at stake for Brueggemann is covenant keeping.[17] Similarly, Andersen and Freedman note that Israel failed to keep her part of covenant commitment by failing the demands of the

---

12. Wolff, *Hosea*, xxii.
13. James L. Mays, *Hosea* (OTL; Philadelphia: Westminster, 1969), 8.
14. Eichrodt, "The Holy One in Your Midst," 271–272.
15. Marvin A. Sweeney, *The Twelve Prophets: Hosea, Joel, Amos, Obadiah, Jonah* (vol. 2; Berit Olam; Collegeville: Liturgical Press, 2000), 3.
16. Eichrodt, "The Holy One in Your Midst," 265.
17. Walter Brueggemann, *Tradition in Crisis: A Study in Hosea* (Richmond: John Knox, 1966), 121.

righteousness essential to being the people of God.[18] Stuart also recognises that the prophet's task is to reinforce Yahweh's intended covenant terms.[19] Yet scholars have by and large interpreted covenant simply in terms of Israel's apostasy to a fertility cult. This shows that there is still a lack of specific identification of those covenant terms. For example, why are the demands of righteousness essential to being the people of God? What does covenant keeping specifically mean? These questions are worthy of examination and a proper specification of covenant terms in Hosea may crystallise the prophet's social critique as well as fill out his understanding of justice.

The Scope and Nature of this Study

Although the scope of this study may seem to be ambitious, its purpose is limited. Because the issue of justice is a clear and major focus of other eighth-century prophets and yet seemingly absent from Hosea, it will be necessary to examine both the similarity between Hosea's social critiques and those of the other eighth-century prophets as well as their differences. It is possible that a lack of clarity here may have blinded scholars from seeing the justice aspect in this book. A careful examination of this issue will not only provide a correct understanding of Hosea's sense of justice, but will also serve as an interpretive approach to the book as a whole.

In essence, our argument is that biblical scholarship has lost sight of Hosea's sense of justice because of its predisposition to read the book in contrast to other eighth-century prophets. For example, without making any effort to discover what can be said about justice in Hosea, scholars simply have treated the book as a special case by omitting it from scrutiny.[20] In order to avoid the same mistake, therefore, we should explore more of other options available in an effort to discover Hosea's true sense of justice.

---

18. Francis I. Andersen and David N. Freedman, *Hosea: A New Translation with Introduction and Commentary* (AB 24; New York: Doubleday, 1980), 47.
19. Douglas Stuart, *Hosea–Jonah* (WBC 31; Nashville: Thomas Nelson, 1989), 7.
20. A good example of this tendency could be seen in Mays' article. See James L. Mays, "Justice: Perspectives from the Prophetic Tradition," *Int* 37 (1983): 5–17.

In these undertakings we will concentrate on a relational notion of justice with its attendant components of responsibility, chastisement and restoration to help us diagnose the prophet's elusive social critique.

Because of the novelty of the concept of relational justice, it will be helpful to offer some clarification about terminology. By definition, *relational justice* rises and falls in and through interpersonal relationships.[21] It rises, as Raines puts it, "from the idea that human life is always life-lived-with-others and, therefore, justice is necessarily a matter of justice in relationship."[22] In order words, humans exist as selves in relationship to others[23] and justice has to do with relationship, and this relationship "brings responsibility and with responsibility comes accountability and obligation."[24] Justice, in this sense, is associated with responsive actions in building, maintaining and restoring right relationships. It also assumes mutual trust and loyalty as an original position in relationships.[25] In contrast, it regards injustice as a breakdown in relationships.[26]

What then is responsibility? As a part of relational justice, responsibility has to do with relationships. The etymology goes back to the Latin

---

21. There is a relational justice movement in the UK, largely known as the Jubilee Policy Group. Their main concern is to promote the relational justice model as an alternative to modern criminal justice. Though we share our starting point to a certain extent, our objectives are different.

22. John C. Raines, "Toward a Relational Theory of Justice," *CC* 39 (1989): 131.

23. Niebuhr rightly puts attention on a social self and social solidarity, not to an isolated individual. He suggests that this social self "not only knows itself in relation to other selves but exists as self only in that relation" – responsibly or irresponsibly. H. Richard Niebuhr, *The Responsible Self: An Essay in Christian Moral Philosophy* (1963; repr., Louisville: Westminster John Knox Press, 1999), 71.

24. G. A. Cole, "Responsibility," *New Dictionary of Christian Ethics and Pastoral Theology*, eds. David J. Akinson and David H. Field (Leicester: Inter-Varsity Press, 1995), 734–736 (736).

25. According to Niebuhr, the idea of responsibility includes four elements: response, interaction, accountability and social solidarity. Niebuhr, *The Responsible Self*, 61–65. Along similar lines, Raines identifies three constituting elements of relational justice, namely, care for appropriate response, trust and loyalty and reciprocity. Raines, "A Relational Theory of Justice," 137.

26. This is true for "even in those cases where the offender does not personally know the victim, a relationship can be said to exist by virtue of being the citizens together, bound together by rules governing social behaviour." Michael Schluter, "What is Relational Justice," in *Relational Justice: Repairing the Breach,* eds. Jonathan Burnside and Nicola Baker; 1994; repr. (Winchester: Waterside Press, 2004), 24.

respondeo, "I answer."²⁷ It is a state of being where a person is answerable or accountable for an action. To be in a position of answerability or accountability, as Lucas rightly suggests, people must be able to answer the question, "Why did you do it?" and in answering such a question, they must give an account of their action.²⁸ Thus, the central idea of responsibility is that the person is obliged to give an answer. The underlying notions of responsibility are accountability and obligation. Cole states this point well, "Accountability looks back to some deed done or attitude held. Obligation looks forward to moral demands that need to be met in relationships."²⁹ As individual selves exist in relationship to others, so is responsibility to be established in the sphere of relationship to others, namely, responsibility to God, responsibility to neighbours and responsibility to oneself.³⁰ Conceivably, all spheres of relationships in the context of Hosea are by-products of Israel's responsibility to Yahweh.

Strictly speaking, the historical background for the idea of relational justice lies in the biblical concept of covenant, used in its relational sense. This biblical notion understands "all life and existence" in terms of social relationship and mutuality and brings responsibilities and rights.³¹ Not surprisingly, the book of Hosea does not prescribe a philosophical description of what the structure of relationships is all about. Rather, it simply pays attention to the fundamental idea of covenant in which Israel stands in relationship to Yahweh, which requires responsibility in terms of accountability and obligation. This relational context is presented in marriage and family images to reflect the deepest relationships of all. Ephraim is now in a position to answer God's question, "Why did you do it?" Israel is answerable for "what and why" in relation to her deeds. In the same way, Israel is responsible to keep the moral demands of covenant that need to

---

27. J. R. Lucas, *Responsibility* (1993; repr., Oxford: Clarendon Press, 1995), 5. (The term connotes that to be responsible is to be answerable).
28. Lucas, *Responsibility*, 5. This assumes the question is correctly addressed to the right person, accurate action and appropriate description of action.
29. Cole, "Responsibility," 734–735.
30. Ibid., 735.
31. R. Z. Werblowsky, "Judaism, or the Religion of Israel," in *The Concise Encyclopaedia of Living Faiths*, ed. R. C. Zaehner (London: Hutchinson, 1971), 10.

be met in relationships. This relational quest for justice appears to be a key element in reading the book of Hosea.

Further, there is another aspect of responsibility, which goes beyond teleological and deontological questions, for example, "What is my goal or end?" (i.e. responsibilities) or, "What is my ultimate law?" (i.e. rights).[32] This aspect is a responsive action that fits into a total reciprocal interaction, attempting to answer, "What is the fitting response to what is happening?"[33] When Hosea counsels his people, he not only reminds them of the terms and conditions of covenant relationship, but also calls them to understand the present situation through which the covenant God is responding so that they are to know how to interpret the covenant relationship correctly. For instance, "knowing Yahweh" according to Hosea (2:20; 4:1, 6; 5:3, 4; 6:3, 6; 8:2; 13:4) also means to say to the people of Israel that they need to make a fitting reply in order to keep the relationship going.

In essence, *righteousness* (צדק)[34] and *justice* (משפט), *devoted fidelity* (חסד) and *mercy* (רחם) (2:21 [19]) are to characterise this relationship. The covenant people are to maintain חסד and משפט and always put their hope in Yahweh (12:6 [7]). They are to sow the seed of צדק and reap חסד. They are to know how to interpret the signs of the times and seek Yahweh until he sends צדק on them like the rain (10:12). Instead, what dictated the social relations in Israel deplorably included cursing, lying, murdering, stealing, adultery and bloodshed (4:2). Their irresponsible deeds would not allow them to return to Yahweh (5:4). *Faithfulness* (אמת), חסד and *knowledge* of God (דעת אלהים) vanished from the land without trace (4:1). Yahweh would not tolerate the dearth of these core qualities, which are essential to make a just coexistence possible. As a result, the prophet insists that Yahweh will surely punish the people (1:4; 2:13 [15]; 4:9, 14; 8:13; 9:9; 12:2 [3]) and chastise them (5:2; 7:12; 10:10).

The book of Hosea also assumes that violations of the covenantal relationship bring punishment. As God is righteous, he is incapable of conforming to the sin and injustice of his people. Yet he is God and not

---

32. Niebuhr, *The Responsible Self*, 60–65.
33. Ibid., 67.
34. All translations from Hebrew to English are my own throughout the book.

human. Thus, he will not execute justice in rage (11:9). He will not trade off his covenant relationship for his anger, nor execute punishment for the sake of punishment. Instead, his chastisement is meant to win his people back to faithfulness (3:5; 6:1–2; 12:6 [7]; 14:1–2 [2–3], 7 [8]). The intention is to reunite, harmonise and restore relationship. He wants to to convince his people to accept relational responsibility and to build new and just relationships with him.

Thesis Statement

The working hypothesis of this thesis is therefore that like the other eighth-century prophets, Hosea criticises the various cultic-religious and socio-economic dynamics that breach the norms of justice. Moreover, Hosea's somewhat unique perspective is that justice fundamentally concerns justice in relationship which we have labelled "Relational Justice." Our proposal is that the organizing structure of such relational justice consists of three components: responsibility, chastisement and restoration. Our hope is that this notion of justice and its organizing structure will not only give us a framework by which to analyse the prophet's social critique but will also provide us with a hermeneutical perspective by which to read the book as a whole.

Procedure of this Study

This study embraces a comprehensive view of the exegetical task involving many possible methods.[35] Broadly speaking, the approach here falls on the side of synchronic analysis.

---

35. Several scholars have been promoting this approach in recent times. For example,. Charles Conroy, "Reflections on the Exegetical Task: Apropos of Recent Studies on 2 Kings 22–23," in *Pentateuchal and Deuteronomistic studies,* eds. C. Brekelmans and J. Lust; BETL 94 (Leuven: Leuven University Press, 1990), 255–268. See Johannes C. de Moor, ed., *Synchronic or Diachronic?: A Debate on Method in Old Testament Exegesis* (OtSt 34; Leiden: E. J. Brill, 1995) in which several articles advocate this new trend.

Synchronic reading entails the examination of the final-form of the text available to us in written form as meaningful, and to interpret it accordingly. Such synchronic reading of biblical texts is popularised by Muilenburg (rhetorical criticism) and Childs (canonical approach), and has attracted increasing attention in recent years.[36] It analyses the text in a given point in time, and generally it does not attempt to reconstruct the historical process by which the text reached its present state. However, a final-form reading is not necessarily an anti-historical approach.[37] As Conroy argues, "its study of the text's syntax and semantics takes account of the historical dimension, all the more so if one includes the aspect of pragmatics [the communicative function of the text] in final-form study."[38] Within this exegetical constraint, this study will undertake a fresh engagement with the final form of the text of Hosea by paying attention to the semantic aspect of key terms and phrases. While the primary intention is to describe and interpret the text as it stands, it will also deal with historical questions whenever deemed necessary to enhance understanding of the possible meaning of the text.

This study treats the book of Hosea as a skilfully crafted literary composition, which exquisitely communicates the prophet's message of relational justice. Accordingly, the conventions associated with general literary analysis will be employed. This literary analysis, often categorised as "new criticism" or "rhetorical criticism," primarily concerns the structure, themes and character of the texts.[39] It studies the texts as unified wholes and deals with their final form rather than with their prehistory.[40] It focuses on the internal articulation and artistic features of any given literary work.

---

36. James Muilenburg, "Form Criticism and Beyond," *JBL* 88 (1969): 1–18; Brevard S. Childs, *Biblical Theology in Crisis* (Fortress Press: Philadelphia, 1970); *idem, Introduction to the Old Testament as Scripture* (Fortress Press: Philadelphia, 1979).
37. For example, James Barr, "The Synchronic, the Diachronic and the Historical: A Triangular Relationship," in *Synchronic or Diachronic?*, ed. Johannes C. de Moor; OtSt 34; (Leiden: E. J. Brill, 1995), 1–14 (2).
38. Conroy, "Reflections on the Exegetical Task," 263.
39. For a comprehensive discussion on method in biblical study, see John Barton, *Reading the Old Testament: Method in Biblical Study* (Louisville: Westminster John Knox Press, 1984).
40. For more detailed treatment of the subject, see David Clines, "Beyond Synchronic/Diachronic," in *Synchronic or Diachronic?*, ed. Johannes C. de Moor; OtSt 34 (Leiden: E. J. Brill, 1995), 64.

As such, the overall approach can also be termed a "close reading," which is just another sub-category of the broader field of literary analysis. It follows the order of the text, paying close attention to individual words, syntax and the order of sentences, and discusses any feature that arises both from prose and poetry.[41]

By adopting a threefold division of the book (chs. 1–3, 4–11 and 12–14), this study will attempt to read six cycles of responsibility-chastisement-restoration under the rubric of relational justice. More attention will be paid to the first component (responsibility) as it reflects more of Hosea's message on justice. The literary structure will demonstrate that the prophetic oracles of Hosea are purposefully structured to convey his important message of relational justice.

This study is divided into two main parts. Following the introduction, Part I consists of four chapters that deal with the theoretical analysis of relational justice from both secular and biblical domains. Part II, which comprises four chapters, analyses the text of Hosea by means of the proposed outline of the book. The study concludes with a discussion on the significance of this study and will touch on suggestions for further study.

Following the introductory chapter, chapter 2 commences with a literature review of major commentaries and more recent studies on Hosea with a view to exploring the depth of scholarly engagement regarding Hosea's message on justice. This is followed by a survey of justice studies in the Hebrew Bible to determine key biblical concepts of justice. In order to demonstrate that a key aspect of justice is relational, chapter 3 extends our literature review to the writings of classical philosophy.

Chapter 4 attempts to investigate the biblical perspective on justice by analysing three keys terms: צדקה, חסד and משפט; and interacting with various key scholars who have studied those important concepts. The primary aim once again is to argue that biblical understanding of justice is primarily relational.

Chapter 5 is a preliminary application to Hosea of the proposed reading of relational justice with the themes of responsibility, chastisement and

---

41. For example, Lyle M. Eslinger, *Kingship of God in Crisis: A Close Reading of 1 Samuel 1–12* (BLS 10; Sheffield: Almond JSOT Press, 1985), 63.

restoration. The second section of the chapter provides a brief social analysis of the eighth-century BC Israelites with a view to relating Hosea's prophetic words to the social, political and religious scenes of his time.

The following four chapters in Part II share similar processes of analysis. Each chapter is occupied with the close reading of the text of Hosea. They begin with a brief consideration of the demarcation and internal subdivisions of the text. Each chapter is divided up on the basis of the proposed organizing components: responsibility, chastisement and restoration. Within this framework, chapter 6 attempts to read the three cyclical proclamations of Hosea in the first three chapters of the book. It will be argued that by using marriage imagery, the prophet depicts what is required (relational justness) and what is denounced (relational unjustness). This basic tenet continues throughout the chapters that follow. Chapter 7 examines the prophetic oracles in 4:1–6:3 based on the suggested three strands and offers a (fourth) cyclical presentation. It argues that Hosea makes his message of justice more explicit in this section compared to previous chapters in the book. Based on our proposed three trends, chapters 8 and 9 will attempt to read two cyclical presentations in 6:4–11:11 and 12:1–14:9 respectively.

Informed by this examination, chapter 10 will provide some concluding remarks with respect to Hosea's message of *relational justice that demands, corrects and restores*. If this study contributes in some way to a more profound understanding of a significant prophetic book like that of Hosea, its purpose will have been met.

PART I

CHAPTER TWO

Research on the Book of Hosea

Overview of Research

Van der Woude has earlier commented on the slow growth of Hosea studies: "Hosea research of the sixties had opened many doors, but the last decade saw few people entering the rooms. It is high time for a new era of Hosea studies."[1] A good number of critical commentaries on Hosea were published in the sixties.[2] These works typically focused on the concerns of redaction, form and tradition criticism. The seventies did not see a good harvest in Hosea studies. However, the eighties saw several contributions to the understanding of the prophet and his book.[3] The development in the nineties represented the expansion of scholarship on Hosea beyond

---

1 A. S. Van der Woude, "Three Classical Prophets: Amos, Hosea and Micah," in *Israel's Prophetic Tradition: Essays in Honour of Peter Ackroyd*, eds. Richard Coggins et al. (London: Cambridge University Press, 1982), 43.

2. Wolff, *Hosea*; Edmond Jacob, Carl-A. Keller and Samuel Amsler, *Osée, Joël, Abdias, Jonas, Amos* (CAT 11a; Neuchatel: Delachaux & Niestlé, 1965); Wilhelm Rudolph, *Hosea* (Guterslöh, [West Germany] Gerd Mohn, 1966); Mays, *Hosea*; James M. Ward, *Hosea: A Theological Commentary* (New York: Harper and Row, 1966); Brueggemann, *Tradition for Crisis*.

3. Andersen and Freedman, *Hosea*; Derek Kidner, *Love to the Loveless: The Message of Hosea* (BST; Downers Grove: Inter-Varsity, 1981); Jörg Jeremias, *Der Prophet Hosea* (ATD 24/1; Gottingen: Vandenhoeck & Ruprecht, 1983); Grace I. Emmerson, *Hosea: An Israelite Prophet in Judean Perspective* (JSOT; Sheffield: JSOT Press, 1984); James Limburg, *Hosea–Micah* (Atlanta: Westminster John Knox Press, 1988); David A. Hubbard, *Hosea: An Introduction and Commentary* (TOTC 22a; Downers Grove: IVP Inter-Varsity Press, 1989).

redaction, form and tradition approaches.[4] From the eighties, scholarly discussions on gender-related issues came to the fore.[5] Since the nineties, Hosea studies have focused attention on broader methodological perspectives such as feminist approaches, metaphor studies, literary theories and socio-historical readings.[6] The latest trend includes canonical and ethical perspectives.[7]

An exhaustive discussion of all the commentaries is beyond the limits of this study. My main concern in the following reviews is to explore the depth of scholars' engagement with Hosea and the lack of clarity in their dealing with the issue of justice. In doing this, I will divide my survey into three main stages, namely, major commentaries, recent studies on Hosea, and justice studies in the Hebrew Bible.

---

4. Graham I. Davies, *Hosea* (NCBC; Grand Rapids: Eerdmans, 1992); Allen R. Guenther, *Hosea, Amos* (BCBC; Scottsdale: Herald Press, 1998); McComiskey, "Hosea," in *The Minor Prophets*, 1–237; Stuart, *Hosea –Jonah*; Francis Landy, *Hosea* (Readings; Sheffield: Sheffield Academic Press, 1995); Gale A. Yee, "The Book of Hosea," 197–297, in *Introduction to Apocalyptic Literature, Daniel, the Twelve Prophets* (vol. VII of *The New Interpreter's Bible*; ed. Leander E. Keck; Nashville: Abingdon, 1996); Garrett, *Hosea, Joel*, 1997.

5. Renita J. Weems, "Gomer: Victim of Violence or Victim of Metaphor?," *Semeia* 47 (1989): 87–104; Naomi Graetz, "God is to Israel as Husband is to Wife: The Metaphoric Battering of Hosea's Wife," in *A Feminist Companion to the Latter Prophets,* ed. Athalya Brenner (Sheffield: Sheffield Academic Press, 1995): 126–45; Yvonne Sherwood, *The Prostitute and the Prophets: Hosea's Marriage in Literary – Theoretical Perspective* (JSOTSup 212; Sheffield: Sheffield Academic Press, 1996); Keefe, *Woman's Body and the Social Body in Hosea*; W. Boshoff, "The Female Imagery in the Book of Hosea: Considering the Marriage Metaphor in Hosea 1–2 by Listening to Female Voices," *OTE* 15 (2002): 23–41; Gerlinde Baumann, *Love and Violence: Marriage as a Metaphor for the Relationship between Yahweh and Israel in the Prophetic Books,* trans. Linda M. Maloney (Stuttgart: Verlag Katholisches, 2000; repr., Collegeville: Liturgical Press, 2003); Yee, *Poor Banished Children of Eve*.

6. Yee, "The Book of Hosea," 197–297; A. A. Macintosh, *Critical and Exegetical Commentary on Hosea* (ICC; Edinburgh: T & T Clark, 1997); Brad E. Kelle, *Hosea 2: Metaphor and Rhetoric in Historical Perspective* (SBLAcBib 20; Atlanta: Society of Biblical Literature, 2005); Seong-Hyuk Hong, *The Metaphor of Illness and Healing in Hosea and Its Significance in the Socio-Economic Context of Eighth-Century Israel and Judah* (SBL 95; New York: Peter Lang, 2006).

7. Paul R. House, *The Unity of the Twelve* (JSOTSup, 97; BLS 27; Sheffield: Almond Press, 1990); Sweeney, *The Twelve Prophets*; Ehud Ben Zvi, *Hosea* (FOTL 31A1; Grand Rapids: Eerdmans, 2005); Daniel J. Simundson, *Hosea, Joel, Amos, Obadiah, Jonah, Micah* (AOTC; Nashville: Abingdon, 2005); J. Andrew Dearman, *The Book of Hosea* (NICOT; Grand Rapids: Eerdmans, 2010).

Major Commentaries on Hosea

A survey of major commentaries on Hosea from the second half of the twentieth century produced several points of consensus concerning the book as a whole. By and large, this trend has concerned the interpretation of the prophetic figure, the redactional issue and the biographical reconstructions of the prophet and his adulterous wife Gomer.[8]

The work that significantly has influenced Hosea scholarship in the second half of the twentieth century has been Wolff's commentary, followed by the works of Mays, Rudolph and Brueggemann. These major works have represented a traditional approach that pays attention to redaction, form, tradition criticism, as well as theological interpretations.

Wolff's commentary is a redactional and form-critical analysis. He divides the book into three transmission complexes: 1–3, 4–11, and 12–14. The primary intention of Hosea's marriage metaphor, according to Wolff, is to "expose the guilt of contemporary Israel, who has succumbed to the Canaanite fertility rites."[9] This is to say that Yahweh's decision to bring judgment on Israel comes as a result of her apostasy to the Baal cult. In this regard, Wolff recognises the punitive aspect of Yahweh's justice in the book. Wolff also sees the influence of wisdom upon Hosea's language and numerous metaphors. He notes that Hosea brings his indictment primarily against the priests and political leaders; the priests for failing to impart the knowledge of God to the people to maintain justice, and the political leaders for running the national affairs without ever seeking the will of Yahweh. Importantly, Israel's guilt above all has been the dissolution of her personal relationship with her God.[10] Despite having said this, Wolff does not explore the basis and structure of this relationship.

Mays' commentary is a solid exposition and a well-balanced presentation. He notes that Hosea's indictment was aimed at the entire corporate life of the people. Hosea primarily addresses two kinds of public and

---

8. See Kelle, "Hosea 4–14," 317.
9. Wolff, *Hosea,* xxii.
10. Ibid., xxvii. Though Wolff's work on the book of Hosea sometimes includes a great number of conjectures, his analysis has more to offer for justice issues than many other works.

concrete sins, the fertility cult and the monarchy with its politics.[11] Mays, however, does not attempt to uncover the basis of Hosea's accusation in relation to both Israel's fertility cult and their foreign alliances. Mays also construes that the sole aim of Hosea's programme was the return of Israel to Yahweh. The judgment that Yahweh brought on was real and awful but the loss of state and cult were meant to win the people back.[12]

Significantly, Mays is aware of Hosea's use of normative terms, which described Yahweh's demand from Israel. However, he asserts that Hosea bypassed *righteousness* and *justice* emphasised by Amos and Isaiah in favour of *knowledge of God, devotion,* and *faithfulness*.[13] Mays appears to be correct in placing emphasis on *knowledge of God* and finding its meaning in Yahweh's instruction (*Torah*). However, Mays unfortunately does not explain the *Torah*'s practical normative requirements, which are just living described by those corresponding terms. To say Hosea's choice of different but equivalent terms makes him less interested in justice issues seems to be an oversimplification. In other words, Hosea's discontent with merely legal terms to characterise Israel's disobedience and his preference for more subtle terms need further exploration.

In *Tradition for Crisis*, Brueggemann argues that the biblical prophets were not individualists who stood aloof from the traditions of faith and condemned priests, politicians and merchants based on their own novel ethical ideals. Neither were they inventors of monotheism or ethical religions, nor were mere repeaters of the old traditions.[14] Their messages and actions were thoroughly grounded in the ancient faith which had its source in Moses. The prophets applied these old traditions in ways which were relevant for the existing community of faith.[15]

For Brueggemann, "the crisis of the time" includes the problem of religious syncretism with the fertility cult of Canaan and the threat of the Assyrian armies. The question at stake was no longer of survival and

---

11. Mays, *Hosea*, 13.
12. Ibid., 8.
13. Ibid., 12.
14. Brueggemann, *Tradition for Crisis*, 13.
15. Ibid., 120.

well-being, but that of faith and covenant-keeping.[16] Brueggemann sees this point illustrated best in the focus on covenant renewal in 2:2–23. In verses 2–13, Hosea presented the historical circumstances of the Canaanite worship together with the Assyrian pressures as a radical crisis in covenant. However, verses 14–23 speak of the possibility and realisation of covenant, and they also describe the situation when Israel could see that all was lost. She was in despair and knew that her way of life had led to defeat and death. At this point, Brueggemann's analysis is promising, suggesting another step of investigation. What was actually "lost" in eighth-century Israel? What caused the Israelites to end their covenant with Yahweh? What did Hosea offer as a path to covenant restoration? Brueggemann has devoted no space to answering these issues. In addition, Brueggemann notes that "by recourse to the tradition," Hosea was able to see what seemed to be a situation of despair as a situation in which the covenant Yahweh could give blessing and restore the relationship.[17] But the problems Hosea addressed, the demands and means of the covenant restoration, which included just, honest, righteous and loving relationships in society, have not been fully covered.

Another major cluster of critical commentaries appeared in the 1980s which expanded Hosea scholarship beyond a focus on redaction, form and tradition. This included Andersen and Freedman, Jeremias, Stuart and Limburg.

Andersen and Freedman's synchronic literary treatment of the text provides an alternative to form-critical and other historically oriented approaches in Hosea studies. They focus on the final form of the text and assume its unity and integrity.[18] They follow the obvious two divisions of the book (1–3 and 4–14), stressing that both parts, almost their entirety, are directly related to an eighth-century prophet and setting.[19]

For Andersen and Freedman, the biblical prophets were the ones who shaped or fractured a nation. For them, the prophets were king-makers

---

16. Ibid., 121.
17. Ibid., 121.
18. Andersen and Freedman, *Hosea*, 59.
19. Ibid., 37.

and king-breakers. Though Amos and Hosea from the north emphasised different aspects of the body politic, they were in line with Isaiah from the south: the whole head was sick, the whole body was diseased.[20] They note that "Israel failed to keep its part of the commitment, failed to maintain unquestioning obedience to the Lord of the covenant, and to fulfil the demands of the righteousness essential to being the people of God."[21] They also accurately note that repeated and persistent breach of the requirements of that status brought Israel into crisis which eventually resulted in earnest worship of the false gods and false politics to seek power rather than justice in internal affairs.[22] Unfortunately, their commentary, in turn, does not offer much on these issues. In their analysis of 2:21, Andersen and Freedman observe that the four interior qualities, righteousness (צדק), justice (משפט), devoted fidelity (חסד) and compassion (רחם) are "the foundational component of the marriage relationship, which derives from the character of Yahweh himself.[23] However, they do not discuss these qualities much in their interpretation of the book in general and the marriage of Hosea in particular.

Stuart's commentary discusses most of the dominant themes of Hosea, Joel, Amos, Obadiah and Jonah. He examines the dependence of the prophets on the Pentateuchal blessings and curses.[24] Although Hosea presents his oracles by employing new styles, his message is not at all innovative. The prophet's task is to reinforce Yahweh's intended covenant terms.[25] For Stuart, Hosea's message is directed to several groups, mostly to Israel as a whole. The predictions of the blessings which focus on restoration are eschatological in orientation, while the curses which include destruction are more immediate.[26]

Stuart examines some notable vocabulary that characterises the book such as זנה "prostitution," שוב "return," חסד "loyalty," עזב "abandon," אהב

---

20. Ibid., 33.
21. Ibid., 47.
22. Ibid., 48.
23. Ibid., 283.
24. Stuart, *Hosea–Jonah*, xxxii.
25. Ibid., 7.
26. Ibid.

"love" and ידע "know."²⁷ He states that the term זנה is used metaphorically, mainly for Israel's unfaithfulness to God's covenant, while the other five words fall into various usages.²⁸ However, like many others, Stuart is reluctant to analyse significant terms such as צדק "righteousness," and משפט "justice" in the book. In his commentary of Amos, he focuses heavily on Amos's strong denunciations of social abuses and corporate sin, but neglects the same issues addressed by means of different words or articulated in very different literary constructs in the book of Hosea. Arguably, Stuart's characterisation of Amos as a prophet of justice as opposed to Hosea as a prophet of love overlooks this important aspect addressed also in Hosea. Therefore, this needs further investigation.

The commentaries of McComiskey, Davies, Macintosh and Garrett also follow the main stream of traditional approaches to Hosea in their analyses.²⁹ McComiskey provides a meticulous exegesis of the Hebrew text and exposition to relate the message of the ancient prophets to contemporary life in practical ways. He notes that "the social decay that resulted from their departure from the Yahwistic tradition of humanitarian concern and social justice were like a dark spectre lurking behind the changing national scene."³⁰ McComiskey has provided very good basic word studies on righteousness (צדק), justice (משפט), faithfulness (אמונה), truth (אמת), devoted fidelity (חסד) and knowledge (דעת). In his analysis of Hosea 4:1, McComiskey persuasively notes that "אֱמֶת connotes truth as a moral attribute (honesty and trustworthiness in word and deed), while חֶסֶד (loving kindness) relates to the quality of mutual concern that should bind people together."³¹ McComiskey points to Hosea's use of positive terms to define the lack of those qualities in social relationships. Garrett also supposes that "the wayward wife constitutes the leadership, institutions and culture of Israel while the children represent the ordinary men and women," trained and nurtured by wayward institutions in that culture.³² Garrett then asserts

---

27. Stuart, *Hosea–Jonah*, 16.
28. Ibid., 16.
29. McComiskey, "Hosea"; Davies, *Hosea*; Macintosh, *Hosea*; Garrett, *Hosea, Joel*.
30. McComiskey, "Hosea," 2.
31. Ibid., 56.
32. Garrett, *Hosea, Joel*, 39.

that "to know God" in 2:20, 4:6 and 6:6 implies the deepest relationship with Yahweh.[33] Unfortunately, their commentaries do not deal much with social issues. In fact, like Stuart, their dealings with ethical concerns are minimal. Nonetheless, their observations set in motion a logical starting point for us to revisit Hosea's marriage metaphor and other metaphorical sayings from the social relational angle.

Macintosh's commentary is another classic exposition in Hosea studies. He treats the composition of the book as primarily literary in character, composed by the prophet himself, possibly assisted by a personal scribe.[34] Macintosh postulates that the words which Hosea delivers publicly are reflected and predominate in chapters 2 and 4–8 whereas the oracles in chapters 9–14 mainly reflect his meditations in private after Hosea would have withdrawn from his public ministry.[35]

According to Macintosh, Hosea's prophetic task was to warn his people that the kingdom of Ephraim, unreformed, was doomed to damnation. The disease which raged in the very establishment of the nation was the abuse of Yahweh's creation of moral order. The people's faulty perceptions, represented by the syncretistic forms of Yahwism and the rapid succession of coups, were the real cause of the national sickness.[36] Macintosh asserts that the antidote for the sickness is the correct understanding of ethical reality and the knowing of Yahweh who has defined it.[37]

For Macintosh, the all-important phrase for Hosea is דעת אלהים (4:6; 6:3, 6). It represents recognition of Yahweh's actions and initiatives, associated closely with allegiance to him. It informs the reason, shapes the intention and thus ensures actions which are consistent with social righteousness, justice and kindness (2:21 [19]). These proper attitudes brought with them Yahweh's particular gift of חסד, which denotes "the very bond of peace and of all virtues and which alone could ensure the wholesome fabric

---

33. Ibid., 93.
34. Macintosh, *Hosea*, lxix. Another way of describing Macintosh's proposal is that except for the Judean glosses, Hosea himself was responsible for the literary composition of the book (see pp. lxxii–lxxiv).
35. Ibid., lxvi–lxix.
36. Ibid., lxxxviii–xc.
37. Ibid., xcii.

of society and of the nation."[38] Macintosh recognises that the vehicle of the metaphor, Yahweh's bride-price, which consists of רחם, חסד, משפט, צדקה, and אמונה, indicates the nature and quality of the marriage offered. The tenor of the metaphor thereby consists of the creation of an Israel, whose very life is to be characterised by these very qualities (2:21–22).[39]

Macintosh's analysis of major terms in Hosea is convincing. If Hosea's primary concern is Israel's moral failure, and if דעת אלהים has close association with משפט, צדקה, and חסד, which must characterise the life of Israel, the entire message of the prophet can be analysed from a social relational perspective. This important observation deserves elaboration.

Dearman's commentary is the most recent major work in Hosea studies. He labels Hosea as an accomplished poet and views his book as among the most poetic of the prophetic collections in the Old Testament. Concerning its origins and transmission, Dearman sees that "little or nothing in the book itself requires a date later than the end of the eighth century BC."[40] As regards the historical setting, Dearman is convinced that the "internal clues to the book put the vast majority of the prophecies in the mid-eighth century (ca. 760–720 BC) with Israel, not Judah, as the primary audience addressed by Hosea."[41]

A significant contribution of Dearman's work is his suggestion of viewing the texts through two lenses. The first is the metaphor of Israel as Yahweh's household, and the second is the metaphor of national covenant as marriage. Yet Dearman's analysis does not focus so much on the justice aspect, but his analysis of these root metaphors is indirectly relevant to the present examination. In following Kaminsky, Dearman recognises that "narrative frameworks are created by communities, not by autonomous individuals."[42] This notion assumes that Hosea was not a lone ranger[43] but there was a certain way of living based on just relationship that was under-

---

38. Ibid.
39. Ibid., xcv.
40. Dearman, *The Book of Hosea*, 6, 8.
41. Ibid., 21.
42. Joel S. Kaminsky, *Corporate Responsibility in the Hebrew Bible* (JSOTSup 196; Sheffield: Sheffield Academic Press, 1995), 181.
43. Dearman, *The Book of Hosea*, 30.

stood and shared by the entire community. Through these two metaphors, this study will analyse a relational aspect in order to see the bases of justice, right, and bonds that bind the biblical community together.

Another representative cluster of major studies that pays attention to theological and hermeneutical interpretation includes the works of Eichrodt, Knight, Hubbard, Doorly, Seow and Pentiuc.[44] Following the path charted by the largely older studies, more recent works by Birch, Gowan and Simundson[45] also offer important nuances to older approaches. Mostly, this trend aims to characterise Hosea as a prophet of love. The most dominant notion among these readings is Yahweh's response to unfaithful Israel in accordance with his loving character by moving beyond judgment to restoration.

A classic example of this theological interpretation is Eichrodt's article, which appeared early in the second half of the last century. In "'The Holy One in Your Midst': The Theology of Hosea," Eichrodt views Hosea's marriage as a mirror of Yahweh's relationship to Israel. According to Eichrodt, the book reveals the inner goodwill and feeling of God that motivates his actions. Hosea's proclamation portrays God's inner struggle, his deep suffering and his desperate effort to reconcile with his faithless wife.[46] Eichrodt sees Hosea not as thinker or genius but as a visionary who complied with the divine command for complete self-denial. Thus, the prophet's actions towards his adulterous wife are beyond the understanding of human rationalisation, contradicting all previous customs. The proclamation that

---

44. Eichrodt, "The Holy One in Your Midst", 259–273; George A. Knight, *Hosea: God's Love* (TBC; London: SCM Press, 1960); David A. Hubbard, *With Bands of Love: Lessons From the Book of Hosea* (Grand Rapids: W. B. Eerdmans Publishing Company, 1968); William J. Doorly, *Prophet of Love: Understanding the Book of Hosea* (New York: Paulist Press, 1991); Choon L. Seow, "Hosea, Book of," *ABD* 3: 291–297; Eugen J. Pentiuc, *Long-suffering Love: A Commentary on Hosea with Patristic Annotations* (Brookline: Holy Cross Orthodox Press, 2002).

45. Bruce C. Birch, *Hosea, Joel, and Amos* (WBC; Louisville: Westminster John Knox, 1997); Donald E. Gowan, *Theology of the Prophetic Books: The Death and Resurrection of Israel* (Louisville: Westminster John Knox, 1998); Daniel J. Simundson, *Hosea, Joel, Amos, Obadiah, Jonah, Micah* (AOTC; Nashville: Abingdon, 2005).

46. Eichrodt, "The Holy One in Your Midst," 261.

breaks through all the barriers of the tradition comes from a depth of extremely bitter suffering.[47]

Eichrodt asserts that Hosea prefers to speak of "knowledge of God" as the proper attitude and deepest means of the people's response to God's love. He recognises that this reciprocity of the process of knowing entails participation in a relationship of love and trust reflected in the bond of a wife with her husband. This trust of inner communion is the source of keeping the covenant ordinances.[48] Eichrodt stresses the breaking of the covenant of love in which everything depends on the attitude of heart and soul and that the faintest break of trust can result in immense harm.[49]

The strength of Eichrodt's examination lies in its emphasis on the inner rediscovery of true communion with God. Indeed, God suffered pain in testifying to his love in response to the lovelessness from a hopelessly corrupted people. In this, his love is not extinguished by his wrath. However, Eichrodt fails to view judgment as a part of God's relational approach to his people, seeing it as contradictory to his will for salvation. He asserts that "this becomes a contradiction in God himself which becomes an oppressing mystery for human thought."[50] Eichrodt seems to be right in saying God's action "mocks all rational considerations and contradicts all human ideas of justice, [and] becomes itself a mystery."[51] However, this mystifying query seems to find its answer when viewed through the divine relational justice point of view. Yahweh has initiated the relationship and will not give up his people no matter what human sinfulness has interrupted, but will carry them on through various means of chastisement until he will win the final victory of complete restoration.

---

47. Ibid., 263.
48. Ibid., 264–265.
49. Ibid., 265.
50. Ibid., 271–272.
51. Ibid., 273.

Major Studies on Hosea

The preceding overview has represented the major conventional studies of Hosea in the last few decades. Alongside these major formulations, there are other approaches that move away from traditional studies. Largely, these diverse trends focus attention on redaction, synchronic, final form, literary and canonical studies of the book. Some of the recent studies employ a synchronic approach to analyse Hosea as part of the Book of the Twelve, while others read the book through insights from modern metaphorical theory.

Redactional, Synchronic, Final Form and Literary Analysis

The book of Hosea has been well studied from the perspective of its redaction history in the works of Emmerson, Yee, Naumann, and Rudnig-Zelt.[52] The majority of scholars in this field find little in the book that can be attributed to Hosea himself and even less that can be attributed to the pre-exilic period. Yee, for example, concludes that the book is primarily the work of later editors.[53] However, there is still a lack of consensus over the origins and transmission of Hosea's prophecy. The works of Landy, Sweeney and Ben-Zvi utilise synchronic literary analyses to interpret the book's rhetoric and the meaning of individual units.[54] Kakkanattu combines synchronic and diachronic perspectives to see a redactional unit in Hosea 11:1–11 within the context of both the book of Hosea and the Book of the Twelve.[55] Again, since this survey makes no effort to be exhaustive, only representative works from different fields will be reviewed.

In *Hosea: An Israelite Prophet in Judean Perspective*, Emmerson aims to re-examine the "Judean redactional activity" in the book of Hosea to

---

52. Emmerson, *Hosea: An Israelite Prophet in Judean Perspective*; Gale A. Yee, *Composition and Tradition in the Book of Hosea: A Redaction Critical Investigation* (SBLDS 102; Atlanta: Scholars Press, 1987); Thomas L. Naumann, *Hoseas Erben: Strukturen der Nachinterpretation im Buch Hosea* (BWA(N)T 131; Stuttgart: Kohlhammer, 1991); Susanne Rudnig-Zelt, *Hoseastudien: redaktionskritische Untersuchungen zur Genese des Hoseabuches* (FRLANT 213; Göttingen: Vandenhoeck & Ruprecht, 2006).
53. Yee, *Composition and Tradition*, 127–130.
54. See below discussions.
55. Joy P. Kakkanattu, *God's Enduring Love in the Book of Hosea* (FAT 2/14; Tubingen: Mohr Siebeck, 2006).

explore whether they are the "authentic expressions of Hosea's thought, or whether alien elements have been introduced which have given to the message a significantly new content."[56] Emmerson's redactional approach does not concern a thematic issue such as justice. Nevertheless, her analysis in relation to "repentance" may have some implications for our examination of Yahweh's relational justice beyond any human capacity.

For Emmerson, Hosea's message of Israel's repentance comes as a result of God's saving activity, while Israel's repentance is a precondition in the view of Judean redactor(s). Among others, Emmerson sees 2:16–17 [14–15] in line with Hosea's message of Israel's new relationship as a result of God's saving activity, while she regards 2:18–25 [16–23] as a distinct theological emphasis that Israel's penitence must precede Yahweh's salvation and therefore is the arrangement of the Judean redactor.[57] Emmerson, however, notes that this distinct theological emphasis stems not from alteration or supplementation of the material, but simply from the new context in which the sayings have been set by their association with each other. We find no reason to dissent from Emmerson's consideration, but our quest is to move a step further in relation to the forgiving love of Yahweh. Indeed, the covenant of Yahweh, rooted in his divine initiative, lays a heavy obligation upon the covenant people to keep the relationship going. Yet is Yahweh's forgiveness dependent on Israel's prior repentance? God's forgiveness of undeserved sinners seems to be based on his divine justice and hence is not only a New Testament concept, but an Old Testament one particularly illustrated in the book of Hosea. This important aspect of the Scriptures deserves proper exploration.

Landy's approach to the book falls into what recent interpreters call reader-response criticism and deconstructive analysis. Landy makes no attempt to see the development of the text,[58] but treats the book as a prophetic performance addressed to Israel, prince, priests etc., and assuming a

---

56. Emmerson, *Hosea*, 4. This kind of redaction criticism is not new, for almost all Hosean scholars pay attention to it in one way or another. Emmerson's attempt, however, is not simply to seek for the *ipsissima verba* of the prophet or distinguish between Hosea and his associates who shared his theological outlook, but rather to trace the distinct Judean influence and its relationship with northern traditions within the material (p. 5).

57. Emmerson, *Hosea*, 39.

58. Landy, *Hosea*, 11–12.

situation of conflict. This performance eventually became *Torah* for some groups of people.[59] Landy regards the book as a highly structured poetry. He understands chapters 4–11 as a topical application of the allegory of chapter 2 to the daily life of political ups and downs of Israel. He states that the centre of the book is focused on contemporary events and problems.[60] Like many interpreters, he sees that there is a dominant pattern, whereby each section ends with a theme of judgment (inevitability of doom) followed by the hope of restoration.[61]

Landy suggests that Hosea sees himself as part of a succession of prophets in line with Samuel and Moses. Through them Yahweh kills with "the words of his mouth" and hews the forest of disloyalty and injustice (6:5). For this reason, prophets, like all dissidents, attract enmity (9:7–9). Hosea's main task is to remind Israel of her special responsibility and relationship with Yahweh.[62] Landy considers that the content of the book reflects a literature written for the elite to which the prophet belongs. He seems to suggest that this bears upon the absence of any reference to the poor in Hosea's prophecy.[63]

Like many others, Landy remarks that what matters most for Hosea is דעת אלהים, which will consummate the betrothal of God and Israel. The erotic union (2:16–25 [14–23]), the exchange of knowledge, kindness, love and faithfulness, are the goal of the book.[64] What Hosea offers to Israel as a way of liberation is to maintain חסד, justice and faith, waiting for Yahweh in his own time (10:12; 12:7).[65]

Landy's approach to Hosea in relating the prophecy to the contemporary socio-political issues is persuasive. He rightly points out that the way forward for Israel's survival is through חסד, justice and faith. However, his stress on the invisibility of the poor in Hosea may undercut his overall approach. It appears that Hosea's use of knowledge, kindness, love

---

59. Ibid., 13–14.
60. Ibid., 13.
61. Ibid., 14.
62. Ibid., 15.
63. Ibid., 16.
64. Ibid., 18.
65. Ibid., 20.

and faithfulness, has not yet been substantiated. Besides, if Hosea's task is to remind Israel of her responsibility, what then are the contents of that responsibility?

Another important postulate of this author is his emphasis on reading Hosea in light of its social world governed by specific rules, namely patriarchy.[66] Landy asserts that "Hosea is undoubtedly patriarchal literature. . . . Its use of female imagery is misogynistic."[67] His suggestion for the need to read Hosea in view of the existing culture is laudable. Yet it is difficult to accept that Hosea's use of female metaphor is necessarily misogynistic, particularly in consideration of other paternal or maternal metaphors.

Ben Zvi's synchronic literary approach to the book is a significant work. He provides a valuable revision of the previous form-critical studies in which the form and historical critics have fractured the text into small units to find the *Sitz im Leben* of those units. This new approach no longer seeks to find the *ipsissima verba* of the prophet, but is concerned with the "prophetic readings" within the context of the whole – *Sitz im Buch*. Ben Zvi argues that "Yahweh's word that came to Hosea signifies a written book."[68] The intention is to educate a group of literati in the post-monarchic Judean community that accepted Hosea as authoritative text. The book of Hosea explains Yahweh's relationship to Israel in the past and his "punishment above all communicates hope by pointing to an ideal future."[69] They were "to read, reread, and understand the book directly."[70]

The present form of the book, according to Ben Zvi, is the end result of these different readings. Furthermore, the prophet "Hosea of the book is a literary and ideological character that lives within the world of the book" and the book of Hosea "is not about mimesis or historicity, but

---

66. Rosengren also suggests that the text of Hosea should be read as advocating a submissive female role within a desirable patriarchal society. Allan Rosengren, "Knowledge of God according to Hosea the Ripper: The Interlacing of Theology and Social Ideology in Hosea 2," *SJOT* 23 (2009): 122–125.

67. Landy, *Hosea*, 19. For opposite view of discussions, see Teresa J. Hornsby, "'Israel Has Become a Worthless Thing': Re-Reading Gomer in Hosea 1–3," *JSOT* 82 (1999): 115–128; Claire Turner, "Hosea: More than a Metaphor," *ExpTim* 121 (2010): 601–607.

68. Ben Zvi, *Hosea*, 319.

69. Ibid., 19.

70. Ibid., 5.

about learning about Yahweh, Israel's past and future."⁷¹ Thus, contemporary readers should not resort to looking for the historical prophet or the reconstructed ancient events not specifically mentioned in the text.⁷² He also notes that individual units of the book are didactic prophetic readings and each reading may evoke images of different social interactions and situations.⁷³

Significantly, Ben Zvi advances four stages of the metanarrative which provide the basic conceptual structure governing the book. First, Yahweh chose Israel long ago and became her patron. Second, Israel, the client, broke her obligations towards her patron, (i.e. Israel sinned against Yahweh). Third, Yahweh punished Israel, but since Yahweh still "loved" Israel, he would not exterminate Israel nor abrogate his patronship. Fourth, since Yahweh did not abrogate his patronship, he would bring this relationship to its proper (ideal) form at an undefined but certain future.⁷⁴ This postulation seems valid and useful in analysing the prophetic texts of Hosea. Conceivably, the first two stages can be incorporated under the theme of responsibility/irresponsibility. Despite having developed the metanarrative of the book, Ben Zvi does not use it to structure the book. Moreover, his placement of the social setting of the book in the late monarchic or post-monarchic Judah does not allow him to take a close look at justice issues in the socio-historical setting of the prophet of old.

Feminist Criticism, Metaphorical Studies and Hosea as Part of the Twelve

As noted earlier, feminist criticism has existed alongside other approaches. Feminist criticism in the last decades paid primary attention to gender-based studies in which Hosea 1–3 became the prime focus of analyses.⁷⁵ For instance, Yee observes that Hosea has become a "much-examined work

---

71. Ibid., 6.
72. Ibid., 80, 223.
73. Ibid., 8.
74. Ibid.
75. A comprehensive survey of the matter is found in Kelle, "Hosea 1–3," 179–216.

among feminist biblical scholars."⁷⁶ Within this approach, the metaphor of Hosea has increasingly been examined under topics like pornography and sexual violence.⁷⁷ Nevertheless, feminist interpretations of Hosea 1–3 vary greatly.⁷⁸ A representative review of two works in this field will serve our purpose.

Keefe's monograph, *Woman's Body and the Social Body in Hosea*, challenges the long-standing consensus that reads Hosea's marriage to Gomer as a sign for Israel's apostasy in terms of syncretistic fertility religion. Keefe explores the metaphorical implications of the "woman of fornications" of Hosea 1–2. She argues that the traditional theme of allegorical interpretation is, at best, an oversimplification of the pressing socio-political crisis in Hosea's time.⁷⁹ Accordingly, Keefe attempts to offer an alternative reading

---

76. Gale A. Yee, "Hosea," in *The Women's Bible Commentary*, eds. C. A Newsom and S. H. Ringe Newsom (Louisville: John Knox Press, 1992), 195.

77. Baumann, *Love and Violence*, 8.

78. No consensus in interpretive methods has been made among feminist scholars. For instance, Helgard Balz-Cochois, *Der Höhenkult Israels im Selbstverständnis der Volksfrömmigkeit* (Frankfurt am Main: Peter Lang, 1982), and Marie-Theres Wacker, *Figurationen des Weiblichen im Hosea-Buch* (HBS 8; Freiburg im Br: Herder, 1996), use a religio-historical approach to recast Gomer as a symbol of repressed goddess worship. Balz-Cochois argues that Gomer worshiped Ashtarte through acts of cultic prostitution that opposed Yahwism. T. Drorah Setel, "Prophets and Pornography: Female Sexual Imagery in Hosea," in *Feminist Interpretation of the Bible*, ed. L. M. Russell (Philadelphia: Westminster, 1985): 86–95, regards the functions and features of Hosea's imagery as pornographic, sharing with modern pornography where the males possess the right over female sexuality. Weems, "Gomer: Victim of Violence or Victim of Metaphor?," proposes reading Hosea's sexual imagery as beneficial yet problematic. She affirmed that Yahweh has the right to punish his people but rejected the use of marital and sexual imagery to express these convictions. Rut Törnkvist, *The Use and Abuse of Female Sexual Imagery in the Book of Hosea: A Feminist Critical Approach to Hosea 1–3* (Women in Religion 7; Uppsala: Uppsala University Library, 1998), questions both the theological assertion that God has the right to punish, as well as the legitimacy of using a marriage metaphor to describe God. She concludes that feminist readers should reject the whole metaphor. Teresa J. Hornsby, "Israel Has Become a Worthless Thing", employs a socio-political method and interprets Gomer's figure as an independent businesswoman prostitute who is resisting a single client's domineering efforts to control her.

79. Feminist critics largely contend that this cultic apostasy thesis of Hosea's metaphor legitimates a social structure within which males possess the right of control over female sexuality. This cultic apostasy thesis eventually forms a basis for a Western ideological framework of metaphysical oppositions – God/nature; spirit/matter – male is to God as female is to sinful humanity. On the one hand, Keefe supports this interpretation by asserting "feminist scholars have rightly pointed to Hosea's metaphor as a critical locus of engagement . . . to rethink those paradigmatic structures which have resulted in our self-alienation from body and nature, and the commitment patterns of relentless violence

of Hosea's metaphor in light of the repeated association of sexual transgression and social violence which is found in biblical narratives. Keefe finally associates Hosea's metaphor with Israel's dishonest society in which Israel has been pictured metaphorically as a fornicating female body in light of a community identity crisis in the eighth-century Israel. Along these lines, Keefe places Hosea's setting as a conflict between traditional subsistence agriculture and the emerging Omride-Jehuide's command of cash-crop economy which threatens the inalienability of land of the patriarchal household.[80]

Keefe follows the two main divisions of the book: 1–3 and 4–14, and sees sex-related imagery continuing as a link between the two sections. The first three chapters thematically deal with the motifs of marriage, female procreation and female sexual transgression while the second section includes diverse oracles addressing social, political and religious issues. Importantly, Keefe identifies the often-neglected familial dimension of metaphor in which she sees the first three chapters are not simply a marriage metaphor but a family metaphor and the similar theme is seen throughout the book. To put this in another way, understanding Hosea's metaphor in the opening chapters is the gateway to the rest of the book. The aspect of family metaphor which assumes bond relationships deserves expansion. Nevertheless, Keefe does not make a credible attempt to reconstruct the specific crises or brokenness alluded to within these chapters. To interpret Hosea's metaphor as socio-political crises in general terms without specification will still be an oversimplification. By expanding Keefe's analysis, a further exploration of relational justice in relation to Hosea's polemics against the nation's social, political and religious issues will shed brighter light on the book of Hosea.

---

which have been characteristic of Western civilization." On the other hand, Keefe remarks that feminist scholars also "failed to recognise that the very dichotomy between fertility religion and ethical Yahwism within which the interpretation of this text has been framed is itself already a function of dualist constructions of gender symbolism and religious meanings." This dualistic worldview, according to Keefe, is a product of a determined interpretive gaze and syncretistic fertility cult in the eighth-century Israel and does not rest on any firm textual or extratextual evidence. See Keefe, *Woman's Body*, 10–11.
80. Keefe, *Woman's Body*, 114.

Yee's work, *Poor Banished Children of Eve: Woman as Evil in the Hebrew Bible* is an extensive groundbreaking book. It focuses on the symbolisation of woman as the incarnation of evil. Yee sees Hosea 1–2 as coming substantially from Hosea's own time during the independent monarchies. She argues that these women are "symbolic alibis" used for other societal issues. Yee investigates gender ideology of biblical Israel and its interconnectedness with the issues of race/ethnicity, class and colonialism during the times of production.[81] According to Yee, the female symbolization as evil in the biblical texts is to demonstrate the actual social, historical and economic crisis.[82]

Yee remains convinced that the feminised trope, "promiscuity," levels against an oppressive mode[83] of production – the corrupt male elites of the eighth-century Israel who exploit the peasant class to pay heavy tribute imposed by foreign powers. Baal worship and foreign policy are the expressions of these socio-economic injustices. This reading far outweighs the long-held view that the marriage metaphor opposes the worship of a fertility goddess and its attendant sexual practices. Yet Yee's analysis is not only limited in scope but also leaves justice issues unexplored in the book as a whole. The actual causes of the total collapse in the eighth-century Israelite society need further investigation.

Alongside feminist criticism, another wave of Hosean scholarship pays much attention to Hosea's metaphors.[84] In recent years, there has been

---

81. Yee, *Poor Banished Children of Eve*, 1. She illustrates her analysis by using four main texts from the Bible: Eve in Genesis 2–3, the woman of fornications in Hosea 1–3, the sisters Oholah and Oholibah in Ezekiel 23, and the Other woman in Proverbs 1–9. She remarks that this symbolization of women is a significant source for Western negative attitudes towards women.

82. Yee's approach is twofold. The first step of her approach, called "extrinsic analysis," analyses the mode of production – the socio-political and historical settings of the texts. The second step, an intrinsic analysis, aims to deal with specific textual issues.

83. This foreign-tributary mode of production involved royal latifundialization, political instability, external political treaties, and religious conflicts with polytheism. Yee sees Hosea as a member of a "Yahweh alone" movement opposed to this mode of production. Yee, *Poor Banished Children of Eve*, 81–83.

84. Nelly Stienstra, *YHWH is the Husband of his People: Analysis of a Biblical Metaphor with Special Reference to Translation* (Kampen: Kok Pharos, 1993); A. Weider, *Ehemetaphorik in prophetischer Verkündigung: Hosea 1–3 und seine Wirkungsgeschichte im Jeremiabuch: Ein Beitrag zum alttestamentlichen Gottes-Bild* (FB 71; Wurzburg, Germany: Echter, 1993); Raymond C Ortlund, *Whoredom: God's Unfaithful Wife in Biblical Theology*

growing interest in the study of the metaphorical language of Hosea. For instance, Eidevall applies metaphorical theories in linguistics to Hosea 4–14, attempting to develop various models, patterns and themes from the various metaphors.[85] Nwaoru attempts to identify semantic relationships, metaphorical imagery and structural coherence in various sections of the book,[86] while Sherwood employs semiotic and deconstructive approaches to Hosea.[87] Three dominant positions of interpretation with overlapping features that stand out in this field of studies are cultic-religious interpretation, socio-economic interpretation and historical interpretation. Perhaps a review of the works of Kelle and Hong, based on socio-economic interpretation, better serve the purpose of this study.

The revised doctoral thesis of Kelle, *Hosea 2: Metaphor and Rhetoric in Historical Perspective*, interprets the marriage metaphor of Hosea 2 against the background of attested practices of marriage and divorce in the ancient Near Eastern world. For Kelle, the metaphor of the adulterous wife and the ensuing sanctions by the spurned husband describes the political situation in the northern kingdom in eighth century BC. In the descriptions of physical and sexual violence against "the wife/mother" (Hos 2:5 [3], 12–14 [10–12]), Kelle finds no evidence of such action in ancient Near Eastern divorce and marriage.[88] For that reason, he asserts that the term Baal (2:18 [16]) functions as a metaphorical term for a political entity such as an ally or overlord and has little to do with a literal statement about the Israelites'

(NSBT; Leicester: Inter-Varsity Press, 1996); Brigitte Seifert, *Metaphorisches Reden von Gott im Hoseabuch* (FRLANT 166; Gottingen: Vandenhoeck & Ruprecht, 1996); Göran Eidevall, *Grapes in the Desert: Metaphors, Model and Themes in Hosea 4–14* (ConBOT 43; Stockholm: Almqvist & Wiksell, 1996); Richtsje Abma, *Bonds of Love*; J. Andrew Dearman, "YHWH's House: Gender Roles and Metaphors for Israel in Hosea," *JNSL* 25 (1999): 97–108; Baumann, *Love and Violence*; Kelle, *Hosea 2: Metaphor and Rhetoric*; Seong-Hyuk Hong, *The Metaphor of Illness and Healing in Hosea and Its Significance in the Socio-Economic Context of Eighth-Century Israel and Judah* (SBL 95; New York: Peter Lang Publishing, 2006); Sharon Moughtin-Mumby, *Sexual and Marital Metaphors in Hosea, Jeremiah, Isaiah and Ezekiel* (OTM; Oxford: Oxford University Press, 2008).

85. Eidevall, *Grapes in the Desert*, 166–185.

86. E. O. Nwaoru, *Imagery in Prophecy of Hosea* (ÄAT 41; Wiesbaden: Harrassowitz, 1999); *idem*, "The Role of Images in the Literary Structure of Hosea VII 8–VIII 14," *VT* 54 (2004): 216–222.

87. Sherwood, *The Prostitute and the Prophets*, 150–253.

88. Kelle, *Hosea 2: Metaphor and Rhetoric*, 62.

worship of Baal.[89] Rather, the descriptions of physical and sexual violence are warlike metaphors rather than marital ones. They depict an impending war against the ruling elite of personified Samaria.[90] This sexual imagery is, therefore, a political condemnation designed to shame Israel's male political leaders.[91] Along this line, Kelle reads the metaphors of adultery, fornication, lovers and Baals as political images which describe Samaria's anti-Assyrian stance.[92] Unlike many others, Kelle sees Hosea siding with the Assyrian-backed usurper, Hoshea, to overthrow King Pekah. He argues that the divine speech in Hosea 2:4–25, coming as though from a spurned husband, intends to undo Pekah's rebellion against Assyria, which is an act of infidelity against the one to whom oaths of a loyalty treaty were sworn. This is, in Hosea's view, contrary to the will of Yahweh.[93]

Kelle regards Hosea 2:21–22 [19–20] as the climax of Yahweh's remarriage which declares that Yahweh will enter into a marriage with his estranged wife. The text lists five things required for carrying out the act of remarriage: righteousness, justice, loving-kindness, compassion and faithfulness. However, Kelle plays down the importance of these concepts by saying, "rather than having significance as individual words, these terms function together as the qualities that mark Yahweh's remarriage."[94] The qualities that mark the remarriage between Yahweh and Israel appear to be crucial in Hosea. However, Kelle is disinclined to explore these qualities. He even further argues against a more consensus opinion that often concludes that the primary task of prophets like Hosea, Amos and Micah is ethical teaching concerning social justice. He states that "Hosea's speech in 2:1–25 [1–23] does not deal with issues like the treatment of the poor and the widow but focuses on the political affairs."[95]

As regards Kelle's interpretation, one is first of all doubtful about whether his denial of the existence of fertility cult in ancient Israel will hold

---

89. Ibid., 275.
90. Ibid., 93.
91. Ibid., 286.
92. Ibid., 181.
93. Ibid., 264.
94. Ibid., 278.
95. Ibid., 293.

when reading Hosea in light of other prophets in general and in relation to Hosea 3 in particular. It is even more difficult to applaud his dismissal of the prospect of Hosea's ethical concern on the grounds of the absence of words such as "widow" and "poor." The positive terms that qualify the marriage are intentionally employed by Hosea to show the lack of those qualities in the social relationship in society. This important issue deserves a proper investigation.

Hong's work, *The Metaphor of Illness and Healing in Hosea and Its Significance in the Socio-Economic Context of Eighth-Century Israel and Judah*, represents the recent trend in Hosea studies that reads various metaphors in Hosea against the background of socio-economic developments in eighth-century Israel. By employing Kittay's semantic field metaphor theory, Hong analyses the metaphors of illness and healing in Hosea 5:8–6:3 and 7:1–7. His analysis of the ancient Near Eastern contexts concludes that illness was mainly considered to be caused by the invasion or attack of foreign agents like supernatural beings and this fundamentally implies disharmony with the transcendental realm.[96] Hence supernatural beings or the right controller of illness are required for healing, that is, to restore this harmonious relationship. What was foreign in the eyes of Hosea, according to Hong, was the monarchy with its oppressive and destructive features, such as commercialisation of agriculture, centralization of political and economic power, failure of political leadership, social chaos, foreign alliances, the disputed relationship with Yahweh etc. The metaphor of healing, therefore, means "the removal of the foreign form of monarchy, that is, returning to the prestate society based on mutuality."[97]

Hong appears to have achieved his aim in highlighting the social hostility and decadence of the socio-political situation of eighth-century Israel. However, owing to its limitation in scope, Hong's conclusion seems to depict only one side of the coin. As one would expect, Hosea's social criticism is not limited to the king and the elite, but rather includes the denunciation of the total chaos of the entire society, the broken relationships between Israel and Yahweh, and between the Israelites and their fellow

---

96. Hong, *Illness and Healing in Hosea*, 78.
97. Ibid., 161.

Israelites. Moreover, it is difficult to accept the view that Hosea's social critique was intended simply to bring the Israelites back to being a subsistence tribal community.

Hosea as part of the Book of the Twelve has been a major field of investigation in recent years. The works of House, Nogalski and Sweeney and articles of Bowman and Braaten deal specifically with this aspect.[98] The trend looks at the collection of the Twelve as a whole and asks about editorial arrangement and intertextual relations. Generally, Hosea 1–3 is taken as an introduction to Hosea 4–14 as well as to the Book of the Twelve. While some scholars analyse Hosea's use of שׁוּב ("turn," "return," "repent") as an inherent unifying reading strategy for the Book of the Twelve, others pay attention to the themes of judgment and restoration as an organising theme. However, it sufficient to note that no scholars in this field attempt to see the theme of relational justice as a unifying thread for the Book of Twelve. This is best illustrated by the work of Sweeney.

In *The Twelve Prophets: Hosea, Joel, Amos, Obadiah, Jonah*, Sweeney attempts to combine the twelve Minor Prophets to form a single coherent entity. He argues that the multifaceted literary unity of the Book of the Twelve has been neglected in modern biblical scholarship.[99] The author asserts that any final form of biblical books, whether individual, such as Hosea, or even the final form of the Book of the Twelve, was accepted to be the work of later editors.[100]

For Sweeney, the book of Hosea, with its thematic condemnation of Israel/Judah and the restoration of the relationship with Yahweh following

---

98. See Paul R. House, *The Unity of the Twelve* (JSOTSup 97; Sheffield: Almond Press, 1990); Marvin A. Sweeney, *Twelve Prophets*; James D. Nogalski and Marvin Sweeney, ed., *Reading and Hearing the Book of the Twelve* (SBLSymS 15; Atlanta: SBL, 2000); Laurie J. Braaten, "God Sows: Hosea's Land Theme in the Book of the Twelve," in *Thematic Threads in the Book of the Twelve*, eds. Paul L. Redditt and Aaron Schart; BZAW 325 (Berlin: de Gruyter, 2003), 104–32; Craig D. Bowman, "Reading the Twelve as One: Hosea 1–3 as an Introduction to the Book of the Twelve (the Minor Prophets)," *SCJ* 9 (2006): 41–59; Jason T. LeCureux, *The Thematic Unity of the Book of the Twelve* (HBM 41; Sheffield: Sheffield Phoenix Press, 2012).
99. Sweeney, *Twelve Prophets*, xx.
100. Ibid., xxxix. Sweeney employs a synchronic literary analysis focusing on their interrelationship to the Book of the Twelve within the Masoretic and Septuagint forms of the book. Yet his commentary "includes diachronic considerations in order for the synchronic analysis to make sense."

punishment at the hands of various nations, stands as a programmatic statement of one of the central issues addressed throughout the Book of the Twelve.[101] In other words, the book of Hosea mostly fits and functions within the overall movement from judgment to restoration found across the Minor Prophets as a whole. Northern Israel's experience served as a model for Southern Judah. Hosea's calls for Israel to return to Yahweh also had implications for Judah.

Importantly, Sweeney observes Hosea 2:16–25 [14–23] as a climactic oracle which outlines the future restoration of the marriage relationship. Yahweh's objective "to betroth" the wife, and the concluding statement, "I will cause you to lie down in security . . . and you shall know Yahweh," clearly provides a sexual play on words.[102] The qualities for the relationship are to be "in righteousness and in justice and in fidelity and in mercy and in faithfulness" which are qualities ascribed to Yahweh and the ideal Davidic king (e.g. Exod 34:6; Isa 11:3–5). However, Sweeney does not use these qualities demanded or promised by Yahweh to seal off the relationship between him and Israel to analyse the Book of the Twelve. If the future restoration of the marriage relationship is to be marked by righteousness, justice, fidelity, mercy and faithfulness, then perhaps Hosea was saying that these are precisely the qualities that were absent in the eighth-century Israelite society. Like many others, Sweeney recognises the two dominant themes of judgment and restoration both for Hosea and the Book of the Twelve. Again like other scholars, he does not substantiate why judgment was imposed upon Israel. Perhaps, a proper investigation of this aspect will disclose Hosea's social message. Thus, the concrete meaning of Hosea's language and sexual imagery needs a fresh exploration.

Summary Assessment

The works reviewed thus far have demonstrated that the book of Hosea has been studied through various methodological approaches. Yet it is clear that the issue of justice has not been sufficiently explored.

---

101. Sweeney, *Twelve Prophets*, 3.
102. Ibid., 36.

Most major commentaries understand that the primary concern of the book is Israel's apostasy to the syncretistic fertility cult. However, more recent interpreters have abandoned this view in favour of a socio-economic and political interpretation that suggests Hosea's metaphor is designed to address the actual historical crisis. What has not been explored so far is an approach that would accommodate these two seemingly contradictory views. Arguably, reading Hosea from a relational justice perspective may resolve the tension. That is, the prophet's metaphorical indictments are levelled against the corporate Israel, calling for right relationships both in the context of religious (vertical relationship with God) and social spheres (horizontal relationship with neighbours).

Many interpreters touch on the importance of relationship in Hosea. Yet little effort has been devoted to examining it as a vital thread to digging deep beneath the prophetic metaphors and other allusive discourses. Similarly, various scholars have rightly stressed the centrality of the covenant theme in the book. However, there has not been a proper specification of the covenant terms and conditions which will make Hosea's social critique more visible. To interpret the covenant theme in terms of Israel's apostasy alone is superficial and will only cover part of the prophet's message. Correspondingly, most scholars ascribe to the centrality of conceptual terms such as "righteousness," "justice," "fidelity," "faithfulness," and "knowledge of God." However, these significant terms are not properly studied on Hosea's own terms, nor are they employed to analyse the book as a whole.

Finally, most interpreters have appropriately taken up the themes of judgment and restoration. However, they have not fully dealt with the question as to why judgment was imposed upon Israel in the first place. It is likely that a proper examination of this question will reveal Hosea's sense of justice. Most interpreters seem to pay more attention to the punitive aspect of judgment. However, judgment in Hosea appears to be a part of the process towards restoration and hence positive in orientation. Therefore, a proper association of Yahweh's demands for justice, his destructive judgment and his ultimate aim of restoration will provide us with a theoretical framework by which we can analyse the profound prophetic oracles of Hosea.

Justice Studies in the Hebrew Bible

The theme of justice is one of the central themes of the Old Testament in general and of the prophets in particular.[103] This suggests that the justice theme may be vital to understanding a prophetic message like that of Hosea. Arguably, prophetic proclamations in the Old Testament were occasioned by an Israelite community that struggled through "the endless web of greed, violence and the abuse of power that cause[d] a myriad of injustices."[104] A number of scholars have concentrated on this important subject in the last few decades. The aim of the following review is to look at certain key biblical concepts concerning justice. The works of Weinfeld, Gossai, Malchow, Nardoni, and Dempsey best represent this field of studies.[105]

Weinfeld's *Social Justice in Ancient Israel and in the Ancient Near East* is a good introduction to the links of social justice between the ancient Near Eastern world and ancient Israel. He sets Israel's understanding of social justice within the context of royal administration and the periodic issuing of edicts of release from debts and other obligations to creditors.

Weinfeld suggests that the concept of social justice was expressed by means of a *hendiadys,* namely "justice and righteousness" (משפט וצדקה).[106] The central focus of his analysis is on משפט וצדקה both in the biblical corpus and equivalent terms in ancient Near Eastern literature including Ugaritic, Hittite, Akkadian and Egyptian. He examines the terms משפט וצדקה and their parallel, *kittum u mīšarum,* in Mesopotamia and

---

103. This centrality is also seen in the New Testament and Christian tradition. This is best illustrated by Christ's proclamation of justice through his tragic death on the cross, extending mercy to his prosecutors and enemies (cf. Matt 12:18–21).
104. Carol J. Dempsey, *Justice: A Biblical Perspective* (St Louis: Chalice Press, 2008), 2.
105. Moshe Weinfeld, *Social Justice in Ancient Israel and in the Ancient Near East* (Minneapolis: Fortress Press, 1995); Hemchand Gossai, *Justice, Righteousness and the Social Critique of the Eighth-Century Prophets* (New York: Peter Lang, 1993); Bruce V. Malchow, *Social Justice in the Hebrew Bible: What is New and What is Old* (Collegeville: Liturgical Press, 1996); Enrique Nardoni, *Rise Up, O Judge: A Study of Justice in the Biblical World,* trans. Sean Charles Martin (Peabody: Hendrickson, 2004); Dempsey, *Justice: A Biblical Perspective.* Most recently, H. G. M. Williamson, *He has Shown You What is Good: Old Testament Justice Then and Now* (Cambridge: The Lutterworth Press, 2012).
106. Weinfeld, *Social Justice in Ancient Israel,* 25.

"freedom" in Egypt.¹⁰⁷ He argues that doing משפט וצדקה in the ancient Near East and Israel implies the maintaining of social justice, equity and freedom within society. Israel's willingness to promote justice indicates her spiritual well-being and so justice is fundamental to national existence.

Weinfeld explores the Hebrew terms צדק, צדקה and משפט. He argues that צדק refers to the abstract principle of righteousness, while צדקה refers to the concrete act.¹⁰⁸ He refutes the Rabbis' connection of משפט וצדקה with the proper execution of justice in a judicial sense. Weinfeld rightly contends that when the prophets spoke of משפט וצדקה, they were not referring to merely settlement between two parties or action in charity, but rather they had in mind primarily an improvement in the conditions of the poor. In other words, the prophets' call to do משפט וצדקה does not mean simply judging accurately in court, but rather that the socio-political leaders, landowners and officials, who made the law, should all act on behalf of the poor.¹⁰⁹

Weinfeld notes that Israel's mission to do "justice and righteousness" first appears in God's call to Abraham in Genesis 18:19, 20–21. Significantly, he stresses the fact that the word pair is used in conjunction with the concept of דרך "way" of life. *Performing* משפט וצדקה means *keeping of the way* of Yahweh.¹¹⁰ Furthermore, Weinfeld also notes that משפט וצדקה and *kittum u mišarum* are considered a social ideal along the lines of "mercy" and "kindness" (cf. Isa 16:5; Prov 20:28; 25:5; Ps 33:5). Indeed, *kindness* and *truth* and *mercy* are found often in the Bible in conjunction with justice or righteousness (Ps 33:5; 89:15; Jer 9:23; Hos 2:21, 12:7; Mic 6:8).¹¹¹

Weinfeld's basic analysis of משפט וצדקה and his suggestion of understanding the terms in light of other terms, such as אמונה, אמת, חסד and דרך, are appealing. This reading provides a valid point of departure in analysing the prophetic words of Hosea. Arguably, the less obvious use of משפט וצדקה in Hosea does not means his message has less to do with justice. Perhaps, Hosea intentionally chooses to employ other vocabularies in

---

107. Ibid., 9.
108. Ibid., 34.
109. Ibid., 44, 45–47.
110. Ibid., 7.
111. Ibid., 29.

his call for social justice. For instance, Hosea often employs general terms such as מעלל "deed" (4:9; 5:4; 7:1; 7:2; 9:15; 12:2), רעה "wickedness" (7:2; 7:3; 9:15; 10:13; 10:15), and דרך "way" (4:9; 9:8; 12:3; 14:10) to accuse Israel of waywardness. Indeed, Hosea's fervent call upon Israel is to return to Yahweh and *keep his way* (14:10), not *their way* (4:9; 12:3).

In *Justice, Righteousness and the Social Critique of the Eighth-Century Prophets,* Gossai examines the use of צדק and משפט in the eighth-century prophets. In order to draw out the basic meanings and nuances, he surveys the use of צדק and משפט in the context of the ancient Near East and their usage in the Old Testament. Gossai's findings suggest that the term צדק is used in three overlapping aspects, namely the forensic, the religious and the ethical. More important than the use of these three, Gossai argues, is the use of צדק in "relationship" contexts.[112]

As in the case of צדק, Gossai investigates the use of שפט in the ancient Near Eastern context and the use of צדק primarily has forensic overtones. Yet the Old Testament incorporates one element of its use as a term of relationship.[113] This observation departs from the commonly held scholarly view that משפט is "an objective norm which must be subscribed to, whether in legal, cultic or religious affairs."[114] Accordingly, Gossai concludes that the primary concern behind משפט is the motivation of Yahweh in covenant relationship.[115] In other words, Yahweh's relation with Israel, even in punitive form, may be regarded as an undergirding element of his relationship with them.

Like Weinfeld, Gossai examines the essence of the word pair משפט וצדקה. Notably, there are sixteen occurrences in the eighth-century prophets, which make up two-fifths of the total incidents in the Old Testament. He asserts that "both concepts function in concrete situations and both are used to articulate in a clear manner, the notion of

---

112. Gossai, *Justice, Righteousness,* 63. He argues that the same terms are seen, and similar uses are found, in the Old Testament, even though it introduces new elements, especially Yahweh's covenant relationship with Israel which eventually shapes the meaning of צדק in the Old Testament.
113. Gossai, *Justice, Righteousness,* 139.
114. Ibid., 198.
115. Ibid., 186.

relationship."[116] Gossai persuasively argues that it is the perversion of such relationship that is attested by the many expressions of injustice in the eighth-century prophets.[117] He notes that the contexts in which these terms are used reveal that either צדק and משפט are missing or that they are necessary. As such, the widespread use of the word pair clearly indicates its close association with the subject of "social justice."[118] For Gossai, the central issue is the corruption of Israel's cult, which epitomises Israel's relationship with Yahweh. This affects every aspect of life, whether in religious, social, judicial or economic spheres. The primary concern of the prophets, therefore, is the restoration of the people's broken relationship with Yahweh and with each other.[119]

Gossai's analysis of צדק and משפט is intriguing. It provides a potential exegetical ground from which to analyse any prophetic text. However, despite acknowledging the fact that the eighth-century prophets have one concern in common, which is to address the social issues, Gossai still keeps Hosea as an exception. He submits that Hosea's critique has primarily to do with cultic apostasy. Gossai's analysis seems inconsistent because he not only locates Hosea's use of צדק and משפט in 2:21 [19] solely with reference to Baalism, but also disregards the other forms of broken relationships criticised by Hosea. For instance, Gossai observes that there is, like Hosea, only one occurrence of צדק and משפט in Micah (7:9), but suggests that the different forms of injustices denounced by Micah are almost identical to those of Amos. In fact, Gossai's analysis has shown that Hosea contains more occurrences of צדק or משפט than Micah and exactly the same number of occurrences as in Amos. In addition, Gossai reads Hosea 10:4 as Yahweh's destructive judgment, which rather seems to mean the breakdown of justice in the society comparable to Amos 5:7 and 6:12. Gossai's work, nevertheless, is a helpful point of departure for further investigation of Hosea's social critique.

---

116. Ibid., 210.
117. Ibid., 310.
118. Ibid., 245.
119. Ibid., 311.

Malchow's *Social Justice in the Hebrew Bible: What is New and What is Old* provides a summary of social justice in the Hebrew Bible with a view to drawing out certain biblical principles which will be applicable in the context of contemporary society.

Following such scholars as Weinfeld and Gossai, Malchow recognises the origins of social justice concepts going back to Israel's ancient Near Eastern neighbours. The ancient Israelites adopted the legacy from their surrounding neighbours, but developed it with new meaning and applied it to their new problems. Malchow notes that Israel did this by accepting, adapting and transforming the Near Eastern ideas.[120]

Malchow notes that there was no notable social inequality in ancient Israel and many of the injustices in Israelite society were caused by the development of a class society in the monarchical period.[121] In order to explore its manifestation in the biblical statements, the author analyses law codes, prophetic books, psalms, narrative works, and wisdom literature.[122] Malchow comprehensively covers the biblical terms, usages and meanings of justice in the Hebrew Bible and provides useful information. In his analysis of the prophetic books, four prophets stand out as those who speak about social justice: Amos, Micah, Isaiah and Jeremiah. Surprisingly, and like many others, Malchow completely ignores the book of Hosea and fails to scrutinise its content to see whether Hosea's polemics against the northern Israelite society contain elements of social justice or not. Malchow's omission of the book for his analysis of social justice shows a typical treatment of the book of Hosea.

In *Rise Up, O Judge: A Study of Justice in the Biblical World*, Nardoni thoroughly studies the themes of social justice as represented in the biblical corpus both from the Old and New Testaments. He provides a chronological overview of social reforms, legal codes and edicts of mercy from ancient religious texts of Mesopotamia and Egypt. In spite of differences

---

120. Malchow, *Social Justice in the Hebrew Bible*, xiv, 76. This approach is not new and Malchow himself acknowledges that he follows a paradigm developed by Wolff and Brueggemann.
121. Ibid., 11.
122. Ibid., 20–63.

in demography, language and religion, Nardoni notes that there is a basic concept of social justice with a strong liberating dimension.[123]

Like many other scholars, Nardoni recognises that Israel shared a social concern common in the ancient Near East and inherited the vocabulary of justice and law. Yet what was unique to ancient Israel was that the nation began its history in a desperate situation as poor and oppressed slaves, being rescued by Yahweh through his saving act which reversed injustice. This compassionate action of Yahweh served as a model and basis in ancient Israel in their effort to assist the poor and oppressed in their own midst.[124] In the ancient Near Eastern world, the monarch was venerated as an agent of deities, entrusted with the responsibility of maintaining cosmic order, and acting as warrior, judge and priest. However, the king in Israel, Nardoni observes, was not the son of God by birth, but by adoption. Order and justice had only to do with Israel's exclusive relationship with Yahweh, who was the sole source of such order and justice.[125]

Interestingly, Nardoni states that the Mesopotamian terms *kittum* and *mišarum* are more influential in the ancient Near East than their parallel Egyptian term *maat*. These terms were later translated in Semitic languages by the words *ṣdq* and *m(y)šr*. Hence the parallel terms in Hebrew include *ṣedeq* (צדק) and *mîšôr* (מישור) and *mišpāṭ* (משפט).[126] Nardoni suggests that the use of these terms is most obvious in the Psalms and the prophets where they are used interchangeably. The term משפט by itself has a wide range of meanings while the words צדק and צדקה, though derived from the same root, do not have the same conclusive meaning. However, when coordinated in a pair with משפט, the terms צדק and צדקה designate the order established by God in human society, particularly in Israel.[127]

Unlike many scholars, Nardoni maintains that Hosea has a lot to say about social justice. In Hosea's views, he argues, the inhabitants of Samaria had forsaken Yahweh and served Baals, ignoring the covenant stipulations

---

123. Nardoni, *Rise Up, O Judge*, 17.
124. Ibid., 42, 90.
125. Ibid., 96–97.
126. Ibid., 97.
127. Ibid., 101–102.

"by violating the rights of God and their neighbours."[128] By using his own preferred terms אמת, חסד and דעת (cf. 4:1–10), Hosea accused Israel of lacking these three substantial dispositions. Like Amos, Hosea criticised Israel's worship (6:6), but, Nardoni notes, Hosea went further than Amos. "While the latter had focused on social injustice as conduct incompatible with true worship, Hosea inquired into the inner dispositions necessary to acceptable worship, dispositions that emerge from the depth of a human being and lead on to make an enduring commitment regarding God and one's neighbours."[129] Like Amos and Micah, Hosea stated that true faith included the practice of צדקה and חסד and social relations (10:12; 12:6). Such practices made it possible to have order (צדק) in the community. Like Isaiah, Hosea spoke of a lawsuit by Yahweh because of Israel's violation of the covenant (cf. 4:1–3). Nardoni devotes only two pages to consideration of Hosea, analysing only one passage from the text and thus cannot do justice to other areas of Hosea's social critique of the society in his time. Nevertheless, his treatment of the message of Hosea is a valid one, and it correlates with our attempt to approach the book.

In *Justice: A Biblical Perspective,* Dempsey employs a canonical approach to reflect the justice theme in both the Old and New Testaments. Unlike other volumes, however, her analysis proceeds from a thematic and reader-centred approach and is informed by contemporary social, ideological and ecological concerns. Dempsey states that the source of injustice in the biblical social world was "the loss of right relationship" – right relationship with their God and right relationship with one another.[130] She asserts that that the biblical prophets continually spoke out against injustice and called the people back to a vision of justice, righteousness and lovingkindness. Accordingly, justice in the Old Testament and New Testament requires a focus on compassion for all humanity, as well as all creation. This sense of justice, she argues, includes not only the community of faith, but

---

128. Ibid., 104.
129. Ibid., 105.
130. Dempsey, *Justice,* 2.

also the perpetrators of injustice and the victims of injustice, especially the weak and vulnerable.[131]

Dempsey pays particular attention to the principle of *lex talionis*, often called the Deuteronomistic theology of retribution.[132] Hence many of the Old Testament texts reflect that divine justice took on the characteristic of being punitive in order to attain justice and liberation. However, she also notes that not all Old Testament texts present divine justice as punitive. She compares Jeremiah 5, which portrays God as a vengeful God who metes out retribution with Genesis 4:1–16, which portrays God acting justly with compassion on the transgressor. Similarly, Dempsey sees Hosea 11:8–9 as another alternative view to Jeremiah's view of God's ways and this justice is executed in compassion.[133] Jesus best exemplifies this view in the crucifixion account (Luke 23:32–34). Jesus, the one persecuted unjustly, intercedes with God for the persecutors, pleading for their forgiveness. Along these lines, she observes Hosea's eschatological vision in Hosea 2:16–20 in which the "renewed covenant would include God's relationship with the people and the people's relationship with non-human life and the land."[134]

Dempsey's emphasis on the compassionate aspect of justice is impressive. If the loving aspect of God in forgiving the unforgivable must be understood as another aspect of justice, perhaps the compassionate aspect of Yahweh reflected in Hosea can be categorised as relational justice. Moreover, Dempsey's basic understanding that the source of injustice is the loss of right relationship offers us a theoretical grounding to analyse Hosea's sense of justice.

The work of Premnath, which investigates the social reality of the eighth-century prophets, can be included in the field of justice studies.[135]

---

131. Ibid., 3.
132. Ibid., 9. Primarily, *lex talionis* advocated "an eye for an eye and a tooth for a tooth" mentality. This is reflected texts such as Exod 21:23–25; Lev 24:19–21 and Deut 19:21. The Deuteronomic theology of retribution is basically derived from Deuteronomy 28 where blessings are promised to the obedient and curses to the disobedient.
133. Dempsey, *Justice*, 36.
134. Ibid., 101.
135. D. N. Premnath, *Eighth Century Prophets: A Social Analysis* (St Louis: Chalice Press, 2003); *idem*, "Amos and Hosea: Socio-historical Background and Prophetic Critique,"

In *Eighth Century Prophets: A Social Analysis*, Premnath examines the process of land accumulation (latifundialization) in the books of Amos, Hosea, Isaiah and Micah. His analysis evidences that the growth of large estates was a key concern in the eighth-century prophets. Using information from archaeology, social science and biblical texts, Premnath presents a working hypothesis concerning the eighth-century social reality. In this, he sees colonisation, regional specialisation, demographics and trade and commerce as indicators.

Accordingly, Premnath reads Hosea 5:10; 7:3–7; 8:14; 9:1–3; 10:13–15; 12:1; 12:7–9 to have described the depriving land accumulation, luxurious lifestyle of the upper class, growth of urban centres, oppressive extraction of surplus, brutal militarization and illicit market conditions.[136] He concludes that the beneficiaries of the unprecedented economic growth and political stability under Jeroboam II and Uzziah were the ruling minority group of the elite community, whose accumulation of land and wealth came at the expense of the common peasant majority. Tested against this background, the fundamental issue raised by the prophets, according to Premnath, is: who has access to the economic base? This concern prompted the prophets to address the unjust accumulation of wealth and unequal access to the economic base that eventually leads us to a justice question.[137] Premnath further asserts that the prophets "knew exactly what the causes were and who was responsible for them. They did not speak in abstraction. They knew the oppression/injustice existed and who the oppressors and oppressed were."[138] Thus Premnath concludes, "Hosea is just as concerned with social justice as Amos, but simply expresses it differently."[139] A full-length discussion of this important aspect, however, is beyond the scope of his work. However, this overarching concern is the motivation that guides this present study.

WW 28 (2008): 125–132.
136. Premnath, *Eighth Century Prophets*, 99–161.
137. Ibid., 182.
138. Ibid.
139. Premnath, "Amos and Hosea," 126.

Summary Assessment

Our survey of representative justice studies has reflected what is well known among biblical scholars, which is that there is a pair of Hebrew words that suggest the core of what is meant by social justice. In a separate chapter, we intend to elaborate the word pair as well as other related terms favoured by Hosea with an aim to crystallise their possible meanings. Having observed the importance of משפט וצדקה, most scholars have avoided exploring the terms in the context of Hosea. Perhaps the obsession with the terms' narrower sense, *social justice,* contributes to this hesitancy. For this, we need a closer look at other associated terms and different form of injustices denounced by Hosea.

Several scholars rightly emphasise the importance of "relationship" concerning justice. If we can identify "right relationship" as an underlying principle of צדק and משפט, as Gossai has done, the customary opinion that understands משפט וצדקה in terms of *social justice* can be revisited. If Dempsey's claim – that the source of injustice in the biblical world was the loss of right relationship – is correct, Hosea will be a good place to explore the idea. Perhaps a broader spectrum of "relational justice" will clarify what we mean by biblical understanding of justice. As such, *social justice* can be regarded as a sub-category of *relational justice.* At any rate, it suffices to say that no substantial examination of justice or social justice has been done on the book of Hosea. Above all, no scholars have looked at the book through its relational justice aspect as a lens for reading Hosea.

CHAPTER THREE

In Search of Principles: Toward a Relational Justice

Justice in the Writings of Classical Philosophy

Every major work on ethics, from Aristotle's *Nicomachean Ethics* to Rawls' *A Theory of Justice*, has held that justice is part of the core of morality in Western civilization. Thus, we will survey a selection of classical works starting from Aristotle with the hope that it might shed light on our consideration of justice in the book of Hosea.

Essentially, justice has been defined as giving each person what he or she deserves. Justice is done when a person receives what is due to him or her and the same holds for social institutions and for states. Injustice is always a violation of someone's rights or deserts. Nevertheless, a practical application of justice in society is not that simple. What is the primary basis of justice? How does one judge whether a person is treated justly or unjustly? What principles can be used to determine justice or injustice?

According to Plato, justice (**dikaiosunh**) is a social virtue for individuals and for states.[1] Justice, for him, is a harmonious relationship, which exists when everyone minds their own business, does which is most naturally suitable for them, without trespassing upon the natural ability of another.[2]

---

1. Plato, *The Republic*, trans. H. D. P. Lee; 1956; repr. (Harmondsworth: Penguin Books, 1967), 174–198, 422–449.
2. Ibid., 181–182, 433–434.

That is, "those who are naturally fit to rule do rule, and those who are naturally fit to obey, do obey."[3]

Sharing Plato's view, Aristotle upholds that justice refers to social virtue in relation to our neighbours. He advocates two types of social virtue: "general" and "particular" justice. The former has to do with lawfulness and concerns the acts of all virtues, which are fixed by law.[4] Those who possess justice in this sense are capable of practising it not only for themselves but also for the advantage of others.[5] Thus, righteousness or justice is the only virtue that benefits someone other than its possessor.[6]

"Particular" justice deals with fairness and equality.[7] It aims at private good and is further divided into two parts: distribution of honour and rectification in private transactions.[8] Just distribution entails that equal cases are treated alike and that unequal cases are treated differently in direct proportion to the differences between them. Rectificatory justice deals with unequal distribution between people and aims to redress the imbalance of unfair profit gained by one party at the expense of another.[9] Therefore, the equal is an average between the more and the less.[10] In other words, the just is the "proportionate."[11] Thus, justice is defined as a restoration of balance.

Plato and Aristotle have laid the groundwork by defining the basic principles of justice. Yet what is the goal of justice? How do we determine the rightness of actions? Mill in his classical exposition, *Utilitarianism*,[12]

---

3. Joel Feinberg and Hyman Gross, eds., *Justice: Selected Readings* (Encino: Dickenson Publishing Company, 1977), 2.

4. Pietro Palazzini, "Justice," in *Dictionary of Moral Theology*, ed. Pietro Palzzini (London: Burns Oates, 1962), 674.

5. Aristotle, *The Ethics of Aristotle: The Nicomachean Ethics Translated*, trans. J. A. K. Thomson; 1956; repr. (Harmondsworth: Penguin Books, 1969), 141–142.

6. Ibid., 142.

7. Ibid., 140–144.

8. Ibid., 145. Aristotle uses terms such as rectificatory, remedial, corrective or compensatory interchangeably.

9. Ibid., 148.

10. Ibid., 149.

11. Ibid., 147.

12. John Stuart Mill, *Utilitarianism* (11th ed.; London: Longmans, Green & Co., 1891). An earlier proponent for this approach of maximizing utility (pleasure, in his case) was Jeremy Bentham, *An Introduction to the Principles of Morals and Legislation* (London: W. Pickering, 1823).

attempts to answer these questions. The right thing to do, for Mill, is what produces the most good or happiness.[13] Therefore, utility (in his case happiness) is the sole criterion of right and wrong. According to Mill, justice is a name for certain classes of moral rules, especially those of binding obligation which protect individual claims considered essential to the well-being of the society. Those claims, however, could be overridden by a greater good and are subjected to the dictates of a utilitarian calculus. Hence justice is a subordinate value. The overriding implication then is that the end determines what is right so that individual rights can be overridden in order to maximise the good of the others.

It is obvious that utilitarianism recognises the greatest utility as the sole criterion for a right action. For this reason, utilitarianism is often criticised for not having a principle of justice. Is there any principle of justice that takes the claims of the individual seriously? This question is what Rawls attempts to address in his social contract theory.[14]

In *A Theory of Justice*, Rawls develops a theory that will do justice to individuals by safeguarding the risk of their rights for the sake of the good of others. The underlying principle in his approach is justice as fairness.[15] For Rawls, humans are free and rational beings and the principle of justice is the outcome of rational choice. In cooperation, they can have ends they want to achieve by adhering to mutually accepted regulatory principles.[16] In order to generate just principles, Rawls has proposed what he calls the original position of equality.[17] From that original position, the

---

13. Karen Lebacqz, *Six Theories of Justice: Perspectives from Philosophical and Theological Ethics* (Minneapolis: Augsburg Publishing House, 1987), 15.

14. The notion of the social contract is an agreement between individuals or an agreement between individuals and a governing power that unites into a society. The process is done through a mutual consent to abide by certain rules and by accepting duties to form a well-organised society to protect one another from various harms. Jennifer Speake, ed., "Social Contract," in *A Dictionary of Philosophy* (London: Pan Books, 1979), 328.

15. John Rawls, *A Theory of Justice* (Cambridge: Belknap Press of Harvard University Press, 1971). A shorter summary of his main argument can be seen in John Rawls, "Justice as Fairness," (first published in *The Philosophical Review* 67 (1958): 164–194, reprinted in Feinberg and Gross eds., *Justice: Selected Readings*, 101–115.

16. Rawls, *A Theory of Justice*, 11.

17. The original position is an assumed situation in which the representative parties select principles that will regulate the fundamental structure of the society they will live in.

representatives make a choice from behind a "veil of ignorance."[18] This means that the parties choosing principles lack certain kinds of particular facts that otherwise might make the process of distribution unfair.[19] Besides, the persons involved in this process are mutually fair-minded, taking no particular interest in each other's aims and purposes.[20]

The bottom line of Rawls' theory is to protect those who are "least advantaged"[21] and provide equal rights and liberties. In other words, the core aim is to "maximise the minimum."[22] Unlike Mill's utilitarian approach, Rawls' theory does not leave the individual vulnerable to trading off their liberty to the demands of the greater good of others. Whether Rawls' theory succeeds or not is beyond the scope of this review. While the utilitarian approach pays attention to the "practical" sphere of justice by positing "happiness" as the foundation of justice, Rawls' theory emphasises a system of justice by deriving principles without positing any single goal.

Rawls' proposal to benefit the least advantaged is intriguing. Yet who then is responsible to do such an enormous task? Rawls might envision a strong and reasonable state to facilitate this end, which has challenged Nozick to come up with an alternative model that he calls the "entitlement" view.

In *Anarchy, State and Utopia*, Nozick argues for a minimal role of the state in the establishment of justice.[23] He sets his attitude against the background of the view of Locke and Kant that individuals are ends in them-

---

18. Rawls, *A Theory of Justice*, 11. The veil of ignorance is a method of determining the morality of certain issues. Imagine a community who are to reshape or redistribute the societal roles. These people must lack certain kinds of knowledge. They should not know their possible place in society or social status, or position; nor should they know their fortune in the distribution of wealth or natural abilities. If they had such particular knowledge, it is highly likely that they would skew the principles in their own favour, which would certainly be unfair.

19. Rawls, *A Theory of Justice*, 137. What the parties do know about the society is subject to circumstances of justice, which means there are conflicts that require adjustment, but by cooperation, they can achieve what is beneficial for the society. Moreover, what these persons must know about the initial economic theory, social organization and human psychology.

20. Ibid., 126–128.
21. Ibid., 15.
22. Ibid., 152–156.
23. Robert Nozick, *Anarchy, State, and Utopia* (New York: Basic Books, 1974).

selves, possessing certain natural rights. According to Nozick, "individuals have rights, and there are things no person or group may do to them (without violating their rights)."[24] That is, "individuals are ends and not merely means," and no actions are permitted that violate their fundamental human rights.[25] These are rights against harm by others, rights to freedom of exchange for choice and action, and rights to own private property. Therefore, the role of government is only to protect those individual rights and to provide compensation for their violations.

The underlying criterion of justice, according to Nozick, is fairness in exchange, and hence procedural or "commutative" rather than distributive justice. For him, a person's holding is just, provided that "it arises from a just situation by just steps."[26] That is, justice is characterised by the original acquisition and exchange of the holdings. For this reason, Nozick rejects all ideas of patterned or end-state principles of distribution. These might include a notion to promote the most good for the greatest number projected by Mill, or a proposition to benefit the least advantaged by Rawls, as well as such formulaic principles, "to each according to need," or "to each according to merit."[27] For him, these end-result principles of justice violate the fundamental Kantian principle of individual's freedom of choice.[28] He even goes so far as to declare that taxes are equivalent to forced labour.[29] Instead, his basic principle follows "from each as they choose; to each as they are chosen,"[30] and this theory he calls "entitlement."

We have surveyed five philosophies of justice. Indeed, these are all essential elements of justice. Yet do we trust human capability too much? Are these philosophical orientations of justice practical in the current society in this sinful world? The question of its limitation and possibility is precisely what Niebuhr attempts to answer. We are now moving from philosophical reasoning towards Christian grounds for a theory of justice.

---

24. Nozick, *Anarchy, State*, ix.
25. Ibid., 29, 31.
26. Ibid., 150.
27. Ibid., 155.
28. Ibid., 167.
29. Ibid., 169.
30. Ibid., 160.

Niebuhr's approach takes seriously prophetic religion in history.[31] He identifies love in two different ways: mutual and sacrificial.[32] The former sees love in terms of harmony where people are motivated by love in interpersonal relationships, promoting a spirit of brotherhood. The latter describes love in terms of self-sacrifice in which Jesus is the "perfect fruit of prophetic religion."[33] The cross is the perfect symbol for such harmony. Yet this selfless identification for perfect harmony is impossible in this sinful world[34] because "the love commandment stands in juxtaposition to the fact of sin."[35]

For Niebuhr, perfect justice with the absence of conflict of interests remains an impossible possibility in political and economic realms.[36] Since perfect love is unattainable, perfect harmony of justice is impossible. Realistic justice, therefore, is only imperfect justice in which conflicting interests are arbitrated by mutual love.[37] Thus, the principles of justice are logical approximations of the law of love through balances of power in a world in which conflict is inevitable.[38] Accordingly, Niebuhr declares, "justice that is only justice is less than justice."[39] This explains his dualistic ethical view of justice. Love requires the norms of justice, but then justice without love is less than complete and hence neither is adequate in itself.

---

31. Reinhold Niebuhr, *An Interpretation of Christian Ethics* (4th ed.; London: Bradford & Dickens, 1936; repr., London: SCM Press, 1948); *The Nature and Destiny of Man: A Christian Interpretation* (vol. 1 of *Human Nature;* 1941; repr., London: Nisbet, 1949); *The Nature and Destiny of Man: A Christian Interpretation* (vol. 2 of *Human Destiny;* 1943; repr., London: Nisbet, 1955); *Moral Man and Immoral Society: A Study in Ethics and Politics* (London: SCM Press, 1932, 1963).
32. Niebuhr, *Nature and Destiny, vol 2,* 71–73.
33. Niebuhr, *Christian Ethics,* 47.
34. Ibid., 61.
35. Ibid., 75.
36. This impossibility of perfect love has to do with the capacities of collective human beings. Elsewhere, Niebuhr discusses love as a possibility for individuals. Nevertheless, this achievement is only possible for rare individuals. Niebuhr, *Christian Ethics,* 121, 211.
37. Niebuhr, *Nature and Destiny, vol 2,* 92.
38. Niebuhr, *Christian Ethics,* 150–159; Niebuhr, *Nature and Destiny, vol 2,* 255.
39. Niebuhr, *Moral Man,* 258.

Summary Assessment

We now have several basic principles of justice, and the differences of emphasis are remarkable. They are more or less the bases of contemporary forms of justice which will be elaborated further on. The six thinkers reviewed represent six principles of justice: (1) Justice, according to Plato, is harmony in society where each individual minds their own work, fulfilling the role for which they are best suited. (2) Aristotle grounds justice in distribution in accordance with merit and restoration of balance when unequal distribution occurs. (3) Mill's utilitarian view recognises that justice is determined in proportion to the extent it produces happiness, and in fact denies that there are absolute rules for justice. (4) Based on the notion of autonomy as essential, Rawls locates justice in the rights of and fairness to the individual, especially those of the "least advantaged." (5) Nozick's entitlement theory defines justice as protecting the fundamental rights of property and choice for each individual and locates justice in fairness in individual exchange. (6) Niebuhr's faith-based approach looks for a balance of power so that the weak are protected from the strong. Yet all principles of justice are inadequate and could be improved in accordance with the demands of love, the perfect justice.

In brief, the diverse theories of justice elucidate the multifaceted nature of justice. No single theory is sufficient to encompass all the requirements of justice. This study reveals that there is an aspect of justice that needs inclusion. Perhaps we need a theory of justice grounded on its restorative flavour.

Contemporary Forms of Justice

We will examine five contemporary forms of justice, namely: commutative, social, distributive, retributive and restorative justice. The purpose of this examination is to argue that there is one neglected aspect – the relational – that runs through all types of justice.

Commutative Justice

Social teaching, particularly by Roman Catholics, distinguishes three dimensions of basic justice: commutative justice, distributive justice and social justice.[40] Commutative or procedural justice regulates and harmonises the exercise of relations between individuals and their relationships to a larger community. It aims to prevent fraud, theft and violence. It particularly calls for "fundamental fairness in all agreements, exchanges between individuals or private social groups," demanding equal respect for human dignity of all persons.[41] In other words, it refers to the idea of fairness and transparency "to ensure that each person is treated fairly or to address transgressions when they are not."[42] For example, lying or breaking promises denies another person's right to know the truth, which destroys the trust essential for good relationships.[43] As mentioned elsewhere, Nozick would limit justice to the commutative sphere of individual exchanges.[44] In both legal and non-legal contexts, there must be transparency of the processes by which the decisions are made and resources are allocated.

Social Justice

Social justice has become a generic term today,[45] but it is essentially one aspect of justice that guides the relationships between individuals and the

---

40. David Hollenbach, "Modern Catholic Teachings Concerning Justice," in *The Faith That Does Justice: Examining the Christian Sources for Social Change*, ed. John C. Haughey (New York: Paulist Press, 1977), 207–231.

41. U.S. Catholic Bishops, *Economic Justice for All: Pastoral Letter on Catholic Social Teaching and the U.S. Economy* (Washington, DC: National Conference of Catholic Bishops, 1986), 35.

42. Paul J. Wadell, *Happiness and the Christian Moral Life: An Introduction to Christian Ethics* (New York: Rowman & Littlefield Publishers, 2008), 223.

43. Wadell, *The Christian Moral Life*, 224. A concomitant aspect of this principle aims to ensure fair procedure of allocation of resources. This attitude of fairness connotes the idea of fair play in contrast to the fair share of distributive justice.

44. For instance, if *A* buys a book from *B* at a market price, the exchange is just. If *A* steals a book from *B* or obtains it by force, that transfer is unjust.

45. The term "social justice" was coined by the Jesuit Luigi Taparelli in 1840 based on the teachings of Thomas Aquinas and given further exposure by Antonio Rosmini-Serbati (1848). See Joseph Zajda, et al. "Education and Social Justice: Issues of Liberty and Equality in the Global Culture," in *Education and Social Justice*, ed. Joseph Zajda (Dordrecht: Springer, 2006), 1.

larger community.[46] It presupposes commutative justice as a default position. Yet it transcends mere just procedures or regulations. Its sole aim is the welfare of community by creating an egalitarian society grounded on "the principles of equality and solidarity, that understands and values human rights, and that recognises the dignity of every human being."[47] Correspondingly, it goes hand-in-hand with distributive justice to create a harmonious society. While distributive justice focuses on goods one receives from society, social justice focuses on what one owes to one's fellow human beings.

Rawls popularised social justice as a secular concept in the late twentieth century, even though its original conception went back to Mill before him.[48] Setting his thought against the context of utilitarian principles of Bentham and Mill, the social contract ideas of Locke, and Kant's categorical imperative, Rawls adheres to a humanistic view that "Each person possesses an inviolability founded on justice that even the welfare of society as a whole cannot override."[49] Social justice is grounded on the concepts of equality and rights. Yet its integral purpose is to contribute to the common good of the entire society.[50] All persons "have an obligation to be active and productive participants in the life of society and that society has a duty to enable them to participate in this way."[51]

Distributive Justice

Distributive justice or economic justice refers to the idea of sharing benefits, resources and burdens in ways that are fair and just. By assuming procedural justice as a condition, it supervises the distribution of benefits and burdens to its individual members "by ensuring that each person receives

---

46. Wadell, *The Christian Moral Life*, 225.
47. Zajda, "Education and Social Justice," 1.
48. See John Stuart Mill, *Utilitarianism, Liberty & Representative Government* (1910; repr., Rockville: Wildside Press, 2007), 57, 59.
49. Rawls, *A Theory of Justice*, 3, 4.
50. David Hollenbach, *The Common Good and Christian Ethics* (Cambridge: Cambridge University Press, 2002), 203.
51. Bishops, *Economic Justice for All*, 36.

an equitable share of the common goods of a society."[52] Yet there are four theories to explain how a just mechanism of distribution can function.

First, *egalitarian* justice says that justice can only exist within the sphere of equality. It demands equality of opportunity and equality of outcome. Nonetheless, this does not mean that all people get whatever they want or desire, but "no external factors will prevent people from fairly competing for the rights and goods available in a given society."[53] This approach advocates similar treatment for similar cases (i.e. "not all human beings are in comparable situations . . . but all those who are in a comparable situation should be treated equally)."[54] Rawls' approach to justice can be plausibly associated with this egalitarian understanding of justice.

A second theory advocated by socialism is *need justice*. This approach says "from each according to his ability, to each according to his need."[55] The underlying notion is that "what individuals are owed is based primarily on their concrete needs in a given sphere."[56] This approach advocates a blindfolded fairness. It presupposes that equality must be at times sacrificed to response to specific needs of an individual or to groups of people in the community.[57] Here too, Rawls' second principle falls into this category, which aims to guarantee benefit to the least advantaged in the society.

Third, *libertarian justice* says that "from each as they choose and to each as they are chosen."[58] All persons have the freedom to choose and are certainly free to pursue their own good in their own way as long as they "do not deprive others of theirs, or impede their efforts to obtain it."[59] Everyone is the rightful owner of their own bodily, and mental and spiritual health.[60]

---

52. Wadell, *The Christian Moral Life*, 224.

53. Dennis P. Hollinger, *Choosing the Good: Christian Ethics in a Complex World* (Grand Rapids: Baker Academic, 2002), 227.

54. Richard Higginson, *Dilemmas: A Christian Approach to Moral Decision Making* (Louisville: John Knox Press, 1988), 173.

55. Karl Marx, *Critique of the Gotha Programme: With Letters from Engels and the Gotha Programme* (Peking: Foreign Language Press, 1972), 18.

56. Hollinger, *Choosing the Good*, 231.

57. As Pope John XXIII declared, "all people have a right to life, food, clothing, shelter, rest, medical care, education and employment." Bishops, *Economic Justice for All*, xi.

58. Nozick, *Anarchy, State*, 160.

59. John Stuart Mill, *On Liberty* (2nd ed.; London: John W. Parker & Son, 1859), 27.

60. Mill, *On Liberty*, 27.

By embracing a minimal role for government, libertarian justice in effect calls for a right to life, a right to freedom of speech, press and assembly and a right to property.[61] Noticeably, the apparent problem with this approach is a tendency to ignore that true justice, at times, limits someone else's freedom, especially in relation with retributive justice or with equality in distribution.

Finally, *meritorious justice,* espoused by capitalism, says that benefit should be distributed according to the value of the contribution an individual makes to the economics of a society. This view focuses on what is owed a person by virtue of their performance.[62] People should be rewarded for being proactive in contributing, provided that fair procedures are in place within a given sphere. Again, Nozick's notion of "whatever happens from a just situation by just procedures is just" works well with this approach, because merit is deemed the best way to reward people for compensation of actions, efforts and impact for productivity. A number of Christian scholars reflect this philosophical influence.[63] However, justice understood as merit alone will not provide a just distribution in a society, because by its very nature, merit justice attempts to ignore the disadvantaged social classes, such as impaired children or the handicapped elderly.

Retributive Justice

Retributive justice deals with a link between crime and sentence, considering whether a given punishment is morally acceptable in response to wrongdoing. Retribution justifies punishment on the grounds that the offender deserves it. It concerns retribution – paying back – rather than maximisation of welfare. It implies that there should be "equivalence" between the punishment and the crime.[64] In line with Kantian categorical imperative principle, this view holds that punishment should be imposed regardless

---

61. See The United Nation's Universal Declaration of Human Rights (1948).
62. Hollinger, *Choosing the Good*, 226.
63. See Ronald H. Nash, *Social Justice and the Christian Church* (Milford: Mott Media, 1983), 57 and E. Calvin Beisner, *Prosperity and Poverty: The Compassionate Use of Resource in a World of Scarcity* (Westchester, IL: Crossway, 1988), 54.
64. Michael Schluter, *Christianity in a Changing World: Biblical Insight on Contemporary Issues* (London: Marshall Pickering, 2000), 98.

of its alleged beneficial consequences.[65] Retributivism is thus "backward-looking"[66] as actions are right or wrong regardless of what might happen in the future.

The notion of retributive justice can be traced back as far as the ancient days, such as the *lex talionis* law. Nevertheless, retributive justice differs from simply revenge law of the jungle,[67] because it justifies punishment only if it inflicts the suffering that is deserved.[68] Like a theory of distributive justice, it links justice with deserts.[69] As such, the assessment of deserts will depend on the offender's blameworthiness in relation to the crimes.

Restorative Justice

Like retributive justice, restorative justice probes the link between the crime and the punishment, but its aim is to amend or restore the distorted relationships between the offenders, victims and the community, which have been damaged by the crime.[70] In order to bring things back to their normal state, restorative justice aims to convince the offender to accept responsibility, either by making amendment or reparation to those who have been hurt and harmed by their offence.

Zehr argues that the notion of restorative justice consists fundamentally of negotiated, compensatory settlements guided by community justice, which places a high premium on maintaining relationships and on

---

65. Ibid.
66. Michael Cavadino and James Dignan, *The Penal System: An Introduction* (4th ed.; 1992; repr., London: Sage Publication, 2007), 37, 44.
67. Philosophers differentiate between vengeance and retributive justice proper. Kant sees that retributive justice is justifiable but dismisses vengeance entirely. For Nozick, revenge is emotional and merely personal, while retribution is justifiable and impersonal.
68. Antony Duff and David Garland, *A Reader on Punishment* (Oxford: Oxford University Press, 1994), 7.
69. This concept has been regarded as obsolete for many years, especially in intellectual circles. However, retributivist thinking has seen its resurgence in the 1970s, notably in the form of "just model." An American report, American Friends Service Committee, *Struggle for Justice* (New York: Hill and Wang, 1971), launched "just deserts" theory which reacted against the "excessive discretion over sentencing in the rehabilitative era." By placing deterrence as an aim, retributism was placed firmly on the agenda. Cavadino, *The Penal System*, 45; Schluter, *Christianity in a Changing World*, 98.
70. Cavadino, *The Penal System*, 48.

reconciliation.⁷¹ The two foundational biblical concepts for restorative justice are *shalom* and covenant.⁷² The main concern of Zehr's analysis is to emphasise the restorative dimensions of justice in contrast to its retributive dimensions.⁷³

In the 1980s, concerns for restorative justice emerged around the world. For instance, Native Americans raised challenges to a white dominated justice system,⁷⁴ while the indigenous challenges to incarceration occurred notably in Canada, Australia and New Zealand.⁷⁵ The approaches adopted in New Zealand and Australia were subsequently identified as a form of restorative justice.⁷⁶ Correspondingly, another restorative wave arose in Latin America during the 1980s, with a movement called *Truth and Reconciliation Commissions* (TRCs).⁷⁷ TRCs expanded across the continent and eventually spread all over the globe.⁷⁸

---

71. Howard Zehr, *Changing Lenses* (3rd ed.; 1990; repr., Scottdale: Herald Press, 2005), 107.

72. Ibid., 130.

73. Ibid., 184–185. Zehr argues that a restorative justice approach identifies "people as victims and recognises the centrality of the interpersonal dimension."

74. Burnside, "Retribution and Restoration," in Johnstone, *Handbook of Restorative Justice*, 76.

75. See Allan MacRae and Howard Zehr, *The Little Book of Family Group Conferences: New Zealand Style* (Intercourse: Good Books, 2004), 10. The Maori leaders in New Zealand pointed out that the Western system of justice was ineffective with their culturally different community. Instead of simply meting out punishment by the judges, they wanted to find the cause of crime, which was part of resolving it.

76. Key proponents of restorative justice in this region are John Braithwaite and Christopher D. Marshall. See John Braithwaite, *Crime, Shame, Reintegration* (1989; repr., Cambridge: Cambridge University Press, 1999); *Restorative Justice and Responsive Regulation* (Oxford: Oxford University Press, 2002); Christopher D. Marshall, *Beyond Retribution: A New Testament Vision for Justice, Crime, and Punishment* (Auckland: Lime Grove House Publishing, 2001); *idem*, "Offending, Restoration and the Law-abiding Community: Restorative Justice in the New Testament and in the New Zealand Experience," *JSCE* 27 (2007): 3–30.

77. For an in-depth examination, see Priscilla B. Hayner, *Unspeakable Truths: Transitional Justice and the Challenge of Truth Commissions* (2d ed.; 2001; repr., New York: Routledge, 2011).

78. See Guillermo Kerber, "Overcoming Violence and Pursuing Justice: an Introduction to Restorative Justice Procedures," *ER* 55 (2003): 152. The five strongest TRCs, according to Hayner, include South Africa, Guatemala, Peru, Timor-Leste, and Morocco. See Hayner, *Unspeakable Truths*, 27–46. Perhaps the most striking example of it was the South African model when Mandela's government tried to implement the restorative justice approach to convince the deeply divided country. As the legislation issued by Mandela's

In short, the overriding aim of a restorative approach is to restore victims, that is, a victim-centred criminal justice system which aims at restoring both the offenders and the community.[79] Restore means *back to*, but Kerber rightly asks: "restore back to what if the previous situation in unjust?" Thus, "restorative justice should mean not only 'back to' a just previous condition . . . , but *pro-storative,* that is, building new and just relationships in the community."[80] It should be noted, however, that like other theories, restorative justice is a complex enterprise, becoming an integral part of long-standing debates at the beginning of the twenty-first century with regard to its strengths and limits.[81]

Summary Assessment

Defining justice is no easy matter. At times the differences are striking, at other times their intentions are overlapping. Five types of justice have been identified: (1) Commutative justice occurs in situations where the exercise of reciprocal rights between individuals has been protected and regulated by just procedures with equal respect to all persons. (2) Social justice occurs in contexts where the rights of every member of the society are safeguarded, distribution of goods is carried out with just procedures and individual members also maintain equality and solidarity of the community by contributing towards those who are in need. (3) Distributive justice occurs in circumstances where people receive their due, treating equals equally and unequals unequally. (4) Retributive justice does not merely mean revenge, but aims to punish the guilty in proportion to the seriousness of their

---

office puts it, "there is a need for understanding but not for vengeance, a need for reparation but not for retaliation, a need for Ubuntu but not victimization." (Promotion of National Unity and Reconciliation Act 1995).

79. John Braithwaite, "Restorative Justice as a Better Future" (Paper presented at Dorothy J Killam Memorial Lectures, Dalhousie University, 1996). Cited 2 May 2011. Online: http://www.iirp.org/article _detail.php?article_id=NDk4.

80. Kerber, "Overcoming Violence," 155.

81. For a comprehensive analysis of this complexity, see Kathleen Daly and Russ Immarigeon, "The Past, Present, and Future of Restorative Justice: Some Critical Reflections," *CJR* 1 (1998): 21–47. Cited 2 May 2011. Online: http://www98.griffith.edu.au/dspace/bitstream/10072/12484/1/8383.pdf. A good review of this broader glimpse of restorative justice theory and practice has been presented in Gerry Johnstone and Daniel W. Van Ness, eds., *Handbook of Restorative Justice* (Cullompton: Willan Publishing, 2007).

wrongdoings. (5) Restorative justice occurs in situations where distorted relationships have been amended, aiming to restore the victims, offenders and the community involved.

It is noticeable that all the different types of justice are interconnected since their demarcation lines are thin. None of them will work for every case. For instance, a society solely focused on egalitarian justice will not be a free society; a society engrossed with libertarian justice will not be just; a society fixated with blindfolded justice will not be healthy; a society focused exclusively on restorative justice will not be ordered and a society obsessed with retributive justice will not be harmonious. Thus, the applications of justice must take a context-conscious approach to see what type of justice will be most suitable in a given context. Arguably, there is an underlying principle that lies behind each classification of justice whose ultimate aim is to create a harmonious and just relationship between individuals and between individuals and their larger society. This principle is none other than "right relationships." In this sense, justice is relational. From this theoretical basis, we can analyse a selection of biblical texts that deal with the issue of justice.

Integrating Different Types of Justice in Biblical Contexts

We will briefly identify relevant theological and biblical support for all five definitions of justice. Not surprisingly, the Bible contains much teaching on justice, which largely accommodates every aspect of justice discussed above. Essentially, God's actions and his character (cf. Deut 32:4) through history provide foundations for the Christian understanding of justice.

To begin with, the definitions of commutative and social justice can be boiled down to the protection of rights which is only possible by reciprocal just living between individuals, and between individuals and their larger society. A biblical understanding of rights refers not only to a right not to be harmed, but also more importantly, to take responsibility towards others. Hundreds of supporting examples can be found in the Bible, but a few will suffice. First, biblical justice is associated with right living in all areas of life, where God measures every deed.[82] Second, justice calls for procedural fairness in trials, bearing no false witness.[83] Third, justice is associated with integrity and truthfulness. The people of God are to be watchful with their use of weights or measures[84] and keeping promises.[85] Fourth, justice is associated with a concern for the poor. It is evident that there is biblical support for liberty[86] for all humanity and therefore, no one is to oppress the poor and exploit their hired workers.[87]

Distributive justice, with its diverse emphases on egalitarian, need-based, libertarian and merit-based justice, finds support from the Scriptures. God himself distributes justice to everyone (Deut 10:18–19; Ps 33:5; Matt 5:45; 2 Cor 9:9–10). The concept of receiving what is due to people is best reflected in the distribution of land in Numbers 26:5–56 (cf. Ezek 47:13–48:20), where larger groups are to receive larger inheritances of land. There are substantial biblical references to egalitarian and need-based justice in the Old Testament law. Needless to say, God has a special concern for the poor (Ps 140:12). Similarly, a notion of reward to the righteous is alluded to in many narrative stories. For instance, Abraham was promised a great reward for his good deed (Gen 19:11). Reward is a common bait to promote just character (Ps 19:11; 59:11; Prov 11:18; 22:4). Paul's statement reflects the idea of merit, "Anyone unwilling to work should not eat" (2 Thess 3:10) and Jesus also echoes the same idea by saying, "Labourers deserve their food" (Matt 10:10; 25:14–30; cf. Luke 10:7).

A biblical understanding of freedom does not negate the idea of pursuing our own good in our own way. However, it locates liberty in a relationship with Yahweh by choosing life (Deut 30:19), serving him (Josh 24:15)

---

82. Deut 28:20; Ezra 9:13; Isa 1:16–17; 26:7; Jer 4:4, 18; 18:11; 25:5; 44:22; 20:43–44; Hos 4:9; 5:4; 6:6; 7:1–2; 9:15; 12:2; Amos 8:7 ; Mic 3:4; Zech 1:4; Matt 16:27; John 3:19–20; 5:29.

83. Exod 20:16; 23:1; Deut 5:20; 19:19–20; Prov 19:9.

84. Lev 19:35–36; Deut 35:13–16; Ezek 45:10; Prov 11:1; 20:23; Mic 6:11.

85. Lev 19:12; 5:4; Deut 6:13; 10:20; Jer 4:2; 5:2; 7:9; 12:6; Hos 4:14; Amos 8:14; Isa 45:23; 48:1; 65:16; Matt 35:33–37; Jas 5:12.

86. Lev 25:39, 42; Deut 23:15–16; Ps 146:7; Isa 58:6; Jer 34:9–10; John 8:32; 1 Cor 9:19; Gal 3:29; Col 3:11; 1 Pet 2:16.

87. Lev 19:13; Exod 3:19; 22:21; 23:9; Deut 24:14; Ps 119:122; Isa 58:3; Jer 22:13; Ezek 18:16; Hos 12:7; 14:3; Amos 4:1; 6:14; Mic 2:2; Mal 3:5; Jas 2:6; 5:4.

and doing his precepts (Ps 119:45). The New Testament echoes the same tone that true freedom is found in Christ (John 8:36) and living out his word.[88] Moreover, justice understood as liberty can also be grounded theologically in two ways: human beings are created in the image of God (Gen 9:5f), and the paradigmatic action of Yahweh in the Exodus illustrates the nature of freedom.

In terms of retributive justice, a biblical perspective has a forensic and punitive dimension. Dishonouring his holiness and violation of his covenant law are violations of justice.[89] Punishment for deserts, implicit in the *lex talionis* formula, is illustrated in Genesis 9:6: "Whoever sheds the blood of a human, by a human shall that person's blood be shed;" and Deuteronomy 13:8. This should, in turn, be an effective deterrent: "The rest shall hear and be afraid, and a crime such as this shall never again be committed among you" (19: 20; cf. 13:11; 17:13; 21:11). The notion of punishment in proportion to the offence committed is also hinted at in the restriction of punishment to forty lashes in Deuteronomy 25:3.

The Bible is forthright in its demand for justice in the form of recompense.[90] The overriding principle behind blood-vengeance in the OT assumes communal responsibility, "fulfilling a duty owed to the injured in affirmation of loyalty and affection."[91] It denounces the crime committed by the offender and asserts the victim's right.[92] Hence the retributive notion of justice has an integral role in implementing justice in the society. Yet the biblical concept of retribution also transcends the tribal notion of blood-

---

88. "If you continue in my word, you are truly my disciples; and you will know the truth, and the truth will make you free" (John 8:31–32; cf. 2 Cor 3:17).

89. M. Burch, "Justice," in *Evangelical Dictionary of Theology*, ed. Walter A. Elwell; 2nd ed. (Grand Rapids: Baker Academic, 2001), 641.

90. The most obvious concept of this is presented in *lex talionis* ('an eye for an eye and a tooth for a tooth') formula (Exod 21:23–25; Lev 24:18–20; Deut 19:21). God is praised specifically because vengeance is his (Deut 32:35, 36, 43). Psalmists picture God as an avenging vindicator (Ps 94:1–3). Jesus also affirms the notion: "I tell you that he will see that they get justice [literally 'vengeance' or 'vindication'], and quickly (Luke 18:7–8). Paul reaffirms vengeance is of the Lord (Rom 12:19; cf. Heb 10:30). Vengeance is awaited for the blood that has been slain for the word of God (Rev 6:10).

91. R. E. O. White, "Vengeance," in *Evangelical Dictionary of Theology*, ed. Walter A. Elwell; 2nd ed. (Grand Rapids: Baker Academic, 2001), 1241.

92. Burnside, "Retribution and Restoration," in Johnstone, *Handbook of Restorative Justice*, 140.

vengeance.[93] This is illustrated by the creation of the cities of refuge (Deut 4:1; 19:2; Josh 20:2) in which unpremeditated offenders receive protection until a just judicial decision has been made. Therefore, the idea of recompense "can neither be dismissed nor absolutized."[94]

Though retributive justice is justified in the Bible, God's retributive justice is "never cruel or capricious but always the action of God as a judge, punishment administered to maintain justice."[95] He never executes judgment just for the sake of punishment or retaliation. Leviticus forbids vengeance but commands loving one's neighbours as oneself (Lev 19:18). This characteristic is reflected again in Ezekiel where God takes no pleasure in the death of the wicked (Ezek 33:11). Rather, the purposes behind his judgment are for reparation, harmonisation and restoration.[96] Hence it carries "both the sense of retribution and restoration."[97] In fact, God often withholds due punishment in the hope that people will repent (cf. 2 Pet 3:9). However, on the day of final judgment, he will recompense everyone according to what they have done (cf. Matt 11:21–24; Rom 2:1–11; Rev 20:11–15).

Restorative justice also reflects the need to remedy the wrong done to the victims. Restorative justice in a biblical framework takes "roots in God's inexplicable mercy,"[98] emphasising "Yahweh's steadfast loyalty toward the covenant people and his saving intervention on their behalf."[99] The biblical notion of restorative justice is not opposed to retributive justice.[100] The bib-

---

93. According to Wenham, though the *lex talion* formula occurs in the Bible, it is just a formula that should not be taken literally except in the case of premeditated murder. The intention of the lawgiver is not to demand its literal fulfilment. Rather, it is to compensate for the offence. See Gordon Wenham, "Law and the Legal System in the Old Testament," in *Law, Morality and the Bible: A Symposium,* eds. Bruce Kaye and Gordon Wenham (Leicester: Inter-Varsity Press, 1978), 40.

94. O. O'Donovan, and R. J. Song, "Punishment," in *New Dictionary of Theology,* eds. S. B. Ferguson and et al. (Leicester: Inter-Varsity Press, 1988), 459.

95. Schluter, *Christianity in a Changing World,* 104.

96. For instance, legal texts such as Exodus 21:18–19; 22:1–4 impose a duty on the perpetrators to redress the victims for physical injury and stolen animals or goods.

97. Burch, "Justice," 641.

98. Piet Naudé, "*Sola Gratia* and Restorative Justice," *Scriptura* 83 (2003): 140.

99. Marshall, *Beyond Retribution,* 49.

100. My approach differs from some of the restorative writers who view retributive justice as the antithesis of restoration, failing to see retributive justice as a particular

lical view is that justice is both retributive and restorative in the sense that they fulfil each other. Donahue expounds this interplay clearly when he says, "Yahweh's justice is saving justice where punishment of the sinner is an integral part of restoration."[101] Indeed, restorative justice can only be explained in conjunction with retributive justice. Burnside rightly asserts that the biblical narrative is a "story of restoration that involves retribution."[102] God's justice, however, takes sides when it comes to good and evil, advocating good and opposing evil. Thus, God's delight in good ultimately means his desire for "restoration to the good of God's original creative intent."[103] Accordingly, God's retributive justice in biblical contexts is not punitive, but "restorative punishment"[104] or what one would call "chastisement." The primary aim of retribution (paying back) is restoration. If restorative justice is to be the measure, retributive justice is the plumb line.

The Exodus motif and the crucifixion of Jesus are among the best examples. God's justice, sustaining just deeds and clashing with wickedness is reflected in Exodus where justice was dispensed by bringing down the oppressor and by liberating the oppressed.[105] Yahweh's condemnation should not be equated with mere vengeance on the wicked. Broadly speaking, it is a means [chastisement] to an end [restoration].[106] The crucifixion is

---

approach to punishment. To some extreme critics, everything else with retributive justice smells bad whereas everything with restorative justice is sweet. I concur with Roche and Burnside who argue that the restorative/retributive dichotomy is a false representation. See Declan Roche, "Retribution and Restorative Justice," and Burnside, "Retribution and Restoration," in Johnstone, *Handbook of Restorative Justice*.

101. John R. Donahue, "Biblical Perspectives on Justice," in *The Faith That Does Justice: Examining the Christian Sources for Social Change*, ed. J. C. Haughey (New York: Paulist Press, 1977), 72.

102. Burnside, "Retribution and Restoration," 133.

103. Ibid., 134.

104. Marshall, *Beyond Retribution*, 131–132. By and large, advocates of restorative justice are often reluctant to speak of punishment at all. However, Marshall is on the right track in supposing that punishment can play a positive role in the attainment of restorative justice. Nevertheless, although he rightly suggests that the goal of punishment should aim to restore and repair, he also fails to stress the overlapping or identical goal between retributive and restorative justice whose aim is to restore.

105. Burnside, "Retribution and Restoration," 135.

106. See Marshall, *Beyond Retribution*, footnote no. 48. Markedly, the fundamental aim of God's justice, as Marshall concludes, is "a restorative or reconstructive justice before it is a punitive or destructive justice." Marshall, *Beyond Retribution*, 52.

an explicit manifestation of God's justice [righteousness], accomplished by means of retributive and restorative justice (cf. Rom 3:25–26).[107] As Burnside observes, "Retribution results in restoration to favour with God: the object of wrath is transformed into a child of God. There is an ultimate restoration, but not one that ignores the need for penalty."[108] The central motivations behind the justice of Yahweh are to overcome the powers of evil which threaten the destruction of the world, and his call to return in repentance for ultimate restoration.

A concomitant tension that must be resolved at this point is between justice and love or mercy, as they are often regarded as contradictory. If love is God's very nature, how can God's retributive justice is justified? Niebuhr sees love and justice in tension with each other. Brunner also regards love and justice as two different things.[109] These observations have certain practical value in a fallen world, but fail to perceive the broad nature of the biblical view. As Higginson puts it, "Love also supplements justice in a way that it transcends the notion of right and duty."[110] That is, love and justice supplement each other. If justice aims to give people what is due to them, mercy is willing to give more than their due. McIlroy considers God's mercy in the Old Testament as a link between his love and his just act of deliverance of "his people *even when they do not deserve it*."[111] In fact, this thread runs through both the Old and New Testaments.[112] The two sides of the coin relative to the concept of mercy are well expounded by McIlroy when he states, "God's justice is the demonstration of his love for the op-

---

107. Like in Exodus, the cross overthrows the ultimate oppressor [Satan] and bestows the ultimate liberation to the oppressed [the entire human race].

108. Burnside, "Retribution and Restoration," 136.

109. For Niebuhr, the ethics of Jesus is "impossible possibility." For Brunner, justice known by reason is realistic and related to institutions while love operates in the personal realm. Emil Brunner, *Justice and the Social Order,* trans. Mary Hottinger (London: Lutterworth Press, 1945), 114–118.

110. Higginson, *Dilemmas*, 183.

111. David McIlroy, *Christian Perspectives: A Biblical View of Law and Justice* (Milton Keynes: Paternoster Press, 2004), 12.

112. As Colwell declares, "God is no less gracious in Genesis than in Romans; judgment is no less a possibility in the Gospels than in the Prophets." John E. Colwell, *Living the Christian Story: The Distinctiveness of Christian Ethics* (Edinburgh: T. & T. Clark, 2001), 92.

pressed, vindicating them and rescuing them from their oppressors. God's mercy is the demonstration of his love even for the oppressors, giving them the opportunity to turn away from evil, and enter into right relations with their victims and with their God."[113] Hence God's justice is not in conflict with his love. Indeed, love and justice need each other to be complete.

Summary and Conclusion

We have explored several principles and types of justice. Our examination of the principles of justice primarily underline the promotion of harmony, fair distribution, maximising utility, assisting the least advantaged, respecting the right of choice and balancing power. Similarly, our exploration of the types of justice call for honouring rights and human dignity, maintaining solidarity or treating equally, allocating resources fairly, executing punishment impartially and restoring just relationships. Clearly, these elements are essential parts in any discussion of justice.

We have also observed that the principles and types of justice in the philosophical sphere do not negate the biblical teaching of justice but are largely complementary. Yet this does not mean that the biblical teaching of justice is an equivalent to a "philosophy of justice, something that can appropriately be put alongside Aristotle or John Rawls."[114] Rather, biblical notions of justice have more to offer in supplementing justice concerns in the secular sphere. For instance, a biblical idea of justice, which is closely associated with mercy, which has a healing, reconciling and forgiving essence, is absent in the philosophical sphere. So too, a notion of justice, dictated by love, that requires more than a sense of fairness by giving people more than what is due to them, is not prominent.

The question now arises whether we can suggest any common threads that run through these widely varied perspectives of justice which will bring about a normative approach. Can we appropriate secular conceptions of justice to analyse biblical texts in general and Hosea in particular? This thesis proposes a "relational justice" approach in which all discussions of

---

113. McIlroy, *A Biblical View of Law and Justice*, 13.
114. Forrester, "Social Justice and Welfare," in Gill, *Christian Ethics*, 197.

justice are incorporated under three categories: responsibility, punishment [chastisement] and restoration.

Arguably, justice or injustice always has to do with relationships. Philosophers, for example, have discussed the significance of shared responsibility under the rubrics of "commutative," "social" and "distributive" justice. Similarly, retributive justice, especially with its biblical flavour, imposes punishments [chastisements] to recreate the relational equilibrium upset by the transgression, while restorative justice aims to restore distorted relationships and builds anew. In light of these observations, relationship appears to be woven into all notions of justice. When relationships have been distorted, the purpose of justice is to administer chastisements to offenders in order to repair broken relationships with a view to restoration. This relational approach best explains the moral personality of a holy God and his dealings with his people. Perhaps the same set of moral principles – responsibility, chastisement and restoration – are key components in analysing the message of Hosea.

CHAPTER FOUR

The Biblical Concept of Relational Justice

This brief section will argue that the biblical perspective of justice is primarily relational. In so doing, it will reinvestigate certain key biblical terms relevant to the subject. Arguably, any consideration of justice in the Old Testament must engage with the three main terms צדקה, חסד and משפט. A well-integrated analysis of these important words will provide us with a new perspective on the often-neglected biblical notion of "relational justice."

Justice in Biblical Perspective

There have been many studies on משפט and צדקה in recent decades.[1] Knierim declares that the "ultimate vantage point" in coordinating Old Testament theologies is "the universal dominion of Yahweh in justice and

---

1. José P. Miranda, *Marx and the Bible: A Critique of the Philosophy of Oppression,* trans. J. Eagleson (New York: Maryknoll, 1974; repr., London: SCM Press, 1977); Weinfeld, *Social Justice in Ancient Israel;* Gossai, *Justice, Righteousness*; James P.M. Walsh, *The Mighty from their Thrones: Power in the Biblical Tradition* (Philadelphia: Fortress Press, 1987); Ahuva Ho, *Ṣedeq and Ṣedaqah in the Hebrew Bible* (AUS 7: Theology and Religion, vol. 78; New York: Peter Lang, 1991); John H. Stek, "Salvation, Justice and Liberation in the Old Testament," *CTJ* 13 (1978): 133–165; Sydney Rooy, "Righteousness and Justice," *ERT* 6 (1982): 263–274; Camilla Burns, "Biblical Righteousness and Justice," *LM* 7 (1998): 153–161; Jason J. Ripley, "Covenantal Concepts of Justice and Righteousness, and Catholic-Protestant Reconciliation: Theological Implications and Explorations," *JES* 38 (2001): 95–108; Willard M. Swartley, "The Relation of Justice/righteousness to Shalom/eirēnē," *ExAud* 22 (2006): 29–53.

righteousness."² A majority of scholars understand משפט וצדקה to refer to the just dealing with the poor. Although this narrow reading explains the notion of the terms correctly in several examples, it nonetheless cannot be universalised in such a manner. An overemphasis on this reading may not be sustainable in other contexts, particularly in the book of Hosea. Therefore, each term deserves a separate investigation in order to ascertain their inherent meanings.

צדק as Relational Faithfulness

The biblical term צדק occurs 523 times in the Old Testament.³ In general, צדק means what is right, just, normal, righteous.⁴ It may mean righteousness in general, (moral) uprightness, right conduct, godliness and integrity.⁵ A comparable term in Egyptian is *maat*, meaning "what is right, what is correct, law, order, justice and truth."⁶ As *maat* is the order and law of life, to live according to *maat* is the duty of all.⁷ The use of the equivalent to צדק in Ugaritic texts refers to right relationship (husband and wife): *'aṭṭ ṣdḵ* means "legitimate, rightful or proper wife."⁸ The noun צדק appears as "right" or "uprightness." The adjective means "lawful" or "rightful."⁹

---

2. Rolf P. Knierim, *The Task of Old Testament Theology: Substance, Method, and Cases* (Grand Rapids: Eerdmans, 1995), 15.
3. B. Johnson, "צָדֵק," *TDOT* 12: 239–265 (243).
4. F. Brown, S. R. Driver & C. A. Briggs eds., *Hebrew English Lexicon of the Old Testament* (Peabody: Hendrickson Publishers, 1979), 841–842. Here after *BDB*.
5. David J. A. Clines, ed., *The Concise Dictionary of Classical Hebrew* (Sheffield: Sheffield Phoenix Press, 2009), 374–375.
6. Siegfried Morenz, *Egyptian Religion,* trans. Ann E. Keep (Stuttgart: W. Kohlhammer GmbH, 1960; repr., London: Methuen, 1973), 113.
7. Helmer Ringgren, *Word and Wisdom: Studies in the Hypostatization of Divine Qualities and Functions in the Ancient Near East* (Lund: Hakan Ohlssons Boktryckeri, 1947), 49. Interestingly, the letters of *maat* engraved on the base of the king's throne represent "Gerechtigkeit, Wahrheit, rechte göttliche Ordnung." See Hellmut Brunner, "Gerechtigkeit als Fundament des Thrones," *VT* 8 (1958): 426–428 (426).
8. David Hill, *Greek Words and Hebrew Meanings: Studies in the Semantics of Soteriological Terms* (SNTSMS 5; Cambridge: Cambridge University Press, 1967), 82. Ginsberg translates צדק as "lawful" or "legitimate". See James B. Pritchard, ed., *Ancient Near Eastern Text Relating to the Old Testament* (Princeton: Princeton University Press, 1969), 143. Here after *ANET*.
9. Cyrus H. Gordon, *Ugaritic Textbook: Grammar, Texts in Transliteration, Cuneiform Selections, Glossary, Indices* (AnOr 38; Rome: Pontificium Inst Biblicum, 1965), 472ff.

Another equivalent word for צדק appears in a Phoenician inscription, and can be rendered as "righteous."[10] The root *ṣdḳ* in Arabic primarily denotes "what is right," "firm" and "stable."[11] Rosenthal translates צדק as "proper" [e.g. proper weight, Lev 19:36].[12] All these examples from the ancient Near Eastern contexts show that to arrive at one single tranlation is virtually impossible.

The distinction between צדק and צדקה is not perfectly clear. Jepsen argues that צדק refers to the proper order, whereas צדקה refers to the appropriate behaviour within that order.[13] For Crüsemann, צדק is an abstraction or a quality, צדקה a deed or an action.[14] Johnson also suggests that צדק "evokes the notion of correctness and order, while צדקה emphasises action and activity rather than condition."[15] Interestingly, neither of the two terms is used more closely than the other to identify God. Thus, צדקה/צדק interchangeably connotes both the action as well as the impulse that gives rise to it.

Diestel understands צדק as God's salvific intervention and rejects the notion of retaliatory divine righteousness.[16] Cremer has developed Diestel's view further and he sees צדק as an *iustitia salutifera*. He suggests that צדק is a relational term that fulfils the claims arising out of actual relationship between two persons and not to the relationship of an object to an idea.[17] Along this line, Fahlgren identifies the content of צדק as a person's performance within the norms of community relationship.[18] He suggests that

---

10. Hill, *Greek Words*, 83.
11. Ibid.
12. Franz Rosenthal, "Sedaka, Charity," *HUCA* 23 (1950–51): 411–430 (416).
13. Alfred Jepsen, "צדק und צדקה im AT," in *In Gottes Wort und Gottes Land,* ed. Henning Graf Reventlow (Göttingen: Vandenhoeck & Ruprecht, 1965), 78–79.
14. Frank Crüsemann, "Jahwes Gerechtigkeit (*ṣᵉdāqā/ṣādāq*) im Alten Testament," *EvT* 36 (1976): 427–450.
15. Johnson, "צָדַק," *TDOT* 12: 256.
16. Ludwig Diestel, "Die Idee der Gerechtigkeit, vorzüglich im Alten Testament, biblisch-theologisch dargestellt," *JDTh* 5 (1860): 173–253.
17. Hermann Cremer, *Die paulinische Rechtfertigungslehre im Zusammenhange ihrer geschichtlichen Voraussetzungen* (Gütersloh: Bertelsmann, 1900), 34ff. cited in G. von Rad, *Old Testament Theology I*, trans. D. M. G Stalker; 1957; repr. (London: Oliver and Boyd, 1962), 371.
18. Karl H. Fahlgren, *Ṣedāḳā, nahestehende und entgegengesetzte Begriffe im Alten Testament* (Uppsala: Almquist and Wiksells Boktryckeri-A-B, 1932), 81.

community loyalty and absolute obedience to Yahweh are the basic meanings under which other concepts such as deliverance, victory and salvation are incorporated.[19]

Eichrodt and von Rad have galvanised the understanding of צדק as a salvific activity [*iustitia salutifera*]. For Eichrodt, צדק refers to social, ethical and religious behaviour when applied to human righteousness. He sees that God's צדק connotes "*a loyalty manifested in the concrete relationships of community*," which transcends mere abstract ethical norms.[20] Von Rad considers צדק as the most significant concept for all the relationships of human life – people's relationship to God, fellow human beings, animals and nature.[21] He understands צדק in the context of communal relationship.[22] So for Koch, linking צדקה/צדק with a fixed norm is not demonstrable because it exceeds obligatory behaviour.[23]

By integrating the conclusions of Cremer, Fahlgren and von Rad, Achtemeier affirms the general orientation of צדק in the OT as the fulfilment of the demands of a relationship. She claims that there is no norm of righteousness outside the relationship itself.[24] Several modern scholars have hailed this position.[25] In sum, this school of thought concludes that צדקה/צדק is not a matter of actions that conform to a given set of absolute legal standards, but of behaviour which is in keeping with right relationships. Hence the wicked person is the one who fails to fulfil the demands of community relationship.

In contrast, Kautzsch developed a forensic concept suggesting that צדק is to be understood as conforming to a norm.[26] He states, "Concerning this

---

19. Ibid., 97, 105.
20. Eichrodt, *OT Theology*, I, 249.
21. Von Rad, *OT Theology*, I, 370.
22. Gerhard von Rad, *The Problem of Hexateuch and Other Essays*, trans. E. Trueman Dicken (Edinburgh: Oliver & Boyd, 1966), 249.
23. Klaus Koch, "צדק to be communally Faithful, Beneficial," *TLOT* 2: 1046–1062 (1050–1051).
24. Elizabeth R. Achtemeier, "Righteousness in the Old Testament," in *IDB* 4 (New York: Abingdon Press, 1962), 80–85 (80).
25. For example,. Horst Seebass, "Righteousness, Justification," *NIDNTT* 3: 352–356 (355) and Burns, "Biblical Righteousness and Justice," 155–156.
26. Emil F. Kautzsch, *Über die Derivate des Stammes* צדק *im Alttestamentlichen Sprachgebrauch* (Tübingen: Druck von Ludwig Friedrich Fues, 1881), 28, 43–47.

term, we cannot proceed beyond the notion of subjection to some norm."²⁷ Nötscher adopts Kautzsch's basic juridical orientation of צדק and sees it as punitive when used in reference to Yahweh's actions.²⁸ Snaith is also of the opinion that צדקה primarily means, "conduct which conforms to the established standards of the time."²⁹ He asserts that צדקה is "the norm which God set up in the beginning, by which also he will judge the world (Psalm 98:9)."³⁰ Jacob deduces that "righteousness is therefore conformity to a norm; in origin it is neither punitive, nor distributive, nor justificatory, but in a general way fidelity to a state or to a way of acting or thinking."³¹ Quell is also of the opinion that צדק involves a fixed norm.³² Wright also avers that צדק means "straight": something fixed, and fully what it should be and so matches the "norm."³³ Yet Wright is more nuanced that he relates the root mening to relationships.³⁴

These observations show that there has been difficulty in defining the specific meaning of צדק. The term is broadly used with ethical, forensic and religious meanings, showing a high level of overlap. Hence scholars have reached two primary conclusions: one camp views צדק within the context of "norm," while another regards צדק as a gift from God to do the right thing in the context of communal relationships. However, despite having differences in emphasis, the distinction between the two views is far from being clear-cut. In fact, scholars from both camps acknowledge the necessity to understand צדק as assumed norm in a given context as well as loyalty manifested in the concrete relationships of community. Therefore, a synthesis view can be proposed. In this, צדק may be treated as fidelity to

---

27. Ibid., 53.
28. Friedrich Nötscher, *Die Gerechtigkeit Gottes bei den vorexilischen Propheten* (ATA VI/1; Münster, 1915), 27.
29. Norman H. Snaith, *The Distinctive Ideas of the Old Testament* (London: Epworth Press, 1944), 73.
30. Ibid., 76.
31. Edmond Jacob, *Theology of the Old Testament*, trans. Arthur W. Heathcote and Philip J. Allcock (New York: Harper, 1958), 94.
32. Gottfried Quell, "δίκη, δίκαιος, δικαιοσύνη . . ." *TDNT* 2: 174–178 (177).
33. Wright, Christopher J. H., *Old Testament Ethics for the People of God* (Leicester: Inter-Varsity Press, 2004), 255.
34. Ibid., 256.

relationships, but is also a concept that incorporates the idea of norm, and at times, even of chastisement.[35] As such, the implied norm "remains to be defined in each particular case."[36] Hill elucidates this point: "the norm is furnished by the objective standard of the thing itself; and in cases where the term is applied to persons, the rightness or righteousness of conduct depends on the fulfilling of obligations arising from a particular situation or set of circumstances."[37] In a similar vein, Anderson observes:

> Righteousness (צדקה) is a term of relationship, denoting that kind of conduct, which serves to maintain established ties. . . . In a covenant context "righteousness" signifies faithfulness to the obligations stipulated by the Covenant, but in general it may imply a behaviour which is right according to the standards accepted by the community.[38]

Even von Rad recognises this reality: "Every relationship brings with it certain claims upon conduct, and the satisfaction of these claims, which issue from the relationship and in which alone the relationship can persist, is described by our term צדק."[39] Similarly, those who choose the option of conformity to a norm also acknowledge the centrality of faithfulness to relationships. Jacob, for example, notes "righteousness is always a concept of relationship, fashioned upon everyday dealings between two people."[40] Likewise, Wright states that צדקה and משפט "are in fact highly relational words."[41] The assumed claims of conduct may include the revealed law or some natural law.[42] Yet the revealed law or ordinances does not by any means exhaust the meaning of צדק in the OT.

---

35. This study focuses attention on judgment with a view of restoration, and therefore "just judgment" or "chastisement" will be the preferred term.
36. Kautzsch, *Über die Derivate des Stammes* צדק, 59; Jacob, *Theology of the OT,* 94.
37. Hill, *Greek Words,* 85.
38. Arnold A. Anderson, *Psalms, I* (NCBC; London: Morgan & Scott, 1972), 262.
39. Von Rad, *OT Theology, I,* 371.
40. Jacob, *Theology of the OT,* 95.
41. Wright, *Old Testament Ethics,* 256.
42. David J. Reimer, "צדק," *NIDOTTE* 3: 744–769 (746).

These observations elucidate the fact that there is no norm as an absolute standard that will work in every circumstance. Briefly, צדקה expresses the idea of fulfilling an assumed standard within the cultural limit (often this is not the case), as well as an action that goes beyond the call of duty, which is beneficial to the upkeep of right relationships between humans, and between humans and God.[43] As such, within the norm or beyond the norm, the primary aim of צדק/צדקה is to keep right relationships.

The narrative description in Genesis 38 reflects the interplay of צדק as norm, as well as צדק as fulfilment to the demands of right relationship with others. Set against the background of a paterfamilias, Judah pronounced the death penalty on his widowed daughter-in-law, Tamar, for prostituting herself. However, soon enough he recognised that Tamar's action apparently was based on something like the levirate marriage rite (e.g. Deut 25:1–10; Ruth)[44] and her pregnancy had to do with Judah himself and so he confesses: "She is more righteous than I" (צדקה ממני, verse 26). Tamar's action was undoubtedly prompted by the norm of the culture in which she lived. Likewise, Judah's admission has to do with this assumed custom. From an ethical point of view, neither of them seems to be right because both of them dealt falsely, Judah for breaching the norm of levirate and Tamar for employing questionable means to facilitate her objectives. Nevertheless, what could be inferred from this scenario is that צדק connotes conformity to a norm, but not an absolute ethical norm. More importantly, the driving force behind Tamar's action acknowledged by Judah is her faithfulness to raise up descendants in order to perpetuate the family relationship. She was committed to producing "seed" while Judah was not. Hence she acted righteously in relation to God. By acting to preserve seed she also acted righteously in relation to Judah. In view of that, צדק here appears not to be measured by some absolute moral standard, but rather fulfilling the demands of right relationship with others.[45] In this sense, the

---

43. Koch, "צדק," *TLOT* 2: 1053; Von Rad, *OT Theology, I*, 376.
44. More on this subject, see Millar Burrows, "Levirate Marriage in Israel," *JBL* 59 (1940): 23–33; Eryl W. Davies, "Inheritance Rights and the Hebrew Levirate Marriage," *VT* 31 (1981): 138–144; Idem, "Inheritance Rights and the Hebrew Levirate Marriage," *VT* 31 (1981): 257–268.
45. Lindsay Wilson, *Joseph, Wise and Otherwise: The Intersection of Wisdom and Covenant in Genesis 37–50* (PBM; Carlisle: Paternoster Press, 2004), 85.

aim of צדקה, relationship, exceeds mere fulfilment of an obligation.[46] Thus, the biblical notion of צדק suggests any deed performed in and through conformity to certain norms of conduct arising from relationship, whose central aim is to perpetuate a persistent, right relationship.

חסד as an extra Deed of one Person to another

The next significant term in analysing justice is חסד. The noun חסד occurs 245 times in the Hebrew Bible and is well distributed throughout later Hebrew, Aramaic and Syriac.[47] Since the term has a strong relational aspect, it can only be defined by a cluster of several words.[48] Generally, חסד means "loyalty, faithfulness, kindness, love and mercy."[49]

Glueck understands חסד as primarily a mutual obligation of individuals who share an ethically binding relationship.[50] He defines חסד as "conduct corresponding to a mutual relationship of rights and duties."[51] He asserts that חסד is never an arbitrary demonstration of grace, kindness, favour or love.[52] Glueck then suggests that חסד, as mutual religious and ethical human conduct, fulfils the demands of loyalty, justice, righteousness and honesty.[53] By linking God's חסד to covenant (ברית) he concludes that חסד is the real essence or content of ברית.[54]

Lofthouse confirms Glueck's idea by considering the distinction of חסד from חן.[55] He argues that while חן has a wide range of meanings, it primarily refers to an action, which cannot be enforced or claimed, done by a superior to an inferior.[56] He further argues that חן is used primarily

---

46. Koch, "צדק," *TLOT* 2: 1050.
47. H. J. Zobel, "חֶסֶד, ḥeseḏ," *TDOT* 5: 44–64 (45).
48. D. A. Baer and R. P. Gordon, "חסד," in *NIDOTTE* 2, ed. Willem Van Gemeren (Grand Rapids: Zondervan), 211–218 (211).
49. Clines, *Classical Hebrew*, 126.
50. Nelson Glueck, *Hesed in the Bible,* trans. Alfred Gottschalk; 1927 (German); repr. (Cinncinnati: Hebrew Union College Press, 1967), 37.
51. Ibid., 55.
52. Ibid. Rabbi Kamsler supports this interpretation. See Harold Kamsler, "Hesed – Mercy or Loyalty?," *JBQ* 27 (1999): 183–185 (184).
53. Glueck, *Ḥesed,* 69.
54. Ibid., 45, 47, 55.
55. W. F. Lofthouse, "Ḥen and Ḥesed in the Old Testament," *ZAW* 10 (1933): 29–35.
56. Ibid., 30.

of people (only rarely of God) between whom there is no specific bond or covenant. In contrast, חסד is used where there is a recognised tie.[57]

Along this line, Eichrodt defines חסד as duty and mutual service of the covenant, but emphasises its limitation in this old sense, particularly when the concept is transcended by the term רחם – mercy, evoked by no kind of obligation – in the prophetic era.[58] In the same vein, Stoebe emphasises God's unconditional devotion towards humankind.[59] He associates חסד with [60]רחם and interprets חסד as "goodness" or "kindness" which goes beyond mere obligatory duty within expected norms. It is a sacrificial, humane willingness to be there for the other.[61] In fact, Montgomery earlier had suggested "kindness" as the best suitable English expression of חסד.[62] Johnson also notes that "חסד connotes more than can be defined in the legal terminology of a ברית ... חסד is 'the virtue that knits together society' (W. Robertson Smith)."[63] Similarly, Zobel defines חסד as an act that preserves life and pursues what is good not evil and translates חסד as "goodness," "grace," or "kindness."[64]

By rejecting Glueck's basic position, Sakenfeld argues that חסד is not a legal right but a moral right.[65] She argues that חסד is an action freely performed by the "situationally superior party" for the "situationally inferior party" for an essential need involving "deliverance or protection

---

57. Ibid., 31–33.
58. Eichrodt, *Theology*, I, 237–238.
59. H. J. Stoebe, "Die Bedeutung des Wortes häsäd im Alten Testament," *VT* 2 (1952): 244–254; idem, "חֶסֶד *hesed*, kindness," *TDNT* 2: 449–464.
60. For Stoebe, חסד is not only unilateral (an act of the superior towards the inferior) but also bilateral (an act of the inferior towards the superior, even human being to God). Stoebe, "חֶסֶד *hesed*, kindness," *TLOT* 2: 449–464 (450).
61. Stoebe, "Die Bedeutung des Wortes häsäd," 248; "חֶסֶד *hesed*, kindness," *TDNT* 2: 244–254 (456). Stoebe stresses that an obligation arises only (subsequently!) through the oath.
62. See James A. Montgomery, "Hebrew *Hesed* and Greek *Charis*," *HTR* 2 (1938): 97–102 (101).
63. Aubrey R. Johnson, "Hesed and Hāsîd," in *Interpretationes ad Vestus Testamentum Pertinentes*, ed. Sigmundo Mowinckel (Oslo: Land og Kirke, 1955), 110.
64. H. J. Zobel, "חֶסֶד *hesed*," *TDOT* 5: 44–64 (51).
65. Katharine D. Sakenfeld, *The Meaning of Hesed in the Hebrew Bible* (Missoula: Scholars Press, 1978), 3, 73.

as a responsible keeping of faith with another with whom one is in a relationship."⁶⁶ As such, the superior party who is the sole source of assistance is free not to act and the act is motivated by moral, not legal, considerations. Nevertheless, the potential actors have a recognised responsibility to act in חסד because of the relationship in which they stand.⁶⁷ Moving a step further, Andersen interprets חסד as a natural expression of love, evoked by no obligation.⁶⁸ For him, Glueck's reading of חסד solely as obligation and duty is misguided. He also challenges Sakenfeld's idea by asking how a person can have a responsibility which they are free not to perform. Andersen goes on to define חסד as a generous and beneficial action that at times violates the custom and duty of the time.⁶⁹

Clark's study shows several new insights. First, חסד is closely related to חנן, which includes "grace" and "mercy," but implies much more. Second, חסד is close to רחם, which includes "compassion," but is not merely compassion. Third, חסד is also close to אמונה, which includes "faithfulness," "reliability," "confidence," but its meaning is not exhausted by these. Finally, חסד is not very close to אהב, which embraces "love," but its connotations are much broader than those of love.⁷⁰ For him, חסד is a "supreme human virtue, standing as the pinnacle of moral values."⁷¹ It is not "merely an attitude or an emotion; it is an emotion that leads to an activity beneficial to the recipient" which is grounded on the character of God that Yahweh expects his people to emulate.⁷²

This brief overview shows the multifaceted dimensions of חסד. Scholars attempt to define חסד from various angles, as in the account of Abraham in Genesis 20:13. Glueck pays more attention to what Sarah "must do" to demonstrate חסד for the sake of Abraham because she lives

---

66. Ibid., 233–234.
67. Ibid., 234.
68. Francis I. Andersen, "Yahweh, the Kind and Sensitive God," in *God Who is Rich in Mercy: Essays presented to Dr. D. B. Knox,* eds. Peter T. O'Brien and David G. Peterson (Homebush, NSW: Lancer Books, 1986), 41–88.
69. Ibid., 44.
70. Gordon R. Clark, *The Word Hesed in the Hebrew Bible* (JSOTSup 157; Sheffield: JSOT Press, 1993), 267–268.
71. Ibid., 267.
72. Ibid.

within fixed rules of loyalty and duty for husband and wife based on reciprocity.[73] Sakenfeld stresses what Sarah "can do," for she is the only one who can perform such an action situationally.[74] Stoebe emphasises "what exceeds duty" and that Abraham's request of Sarah is something that is beyond a wife's duty.[75] Andersen notes that Sarah does "something unusual" and thus "doing חסד is praiseworthy; not doing it is not blameworthy."[76] None of these views seem misplaced but reflect the complex nature of the concept. Conceivably, the definitions can be boiled down to two main interpretations: mutual responsibility and compassionate deed. As such, חסד includes *both* a loving commitment (not as legal obligation) *and* kind and dutiful action (as moral obligation) towards those in need with whom one stands in relationship. Clearly, a restriction to one narrow aspect is unsustainable.

חסד *as Mutual Responsibility*

Scholars normally examine חסד in the context of interpersonal relationships. These contexts include relationships between immediate family,[77] relatives,[78] host and guest,[79] friends,[80] sovereign and subjects,[81] two parties or individuals,[82] and within the community (Ps 109:16, Isa 57:1, Mic 6:8, Zech 7:9). The first obvious aspect of חסד as mutual responsibility is based on prior action. That is, either the one who demonstrates an act of חסד expects a similar act of חסד in return, or the one who receives an act

---

73. Glueck, *Ḥesed*, 40.
74. Sakenfeld, *The Meaning of Ḥesed*, 27.
75. Stoebe, "חֶסֶד *ḥesed*, kindness," *TDNT* 2: 455.
76. Anderson, "Kind and Sensitive God," 53.
77. Sarah–Abraham (Gen 20:13), Joseph–Israel (Gen 47:29) and (also Ruth 1:8; 3:10).
78. Laban–Isaac (Gen 24:49), Ruth–Boaz (Ruth 3:10), and Israel–Kenites (1 Sam 15:6).
79. Men–Lot (Gen 19:19), Abimelech–Abraham (Gen 21:23), and Rahab–Spies (Josh 2:12, 14).
80. Jonathan–David (1 Sam 20:8, 14), David–Meribbaal (2 Sam 9:1, 3, 7), David–Hanun (2 Sam 10:2), Hushai–David (2 Sam 16:17), Solomon–sons of Barzillai (1 Kgs 2:7), and also any individuals friend (Job 6:14).
81. Men of Jabesh Gilead–Saul (2 Sam 2:5), Abner–house of Saul (2 Sam 3:8), Hushai–David (2 Sam 16:17) and Jehoiada–Joash (2 Chr 24:22).
82. Prisoner–Joseph (Gen 40:14), house of Joseph–man from Bethel (Judg 1:24), and Israelites–family of Jerubbaal (Judg 8:35).

of חסד from another responds with a similar act of חסד (e.g. Abimelech–Abraham, Rahab–the Spies and Jonathan–David).

There are instances where mutual responsibility is simply assumed. The one who stands in a specific relationship with another is expected to demonstrate certain acts of חסד. For example, Abraham assumes חסד from Sarah as his wife and requires no further oath to seal it. David assumes חסד from his friend, Hushai. Absalom perceives Hushai's desertion of David as a failure to do חסד, and his assumption is placed precisely on the intimate relationship between them. These instances take the mutual responsibility for granted since no treaty or covenant has been enacted. Perhaps mutual obligation is understood as an inherent part of what binds a society and all its members.[83]

In some other instances the mutuality of חסד is often sealed with a ברית. For instance, Abimelech requests Abraham to seal the חסד he has been shown to him with a ברית (Gen 21:23). The spies must also swear to Rahab (Josh 2:13–14), and so too, Jonathan makes a covenant with David before Yahweh (1 Sam 20:16–17). Similarly, Jacob urges Joseph to deal with him in חסד when he dies (Gen 47:29). Arguably, the presence of ברית in these contexts shows that there is no noticeable expectation of mutual assistance. Instead, a hostile situation is in view, for there is a real possibility that the other party may not respond with חסד.[84] At any rate, the existence of a ברית reinforces and strengthens the long-lasting commitment of חסד.[85] In several occurrences, חסד appears to be an unexpected demonstration of commitment that emerges out of a given situation.[86] Yet again, the existence of a ברית provides assertion of the permanence of חסד.

---

83. Zobel, "חֶסֶד" *TDOT* 5: 48, recognises that even in cases where such mutuality is not explicit, the mutual demonstration of חסד could be assumed as "we are dealing with the closest of human bonds."
84. Baer and Gordon, "חסד."
85. See Robin Routledge, "*Hesed* as Obligation: A Re-Examination," *TynBul* 46 (1995): 179–196 (183).
86. Brian Britt, "Unexpected Attachments: A Literary Approach to the term חסד in the Hebrew Bible," *JSOT* 27 (2003): 289–307.

חסד *as Compassionate Deed*

Interpreters describe חסד as being more a characteristic of Yahweh than of humans.[87] Divine חסד saves people from disaster or oppressors (Gen 19:19; Ps 31:7 [8], 21 [22]; 32:10; 94:18; 143:12), sustains life (Gen 24:12, 14, 27; Ps 6:5 [6]; 119:88), outlasts God's wrath (Isa 54:8; Mic 7:18). It is enduring, persistent and even eternal (Ps 89:2 [3], 28 [29]; Isa 54:10a; Hos 6:4; Jer 31:3). It occupies a prominent role in the inner and communal life of God's people (e.g. Exod 15:13; Ps 13:5 [6]; 17:7; 26:1–3; 33:18; 119:124; 143:8; Isa 63:7). The divine חסד finds most vivid expression in his endless reconciling love, always ready to forgive (cf. Ps 51:1 [3]; Jer 22; 31:32; Hos 6:4). God's חסד is delivering power exercised on behalf of those who are obedient and it is also a surprising forgiveness offered to the disobedient. This demonstration of חסד by Yahweh towards his people places all members in a covenant relationship with fellow human beings.[88] That is, every individual in the community is to demonstrate towards others the חסד which they have experienced from Yahweh, by maintaining righteousness and justice, kindness and mercy (cf. Hos 12:6 [7]; Mic 6:8; Zech 7:9).

A significant indicator of the compassionate nature of חסד is its use with צדקה (cf. 1 Kgs 3:6; Ps 33:5; 35:10; 40:10; 98:2–3; 103:17; Prov 21:21; Jer 9:24; Hos 10:12). As noted earlier, the biblical notion of צדקה suggests any deed performed in and through conformity to certain conduct arising from relationship, aiming to perpetuate a persistent and right relationship. The term צדק not only presupposes actions maintaining ethical norms, but also goes beyond the call of obligation, with the primary goal to keep right relationships between humans, and between humans and God. Correspondingly, חסד connotes not only a moral behaviour corresponding to a mutual relationship, but also a compassionate deed that is solely grounded on divine חסד, which aims to restore or amend broken relationships. In the light of this, it is apparent that the central aim of חסד (and צדקה) is to call for the mutually inclusive moral values of "right

---

87. According to Clark's findings, two-thirds of the term's total occurrences have to do with Yahweh's חסד. He notes 282 occurrences and 187 have God as the agent. Clark, *The Word Hesed*, 53. See also Baer and Gordon, "חסד."

88. Zobel, "חֶסֶד *ḥesed*," *TDOT* 5: 63.

motives" and "right actions" to keep and maintain true and loving relationships within the community.⁸⁹

Clearly, חסד consists of inward disposition of love and outward expression of responsibility. The term has a strong relational element, which lies in the domain of interpersonal relations and can only be defined by a cluster of words. Indeed, חסד is a social virtue for all individuals that knit the community together, aiming to preserve and promote life. It describes the inner temperament of commitment and outward expression of dutiful deed, which can be applied to both God and people. As such, it is a humane willingness to be there for others especially those who are in need. Moreover, חסד is characterised by conduct in accord with social norms. Nonetheless, it is not defined by forensic notions. In sum, חסד expresses a mutual, friendly, sincere, familial, dutiful, loyal and loving deed towards others, as well as a compassionate, gracious, kind, generous, benevolent, merciful and forgiving disposition to maintain right relationships between humans and their neighbours and God and his people.

משפט/שפט as Sustaining Relationship

The Hebrew word משפט is arguably the most significant term in the discussion of divine and human justice. שפט may basically mean judge, make decision, execute justice, pronounce judgment.⁹⁰ There is no consensus over the original meaning of שפט.⁹¹ The 400 occurrences of משפט in the OT exhibit a wide semantic variation.⁹² Cognate roots of שפט also occur

---

89. Cf. Alfred Jepsen, "Gnade und Barmherzigkeit im Alten Testament," *KD* 7 (1961): 261–271 (266); Routledge, "*Hesed* as Obligation," 181. See also Robin Routledge, *Old Testament Theology: A Thematic Approach* (Nottingham: Apollos, 2008), 108.

90. Clines, *Classical Hebrew*, 475.

91. Henry Ferguson, "The verb שפט," *JBL* 8 (1888): 130–136 (131), suggests that "judging" or "deciding" judicially is the original meaning of שפט. Loring W. Batten, "The use of מִשְׁפָּט," *JBL* 11 (1892): 206–210 (210), suggests "to judge" or "decide out of which other meanings grow." Ludwig Köhler, *Hebrew Man*, trans. Peter R. Ackroyd (London: SCM Press, 1956), 133, and Fahlgren, *Ṣedāḳā*, 124, opt for "to decide between" or "decision" as its basic meaning. Oskar Grether, "Die Bezeichnung 'Richter' für die Charismatischen heelden der vorstaatlichen Zeit," *ZAW* 57 (1939), understands שפט as "deciding juristically, judging."

92. B. Johnson, "מִשְׁפָּט, judgment, justice" *TDOT* 9: 86–98 (87).

outside the OT.⁹³ Semantically related words include "dispute, lawsuit" (ריב), "judgment" (דין), "statute" or "ordinance" (חק/חקה) and "righteousness" (צדקה).⁹⁴ As a verb, שפט often means "to judge," and the noun משפט also follows this sense.⁹⁵

Of interest is Liedke's description of שפט as "an action that restores the disturbed order of a (legal) community."⁹⁶ This restoration of order includes a one-time act as well as a continuous activity and thus "to govern, rule."⁹⁷ What is not discussed, however, is whether the "judging" (one-time act) and "ruling" (continuous act) in forensic or non-forensic contexts have a relational element as their force. Broadly speaking, the noun משפט can refer to several features such as divinely-given laws or ordinances, divine justice, judgment, authoritative actions, decision, court, cause or case, executing justice, rights, custom, manner and even path. Its wide-ranging use oscillates around three domains: the forensic, religious and ethical. Booth suggests three dynamics that underline the fundamental meaning of משפט: custom, law, and right.⁹⁸ We will now discuss the principal function of משפט as customary action, judicial concept, and ethical concept with a view to drawing out the often-neglected relational component of משפט.

---

93. The noun *šiptu* in Mari letters means a "command, order, edict" pronounced by the king or a governor. The verb *šāpiṭu* in the Old Babylonian and Assyrian text denotes "determine, decide" and "rule." The verb *tpṭ* in Ugaritic means "reign" and "judge." In Phoenician and Punic inscriptions, the verb *tpṭ* connotes "rule." Hence the basic idea of the verb שפט, maintained in the ANE as well as Hebrew, includes the meaning "rule, lead, govern" and "judge, determine, grant justice." H. Niehr, "שָׁפַט *šāpāṭ*, lead, rule; judge, ruler," *TDOT* 15: 411–431 (415–419).

94. See Richard Schultz, "Justice," *NIDOTTE* 4: 837–846 (838).

95. J. van der Ploeg, "Studies in Hebrew Law," *CBQ* 12 (1950): 248–259 (249).

96. Gerhard Liedke, "שפט, to judge," *TLOT* 3: 1392–1399 (1393).

97. Gerhard Liedke, *Gestalt und Bezeichnung alttestamentlicher Rechtssatze* (WMANT 39; Neukirchen-Vluyn: Neukirchener Verlag, 1971), 70–72. Following Liedke, Schultz also emphasises the continuous activity of שפט. Richard Schultz, "שפט," *NIDOTTE* 4: 213–220 (214).

98. Osborne Booth, "The Semantic Development of the Term משפט in the Old Testament," *JBL* 61 (1942): 105–110 (107).

משפט *as Customary way of action*

The first type of Booth's classification of משפט is "manner" or "custom."[99] For instance, in Genesis 40:13, Joseph told Pharaoh's cupbearer that his office would be restored to its previous manner (משפט). A cursory reading of משפט means that of habit – the way a thing is done customarily. However, a deeper import in this context suggests that the once broken relationship between Pharaoh and his butler will be restored.

In Judges 13:12, Manoah asked the Angel of God "what will be the boy's משפט"? Here, it can be rendered as "custom or manner" or even responsibility. Again, the objective "manner" or "custom" in the sense of specific rules does not seem to be the issue inquired by Manoah. Rather, it is a unique משפט "which is necessary to launch Samson as one who is intimately associated with Yahweh."[100] 1 Kings 18:29 describes how the prophets of Baal cut themselves with swords and spears, according to their custom (כמשפטם). 2 Kings 17:24 also asserts that the new settlers in Samaria did not know the משפט of the land. In these two cases, the משפט of Baal and the משפט of other nations stand in contrast to the משפט of Yahweh.[101] In fact, the God of the land had his own customary way of conduct binding on others. Yahweh has his own way by which he must be worshipped. Knowing his ways is to know his משפט. As Gossai rightly notes, "knowing" in this context implies a close relationship with a party and not simply an objective knowledge."[102] These instances show that although the term משפט is used broadly, the specific meaning behind the usages refers to a relational situation.[103]

Another term that falls into this category is דרך, which is used as a synonym in Jeremiah 5:4–6. Here the prophet laments Israel for they do not understand the דרך of the Lord, the משפט of God. The משפט of God in this context, as Berkovits notes, "is not another object of their ignorance

---

99. Ibid., 108.
100. Gossai, *Justice and Righteousness,* 179.
101. Herntrich, "κρίνω, κρίσις, κρίμα," 926.
102. Gossai, *Justice and Righteousness,* 192.
103. By definition, custom means a common practiced set of values associated with a particular society, place (or a person's habitual practice), which denotes a circumstance where everything is in place entailing an idea of concord, and where everything rotates without interruption.

but an exemplary parallelism to 'the way of the LORD.'"[104] In fact, this is one of the main subjects of Hosea's message to the people of Israel (cf. Hos 4:9; 10:13; 12:3 [2]; 14:10 [9]). In their rejection of the way of the LORD, the people trusted their own דרך. משפט means not merely the law in its abstract sense, but "his way of doing a thing" – a right relationship where everything is in place.

משפט *as Judicial Concept*

Booth's second category includes the various meanings of משפט, which are largely associated with the promulgated body of law.[105] For McKenzie, the noun משפט can mean the decision of the judge, the guilt of the person condemned and the whole of the judicial proceedings.[106] Yet even behind these judicial usages, there is a strong sense of emphasis on preserving relationship.

To begin with, משפטים refers to a group of rules and ordinances, covering a wide range of civil, criminal and ritual law. They are God's gift to the Israelites by which they should live and relate to one another. In this widest sense, משפט can describe the whole process of litigation based on past precedents (cf. Exod 21–23). For instance, in Deuteronomy 1:17, the judges of Israel were commanded not to show partiality when rendering משפט (judgment), and similarly, in Numbers 27:5 where Moses addressed the claim made by the daughters of Zelophehad. These instances do reflect a forensic scenario. However, the dynamic behind this legal setting is above all relationship. The issue is not only about the daughters of Zelophehad getting their fair share, but more importantly, it is concerned with coexistence in harmony with other members in the community. Thus, the responsibility of the judges not only includes judging impartially but also restoring the disturbed order and recreating a co-inhabitable environment.

---

104. Eliezer Berkovits, "Biblical Meaning of Justice," *Judaism* 18 (1969): 188–209 (201).
105. Booth, "The Term משפט," 108.
106. Donald A. McKenzie, "Judicial Procedure at the Town Gate," *VT* 14 (1964): 100–104 (101).

Another example is Exodus 2:14. The contextual meaning suggests that the role of a leader includes both ruling and judging.[107] Judging is a part of ruling. Moses judges the people (Exod 18:13) and so does Samuel (1 Sam 7:15) and his sons too (1 Sam 8:1–3).[108] Absalom's seditious statement (2 Sam 15:4) echoes a position of authority that includes the judiciary function as well. Solomon was also aware of his main function as a ruler and judge (1 Kgs 3:11). This double sense of responsibility reflects the fact that the rulers of Israel are to administer the people by restoring the disturbed order (in their judgment) as a one-time act, and by maintaining concord relationship in their ruling as a continuous act. Once again, the emphasis is not so much on the "rules" and "norms" by which the judicial proceedings should be administered, but rather on striving to maintain stability in the society.

משפט *as Ethical Concept*

Booth's third classification includes meanings such as "rightful due," "that which should be," and "proper administration of law by man."[109] Liedke has argued that משפט means one's due that includes duty and claim, and one's desert that includes reward and punishment.[110] Hence משפט embraces a wide breadth of meaning for the designated groups.[111] Within this broad horizon, it would be appropriate to observe a relational aspect of משפט, which has a strong sense of social concern for the underprivileged.

Berkovits most clearly draws the meaning of the verb שפט (to judge) as "to save" specifically from 1 Samuel 24:16 [15] and 2 Samuel 18:19.[112] In these two contexts, the root שפט is used to refer to deliverance from

---

107. Friedrich Büchsel and Volkmar Herntrich, "κρίνω, κρίσις, κρίμα . . . ," *TDNT* 3: 921–954 (923).
108. Samuel's description of his role in 1 Samuel 12:2 is identical to that of the king, which suggests he was both ruler and judge. Gossai, *Justice, Righteousness*, 135–136.
109. Booth, "The Term משפט," 108.
110. Liedke, *Gestalt*, 78–83.
111. For instance, the משפט of the poor (Exod 23:6; Isa 10:2; Jer 5:28), and of the Israelites (Exod 28:30; Isa 40:27; Mic 7:9), of the priests (Deut 18:3; 1 Sam 2:13; 2 Chr 30:16), of a daughter (Exod 21:9), the orphan, widow, or alien (Deut 10:18; 24:17; 27:19), the priest, the firstborn (Deut 21:17).
112. Berkovits, "The Biblical Meaning," 193–195. Donald A. McKenzie, "Judge of Israel," *VT* 17 (1967): 118–121, argues for a similar meaning.

David's enemies. The Psalmist uses שפט (to judge) in parallel with ישע (to save, Ps 76:10 [9]). The declaration of God's mercy in Isaiah 51:5 assumes that God's שפט goes hand-in-hand with salvation (ישע) and righteousness (צדק). This evidence suggests that the fundamental mandate of the judges, leaders, or kings of Israel includes both judging (juridical) and leading the people with a view to save those whose rights have been violated or taken.

Needless to say, משפט takes on an ethical force when used for the afflicted or poor. The term is often associated with צדקה by means of a *hendiadys*.[113] Interpreters normally recognise that this word-pair (משפט וצדקה) best expresses the concept of justice in ancient Israel and in the ancient Near East. Miranda takes צדקה and משפט as synonymous.[114] משפט is also equated with other terms such as חסד (Jer 9:23; Hos 2:21; 12:7; Mic 6:8; Ps 33:5; 89;15; 101:1), and תוב (Isa 1:17; Job 34:4). Scholars largely recognise that the practical application of this word-pair משפט וצדקה is to the realm of social justice.[115] Noticeably, "God's preferential option for the poor" was deeply ingrained in the thoughts of Israelites in biblical times.[116] In fact, a similar concern was pervasive in the ancient Near Eastern world.[117] Deuteronomy 10:18 explicitly states that Yahweh was the one who created the משפט for widows and orphans. A similarly strong ethical demand can be seen in the Prophets (e.g. Isa 1:17; 10:2; Amos 5:11, 15; 8:4; Jer 5:28;

---

113. Examples, with צדק (Isa 16:5; 26:9; 32:1; 51:4f; Hos 2:21; Zeph 2:3; Ps 72:2; 89:15; 97:2; Job 8:3; 29:14; 35:2; Prov 1:3; 2:9; Eccl 5:7), צדקה (Isa 5:7; 9:6; 28:17; 32:16; 35:5; 54:17; 56:1; 58:2; 59:9; Jer 4:2; Amos 5:7, 24; 6:12; Ps 33:5; 36:7; 99:4; 106:3; Job 37:23; Prov 8:20; 16:8). With a formulae of משפט וצדקה or משפה ו צדקה ומשפה (Gen 18:19; 2 Sam 8:15; 2 Chr 9:8; Jer 9:23; 22:3, 15; 23:5; 33:15; Ezek 18:5, 19, 21, 27; 33:14, 16, 19; 45:9).

114. Miranda, *Marx and the Bible*, 93–94.

115. Among many others, Miranda, *Marx and the Bible*, 93, regards the use of משפט וצדקה in the Old Testament as a technical term that clearly signifies justice for the poor and oppressed, hence social justice. Wright, *Old Testament Ethics*, 257, also deduces that the "nearest English expression to this double word phrase משפט וצדקה then is *social justice.*"

116. The classical proponent of this position is Gustavo Gutiérrez, *A Theology of Liberation: History, Politics, and Salvation*, trans. Inda Caridad and John Eagleson (Maryknoll: Orbis Books, 1973).

117. See Epsztein, *Social Justice in the Ancient near East*, 3; F. Charles Fensham, "Widow, Orphan, and the Poor in Ancient Near Eastern Legal and Wisdom Literature" *JNES* 21 no. 2 (1962): 130; Richard D. Patterson, "The Widow, the Orphan, and the Poor in the Old Testament and the Extra-Biblical Literature," *BibSac* 130 (1973), 226.

21:12; 22:3, 15; Ezek 22:29). Since משפט in Hebrew can also denote "to save," it is logical to conclude that the judges or heads of Israel were to save the poor out of the hand of those who oppressed them. Yet at this point, it also is worth stressing that "justice and righteousness" in English are abstract nouns, whereas in Hebrew they are commonly used as concrete nouns. For instance, as Goldingay notes, "one cannot 'do [a] social justice' as one can 'do a משפט' or 'do a צדקה.'"[118] The term "social justice" is an abstract expression and thus only reflects an approximation of Hebrew meaning. Thus, the Hebrew word-pair here, as Goldingay rightly deduces, "points to an exercise of authority that has a certain relational and social commitment and to a certain relational and social vision that expresses itself in decisive action."[119]

משפט *as Relational Justice: A Proposal*

We have observed that משפט represents a complex and wide variety of meanings from moral, legal and religious domains. However, one notion which is deep-seated in all the diverse meanings is its relational aspect. This relational dimension is not simply one of the different meanings of משפט; rather it is the lifeblood of the concept. So, משפט may be described as an action that preserves relationships, restoring disturbed order and hurt individuals in the community. The notion subsumes legal demand but goes beyond it.

Like צדקה, משפט regulates relationships in a particular society. For instance, judges in Israel were responsible to regulate the social relationships within the community. In their judging, they were to act in accordance with their relationship to Yahweh. In simple terms, his ways of judging should be their ways of judging. Once again, we must not confuse the biblical notion of משפט with the modern understanding of justice based on a *iustitia distributiva*. In contrast, the biblical justice (משפט) is *iustitia*

---

118. John Goldingay, "Justice and Salvation for Israel and Canaan," in *Reading the Hebrew Bible for a New Millennium*, eds. Wonil Kim et al. (Harrisburg: Trinity Press International, 2000), 174–75. Goldingay argues that whatever משפט וצדקה means, it is not 'justice and righteousness' in its abstract sense.

119. Goldingay, "Justice and Salvation," 175.

salutifera. The same holds true with צדקה. Only in this light can we visualise the full thrust of משפט.

The consideration of this relational aspect must take seriously the term's close association with other terms of the group such as צדקה, חסד and רחם. In many texts, משפט is virtually equated with them (Hos 2:21 [19]; Isa 16:5; Ps 38:4–5). In Jeremiah, God is referred to as Yahweh who exercises חסד, משפט and צדקה and delights in them (Jer 9:23). What the prophet Micah calls for the people is once again to exercise משפט and to love חסד (Mic 6:8). While Hosea urges the people to maintain משפט and חסד (Hos 12:7 [6]), Isaiah admonishes them to keep משפט and to do צדקה (Isa 56:1). We have argued above that חסד connotes a humane willingness to be there for others, whereas צדקה suggests an action whose sole aim is to perpetuate a persistent, right relationship. In this light, we can understand the deeper meaning of משפט.

In justifying this view, a representative instance may be examined. In Deuteronomy 1:16–18, the judges in Israel are instructed to be impartial and just in their execution of משפט. The cursory meaning refers to the process of the entire lawsuit. Yet the command is given precisely because of a likely possibility of the judges being influenced by the more powerful of the two parties in question. At the core, the instruction aims to protect the individual from being harmed wrongfully. Heschel comments: "Justice exists in relation to a person, and is something done by a person. An act of injustice is condemned, not because the law is broken, but because a person has been hurt."[120] Gossai also states: "when a judge executes משפט it is not so much a punitive action against one party (though this is often a secondary factor), but rather a means of repairing a broken relationship, and sustaining justice."[121] Clearly, even in a forensic setting like this, the primary question is not simply about fair play within the administration. Rather, it is about the protection and sustenance of relationship for coexistence in the community. Therefore, the biblical idea of משפט can be described as *"fidelity to the demands of a relationship."*[122] The primary de-

---

120. Abraham J. Heschel, *The Prophets* (New York: Harper & Row, 1962), 216.
121. Gossai, *Justice and Righteousness,* 182.
122. Donahue, "Biblical Perspectives on Justice," 69.

mand or expectation of משפט, whether legal, ethical or religious, involves commitment to sustain right relationships between God and his people and between humans and their fellow human beings.

Summary and Conclusion

We have so far attempted to comprehend the basic notion of biblical justice. In light of the discussion, analysing three key words, it can be now asserted that the biblical understanding of justice is clearly relational. A crucial aim of biblical justice is to preserve, sustain, maintain, create or recreate harmonious relationships in society. The concept of צדקה implies that a person is relationally faithful. The fundamental idea of חסד involves an extra action of one person done to (and for) another. The aim of משפט at its highest level is to sustain right relationships. Together, they represent a state of being where everything is in place, harmonious relationships are maintained, and the well-being of the people is well taken care of.

How, then is relational justice expressed? To begin with, relational justice is accomplished through conforming to certain expected norms in the culture one lives in, but surprisingly, it is also at times, fulfilled through violations of norms, rules or customs. It incorporates but also goes beyond the legal notion of justice. That is, its prime objective is not simply giving everyone their just due. Rather, it strives to create a community where no member is being hurt. The demonstration of relational justice entails mutual obligation between persons involved, but it does not stop at a mere display of mutuality. Rather, it swings as far as to a situation where the irresponsible or the underserving are absolved. Relational justice demands justice for the marginal people in society, but this concern alone does not exhaust its encompassing objective. Furthermore, relational justice involves forgiving the unforgivable, but embraces just judgment or chastisement with a view to restoration. In brief, the biblical notion of relational justice suggests whatever action nourishes or maintains a true and harmonious relationship in a given relational context.

CHAPTER FIVE

Hosea: The Socio-Political Background and His Message

The first section of this chapter briefly examines the socio-political context that caused Hosea to cast his message. In a preliminary fashion, the second section outlines the content and sources that shaped his theological standpoint, his message.

The Socio-political Background of Hosea

This study proposes that Hosea has much to say about justice. However, reading Hosea, as Premnath appropriately remarks, is like "looking into a kaleidoscope with the tumbling profusion of images that emerge and merge into new patterns and tropes."[1] To this end, this study seeks to establish that Hosea's critique specifically aims at the relational breakdown and social turmoil of the eighth-century Israel, on the one hand ushered in by political and economic injustices, and cultic abuses on the other. Hosea's approach to justice may not be as scathing as Amos's, but his demand for justice is no less than that of Amos. His polemics against injustices may not be as direct as the other eighth-century prophets, but his concern for the social brokenness of his time is perhaps deeper.

In order to recognise Hosea's message on justice, it is necessary to analyse Hosea in its proper socio-political context. In other words, we need to

---

1. Premnath, "Amos and Hosea," 125.

explore the socio-political background that compels the prophet to call for relational justice. Dearman appropriately notes that the book of Hosea can be understood as an occasional document. "It is occasioned by the circumstances of Israel in the second half of the eighth century."[2] That is, the book of Hosea may not be understood properly without taking into account the prophet's social world. "The event and issues of the day," as Heflin describes, "were the historical vehicle out of which the Word of God came to Hosea."[3]

Various scholars have discussed that the prophetic figures in this era differ from earlier prophets significantly. According to Bright, the prophets prior to the eighth century were professional prophets attached to a court or shrine. They were paid court prophets and therefore did not dare to criticise the state or believe that it could not necessarily fall. This marked the end of their historic mission.[4] In the same vein, Holladay identifies the former "court prophets" as bands or groups of prophets, while the later "writing prophets" were individual or popular prophets. The object of prophecy in the eighth-century prophets, with the exception of Isaiah, shifted away from the ruling houses to the people of Israel as a whole.[5] Petersen also notes that the older professionalised prophets had misled the people of Yahweh by proclaiming peace to those who paid them and made war against those who did not.[6]

It is crucial to keep in mind that Hosea followed Amos to the pulpit of Israel and therefore closer attention should be paid to the message of Amos. In turn Hosea was followed by Isaiah and Micah in the South later in the same century. In response to interpreters who question whether Hosea addresses the justice issues at all, the answer resides with Hosea's unique prophetic style and theme. That is, one need not expect Hosea to make a verbatim report of Amos in relation to social issues, but interpret his allusive

---

2. Dearman, *Hosea*, 29.
3. J. N. Boo Heflin, "The World of Hosea," *SwJT* 18 (1975): 6–21 (6).
4. John Bright, "The Prophets were Protestants: Fresh Result of Valid Criticism," *Int* 2 (1947): 153–182 (170).
5. John S. Holladay, "Assyrian Statecraft and the Prophets of Israel," *HTR* 63 (1970): 29–51 (35).
6. David L. Petersen, *The Roles of Israel's Prophets* (JSOTSup 17; Sheffield: JSOT Press, 1981), 54.

oracles along the lines of Amos and other contemporary prophets. Perhaps, the disparate prophetic articulations of Amos and Hosea have much to do with their personal backgrounds. Amos's resolute, intense and trenchant prophetic style would have been expedient only for an itinerant preacher from the South. In contrast, Hosea was a native with so much to consider that only a wise choice of metaphors would allow him to maintain his existence as a prophetic figure under the oppressive ruling regime. Hosea has a commission to proclaim, but his message must be skilfully crafted to ensure his own survival. Amaziah's words to Amos, "Go away, you seer! Flee to the land of Judah. Earn your living and give your prophecies there," (Amos 7:12) reflects this scenario. If the itinerant preacher Amos faced such hostility, it was much more likely so for Hosea.

Sharing the core of the mission of the eighth-century prophets, Hosea condemns Israel's failure to keep its part of the commitment, which is to fulfil the demands of the righteousness essential to being the people of God.[7] As Petersen describes, these prophets "regularly speak on behalf of values central to the society and on behalf of the god who sanctions the moral structure of the society."[8] Considering themselves to be divinely chosen messengers, they conveyed their suzerain Lord's complaint directly to the people.[9] Further, these prophets formulated their message against the backdrop of the growing trend of internationalism.[10] In this scenario it would be naïve to regard Hosea as being concerned only with the spiritual adultery of the fertility cult of the time and with God's merciful response. Swaim rightly asserts that Hosea was not "merely a religious crank who opposed any practical approach to the huge dilemmas of a state threatened externally by the Assyrian menace and internally by civil strife."[11] Contrary to what has often been assumed, Heflin argues that "every aspect of his message is wed dramatically to the political, social and religious scenes of

---

7. Andersen and Freedman, *Hosea*, 47.
8. Petersen, *Israel's Prophets*, 68.
9. Holladay, "Assyrian Statecraft," 40.
10. Norman K. Gottwald, *All the Kingdoms of the Earth* (New York: Harper, 1964), 392, concludes: "The prophets' interpretation of the relations between states rose on religious grounds informed by a high degree of political knowledge."
11. Gerald G. Swaim, "Hosea the Statesman," in *Biblical and Near Eastern Studies*, ed. Gary A. Tuttle (Grand Rapids: Eerdmans Publishing, 1978), 179.

750–722 BC."[12] This evidence points to the benefit of reading Hosea in light of the socio-political and economic circumstances of the time, and with the social critiques that came from other contemporary prophets.

Political Achievement: The Resurgence of Israel's Imperialism

The superscription (1:1) to the book mentions four Judean kings: Uzziah, Jotham, Ahaz and Hezekiah, and only one king of Israel, Jeroboam II.[13] This suggests that an awareness of the prophet's world, particularly within the period of Jeroboam II, plays an important role in interpreting his message. Perhaps it is best to locate Hosea's activity broadly in the waning years of the Jehu dynasty,[14] of which Jeroboam II was the last significant ruler, and when political instability in Israel followed.[15] The years of Jeroboam II and Uzziah of Judah might be considered the most prosperous time in the history of Israel and Judah. King has persuasively proposed that the emergence of the classical prophets with the resurgence of Israel and Judah, and the Neo-Assyrian Empire branded the eighth-century the greatest of centuries.[16]

It was from Jehoash's time that the fortunes of Israel began to ascend.[17] Under Jeroboam II's forty-year reign, Israel and Judah enjoyed a period of

---

12. Heflin, "World of Hosea," 7.
13. A cursory observation over the span of four Judean kings gives the impression that Hosea's period of prophecy was a very long one. However, taking into account the matter of co-regencies of Judean kings would put Hosea's ministry ca. 760–720 BC. See Nadav Na'aman, "Historical and Chronological Notes on the Kingdoms of Israel and Judah in the Eighth Century BC," *VT* 36 (1986): 71–92 (83, 92).
14. For detailed analysis on this subject, see John H. Hayes, *Amos, the Eighth-Century Prophet: His Time and His Preaching* (Nashville: Abingdon Press, 1988), 17; *ANET*, 280; Michael C. Astour, "841 BC: The First Assyrian Invasion of Israel," *JAOS* 91 (1971): 383–389 (384); James M. Miller and John H. Hayes, *A History of Ancient Israel and Judah* (Philadelphia: Westminster, 1986), 289.
15. Opinions over the exact dates have varied, and therefore, in this study we refrain from delving into its chronological problems. For discussion on this issue, see Na'aman, "Historical and Chronological Notes," 92 and Edwin R. Thiele, *The Mysterious Numbers of the Hebrew Kings*. New Revised Edition (Grand Rapids: Kregel Publications, 1983), 103–116.
16. Philip J. King, "The Eighth, the Greatest of Centuries?" *JBL* 108 (1989): 3–15.
17. See Menahem Haran, "The Rise and Decline of the Empire of Jeroboam Ben Joash," *VT* 17 (1967): 266–297 (296). For a contrary view see Nadav Na'aman, "Azariah and

relative peace and prosperity.[18] His achievement of territorial enlargement is reported in two verses in 2 Kings 14:25 and 14:28. This expansion included much of the Transjordan, extending down to the plains of Moab, and giving control over the trade routes from Philistia up through Galilee, through the Transjordan north of Moab, to the border of the Damascus kingdom.[19] Poobalan argues that the extent of Jeroboam's restoration refers to a territory as vast as it was under the United Monarchy.[20] This would imply that Jeroboam II was as politically significant as David and Solomon. Interestingly, his conquests were carried out with prophetic and divine sanction (2 Kgs 14:25).

From Stability to Chaos: the Aftermath of Jeroboam II

Despite Israel's political accomplishments, the glory of Jeroboam II in Hosea's time was about to pass. In his final years, Israel faced enormous pressure from neighbouring states. The central power erosion of Assyria placed Israel's pro-Assyrian stance in jeopardy. The final turning point, marked by the demise of Jehu's dynasty as reflected in Hosea 1:4, came when Shallum usurped the throne from Zechariah, the son of Jeroboam II (2 Kgs 15:8–10).[21] One month later, Shallum himself was deposed in favour of Menahem who ruled in Samaria for ten years (ca. 749–738).[22] Menahem's intention to found a dynasty and his pro-Assyrian posture came to an end when Pekah from Gilead deposed his successor, Pekahiah

---

Jeroboam II of Israel," *VT* 43 (1993): 227–234.

18. Though the Judean biblical narrator is reluctant to reveal the political significance of Jeroboam II, most scholars today are of the opinion that his reign was victorious. Cf. Hayes, *Amos the Eighth Century Prophet*, 22.

19. Gösta W. Ahlström, *The History of Ancient Palestine from the Palaeolithic Period to Alexander's Conquest* (JSOTSup 146; Sheffield: JSOT Press, 1993) 591–620.

20. For Poobalan, the phrase "Lebo Hamath" and "Sea of the Arabah" are geographical idioms (cf. Num 34:8 and Josh 13:2–5) that mark the northern and southern limits respectively of the ideal Promised Land. Ivor Poobalan, "The Period of Jeroboam II with Special Reference to Amos," *JCTS* 3 (2005): 43–74 (47).

21. Shallum dethroned him perhaps with the support of a rising anti-Assyrian faction. John H. Hayes and Paul K. Hooker, *A New Chronology for the Kings of Israel and Judah: and its implications for Biblical History and Literature* (Atlanta: John Knox Press, 1988), 55.

22. Menahem is on the list of conquered rulers by Tiglath-pileser III in his stele inscription. He is named also in a tribute list contained in the Assyrian king's annals. L. D. Levine, *Two Neo-Assyrian Stelae from Iran* (Toronto: Royal Ontario Museum, 1972).

(2 Kgs 15:22–26).[23] The failure by Pekah and Rezin of Damascus to persuade Ahaz from the South to join the anti-Assyrian coalition resulted in the Syro-Ephraimite War (2 Kgs 16:5–9; Isa 7:1–9; 2 Chr 28:1–21).[24] The consequences of the war were devastating as Ahaz could bribe and influence Assyria.[25] As a result, Tiglath-pileser III conducted a campaign (733–732 BC) against Damascus, demolishing the anti-Assyrian coalition led by Rezin and Pekah.[26] Damascus was destroyed, Rezin killed and Syria was incorporated into an Assyrian province. Most of Israel's territory that was previously controlled by Syria came under Assyrian control.[27] For unknown reasons Samaria was somehow spared, but heavy tribute was imposed and it remained only as a rump state with a truncated territory. By this time the kingdom of Israel may have consisted only of the Ephraimite hill country surrounding the city of Samaria. Plausibly, Miller and Hayes have proposed that this reduced status of the northern kingdom is reflected in Hosea's preferred term as he refers to Ephraim more often in latter materials in his book.[28] Pekah was overthrown and Hoshea replaced on the throne (2 Kgs 15:30). Again, the conspiracy against Pekah may have been prompted by pro-Assyrian fervour.[29] Despite showing loyalty to Assyria early in his reign in 731 BC,[30] Hoshea then withheld tribute from Shalmaneser and sent an appeal for assistance to the "So, king of Egypt (2 Kgs 17:4).[31] The response

---

23. Scholars are perplexed by the long reign assigned to Pekah (2 Kgs 15:27) which does not fit well into the overall royal chronology of Israel and Judah. According to one popular theory, Pekah may have established a "rival kingdom" in about 750 BC by leading a regional faction and ruling elsewhere other than just Samaria. Another line of inquiry takes Pekah as the legitimate heir of the dynasty of Jehu, thus counting his years from the date of the murder of Zechariah, the last king of this dynasty (749 BC). For former view, see H. J. Cook, "Pekah," *VT* 14 (1964): 121–135; Hayes and Hooker, *A New Chronology*, 54. For latter view, see Na'aman, "Historical and Chronological Notes," 77–80
24. For detailed examination of this subject, see R. Tomes, "The Reason for the Syro-Ephraimitic War," *JSOT* 59 (1993): 55–71; Kelle, *Hosea 2*, 181–199.
25. Kelle, *Hosea 2*, 183.
26. Miller and Hayes, *History of Ancient Israel*, 332.
27. Ibid.
28. Ibid., 334.
29. Tiglath-pileser III claimed to have appointed Hoshea on the throne (*ANET*, 284).
30. John H. Hayes and Jeffrey H. Kuan, "The Final Years of Samaria," *Bib* 72 (1991): 153–181 (156).
31. Miller and Hayes suggest that the oracles of Hosea in 7:11 and 12:1 reflect this scenario. Miller and Hayes, *History and Ancient Israel*, 334.

from Shalmaneser came with the arrest of Hoshea, the looting of the sanctuary at Bethel, and part of Samaria was demolished and subjected to a three-year siege.[32] However, there seems to have been a re-establishment of the Israelites' government (or possibly unnamed monarchy) during this period, which favoured the anti-Assyrian effort in the region.[33] As a result, Sargon II concluded the process of suppressing rebels in Syria-Palestine, and Samaria was declared an Assyrian province, its intelligentsia were deported and the city fell in the ninth year of Hoshea's reign (722).[34]

Economic Situation: the Zenith of Prosperity

During the long reign of Jeroboam II and Uzziah, Israel and Judah enjoyed unparalleled economic growth and political stability. Jeroboam's imperial territorial expansion allowed him to exercise control over much of the Transjordan and thereby Israel's former frontiers. This implies that they had control of the King's Highway that promoted international trade and commerce, and other major trade routes plying the length of the plateau.[35] These opportunities paved the way for Samaria to build many sophisticated fortresses and houses, and to undertake a variety of regional economic activities. Beside farming and herding, Samaria's various specialised economic activities included viticulture, olive growing, mining and metallurgy, dyeing and weaving, and a perfume industry.[36]

Commodities such as wine and oil were prominent items in export/import exchange. Oil was exported to Egypt from Palestine in exchange for

---

32. Hayes and Kuan, "The Final Years," 166.
33. Ibid., 167. Again they suggest that the prophetic words of Hosea in 8:4, "they made a king, but not through me," depicts the situation during this period.
34. For further references and discussions on the final years and fall of Samaria, see Hayim Tadmor, "The Campaigns of Sargon II of Assur: A Chronological Historical Study," *JCS* 12 (1958): 22–40; Nadav Na'aman, "Historical Background to the Conquest of Samaria (720 BC)," *Bib* 71 (1990): 206–225; Gerson Galil, "The Last Years of the Kingdom of Israel and the Fall of Samaria," *CBQ* 57 (1995): 52–65; K. Lawson Younger, "The Fall of Samaria in Light of Recent Research," *CBQ* 61 (1999): 461–482; M. Christine Tetley, "The Date of Samaria's Fall as a Reason for Rejecting the Hypothesis of Two Conquests," *CBQ* 64 (2002): 59–77; Brad E. Kelle, "Hosea, Sargon, and the final Destruction of Samaria: A Response to M. Christine Tetley with a View Toward Method," *SJOT* 17 (2003): 226–243.
35. Cf. Numbers 20:17 and 21:22. See Premnath, *Eighth Century Prophets*, 51.
36. Premnath, *Eighth Century Prophets*, 58.

military equipment.[37] As a result, the ancient subsistence economy shifted towards a market economy. The drive of labour was no longer to support family units, but production for unknown consumers. This resulted in the rise of private and royal enterprises. The monarchical centralised power began to play an important role in the economy. Both regional and international trade came under royal monopoly. This implies that the growth and prosperity did not benefit everyone in the society. The beneficiaries of all trade and commerce in Israel were only the members of the ruling class.

Another indicator of the growth of economy is the growth in population. Wright comments on the increase in population and standard of living in the eighth century.[38] Similarly, Broshi and Finkelstein observe that the population of Israel and Judah reached an all-time high of 460,000 in the eighth century BC. They also point out that large-scale agricultural development, general economic well-being, peace, and security contributed to this population increase.[39] In addition, this picture is congruent with the growth of urban layout and sophisticated architecture. Large cities during this time, for example Samaria, Hazor and Megiddo, were fortified with offset-inset walls and casements, as well as with multi-chambered gates systems.[40] The long period of relative peace and independence enabled the nobility to continue the tradition of building. Thomas notices that there are more than 200 Iron Age settlement sites today, which are attributed to the tribes of Ephraim and Manasseh.[41] Ceramic store jars, trench silos and four-room houses are considered characteristic of the Israelite settlement in the mountains of Samaria.[42] An overarching question for us to ask is that what was the impact of the recent political successes and economic prosperity on the people of Israel?

---

37. Ibid., 63.
38. George E. Wright, *Biblical Archaeology* (rev. ed.; Philadelphia: Westminster, 1962), 91.
39. Margen Broshi and Israel Finkelstein, "The Population of Palestine in Iron Age II," *BASOR* 287 (1992): 47–60 (55).
40. King, "The Greatest of Centuries?" 13.
41. P. P. Thomas, *Jeroboam II the King and Amos the Prophet: A Social-Scientific Study on the Israelite Society during the 8th Century BCE* (Delhi: ISPCK, 2003), 83.
42. Shimon Dar, "Samaria, Archaeological Survey of the Region," *ABD* 5: 927.

Moral Sickness: The Impact of Political Expansion and Economic Growth

There is a widespread agreement among scholars that the period under Jeroboam II was a period of prosperity. Nevertheless, the era that can be called "a kind of Golden Age"[43] in terms of economic prosperity and territorial expansion was also a kind of a "Dark Age" plagued with grave injustice. This is mirrored by the existence of massive prophetic accusations against the nation by Hosea and Amos. Prosperity, profligacy, exploitation and syncretism seem to have sparked the rise of writing prophets in Israel and Judah. As noted earlier, the beneficiaries of various achievements were the minority of the ruling elite,[44] bringing a stratified society in which only members of a dominant group had access to goods and services and dictated its maximum distribution.[45] In such a stratified society, as Lenski remarks, the ruling elite, no more than 2 percent of the population, controlled up to half or more of the total goods and services.[46] This was made possible through organised means of the extraction of surplus which would go to support a life of leisure and luxury for a small minority of the population (i.e. the members of the ruling class).[47] This upper class, accustomed to prosperity and economic indulgence, continued to live their exploitative and luxurious lives amidst politically unstable circumstances following the reign of Jeroboam II and until Samaria fell to its knees before an Assyrian throne.

To the prophets, Israel's grave offences included injustice in human relationships. For Hosea and Amos, the infidelity of social relationship became the acid test of the welfare of the future of Israel. The growth of urban centres, militarisation and extraction of surplus in the name of national

---

43. Martin Noth, *The History of Israel*, trans. P. R. Ackroyd; 2nd ed. (New York: Harper & Row, 1960), 250.
44. See Willy Schottroff, "The Prophet Amos: A Socio-Historical Assessment of His Ministry," in *God of the Lowly: Socio-Historical Interpretations of the Bible*, eds. Willy Schottroff and Wolfgang Stegemann; trans. Matthew J. O'Connell (Maryknoll: Orbis Books, 1984), 34–35.
45. Premnath, *Eighth Century Prophets*, 78.
46. Gerhard E. Lenski, *Power and Privilege: A Theory of Social Stratification* (New York: McGraw-Hill Book Company, 1966), 189–196.
47. Cf. Premnath, *Eighth Century Prophets*, 80.

expansion meant injustice and corruption. As discussed earlier, the growth of urban centres and a market-oriented economy in this period went hand-in-hand, by which the privileged social groups monopolised the best of goods and services. This was done through the city's important political, economic and religious functions. Cities, in this sense, enjoyed prosperity and development at the expense of the rural areas. The prophets' anti-urban sentiment seems to be grounded on an awareness of the principal burden of the urban culture being on the lower economic strata of the society. Though they noticed the external political threat that was increasingly visible on the frontiers of Israel, they saw that the basis for the downfall of Israel was to be found in internal affairs. They saw the collapse of relational justice in the lives of Israelites. It is interesting to note how Hosea and Amos employed different perspectives towards the social wrongs and religious misconceptions of Israel, often, addressing the same subject matter by means of different articulations and expressions. A few examples will suffice to illustrate this point.

As Premnath expresses, for the prophets, the growth of urban centres "symbolised the malady that afflicted the society."[48] While Amos called Ashdod and Egypt to witness the violence and oppression in Samaria (Amos 3:9–11),[49] Hosea regarded the multiplied fortified cities as an indicator of Israel's moral decadence, forgetting her maker (Hos 8:14). Amos pronounced judgment upon the palatial houses, including their "houses of ivory" (Amos 3:14–15; 6:8). Their military valour, too, would be brought to an end (Hos 10:13b–14). In reference to the extraction of excessive pecuniary burdens of surplus, both prophets accused the targeted group of people of wrongdoing. Amos' accusation, "you impose heavy rent on the poor and exact a tribute of grain from them" (Amos 5:11) brought to light the awful effect on the peasants. Hosea's indictment "you have loved the wages of a prostitute on every grain-threshing floor" (Hos 9:1) targeted the source of exploitation, namely the depraved moral fibre of the people.

---

48. Premnath, "Amos and Hosea," 128.
49. Andrew Dearman, *Property Rights in the Eighth-Century Prophets* (SBLDS 106; Atlanta: Scholars Press, 1988), 26, argues that Ashdod and Egypt were the two former oppressors of Israel, which are now called to witness the city of Samaria, which now oppresses her very own people.

With respect to the lifestyle of those of the upper class, Amos drew attention to their luxury and extravagant ways of life (Amos 6:4), their feast-loving culture, characterised by מרזח (Amos 6:4–7),[50] and their selfish pursuits of owning multiple residences for summer and winter (Amos 3:15).[51] Their carefree way of living is also demonstrated by the wanton behaviour of elite Samaritan women, "who extort the poor, who crush the needy, and say to their husbands, 'Bring something to drink!" (Amos 4:1). Hosea, too, captured a glimpse of this lavish lifestyle when he said, "On the day of our king the officials became sick with the heat of wine" (Hos 7:5).

What is more, both Hosea and Amos indicted the sexual exploitations of the time. Amos spelled out the deplorable behaviour of men where "a man and his father resort to the same girl (נערה)," (Amos 2:7b). According to Barstad, this sexual exploitation should be understood in the context of מרזח feast where a man and his father come together to celebrate the luxurious upper class meal.[52] For Paul, Amos' criticism is basically the lack of moral conduct indicated by both the father (setting example for his son) and his son copulating with the נערה.[53] Andersen and Freedman propose a distributive use of איש meaning "each," which would suggest "not just two men, but everybody is doing it."[54] In addressing the same issue, Hosea brought charges against the men for the adulterous behaviour of their young women because they only had learned it from their husbands (4:14). This is in effect saying, promiscuity deserves punishment but the cause of promiscuity deserves greater punishment. While Amos focused on

---

50. The etymology of the word מרזח is uncertain. Its extrabiblical occurrences generally denote a religious-institutional meal with the deity. This religious fellowship, as Fabry observes, developed into a social fellowship. See H. J. Fabry, "מַרְזֵחַ *marzēaḥ*," in *TDOT* 9: 11, 14. For Philip J. King, *Amos, Hosea, Micah: An Archaeological Commentary* (Philadelphia: Westminster Press, 1988), 137, the מרזח "was a pagan ritual that took the form of a social and religious association. . . . Wealth and affluence apparently were prerequisites for participation in the מרזח."

51. For a comprehensive analysis of the issue, see Bernhard Lang, "The Social Organization of Peasant Poverty in Biblical Israel," *JSOT* 24 (1982): 47–63.

52. Hans M. Barstad, *The Religious Polemics of Amos: Studies in the Preaching of Am 2, 7B–8; 4,1–13; 5,1–27; 6,4–7; 8,14* (Leiden: E. J. Brill, 1984), 34.

53. Shalom M. Paul, *Amos: A Commentary on the Book of Amos* (Hermeneia; Minneapolis: Fortress Press, 1991), 81-82.

54. Francis I. Andersen and David N. Freedman, *Amos: A New Translation with Introduction and Commentary* (AB 24A; New York: Doubleday, 1989), 318.

Israel's failure to set an example for their sons, Hosea paid attention to the same failure for their daughters.

Again, the prophets' parting shots were aimed at the corrupt practices in the market. Amos described the conduct of the greedy and oppressive merchants who were irritated by religious observances, for their only heartfelt joy was to "trample the needy, do away with the humble," sell the grain to them by making "the bushel smaller and the shekel bigger, and to cheat with dishonest scales" (Amos 8:4–5). Hosea echoed the same concern when he says, "A merchant, in whose hands are dishonest scales, loves to oppress" (Hos 12:7). With regard to the function of the institution of justice, Amos accused the judicial officials of turning "justice to wormwood" (Amos 5:7). Hosea, too, saw deceitfulness in the context of covenant declaring "justice springs up like poisonous weeds in the furrows of the field" (Hos 10:4). In fact, the moral sickness of the society was so severe and corruption so rampant that anyone who would stand up for justice was subjected to hostility and hatred from their people or associates (Amos 5:10; Hos 9:7). Perhaps, Hosea's crowning invective against social injustice came when he declared, "cursing, lying, murder, stealing, adultery are rampant; bloodshed follows after another" (Hos 4:2). We find no better expression than this to describe the moral situation of Israel. Hosea, like Amos, spoke boldly against the abusive and destructive social structure of the eighth-century Israel.

Summary Assessment

This section has attempted to underline the need to analyse the message of Hosea in the light of its socio-political backdrop, particularly with the period under Jeroboam II in Israel. The first half of the eighth century, without a doubt, was a time of political achievement and prosperity. However, by the time of Hosea time Israel had become a chaotic, fragile, dying nation. It was home to oppression, violence and exploitation. The people, used to such an extravagant way of life, continued to indulge in their exploitation of fellow human beings. In the eyes of Hosea, Israel definitely failed in its commitment to fulfil the demands of relational justice essential to being the people of God. Our analysis has also suggested that Hosea's message of social issues, subtly inserted in metaphorical language, could be viewed in the light of the prophetic oracles from other contemporary prophets.

Clearly, Hosea was not simply a religious fanatic who had no practical things to offer for the nation's growing international pressure, internal civil strife and individual affair. Indeed, he did offer something for the nation's survival – "justice" expressed in all structures of life.

Hosea's Message

This thesis has argued that the biblical notion of justice is relational. Relational justice starts and ends with right relationship. Its commitment to relationships is so strong that a break in the chain is intolerable. As Donahue describes, "'to live [for the Israelites] is to be united with others in a social context either by bond of family, or by covenant relationships."[55] Relational justice embraces the fact that faithlessness often interrupts relationship, but just, loving chastisement redirects it, and grace eventually restores the original shape of a right relationship. This conceptual understanding has been proposed as the underlining principle behind the message of Hosea.

The book of Hosea can be described as being all about Hosea's (or Yahweh's) hard-fought combat against the threatening challenges to relationship. The focal point is to amend the distorted relationship by bringing the renegade back on the right track. In so doing, Hosea addresses his people with three essential components of a true relationship: responsibility, chastisement and restoration. Interestingly, the book of Hosea comprises six cyclic *responsibility-chastisement-restoration* engagements by the one who initiates and sanctions relationships. Each aspect deserves a separate close examination. However, our investigation at this stage is preliminary, as we will offer more detailed exegetical observations in subsequent chapters.

Responsibility

The first component of Hosea's social critique involves responsibility. In essence, any relationship entails responsibility in terms of accountability and obligation. Our analysis of modern conceptions of justice has located

---

55. Donahue, "Biblical Perspectives on Justice," 69.

justice in interpersonal relationships. Justice occurs when individuals exercise their reciprocal rights and duties at the dictate of just procedures. Justice occurs when the well-being of every member is well taken care of and when people receive their just due. Our analysis of the biblical notion of justice also has defined justice as fidelity to right relationship. By assuming mutual trust and loyalty as the original position, this relational justice aims to build, maintain and restore right relationships. If this is the case, then it is quite reasonable to suppose that Hosea, who apparently holds this conviction, regards injustice as a breakdown in relationships. Israel, in the eyes of Hosea, is accountable for her actions, and has responsibilities in terms of accountability and obligations to her wronged partner. Israel must give an account of her (1) action done, (2) attitude held, and (3) responsibility to the moral demands of relationship.

Hosea spells out this relational context in terms of marriage and family to reflect the deepest relationships of all. The purpose, however, is to illustrate Hosea's faithfulness which stands in contrast to the faithlessness of his wife. This contrasting image points to Yahweh's consistent graciousness and Israel's consistent irresponsibility to maintain right relationships. Hosea as a relationally faithful father/husband and Gomer as a relationally faithless wife/husband are presented in the very first section of the book.

1:2   *Yahweh said to Hosea, "Go, take to yourself a woman of harlotry and have children of harlotry for the land commits adultery by forsaking Yahweh.*

3:1–2   *¹Yahweh said to me again, "Go and love a woman who is loved by her friend and is an adulteress, just as Yahweh loves the children of Israel, though they turn to other gods and love raisin cakes. ²And I bought her to me for fifteen shekels of silver and a homer and a lethek of barley.*

In the marriage metaphor (chs. 1–3), Hosea directs the principal content of his critique to the Israelites by indicating "what is lacking" and "what should be" in the society. Again, the intention at this stage is not to argue at length, but simply to show that Hosea certainly has messages concerning justice, which take their roots in interpersonal relationships. This whole idea is succinctly presented in Hosea 2:21–22 [19–20].

2:21 [19]   *[And] I will betroth you to me forever; and I will betroth you to me in righteousness* (צדקה) *and justice* (משפט), *in devoted fidelity* (חסד)
2:22 [20]   *[And] I will betroth you to me in faithfulness* (אמונה), *and you will know* (ידע) *the* L<small>ORD</small>.

Every relationship entails responsibility, expectation and demand. In some cases, it is sealed with certain commitments, while in other cases the demand is simply assumed. The all-embracing, radical nature of the new relationship Yahweh is going to re-establish with Israel is characterised by key qualities: righteousness, justice, devoted fidelity, compassion and faithfulness. This is relational justice rather than anything else, and Hosea concentrates on that. The five bridal gifts (צדקה, משפט, חסד, רחם, and אמונה) following a theme "knowledge of Yahweh" (וידעת את־יהוה) are the primary threads that knit the people together. They are the foundational ethical attributes that create harmonious and just relationships in the community, but these were the lost realities in the Israelite society. These qualities both govern Yahweh's conduct towards Israel and are requirements for Israel. In other words, they are the attributes of God which are precisely for his people to emulate as they enter a new reciprocal relationship with him. Elsewhere in the prophets, similar ethical qualities are stipulated. They are the standards of behaviour Yahweh demands of his people (e.g. Amos 5:15, 24; Mic 6:8; Isa 5:7). Such features define the ideal ruler (Isa 11:3–5) and the forgiving Yahweh (Mic 7:18–20). Hosea does not explain the meaning of these individual concepts, but uses them as if they are plain to his audience.

In light of our earlier examinations, we can fill out those key concepts, which Hosea uses as though they are self-evident in meaning. We have argued that the biblical notion of צדקה suggests a relational faithfulness at the disposal of societal norms, and at times, even in violation of those norms. משפט represents relational integrity in communal life within the reach of legal demand, aiming to create a rightly related society by restraining vice and protecting those who have been hurt. The idea of חסד involves mutual loyalty, but surpasses mutual obligation by going beyond the call of duty. Side by side, there is רחם [רחמים], "the tender side of commitment to the well-being of another," which cannot tolerate the total termination of relationship.[56] The last gift: אמונה can be regarded as an essential element of חסד as it denotes a "constancy of commitment" to do good deeds to (and for) another.

By drawing these notions all together, Hosea addresses the people's broken relationships with Yahweh and their fellow Israelites. His goal is to show Israel that the only way to true fellowship of "knowing" Yahweh is by living out these relational virtues. In a stark contrast, this communal fidelity ethos has been melting down. The prophet laments this deficiency unambiguously in 4:1.

4:1 [b] *There is no truth (אמת), no devoted fidelity (חסד), and no knowledge (דעת) of God in the land!*

The accusation in this context is levelled against the moral and religious deficiency of the people as a result of the priests' failure to disseminate the knowledge of God to them. The concept of אמת refers to the good deeds and reliability of an individual on whom another party can rely, which will prove to be true in the future (cf. Josh 2:12; Jer 2:21; Prov 11:18).[57] אמת always involves "one's relationship to his fellow men, and pertains to his speech and actions."[58] חסד and אמת are a recognised *hendiadys* which typically describe the attributes of Yahweh (e.g. Exod 34:6; Pss 40:11–12 [10–11]; 86:15 [14]).

While some scholars view אמת as a component (along with אמונה) of חסד, others regard it as a separate attribute of God.[59] This suggests that

---

56. Dearman, *Hosea*, 128. Macintosh notes that רחם describes the natural love of a mother or a father (cf. Isa 49:15; Ps 103:13). Macintosh, *Hosea*, 21.
57. Alfred Jepsen, "אמן, ... אמת" *TDOT* 1: 292–323.
58. Ibid., 310.
59. The former view, see Clark, *The Word Hesed*, 260. For the latter, see Jepsen, "אמן, ... אמת" *TDOT* 1: 314.

their meanings in many areas overlap. Hence it essentially connotes a being or action that is reliable. For Macintosh, חסד and אמת signify moral integrity and goodness respectively, and the absence of such qualities is due to their failure to recognise God's character, and the inability to accept his demands.[60] Thus, the dearth of both אמת and חסד not only means the collapse of relationships between Yahweh and his people, but also between humans and fellow humans. If this is the case, the primary objective of Hosea's criticism lies with the decay of relational fidelity. A clearer presentation is reflected in Hosea 6.

6:4b   *Your devoted fidelity (חסד) is like the morning mist and like the night dew that vanishes.*

6:6   *For what I desire is devoted fidelity (חסד) not sacrifice, the knowledge of God (דעד אלהים) rather than burnt offerings.*

The חסד in this context refers to Israel's devotion and fidelity to Yahweh, which forms the basis for relational commitment for Israel with their God and with their fellow Israelites. As will be elaborated later, in Hosea חסד is used in a variety of senses (cf. 2:21[19]; 10:12; 12:7 [6]). As Davies explains, "It seems most likely that it embraced for Hosea living up to one's responsibilities both to Yahweh and to fellow members of the community."[61] Hence Israel's attitudes towards Yahweh and towards fellow human beings are inextricably connected.

Like חסד, the usage and meaning of דעד אלהים in Hosea is complex. Yet it may suffice to note here that it involves Israel's relationship with Yahweh as well as knowledge about him. It is recognition of Yahweh's moral character as well as submission to his demands. The notions noted above with regard to both אמת and חסד are the outworking of דעד אלהים. This relational demand does not tolerate any interference from within or without. It should neither be traded off for an overreliance on sacrifice, nor for political alliance with a third party (5:11b). Neither should it be exchanged

---

60. Macintosh, *Hosea*, 128.
61. Davies, *Hosea*, 96.

for help from other nations (5:13), nor should it sanction hostility between blood relatives.[62] Yet Israel's faithfulness to relationships is short-lived and far too fleeting. It vanishes quickly like "morning clouds" in the summer, and like "night dew" that falls on dry ground.

Again, with imagery drawn from agricultural life (10:11–13a), Hosea exhorts the people to fulfil their part of the responsibility of sowing, reaping and tilling:

10:12   *Sow for yourselves righteousness* (צדקה) *and reap fidelity* (חסד); *break up your untilled ground for it is time to seek the* LORD *until he comes and sends righteousness on you like the rain.*

Israel's initial commission is to demonstrate (i.e. *sowing* and *reaping*) relational loyalty branded by צדקה and חסד. This is a high calling for service, which originates from Israel's election by Yahweh. "Sowing" צדקה and "reaping" חסד may well suggest that Hosea is thinking of Israel's entire conduct in relation to others: actions that are just, decisions that are sustaining, good deeds that are generous, commitment that is reliable and worship that is genuine. By "breaking" the fallow ground alone (i.e. implementing the relational ethos), they can now expect a good harvest (i.e. from the life-giving fellowship with Yahweh). Yet again, the societal climate pictured by Hosea, however, is strikingly different. Righteousness, justice, loyalty, compassion and faithfulness have all gone from the scene. Alas! Their places have been occupied by acts of hatred towards neighbour and God.

4:2   *Cursing, lying, killing, stealing, and adultery are rampant; bloodshed follows after another.*
4:11   *Promiscuity, wine, and new wine take away one's character.*
7:1b   *For they practise deception; a thief breaks in; a bandit raids outside.*
10:13a *You have ploughed wickedness and reaped injustice; you have eaten the fruit of deception.*

---

62. Cf. Wolff, *Hosea*, 120.

It is worth stressing that Hosea has never shied away from criticism of the economic injustices of his time, nor does he walk away from pleading for legal rights of the people, in a way similar to his contemporary prophets. He calls for a relationally faithful socio-economic and political orientation, which presumably was once enjoyed during the premonarchic period. Though his way of addressing the subject is not direct, his words conceivably echo an institutional critique of Israel and Judah.

5:10–11	*¹⁰The officials in Judah are like those who move boundary makers; I will pour out my fury on them like water. ¹¹Ephraim is oppressed, justice is crushed, for he is determined to follow what is worthless.*
7:3	*They gladden a king with their wickedness; the officials with their lies.*
7:5	*On the day of our king the officials become sick with the heat of wine.*
7:7	*All of them are like a hot oven, they have devoured their judges. All their kings have fallen; but none of them calls upon me.*
8:11	*When Ephraim increased altars (to expiate) for sin, they became for him altars for sinning.*
9:1b	*You have loved the wages of a prostitute on every threshing floor of grain.*
10:4	*They speak mere words, taking deceitful oaths to make a covenant. So justice springs up like poisonous weeds in the furrows of a field.*
12:8 [7]	*A merchant, in whose hands are dishonest scales, loves to oppress.*

Fascinatingly, Hosea never fails to paint the other side of the picture: Yahweh standing in relationship with his chosen Israel. As the relationship initiator and guarantor, Yahweh will keep protecting that relationship at any expense. The first step of this task is to invite the defector to come back to the table to reconsider the terms and conditions of the original relationship.

6:1	*Come, let us return to Yahweh. For he has torn us into pieces and he will heal us; he has beaten us and he will bind us up.*
12:7 [6]	*But you must return to your God. Maintain devoted fidelity (חסד) and justice (משפט), and always put your hope in God.*

What is intriguing is the fact that Hosea's utmost concern is not simply on Israel returning to God, but also to specify "exactly how" they should return. Not surprisingly, the means by which they are to return has the same practical application of loyalty and justice. However, the search for fidelity in relationship in Israel until now is of little avail. As a result, another approach has to be considered. This consideration then leads us to our suggested second motif of Hosea's message, namely, chastisement.

Chastisement

One distinctive feature of classical prophets in the Scriptures is their announcement of "end" (cf. Amos 5:2; 8:2; 9:7; Isa 28:21; Jer 27:6; Mic 3:12).[63] As such, judgment is presented in the form of retribution. Yet surprisingly, pronouncement of judgment in Hosea should not be understood as a concluding point. Rather, Yahweh's harsh judgments are corrective measures that would send his people back to his loving arms.[64] Perhaps with this in mind, Hosea pronounces tough but corrective judgments which will lead the recalcitrant Israel into an enduring and true relationship with their partner, Yahweh. For the moment, Israel is in despair and must learn that her "way of life" has led to defeat. The next way forward is to live in the absence of Yahweh's רחם, which means the presence of harsh measures by which a new course of relationship would be recommended. Hosea presents this situation in the words of a spurned husband:

2:5 [3]   *I will strip her naked and render her like the day of her birth, I will make her like the wilderness, I will make her like parched land and kill her with thirst.*

2:6 [4]   *I will have no compassion on her children because they are the children of promiscuity.*

2:8 [6]   *I will block her way with thorns; I will enclose her with a wall, so that she cannot find her paths.*

---

63. Hans W. Wolff, "Prophecy from the Eighth through the Fifth Century," *Int* 32 (1978): 17–30.
64. Ibid., 24.

3:4	*For many days the children of Israel shall live without king, without prince and without sacrifice, without standing-pillar and without epoch and teraphim.*
1:4	*And Yahweh said to him, "Name him Jezreel, because in a little while I will call to account the blood of Jezreel on the house of Jehu and I will put an end to the kingdom of the house of Israel."*

In Israel, leaders at any level were called to be active in implementing justice. Wise and experienced men were to exercise justice with integrity and impartiality (Deut 1:10–20). Judges functioned both as judges in judicial arbitration and as military deliverers (1 Sam 7:15-17; Jude 4:5). Their role involved liberating the people from their various oppressions. Kings were responsible for ensuring a just society (2 Sam 8:15; 1 Kgs 10:9) by means of doing "justice and righteousness" (Jer 22:2–5). The role of priests involved not only expiating sin through divinely approved means (Lev 16:33), but also instructing people in settling cases (Deut 17:7). An individual member of the community, too, must be just towards their neighbours. As far as Hosea is concerned, these social bearings and mandates have all disappeared from sight. This failure results in harsh judgment upon people, priest and king alike.

4:9	*Both people and priests will be treated alike. I will punish them for their ways and repay them for their deeds.*
7:16b	*Their leaders will fall by the sword because of the cursing of their tongue. They will be ridiculed for this in the land of Egypt.*
10:7	*Samaria's king will be gone like foam on the surface of the waters.*
10:15	*Therefore, the roar of battle will rise against your populace and all your fortified cities will be destroyed on the day of battle like Shalman's destruction of Beth-arbel. Mothers will be smashed in pieces with their children.*
14:1	*Samaria shall become desolate; for she hath rebelled against her God: they*
[13:16]	*shall fall by the sword: their infants shall be dashed in pieces, and their pregnant women shall be ripped up.*

Hosea does not dwell on expounding the rationale behind the looming judgments, but simply understands that violation of relational justice means violation of Yahweh's nature. Judgment can be justified, in a sense, as Yahweh's struggle is with the sin of his people. It is feasible then, that the underlining principle is to sustain relationship and hence chastisement, because Hosea does not pronounce judgment for the sake of retaliation. Rather, judgment serves various relational purposes. For instance, Yahweh's chastisement will put a halt to Israel's traitorous action of political alliances with other nations.

5:13–14	*13When Ephraim saw his sickness and Judah (saw) his wound, Ephraim went to Assyria and sent (a delegation) to the great king. But he is unable to cure you or heal your wound. 14For I am like a lion to Ephraim and like a young lion to the house of Judah. I will surely tear them to pieces. I will carry them off, and there will be no deliverer.*
7:11–12	*11So Ephraim has become like a silly, senseless dove; they call to Egypt, and they go to Assyria. 12As they go, I will throw my net over them; I will bring them down like birds of the sky. I will chastise them in accordance with the word of their assembly.*
12:2 [12:1]	*Ephraim chases the wind and pursues the east wind all day long. He continually multiplies lies and violence. He makes a covenant with Assyria, and olive oil is carried to Egypt.*

In the same manner, Yahweh's stern chastisement will put a halt to their erroneous religious practices that have gone too far.

8:13	*Though they offer sacrificial gifts and eat the flesh, Yahweh does not accept them. Now he will remember their iniquity and punish their sins, they will return to Egypt.*
9:4	*They will not pour out their wine offerings to Yahweh, nor will their sacrifices please him. Their food will be like mourners' bread; all who eat will be defiled. Their bread will be for their appetites only; he (Ephraim) will not enter the house of Yahweh.*

10:8	*The high places of Aven, the sin of Israel, shall be destroyed: thorn and the thistle shall grow over their altars; and they shall say to the mountains, "Cover us!" and to the hills, Fall on us!"*
13:3	*Therefore, they (molten images and idols) will be like the morning mist, like the early dew that vanishes, like chaff blown from a threshing floor, or like smoke from a window.*

Again, the execution of chastisement will ensure that the economic difference will be levelled, recreating relational stability that has been upset by ill-gotten gain.

8:14	*Israel has forgotten his maker and built palaces; Judah has also multiplied fortified cities. But I will send fire on their cities, and it will consume their large buildings.*
9:2–3	*²The floor and the winepress shall not feed them, and the new wine shall fail in her. ³They will not live in the land of Yahweh. Instead Ephraim shall return to Egypt and they will eat unclean food in Assyria.*
12:9–10 [8–9]	*⁹Ephraim has said, "How rich I have become! I have earned it all by myself; in all my incomes, no one can find vice in me that is sin." ¹⁰But I am Yahweh your God ever since the land of Egypt; I will make you live in tents again, as in the appointed days.*
13:6–8	*⁶When they had pasture, they became satiated; they were satisfied and their hearts became proud. Therefore they forgot me. ⁷So I will be like a lion to them; I will lurk like a leopard along their path. ⁸I will attack them like a bear bereft of her cubs and I will rip open their chests. I will devour them there like a lioness, (like) a wild beast would tear them.*

Retributive justice in philosophical consideration associates punishment with just deserts and its aim to reduce crime. To some extent, the biblical perspective shares this point in the concept of *deed-consequence*, whether good or bad. Having said that, the difference lies in the fact that the biblical sense of punishment makes use of even bad consequences as an appropriate tool for correction, as evident is Hosea. Certainly, Hosea pronounces chastisements to recreate the relational equilibrium between Yahweh and the people.

Restoration

The third and final theme of Hosea's message includes the aspect of restoration. Again, another feature of the prophets is their announcement of the "New," and hence salvation [or New Covenant] (Jer 31:31–34; Ezek 33:10–22; 36:26f.; Isa 41:22f.; 42:9f.; 43:18f.).[65] This is essentially the spirit of the book of Hosea. On this discussion, there are two phases of the path towards the new or the restoration that must be considered. The first phase towards this new relationship is associated with repentance.

> 2:9b [7b] *Then Israel will think: I will go back to my former husband, for then it was better for me than now.*
>
> 3:5 *Afterwards, the people of Israel will return and seek the LORD their God and David their king. They will come with awe to the LORD and to His goodness in the last days.*

As stated elsewhere, in Hosea's scheme chastisements serve as an integral part of a new relationship. They are meant to be the turning point for restoration so that the offender, Israel, returns to Yahweh in repentance prompted by these harsh measures. Understood in this sense, therefore, Yahweh's chastisement is never cruel or capricious, but aims to restore and sustain relationships. We have also noted that the primary aim of restorative justice in the secular sphere, too, is to convince the offender to accept responsibility, and make reparation of relationship with those who have been hurt and harmed by their offence.

On the other hand, it must be stressed that even the threatened judgments may not bring the final goal to completion. After all, chastisement does not promise outright repentance. In other words, repentance is not a guaranteed result of punishment. In fact, the evidence in Hosea suggests otherwise. Yahweh's expectation of repentance from his people is ultimately

---

65. Wolff, "Prophecy," 24.

in vain, despite ample expressions of love, and in spite of harsh punishments.[66] Israel still refuses to repent, and is thus unable to return to God.

5:4	*Their actions do not permit them to return to their God, for a spirit of promiscuity is within them, and they do not know the* LORD.
11:5b	*The Assyrian will be his king, because they refused to repent.*
11:7a	*My people are bent on apostasy from me.*

A further consideration of this aspect leads us to the second phase of the path to restoration. For a final attempt to persist and sustain relationship, a new engagement must be launched to cap the ultimate and true relationship. It is no wonder that Yahweh's inexplicable mercy must intervene. In this breakthrough, Yahweh, by his own free will, would heal the unrepentant.[67]

2:25 [23]	*I will sow her for myself in the land, and I will have compassion on Lo-ruhamah; I will say to Lo-ammi, "You are my people," and he will say, "You are my God."*
11:9	*I will not implement my fierce anger; I will not again destroy Ephraim. For I am God and not man, the Holy One in your midst; I will not come in rage.*
14:5 [4]	*I will heal their apostasy; I will freely love them because my anger has turned away from them.*[68]

The focus of attention has now shifted from pronouncement of judgments on the perpetrators to declaration of their restoration. The divine, inexplicable justice offers a possibility for the renewal of relationship even with people who do not deserve it. In fact, this sort of justice is totally foreign to justice in retributive terms, which says, "justice is done when a person receives what is due to him or her." To be sure, when human justice dwindles,

---

66. Ibid.
67. Ibid.
68. The MT "from him" reads a collective reference to Israel.

relational justice still flourishes. Yahweh will not "carry out a judgment that from a human point of view is expected and deemed necessary."[69] In this sense the execution of justice is grounded on compassion and love, rather than linking it to what is deserved, and so transcends the notion of right and duty. By saying "no" to his own burning anger, Yahweh has demonstrated his unreserved commitment to an enduring relationship with his people Israel. Though what is actually due to the people is only a corporate death sentence, Yahweh gives them deliverance instead – the pinnacle of relational justice.

Summary Assessment

A fuller image of Hosea's message is now unfolding. Nevertheless, what we have underlined so far presents only a cursory snapshot of the full image. The first stage of Hosea's message oscillates between his accusations of infidelity in relationship and exhortations to implement right relationships. He calls his people to preserve, sustain and maintain harmonious relationships in society and with their God. This can come only through implementing צדקה, חסד, משפט, רחם **and** אמת in their social, political and sacred lives. The failure to do so necessarily incurs chastisement on the part of the perpetrators. When chastisement seems to be ineffective in bringing a new and true relationship, the divine compassion takes over in recreating a new beginning of relationship. This evidence shows that Hosea proclaims a well-balanced message which one might call a "holistic relational justice." The next four chapters to which we now turn will offer exegetical applications of the proposed three threads of the relational justice – responsibility-chastisement-restoration – in the book.

---

69. Dearman, *Hosea*, 290.

Part II

CHAPTER SIX

Relational Justice: Responsibility, Chastisement and Restoration in Hosea

It is worth taking a moment to reflect on the thesis so far. The literature survey has confirmed our initial argument that the justice aspect has largely been overlooked in previous Hosea studies. Our examination of the secular understanding of justice has shown that no particular type of justice is complete without the others. Thus, any understanding of justice needs to be a more inclusive concept. Our exploration of some key words has also confirmed our suggestion that justice is relational. We have also argued that the prime intention of relational justice is to sustain, maintain, create or recreate harmonious relationship. Relational justice embraces three constituting realities within its theoretical framework: (1) responsibility (mutual obligation) as its base, (2) chastisement (judgment) as its restructuring factor and (3) restoration (reconciliation) as its culmination. Our preliminary application of this relational agenda to the book of Hosea has shown that these principles are key components for analysing the message of Hosea. Our analysis of the socio-political background of eighth-century Israel has also revealed that Hosea, like Amos, addresses the injustice of his time with his own expressions and means although his message is not confined solely to this issue. The task that lies ahead, therefore, is to discover the specific content and structure of justice in Hosea.

A Structure of Six Cycles

Interpreters have normally acknowledged the obscurity and difficulty of the text of Hosea.[1] Many concur in recognising the absence of any literary formulae to demarcate the structural units or sub-units in the book.[2] Largely, interpreters follow the twofold division of the book, which appears to be discrete in size and genre. The first section (chs.1–3) is more biographical and largely narrative in nature, which serves as a kind of interpretive framework by which the following individual, or so-called "detached sayings"[3] of the book, are to be understood. The second section (chs. 4–14) seemingly lacks the clear plan of the first. Given this impression, any attempt to find a unifying theme does not seem conceivable. Yet viewing the structure of Hosea as a formless collection will also be equally problematic.

Following a threefold division of the book (1–3, 4–11, and 12–14) proposed by several key scholars,[4] this study reads six cycles of responsibility-chastisement-restoration under the rubric of relational justice. In fact, this cyclical organisation has already been noted by scholars in one form or another. For example, Wolff notes that each of the three transmission complexes (1–3, 4–11, and 12–14) moves "from accusation to threat, and then to the proclamation of salvation."[5] Rudolph organises the first three chapters of Hosea with the triple sequential alteration from judgement to salvation but does not pursue the same organisation in the chapters that follow.[6] Buss identifies several individual oracles (3 in chs. 1–3, 4 in 4–11 and 3

---

1. For instance, a century ago W. R. Harper, *A Critical and Exegetical Commentary on Amos and Hosea* (New York: Charles Scribner's Sons, 1905), clxxii, concluded that "the text of Hosea is one of the most corrupt in the OT." See also Stuart, *Hosea–Jonah*, 13; Macintosh, *Hosea*, lxxiv; Dearman, *Hosea*, 3.

2. Sigmund Mowinckel, *Prophecy and Tradition: The Prophetic Books in the Light of the Study of the Growth and History of the Tradition* (Oslo: Jacob Dybward, 1946), 55–57; Wolff, *Hosea*, 75; Mays, *Hosea*, 5; Andersen and Freedman, *Hosea*, 69.

3. The often-quoted statement of Jerome includes, "Hosea is concise and speaks as it were in detached sayings." See Andersen and Freedman, *Hosea*, 69; Dearman, *Hosea*, 16.

4. For example, Wolff, *Hosea*, xxix–xxxii; Hubbard, *Hosea*, 49–50; James M. Ward, *Hosea: A Theological Commentary* (New York: Harper and Row, 1966), vii–viii; Davies, *Hosea*, 39; Gerald Morris, *Prophecy, Poetry and Hosea* (JSOTSup 291; Sheffield: Sheffield Academic Press, 1996), 115–116; Pentiuc, *Long-suffering Love*, 7; Ben Zvi, *Hosea*, 95–97; Dearman, *Hosea*, 16–18, all advocate the threefold division.

5. Wolff, *Hosea*, xxxi.

6. Rudolph, *Hosea*, 35–93.

in 12–14) in which each unit begins and ends in a typical manner.[7] While Wyrtzen recognises that there are five cyclic movements from judgment to salvation in the book,[8] Silva identifies six cyclic judgment and restoration patterns within the twofold division of the book.[9] Dearman also recognises the presentation of a sin-judgment-renewal pattern.[10] Although the present study concurs with the basic literary structure proposed by Wyrtzen and Silva, it differs considerably from their approaches. In regard to the former, it differs with its emphasis placed on God's "relational justice" as the organizing centre. Unlike the latter, this study proposes another stratum of the cycle. Though they, including other scholars cited above, have observed the alternating cycles of a *judgment* and *salvation* structural development, our proposed first constituent of the cycle – responsibility – is entirely overlooked in their analyses.

Therefore, this study attempts to show that the message of Hosea is not simply the pronouncement of judgment and restoration. Rather, each major oracle sets out a norm of relationship by whose standard judgment is pronounced and on the basis of that inseparable relationship salvation is announced. This demonstrates that God's relational justice is a dominant controlling strand of the threefold structural presentation throughout the entire book. The six cycles of responsibility-chastisement-restoration thus can be outlined as follows.

Prologue: Superscription (1:1)
I. Hosea and his Family (1:2–3:5)
    a. Cycle 1 (1:2–2:3 [2:1])
    b. Cycle 2 (2:4–25 [2:2–23])
    c. Cycle 3 (3:1–5)

---

7. Martin J. Buss, *The Prophetic Word of Hosea: A Morphological Study* (BZAW 111; Berlin: Töpelmann, 1969), 31.
8. D. B. Wyrtzen, "The Theological Center of the Book of Hosea," *BSac* 141 (1984): 315–329 (316).
9. Charles H. Silva, *A Literary Analysis of Hosea* (Ann Arbor: UMI Dissertation Service, 2006), 190.
10. Dearman, *Hosea*, 17.

II. Yahweh and his People (4:1–11:11)
    d. Cycle 4 (4:1–6:3)
    e. Cycle 5 (6:6–11:11)
III. Yahweh and his People (12:1–14:9 [11:12–14:8])
    f. Cycle 6 (12:1–14:9)
Epilogue: Wisdom Saying (14:10 [9])

Despite having identified the six cyclical movements in the book, it must be noted that our primary focus is not to argue at length for the unity and literary structure of the book. Rather, relying on the work done by scholars noted above and accepting the overall structural unity of the book, we will argue that relational justice is the theme that resonates through every section of the book.

Excursus: Remarks on Metaphor Studies and Feminist Readings

Before moving to the heart of our discussion, we must also make some passing comments about two recent approaches in Hosea studies, namely, gender-based studies and metaphorical readings.[11] The primary purport, among others, of feminist criticism is to make a clear distinction between "the original context, with its internal logic, and our present-day ways of thinking."[12] There is a real danger of using a prophetic text such as Hosea to legitimise sexual violence by husbands against their wives, fathers against their daughters and even men against women. It is true that there are hierarchies and power imbalances in ancient marriage relationships in which women are regarded as the possessions of their fathers and subsequently of their husbands. This perception may lead men to regard women as morally tainted and fail to recognise their full human dignity in a postmodern world. At the same time, the same danger applies to reading the biblical texts exclusively through the lens of modern perceptions particularly with regard to female sexuality. As Baumann rightly observes, "While at present self-determination regarding one's own sexuality is a postulate, at least

---

11. An extensive bibliography has already been provided in chapter 2.
12. Baumann, *Love and Violence*, 25.

in Western societies, so that legal consequences are attached to offenses against it, there was no, or almost no such thing in ancient Israel."[13] That is, while we are to avoid the danger of a wholesale acceptance of ancient customs, we are also to put our current prejudices to one side in order to glean the best out of the biblical marriage metaphor, and build an instructive scriptural principle from the received texts. The first step of the task, therefore, is to analyse the marriage metaphor in light of its historical background and social customs pertaining to it.

No studies in Hosea can overlook the centrality of the marriage metaphor and how it is used side by side with other imagery. Again, though we have no intention of entering into discussion of metaphorical theories, it would be worth stating the basic content and meaning of a metaphor. For McFague, "thinking metaphorically means spotting a thread of similarity between two dissimilar objects, events, or whatever, one of which is better known than the other, and using the better known one as a way of speaking about the lesser known."[14] Essentially, a metaphor consists of two components in a unit of discourse that have certain characteristics in common in terms of ideas, not as isolated subjects or words. The two elements include a content of expression that finds support literally and another that supports only in the given metaphor.[15] Further, "one of the two elements need not be explicitly stated, while it can be suggested in accordance with a context."[16] According to Richards, a metaphor is composed of two thoughts, which he labels the *tenor* and the *vehicle*. The former is the underlying idea or principal concept, whereas the latter is the figurative language that illuminates the tenor.[17] Along a similar line Black maintains that a metaphorical speech is comprised of two subjects, the principal and the subsidiary one

---

13. Ibid., 23.
14. Sallie McFague, *Metaphorical Theology* (Philiadelphia: Fortress, 1982), 15.
15. Eva F. Kittay, *Metaphor: Its Cognitive Force and Linguistic Structure* (Oxford: Clarendon Press, 1987), 24.
16. Hong, *Illness and Healing in Hosea*, 13.
17. I. A. Richards, *The Philosophy of Rhetoric* (1936; repr., New York: Oxford University Press, 1965), 96–97. A common metaphorical term that is used to illustrate this point is "Man is a Wolf." For Richards, Man is the *tenor* and Wolf is the *vehicle*.

(corresponding to *tenor* and *vehicle* respectively).[18] However, Kittay points out the difficulty involved in determining which component ought to be the vehicle and which is to be the tenor in a given context.[19] By retaining Richards' *vehicle,* she defines it as "the idea conveyed by the literal meanings of the words used metaphorically. By replacing *tenor* with *topic,* she defines it as "what the text is speaking about."[20] Within this framework, we will analyse Hosea's marriage metaphor as the *vehicle* (source domain) and relational justice (or injustice) as the *topic* (target domain). As regards the root metaphor, some scholars think that the "marriage metaphor" serves as a "constitutive metaphor," a single metaphor around which the whole text revolves.[21] In other words, there are certain metaphors that *collect* subordinate metaphors and *diffuse* new strands of thought.[22] Nevertheless, a better approach appears to be taking the institution of marriage as a constituent part under the primary root metaphor of "family" or "household."[23]

Hosea and His Family (1:2–3:5)

Structural Analysis of Hosea 1–3

There are three cyclic presentations in the first three chapters of the book (1:2–2:3 [2:1], 2:4–25 [2:2–23], and 3:1–5), and we must first briefly address the demarcations and contents of each cycle. Typically, interpreters treat the first cycle (1:2–2:3 [2:1]) as having two clear literary units.[24]

---

18. Max Black, *Models and Metaphors: Studies in Language and Philosophy* (Ithaca: Cornell University Press, 1962), 44.
19. Kittay, *Metaphor,* 25.
20. Ibid., 16, 26.
21. Cf. Paul Ricoeur, "Stellung und Funktion der Metapher in der biblischen Sprache," in *Metapher. Zur Hermeneutik religiöser Sprache,* Paul Ricoeur and Eberhard Jüngel, eds., (Munich: Kaiser, 1974), 45–70 (64).
22. Cf. Baumann, *Love and Violence,* 30.
23. For the former see Nwaoru, *Imagery,* 96–109, who analyses the two aspects of Hosea's marriage metaphor: Yahweh as husband and Yahweh as father. Braaten, "God Sows," in Redditt, *Thematic Threads,* 104–132, also recognises family imagery as a root metaphor under which he places emphasis on the importance of land in the book. For the latter, see Dearman, "YHWH's House," 97–108; *Hosea,* 44–50.
24. For instance, Wolff, *Hosea,* 9–11; Stuart, *Hosea–Jonah,* 22–41; Dearman, *Hosea,* 88–106.

The terse biographical account (1:2–9) introduces Hosea's marriage and children, symbolising Israel's infidelity and judgment that will fall upon Israel. Most exegetes agree that the introductory address formula (תחלת דבר־יהוה בהושע) in verse 2a signals the beginning of the narrative unit.[25] Significantly, this unit is characterised by four separate commands given by Yahweh to Hosea (vv. 2, 4, 6, 9). Each command is issued in the form of an imperative followed by a כי–clause that explains the meaning associated with Yahweh's command.[26] The form of the four commands, however, falls into two categories. The first use of a כי–clause in verse 2, as Wolff rightly notes, does not contain a threat but an accusation while the remaining כי–clauses (vv. 4, 6, 9), with symbolic names, are attached to judgment.[27] This suggests that verses 2b–3 form a separate subunit, staging a platform of relationship in order to set forth a basis for future judgment.[28] In contrast, verses 4–9 present the guilt of Israel and declare Yahweh's coming judgment. The opening adversative ו in 2:1 [1:10] sets 2:1–3 [1:10–2:1] in contrast to the previous subunit.[29] Further, the content of the salvation oracle which reverses the theme of judgment regarding Israel and Judah marks the cycle's conclusion. In sum, there are three subunits in the cycle instead of two.

The second cycle (2:4–25 [2–23]) begins with the covenant lawsuit form (ריב oracle) in 2:4 [2]. Though interpreters generally regard that two literary units make up the cycle (2:4–15 [2–13] – 2:16–25 [14–23]),[30] opinions vary in relation to the identification of smaller units particularly

---

25. See Andersen and Freedman, *Hosea*, 155; Stuart, *Hosea–Jonah*, 26; Dearman, *Hosea*, 90.
26. Wolff, *Hosea*, 10; Silva, *A Literary Analysis*, 200.
27. Despite noting that there is considerable difference between the content of verse 2 and verses that follow, Wolff does not attempt to read two separate units. Rather, he takes pains to connect verse 2 as an introduction to vv. 3–9 (*Hosea*, 10).
28. Though Silva has suggested that the judgment associated with the children's names in verses 4–9 must be interpreted in light of Yahweh's initial accusation in verse 2, he, too, fails to note its clear demarcation.
29. Mays, *Hosea*, 30; Rudolph, *Hosea*, 55.
30. See Silva, *A Literary Analysis*, 210; Dearman, *Hosea*, 106–120. For Wolff, *Hosea*, 30–46, Mays *Hosea*, 34–53 and Stuart, *Hosea–Jonah*, 42–55, the section is comprised of two subsections (2:4–17 [2–15] and 2:18–25 [16–23]).

in the first section (2:4–15 [2–13]).³¹ With regard to thematic content, the first unit can be divided into two subunits (2:4–7 [2–5] and 2:8–15 [7–13]). In the former unit, Hosea states his case against the mother as a sign of Yahweh's case against Israel while the latter focuses on disciplinary measures to bring back the recalcitrant. Put another way, 2:4–7 presents the expected condition or thwarted situation while 2:8–15 focuses on the consequences or results of the situation described in 2:4–7. As a consequence of Israel/Gomer's infidelity, Yahweh/Hosea will withhold his provisions and support. The remaining panel (2:16–25 [14–23]), with the promise of future restoration by reversing the judgment against Israel, signals the end of the cycle.

Sandwiched between the end of the salvation oracle in 2:25 [23] and a clear ריב oracle in 4:1, the third cycle with a prose memoir forms a clear section. This first-person report also makes the unit distinct from the first two chapters.³² The literary unit is introduced in 3:1 by the introductory address formula (דבר־יהוה אשר היה אל־הושע). The prediction of Israel's return to Yahweh under a Davidic ruler closes the cycle. The form of this passage looks straightforward, as interpreters have often followed the pattern: command, action and interpretation.³³ In essence, this pattern is not foreign to the previous chapters particularly in chapter 1 as Yahweh's command to Hosea (v. 2) is followed by interpretation. While these elements

---

31. Wolff takes 2:4–17 as a kerygmatic unit and thus does not pay attention to smaller units. Wolff, *Hosea*, 31 and Stuart, *Hosea–Jonah*, 46, consider the possibility that this passage contains some material from what were once separate oracles and were combined by Hosea. Andersen and Freedman, *Hosea*, 217–256, read five smaller units in this passage (vv. 4–5, 6–7, 10–11, 12–14 and 15).

32. The debate concerning the identity of the unnamed woman in this chapter has been intense among scholars. Those who argue that Gomer is not the woman in the passage include Harper, *Amos and Hosea*, 216–217; and Stuart, *Hosea–Jonah*, 64. Other interpreters who view the unnamed immoral woman as Hosea's wife, Gomer, are Wolff, *Hosea*, 59–60; Mays, *Hosea*, 55; Andersen and Freedman, *Hosea*, 295–296; Garrett, *Hosea*, 98; and Dearman, *Hosea*, 133. For more comprehensive discussion on this subject, see H. H. Rowley, "The Marriage of Hosea," in *Men of God: Studies in Old Testament History and Prophecy* (London: Nelson, 1963), 66–97.

33. For Wolff, *Hosea*, 58, the three main elements of a symbolic action are: God's command (v. 1); report of its execution (vv. 2f); and the interpretation (vv. 4f). Subscribing to Wolff's basic structuring, Stuart, *Hosea*, 63–64, notes the need to adjust the arrangement, as an interpretation interpolates both in v. 1 and v. 3. Based on this pattern, Garrett, *Hosea*, 97, also divides the passage.

serve as useful tools to analyse the form of text, they may not be the best criteria to structure the passage. Instead, 3:1–2 (Yahweh's command and Hosea's response) can be taken to form a unit, once again describing the state of inseparable relationship from the perspective of a faithful covenant partner. The procurement in this account presupposes chastisement in 3:3–4. As Gomer is to go through forced isolation and a period of purification, Israel would be deprived of the socio-political independence and religious institutions that define a state. The love of the faithful partner (3:1–2) which evolves into disciplinary measures (3:3–4) will, in turn, finally produce obedience, or will put a stop to the unfaithful partner's wicked behaviour, leading the unfaithful to embrace the one who had faithfully pursued her (3:5).

By way of summary, the proposed structure would look like this. Each of the three cycles has three subunits.

Cycle	Responsibility	Chastisement	Restoration
1	1:2b–3	1:4–9	2:1–3[1:10–2:1]
2	2:4–7 [2–5]	2:8–15 [6–13]	2:16–25 [14–23]
3	3:1–2	3:3–4	3:5

While we do not claim this structure to be problem-free, we are convinced that it is driven by the inner message. This restructuring is significant particularly in the sense that a proper analysis of the first part of each cycle will let us see exactly where Hosea grounds his proclamation of judgment, and of restoration. By his symbolic life experience, Hosea portrays what is meant by a "just" relationship or what a just and faithful person does. It must be noted that Hosean scholarship has often overemphasised judgement at the expense of this key aspect and hence pictures Hosea as if it has no message about justice at all.

Put simply, the first three chapters of Hosea are like a plan of a sermon in which the first chapter serves as an introduction to the bulk of the message in the second chapter, while the final chapter summarises the overall message. This can be substantiated in two ways.

First, though the vocabulary of the first-person account in chapter 3 differs from that of the third-person report in chapters 1–2, it covers ground similar in theme to that in chapters 1–2.[34] The content of these identical themes are presented in a spiral movement, comprising responsibility in relationship, chastisement incurred by irresponsibility and the existence of an inseparable relationship branded by reconciliation. That is, chapter 3 presupposes much that is in chapters 1–2.[35]

Second, there is also a progressive movement throughout these chapters. Chapter 1 introduces the initiation of the marriage relationship between Hosea and Gomer while this relationship had been severed in chapter 3 (cf. 1:2 and 3:1). In others words, the marriage metaphor is in progression, giving rise to and unifying other themes of images.[36] With this basic structural unity in mind, the next section will attempt to provide an exegetical analysis of Hosea 1–3 under the rubric of our proposed themes noted above.

Responsibility (1:2b–3; 2:4–7 [2–5]; 3:1–2)[37]

The significance of the marriage metaphor that dominates the first three chapters of the book is well recognised. It must be said that Hosea did choose an appropriate metaphor to illustrate the deepest relationship between Yahweh and his people. Koch recognises this when he writes, "Hosea nonetheless knows no other way of comprehending the true relationship of Yahweh to Israel except in terms of love, marriage, betrothal and having children."[38] In what follows, we will first set Hosea's marriage metaphor

---

34. Dearman, *Hosea*, 131.
35. See Andersen and Freedman, *Hosea*, 292.
36. Edwin M. Good, "The Composition of Hosea," *SEÅ* 31 (1966): 21–63 (27), recognises this point well when he says, "It slips back and forth from the individualization of man and wife to the collective of Yahweh and Israel."
37. We normally indicate the differences between MT and English versification in the course of the study. However, it will be ignored in the case of excessive references when we will follow MT versification.
38. Klaus Koch, *The Prophets* (vol. 1 of *The Assyrian Period*; trans. Margaret Kohl; London: SCM Press, 1978), 88.

in its proper context of the ancient patrilineal household. Second, we will analyse the relational terms that reflect the covenantal relationship between Yahweh and Israel.

Hosea as Relationally Faithful Father/Husband

The concepts of marriage and family constitute the deepest bonds of all human relationships. The motion of this relationship is set by Yahweh's commands to Hosea to marry a wife in 1:2b–3 and to recommence that commitment in 3:1.

Hosea 1:2b–3
²ᵇ וַיֹּאמֶר יְהוָה אֶל־הוֹשֵׁעַ לֵךְ קַח־לְךָ אֵשֶׁת זְנוּנִים וְיַלְדֵי זְנוּנִים
כִּי־זָנֹה תִזְנֶה הָאָרֶץ מֵאַחֲרֵי יְהוָה׃
³ וַיֵּלֶךְ וַיִּקַּח אֶת־גֹּמֶר בַּת־דִּבְלָיִם וַתַּהַר וַתֵּלֶד־לוֹ בֵּן׃

Hosea 3:1
¹ רֵעַ וּמְנָאָפֶת וַיֹּאמֶר יְהוָה אֵלַי עוֹד לֵךְ אֱהַב־אִשָּׁה אֲהֻבַת
כְּאַהֲבַת יְהוָה אֶת־בְּנֵי יִשְׂרָאֵל וְהֵם פֹּנִים אֶל־אֱלֹהִים אֲחֵרִים
וְאֹהֲבֵי אֲשִׁישֵׁי עֲנָבִים׃

The mandate to "take" (לקח) a woman of harlotry (1:2b) is parallel to the command to "love" (אהב) a woman who commits adultery (3:1). The common verb לקח is used as the *terminus technicus* for Hebrew marriage (Gen 4:19; 6:2; 11:29; 12:29; Exod 6:20).[39] It can also mean "buy," thus describing the process of acquiring a wife or family.[40] The employment of this technical term in this context indicates that a real marriage is meant.[41] In simple terms, Hosea is to "marry" and "love" his wife and have a family. The probable purpose of staging this platform is to depict a just relational manoeuvring of one entity in order to mirror an unjust state of another. The context simply assumes that the audience has understood what is meant by Hosea's laconic statement. What the text presents to us is a man

---

39. H. Seebass, "לָקַח *lāqaḥ*." *TDOT* 8: 16–20 (19).
40. Andersen and Freedman, *Hosea*, 156.
41. F. Charles Fensham, "The Marriage Metaphor in Hosea for the Covenant Relationship between the Lord and his People (Hos 1:2–9)," *JNSL* 12 (1984): 71–78, 72.

who is a husband and father and is assumed to be fully responsible for his household.[42] As such, Hosea's marriage is nothing other than a metaphor drawn from the everyday actions of a husband and father who is exercising his responsibility and right to sustain and discipline his family. If this is indeed the case, it is worth exploring what is involved in being a father and a husband in ancient Israel with the hope of enhancing our comprehension of the message of the metaphor.

In anthropological terms, the social structure of ancient Israelites has been described as paterfamilias, patrilineal succession and patrilocal.[43] The society was organised according to kinship groups. The three Hebrew terms in sequence referring to levels of social structures are בית אב, [44]משפחה and שבט.[45] The term בית אב means the persons in the family[46] which includes "family household" and "extended family,"[47] reflecting "the integral relationship between kinship-linked persons and the material basis for their

---

42. Nwaoru, *Imagery,* 96–97, describes that the metaphor for Yahweh in Hosea has two aspects which express Yahweh as father and Yahweh as husband. He remarks that the word אב (father) is not used in the book of Hosea. However, the concept is consequent upon Yahweh's calling his people to sonship (11:1) and a parental role for Ephraim, his child (11:3).

43. For detailed analysis of the social structure of ancient Israel, see Roland de Vaux, *Ancient Israel: Its Life and Institutions,* trans. John McHugh (London: Darton, Longman & Todd, 1961); Carol Meyers, *Discovering Eve: Ancient Israelite Women in Context* (New York: Oxford University Press, 1991); idem, "The Family in Early Israel," in *Families in Ancient Israel,* eds. Leo G. Perdue, et al. (Louisville: Westminster John Knox, 1997); Naomi Steinberg, *Kinship and Marriage in Genesis* (Minneapolis: Fortress Press, 1993); S. Bendor, *The Social Structure of Ancient Israel* (Jerusalem: Simor, 1996).

44. The משפחה was comprised of blood-related extended families or "the maximal lineage." Cf. Niels P. Lemche, *Early Israel: Anthropological and Historical Studies on the Israelite Society before the Monarchy* (VTSup 37; Leiden: E. J. Brill, 1985), 269. Geographical areas of villages originally occupied by the kin groups were later formed into administrative units under the monarchy. See Christopher J. H. Wright, *God's People in God's Land* (Grand Rapids: Eerdmans Publishing, 1990), 51.

45. A further association of several clans would comprise a tribe (שבט). See J. Andrew Dearman, "The Family in the Old Testament," *Int* 52 (1998): 117–129 (117). The self-understanding of brotherhood had results for the mutual relationships of its individual members. See Hans W. Wolff, *Anthropology of the Old Testament* (London: SCM Press, 1974), 187.

46. J. Andrew Dearman, "Marriage in the Old Testament," in *Biblical Ethics & Homosexuality: Listening to Scripture,* ed. Robert L. Browley (Louisville: Westminster John Knox Press, 1996), 56.

47. Leo G. Perdue, "The Israelite and Early Jewish Family," in *Families in Ancient Israel,* eds. Leo G. Perdue et al. (Louisville: Westminster John Knox, 1997), 175.

survival."⁴⁸ Every Israelite identified himself or herself as a member of a group. A shared landholding and dependency upon each other for purposes of economic survival made the individual members in the family inextricably connected.⁴⁹

As regards the status of women, some scholars have attempted to defend the notion that women enjoyed equal rights with men,⁵⁰ whereas others see the position of women as an unequal "painful, toilsome, slavelike existence."⁵¹ A median position argues that a woman was "really regarded as a person, but under the pressure of circumstances was on occasions debased to the level of a chattel."⁵² McNutt suggests that although men very likely dominated in more public expressions of religion, women would have had important roles at the family level.⁵³ In a nutshell, the family pattern in the Old Testament, rightly or wrongly, wore cultural clothes. Therefore, the task for an interpreter, as White notes, is "to evaluate the setting and culture in which the biblical message was cast."⁵⁴

In this cultural context, a father was in charge of almost every aspect of the family life. Women's rights in the modern sense had no place in the ancient scenario. A woman's supreme role was to contribute towards the well-being of the family by means of producing children and by being faithful to the husband. Thus, the driving force for both the father and mother in the family was to sustain the coexistence and well-being of all the family members. Success and failure relied much more on the father who was made responsible for every aspect of the family life, including teaching his household religion and morality (Gen 18:19; 45:8), and even rebuking of wayward conduct (Gen 38:24).⁵⁵ Hence the father was not simply wield-

---

48. Meyers, "The Family," in Perdue, *Families*, 19.
49. Ibid., 33.
50. See Ismar Peritz, "Women in the Ancient Hebrew Cult," *JBL* 17 (1898): 111–148 (127).
51. See E. B. Cross, *The Hebrew Family* (Chicago: University of Chicago Press, 1957), 43, quoted in Ernest White, "Biblical Principles for Modern Family Living," *RevExp* 75 (1978): 5–18, (6).
52. David R. Mace, *Hebrew Marriage* (New York: Philosophic Library, 1953), 186.
53. Paula McNutt, *Reconstructing the Society of Ancient Israel* (London: SPCK, 1999), 96.
54. White, "Biblical Principles," 9.
55. Cyril S. Rodd, "Family in the Old Testament," *BT* 18 (1967): 19–26 (23).

ing his power over his wife and children, nor would the wife live a slavelike life in fear of her husband. With different positions and roles, husband and wife committed themselves to each other to sustain and perpetuate the family. Faithlessness to that commitment was unjust and therefore unacceptable. It is reasonable to suppose that this understanding lies at the background of Hosea's language and his attack on his wife's unfaithfulness appeared to be firmly based on this commitment.

Gomer as Relationally Faithless Mother/Wife

Hosea is not simply commanded to marry a wife and have children, but appallingly, to have a wife and children of "whoredom." The two objects of the verb לקח are אשת זנונים and ילדי זנונים, for the land is "utterly whorish" (זנה תזנה) forsaking Yahweh (1:2). Similarly, the object of the verb אהב in 3:1 is a woman who is an adulteress (מנאפת). The ארץ here stands as a metonym for the nation or inhabitants.[56] As Mays puts it, "the children [and inhabitants] are the individual members of Israel, which [are] represented by the mother as a corporate person; the individual and collective ways of thinking are juxtaposed to create flexibility in the allegory."[57] All these elements endorse the idea that Israel is depicted symbolically as wife, children and land.[58] The two roots of accusation (זנה and נאף) appear together in Hosea 2:4:

---

56. The use of the definite article הָ for the ארץ indicates a particular land is meant that is "all the inhabitants of the land (of Israel)." Macintosh, *Hosea*, 8; Nwaoru, *Imagery*, 146.
57. Mays, *Hosea*, 37.
58. John J. Schmitt, "The Gender of Ancient Israel," *JSOT* 26 (1983): 115–125; "The Wife of God in Hosea 2," *BR* 34 [1989]: 5–18; "Yahweh's Divorce in Hosea 2 – Who is that Women?," *SJOT* 9 (1995): 119–132) argues that Israel is consistently and grammatically portrayed in masculine imagery. This leads him to conclude that the wife in Hosea 2 stands for a city, namely Samaria. Schmitt's position has been refuted by Dearman ("YHWH's House: Gender Roles and Metaphor"), pointing out that none of the other female agents (Gomer or mother, Lo-Ruhamah, adulteress) in 1–3 represent Samaria. As Ben Zvi also notes, even if the "wife" in Hosea 2 stands for a city, it still stands for the inhabitants too, namely Israel. Ehud Ben Zvi, "Observations on the Marital Metaphor of YHWH and Israel in its Ancient Israelite Context: General Considerations and Particular Images in Hosea," *JSOT* 28 (2004): 363–384 (364), footnote 1. In fact, the latter view is further reinforced by the negation of names, namely, לא עמי (1:6) and לא רחמה (1:9), which represent the Israelites, alternating between being ילדי זנונים (1:2) בני ישראל (2:1) בני אל-חי (2:1) and בני זנונים (2:6).

רִיבוּ בְאִמְּכֶם רִיבוּ כִּי־הִיא לֹא אִשְׁתִּי וְאָנֹכִי לֹא אִישָׁהּ
וְתָסֵר זְנוּנֶיהָ מִפָּנֶיה וְנַאֲפוּפֶיהָ מִבֵּין שָׁדֶיהָ:

This passage provides three key features to analyse Hosea's message: a רִיב-pattern proclamation, a negated divorce formula and the theme of harlotry. We will start with and continue our observation with the third theme. The subject that holds the wife/mother, children and land together is זנונים, which has been often qualified by the phrases "turning away from Yahweh" (1:2) and "turning to other deities" (3:1). The verb זנה and its derivatives, זונה, זנות, and זנונים occur over ten times in Hosea (1:2; 2:4, 6 [2, 4]; 4:11, 12, 15, 18; 5:4; 6:10). זנונים appears most frequently, five times. According to Erlandsson, the verb זנה designates primarily a sexual relationship outside of a formal union. The *qal* participle זונה designates a woman who has sexual intercourse outside a formal marriage bond or covenant relationship.[59] The root and its derivatives of נאף "commit adultery" occur in 2:4, 3:1; 4:2, 13, 14; 7:4. Unlike this narrower term, which can be committed also by men, זנה is used generally for the actions of women or female personifications.[60] However, the immediate exception comes when Ephraim (male) is accused of "whoring" (זנה and its derivatives [4:18; 5:3; 6:10]). This evidence shows that in the context of Hosea נאף and זנה are used synonymously.[61] As Freedman and Willoughby have shown, the terms are not mutually exclusive and "Hosea's wife Gomer is an example of terminological interaction, for she is both an adulteress and a prostitute (Hos 2:4 [2]; 3:1–3)."[62]

Commentators generally agree that the emphasis on the plural זנונים and נאפופים points to an abstract conception relating to a quality or an attribute.[63] The notion of זנונים is associated not only with Gomer (1:2; 2:4 [2]) but the unborn children are also tagged children of זנונים(1:2; 2:4

---

59. Seth Erlandsson, זנה, *zānāh*, *TDOT* 4:99–104 (100).
60. Baumann, *Love and Violence*, 43.
61. Erlandsson, זנה, *zānāh*, *TDOT* 4: 100.
62. D. N. Freedman and B. E. Willoughby, "נָאַף *nā'ap*," *TDOT* 9: 113–118 (115).
63. See for instance, Wolff, *Hosea*, 13.

[2]).⁶⁴ Other connections include the land (1:2), the people (4:10–11), the priests (4:14), the brides and daughters of the people (4:13) and of course Israel (4:15) or Ephraim (4:18; 5:3; 6:10). The avalanche of these connections suggest that Gomer and Israel (the people) are not only actual adulterers but the רוח זנונים "spirit of whoredom" lies within them all. Correspondingly, the use of נאף in 3:1; 4:2, 13, 14; 7:4 oscillates between the concrete actions and habitual behaviours of the Israelites.⁶⁵ The crux of the ambiguity is resolved in light of 4:12 and 5:4 which denounce the רוח זנונים embedded within the being of the people. This line of evidence shows that זנה and נאף can be associated with a variety of infidelities against Yahweh and his demands. For instance, זנונים in the context of 3:1 (or in the context of chs 1–3) may well suggest Israel's religious apostasy in terms of their vertical relationship with Yahweh. Yet the meaning and usage of the terms in other instances, with anticipation of what follows, focuses on social delinquency in terms of their horizontal relationships with fellow human beings.

At this juncture it is necessary to observe the biblical understanding of adultery on which Hosea seems to have grounded his prophetic words. It must be remembered that the idea conveyed by the literal meaning is essential to understanding its meaning metaphorically. Due to the one-flesh bond concept between husband and wife, violation of that relationship was taken seriously in biblical Israel.⁶⁶ The primary threat to the proper function of the family was adultery. Accordingly, adultery was not only considered a wrong against the husband (Prov 6:32–5) but was also regarded

---

64. Some interpret the phrase ילדי זנונים as if the children were already born to Gomer prior to her marriage to Hosea. For instance, McComiskey, "Hosea," in *The Minor Prophets,* 15–16. However, the context does not seem to support this interpretation. For Fensham, "The Marriage Metaphor in Hosea," 73, the emphasis on זנונים points that "these children will follow in the footsteps of their mother." Similarly, Garrett, *Hosea,* 53, notes that the phrase means the "children who bear the disgrace of their mother's behaviour."

65. Baumann, *Love and Violence,* 91.

66. The Bible presents marriage as a divine institution. The two accounts of creation (Gen 1:1–2:3 and 2:4–3:24) are fundamental to the understanding of marriage in the Old Testament. The foundational description of marriage in 2:24 reveals the biblical understanding of marriage as covenant (bond) relationship. The idea is expressed more explicitly later in Scripture in such as passages as in Malachi 2:14.

as sin against God (Exod 20:14, 17; Deut 5:18, 21).⁶⁷ Biblical legal codes treated adultery as the same as murder and stealing that injured one's neighbour, hence adulterers were subject to the same penalties (Lev 20:10; Deut 22:22). In view of adultery as a crime against the husband's rights committed by two parties – his wife and the paramour – the wronged victim was also likely to have several legal options available to him regarding the remedies or penalties (including the death penalty) and prosecution at his discretion.⁶⁸ In this light, it is not difficult to see that Hosea as the husband is entitled to punish his wife for a breach of her marital duty of fidelity to him. Surprisingly, Hosea does not opt for divorce, nor demand the maximum penalty. Instead, he takes great pains to charm his wife to abandon her waywardness and return.

Interestingly enough, Hosea, the seemingly least "legal-minded" of the prophets, is the first to employ a ריב–pattern.⁶⁹ His declaration: "Accuse your mother (ריבו באמכם)! Accuse because she is not my wife and I am not her husband" (2:4) falls in this category. As Gemser has demonstrated, the employment of ריב expresses "the conviction of Israel's spiritual leaders that there is something basically wrong in the religious and ethical relation

---

67. For detailed discussion on the issue, see Raymond Westbrook, "Adultery in Ancient Near Eastern Law," *RB* 97 (1990): 542–580.

68. Several interpreters view that biblical law as exhibiting unique principles different to the general body of ancient Near Eastern law, which demanded the mandatory death penalty. See W. Kornfeld, "Adultère dans l'orient antique" *RB* 57 (1950): 92–109; Moshe Greenberg, "Some Postulates of Biblical Criminal Law," *Yehezkel Kaufmann Jubilee Volume* (Jerusalem: 1960); Shalom Paul, *Studies in the Book of the Covenant in Light of Cuneiform and Biblical Law* (VTSup 18; Leiden: E. J. Brill, 1970); Anthony Phillips, *Ancient Israel's Criminal Law: A New Approach to the Decalogue* (Basil Blackwell: Oxford, 1970); idem, "Another Look at Adultery," *JSOT* 20 (1981): 3–25.

However, other scholars argue that biblical law shared much in common with other ancient Near Eastern laws, offering other alternatives such as divorce, compensation and harsh punishments. See Bernard S. Jackson, *Essays in Jewish and Comparative Legal History* (SJLA 10; Leiden: E. J. Brill, 1975); Samuel E. Loewenstamm, "The Law of Adultery and the Law of Murder in Biblical and Mesopotamian Law," *AOAT* 204 (1980): 146–153; Henry McKeating, "Sanctions against Adultery in Ancient Israelite Society, with some Reflections on Methodology in the Study of Old Testament Ethics," *JSOT* 11 (1979): 57–72; Westbrook, "Adultery," 542–580.

69. B. Gemser, "The *Rib* or Controversy-Pattern in Hebrew Mentality," in *Wisdom in Israel and in the Ancient Near East*, eds. M. Noth and D. W. Thomas (Leiden: E. J. Brill, 1969), 129.

and conduct of their nation."[70] Hosea employs this term several times (2:4 [2]; 4:1, 4; 12:3 [2]). Scholars generally follow Würthwein who has maintained that the primary meaning of a ריב as "Anklage."[71] Its use here with ב "against" fits in to this basic sense.[72] At this stage, it may suffice to note that the presence of a ריב proclamation is to signpost the fact that there is a breach in marital relationship with a view to eventually unveiling Israel's broken relationships in all walks of life. Hosea calls his children to start a ריב with their mother. They are precisely called to charge her with a breach of family integrity, namely infidelity to *her* husband, *their* father.

Interpreters have taken the view that a divorce formula common in the ancient Near East lies behind Hosea's declaration (כי־היא לא אשתי ואנכי לא אישה). Among several extant ancient oriental formulae, one document, for example, attests the double declaration: "You are not my husband" and "You are not my wife."[73] Yet scholars are at the same time perplexed by the noticeable differences in the pattern found in Hosea.[74] For instance, the sources from the ancient Near East primarily concentrate on the positive formula, and an utterance of the *verba solemnia* institutes the "termination" of the existing marriage relationship.[75] In contrast, in Hosea, Yahweh/Hosea engages in a sort of judicial procedure designed to win Gomer through various types of chastisement. The correspondence, however, is striking which leads scholars to take the formula as a negated traditional marriage formula.[76] At any rate, it may not be feasible to take Hosea 1:9b or 2:4 [2] as an official divorce declaration since it is far from clear that Hosea and Gomer were officially divorced. As Westbrook puts it, "It is therefore a reference to the formula rather than the formula

---

70. Ibid., 133.
71. Ernst Würthwein, "Der Ursprung der prophetischen Gerichtsrede," *ZTK* 49 (1952): 1–16 (4).
72. Wolff, *Hosea*, 33; Stuart, *Hosea–Jonah*, 47.
73. Samuel Greengus, "Old Babylonian Marriage Contract," *JAOS* 89 (1969): 505–532 (517); Paul A. Kruger, "The Marriage Metaphor in Hosea 2:4–17 against its Ancient Near Eastern Background," *OTE* 5 (1992): 7–25 (12); Gordon P. Hugenberger, *Marriage as a Covenant: A Study of Biblical Law and Ethics governing Marriage developed from the Perspective of Malachi* (Leiden, The Netherlands: E. J. Brill, 1994), 129.
74. Kruger, "The Marriage Metaphor," 11–12.
75. Ibid., 11.
76. Buss, *Word of Hosea*, 87–88; Kruger, "The Marriage Metaphor," 12.

itself."[77] Although the Hosean example echoes the institution in several ways, Hosea's aim is far from the dissolution of relationship. Perhaps Hosea employed "the recognised rhetoric of the day"[78] to illustrate his point to provoke Israel for her faithlessness to relationship.

One last significant aspect that reflects the Hebrew concept of marriage as a responsibility is its economic aspect. This is echoed in the third person report of Gomer's point of view in 2:7b.

Hosea 2:7b

כִּי אָמְרָה אֵלְכָה אַחֲרֵי מְאַהֲבַי נֹתְנֵי לַחְמִי וּמֵימַי צַמְרִי וּפִשְׁתִּי שַׁמְנִי וְשִׁקּוּיָי׃

Gomer's actions as a harlot become apparent. Her friends in זנונים are now identified as "lovers" (cf. 2:9, 12, 14, 15). The context suggests that these lovers are the Canaanite deities (בעל [v. 5] and בעלים [vv. 15, 19]).[79] Gomer wrongly describes these deities as "providers" or "givers" (נתן) of her life sustaining commodities (cf. 2:7, 10, 13). The response from the husband claims that he is the true provider (v. 10). The fundamental error of Gomer is to disdain her husband's dutiful care and provisions, and wrongly attribute them to other lovers. Once again, this understanding lies in the backdrop of marriage responsibility in Israel. Normally, the marriage process in early Israel was initiated by the man's family.[80] Upon receipt of a gift (מהר, Gen 34:12; Exod 22:16; 1 Sam 18:25), the father declared that his daughter was bindingly betrothed (cf. 1 Sam 18:17–21). A dowry, typically a large wedding present, was given to the bride by her father and this remained hers.[81] Upon the completion of the marriage transfer ceremony, a man would take a woman to his house and she became his

---

77. Westbrook, "Adultery," 578.
78. Dearman, *Hosea*, 57.
79. J. A. Thompson, "Israel's 'Lovers'," *VT* 27 (1977): 475–481 (480), thinks that Israel's lovers in Hosea 2 were other deities, the Baalim. However, the book anticipates more of other providers to come.
80. Vitaly Voinov, "Observations on Old Testament Kinship Relations and Terminology," *BT* 55 (2004): 108–119 (109).
81. Gordon J. Wenham, "Family in the Pentateuch," in *Family in the Bible,* eds. R. S. Hess and M. D. Carroll R. (Grand Rapids: Baker Academic, 2003), 24.

wife (Gen 24:67).[82] Most scholars recognise מהר as a sign symbolising the transfer of "right" over the woman from the father to the future husband.[83] Undoubtedly, מהר is a symbol of right for a man, but more important than this aspect is his new "responsibility" to take care of his newly wedded wife for her lifetime. Put another way, this right implies responsibility, and involves a transfer of obligation. Prior to his marriage a man's sole responsibility was to his parents or siblings. When a man is married, his order of responsibilities has changed and he now has become a part of "one flesh" by being joined to his wife. As Wenham observes, "though his parents' needs are still important, his wife's needs are even more important."[84] Extra-biblical sources stipulate certain specific responsibilities of a husband for his wife. For instance, the Middle-Assyrian Laws prescribe that a husband provides three basic staples of life for his wife: food (bread and water), clothes (wool and flax) and oil (cosmetics).[85] The same provision is required even for a harlot from the square who has borne him children.[86] An identical stipulation is prescribed in Exodus 21:10 as the legal responsibility of a husband for the wife's marital right. Hosea's metaphor anticipates similar provisions. In light of this evidence, it would be sensible to deduce that Hosea's "taking a wife," or marrying, primarily assumes a relationship with responsibility. "Justness" or "unjustness" must be tested on this, and it is the reference line from which Hosea launches his accusations.

We may say in summary that though Hosea presents no sociology on ancient Israel's family structure, the metaphorical language undeniably reflects the relationships between husband and wife, parents and children. Israel's social structure, in light of our analysis, is hierarchical in nature but team-like in spirit. To be a contributing member is not only an identity but a privilege. Commitment is a key to marriage and family relationships. Dependence upon each other for various purposes of survival unites all individual members in the family or community. The father of the household assumes full responsibility of supporting, judging and protecting the

---

82. Dearman, "Marriage," 57.
83. For example, de Vaux, *Ancient Israel,* 17.
84. Wenham, "Family in the Pentateuch," 18.
85. *ANET*, 183.
86. Ibid., 160.

household members, but also demands exclusive loyalty and fidelity from the subordinate members, namely the wife and children. These terms and conditions seem crystal clear for both Hosea and his audience. In its simplest term, Hosea stands as the relationally faithful father/husband, while Gomer positions herself as the relationally faithless mother/wife.

Yahweh as Israel's Covenant Father/Husband

Scholars in one way or another have recognised the commonality between the biblical concept of covenant (ברית) and marriage metaphor. The basic terminology and content of the ברית and marriage metaphor stand side by side in a number of biblical texts. Though we have no intention to exhaust a rather complex concept of ברית in this brief section,[87] it would be worth drawing out its basic tenet to illuminate Hosea's relational message.

The term ברית occurs five times in Hosea (2:20 [18]; 6:7; 8:1; 10:4; 12:2 [1]). Hosea employs the term in two senses: "one relates to political agreements between peoples, and the other represents Yahweh's initiation of a relationship with Israel or another aspect of creation."[88] It is the latter aspect that we want to pay attention to at this point. According to Kline, "a relationship ratified by a human oath of allegiance is a covenant (ברית)."[89] Hugenberger defines a ברית as "an elected, as opposed to natural, relationship of obligation under oath."[90] While scholars have generally recognised a ratifying oath or "oath sign" as the *sine qua non* of the ברית,[91] the absence of a specific oath in biblical marriages (such as the marriage metaphor in Hosea) has prompted some to challenge the validity of identifying

---

87. There are different types of ברית in biblical tradition. For more comprehensive analyses on these varieties, see George E. Mendenhall, "Covenant Forms in Israelite Tradition," *BA* 17 (1954): 50–76; Moshe Weinfeld, "The Covenant of Grant in the Old Testament and in the Ancient Near East," *JAOS* 90 (1970): 184–203; Herbert B. Huffmon, "The Covenant Lawsuit in the Prophets," *JBL* 78 (1959): 285–295.
88. Dearman, *Hosea*, 51–52.
89. Meredith G. Kline, *By Oath Consigned: A Reinterpretation of the Covenant Signs of Circumcision and Baptism* (Grand Rapids: Eerdmans, 1968), 16.
90. Hugenberger, *Marriage as a Covenant*, 11, 175.
91. See James Barr, "Some Semantics Notes on the Covenant," in *Beiträge zur alttestamentlichen Theologie*, ed. Herbert Donner et al. (Göttingen: Vandenhoeck & Ruprecht, 1977).

marriage as a covenant.⁹² In response to this objection, Hugenberger argues that many oaths may simply consist of "a solemn positive declaration" (i.e. *verba solemnia*), as opposed to self-maledictory oath-signs, or a "symbolic depiction of the commitment being undertaken" (i.e. an oath-sign such as a shared meal or handshake).⁹³ In the same line, Silva argues that the mere absence of the term ברית need not exclude the thing signified,⁹⁴ and in fact the idea of covenant can be understood as "an invisible framework" in the prophetic books.⁹⁵ Not surprisingly, Mendenhall also remarks that there are "numerous references to covenants and covenantal relationships where this term does not occur."⁹⁶ Typical examples are Genesis 12 and 2 Samuel 7 where the term ברית is not actually used but the passages demonstrate what the covenant is all about. These observations suggest it is reasonable to deduce that Hosea understands his marriage as a bond relationship, symbolising the covenant between Yahweh and his people Israel. In other words, the marriage is the vehicle and God's covenant is the topic.⁹⁷

There are conceptual and terminological links between marriage and covenant. This is clearly visible when the language of Hosea is compared with those known as the covenantal formulae in the Old Testament. For instance:

Exod 6:7a:	וְלָקַחְתִּי אֶתְכֶם לִי לְעָם וְהָיִיתִי לָכֶם לֵאלֹהִים
Hos 1:2–3:	לֵךְ קַח־לְךָ אֵשֶׁת ... וַיֵּלֶךְ וַיִּקַּח אֶת־גֹּמֶר

---

92. Proponents for this position, for example, include Jacob Milgrom, *Cult and Conscience: The Asham and the Priestly Doctrine of Repentance* (Leiden: Brill, 1976) and Moshe Greenberg, *Ezekiel 1–20* (AB 22; New York: Doubleday, 1983).
93. Hugenberger, *Marriage as a Covenant*, 215.
94. Moisés Silva, *Biblical Words and their Meaning: An Introduction to Lexical Semantics* (rev. and enl. ed; Grand Rapids: Zondervan, 1994), 26.
95. Delbert R. Hillers, *Covenant: The History of a Biblical Idea* (Seminars in the History of Ideas; Baltimore: Johns Hopkins Press, 1969), 291.
96. George E. Mendenhall, "Covenant," *IDB* 1: 714–723, 715.
97. Scholars have noted that the portrayal of deity as the husband of the people is unique and Hosea is the first of the prophets to describe in terms of this image. Kruger, "The Marriage Metaphor in Hosea 2:4–17," 7; Dearman, *Hosea*, 55.

With Israelite's marriage culture in mind, it is not difficult for us to see that the "taking" here means entering into a new relationship. As Yahweh takes the initiative in a covenant relationship with his people, so is Hosea commanded by Yahweh to take a wife for himself. The most obvious correspondence between marriage and covenant is its hierarchical relationship of the two sides. It is always the stronger that takes the initiative in a relationship and demands sanctions against it.[98] The terminological links become even clearer in Ezekiel's descriptive rehearsal of marriage between Yahweh and Jerusalem: "I entered into a covenant with you . . . and you became mine" (Ezek 16:8b). Therefore, as discussed elsewhere, the relationship between a husband and his family or wife in a patriarchal setting was hierarchical in which the father could claim allegiance from his wife and children. As Hosea, the stronger partner, takes Gomer the weaker partner, so Yahweh takes Israel into a special relationship. The context assumes that the stronger partner remains faithful. Accordingly, what the stronger partner demands from the weaker partner and what the weaker partner owes to the stronger partner is an exclusive loyalty and fidelity.

The next examples are Jeremiah 7:23 and Ezekiel 14:11 (see also in Lev 26:12; Deut 29:11 [12], etc.).

Jer 7:23:	וְהָיִיתִי לָכֶם לֵאלֹהִים וְאַתֶּם תִּהְיוּ־לִי לְעָם
Ezek 14:11:	וְהָיוּ לִי לְעָם וַאֲנִי אֶהְיֶה לָהֶם לֵאלֹהִים
Hos 1:9:	כִּי אַתֶּם לֹא עַמִּי וְאָנֹכִי לֹא־אֶהְיֶה לָכֶם
Hos 2:4 [2]:	כִּי־הִיא לֹא אִשְׁתִּי וְאָנֹכִי לֹא אִישָׁהּ

What is fundamental to each instance is its reciprocal component. The context of Jeremiah shows that the sacrifices will not save the Israelites as long as they go on in disobedience. Ezekiel uses the formula envisioning the ideal relationship between Yahweh and his people. This will come, however, only after Israel has been purged of all infidelity. Another internal parallel is the declaration in 1:9: "For you are not my people (לֹא עַמִּי), and I will not be your God ([לֹא־אֶהְיֶה]) i.e. literally I am not 'I AM' to you)." The

---

98. Baumann, *Love and Violence,* 61.

statement is formed by two negated names: one of which is intended for the son (לֹא עַמִּי), while the other is a play upon the divine name (לֹא־אֶהְיֶה). Most commentators have understood the phrase לֹא־אֶהְיֶה to represent the divine name revealed to Moses in Exodus 3:14.[99] What is significant for us is to note that the relational language formulated in the form of "my people . . . your God" or "yours" . . . "mine," comes from biblical covenantal texts such as cited above, but they have been reversed by Gomer/Israel's deeds. The prophetic word, borrowing Buss's dialectical term, "is a negation of the negation" and Hosea/Yahweh chooses the "blackest terms possible"[100] to demonstrate the dissolution of Israel's personal relationship with Yahweh resulting from rebellion and irresponsibility. The covenant is now broken and Israel has indeed failed her obligation.

One last clear linguistic parallel concerns Deuteronomy 6:5, 7:8 and Hosea 3:1.

Deut 7:8:	כִּי מֵאַהֲבַת יְהוָה אֶתְכֶם וּמִשָּׁמְרוֹ אֶת־הַשְּׁבֻעָה אֲשֶׁר נִשְׁבַּע לַאֲבֹתֵיכֶם הוֹצִיא יְהוָה אֶתְכֶם בְּיָד חֲזָקָה וַיִּפְדְּךָ מִבֵּית עֲבָדִים
Hos 3:1a:	עוֹד לֵךְ אֱהַב־אִשָּׁה אֲהֻבַת רֵעַ וּמְנָאָפֶת כְּאַהֲבַת יְהוָה אֶת־בְּנֵי יִשְׂרָאֵל
Deut 6:5	וְאָהַבְתָּ אֵת יְהוָה אֱלֹהֶיךָ
Hos 3:1b:	וְהֵם פֹּנִים אֶל־אֱלֹהִים אֲחֵרִים וְאֹהֲבֵי אֲשִׁישֵׁי עֲנָבִים

Weinfeld declares that the theme of love (אהב) between God and Israel is "the most prominent point of contact between Deuteronomy and Hosea."[101] By employing the same root אהב Hosea and Deuteronomy describe Yahweh's love of Israel as well as the human side of the relationship.[102] Moran has argued that the אהב in Deuteronomy is the אהב that can be

---

99. See Wolff, *Hosea*, 21–22; Mays, *Hosea*, 29–30; Andersen and Freedman, *Hosea*, 197–199; Stuart, *Hosea–Jonah*, 33–34; Macintosh, *Hosea*, 26–29.

100. Buss, *Word of Hosea*, 140.

101. Moshe Weinfeld, *Deuteronomy and the Deuteronomic School* (Oxford: Clarendon, 1972), 360. We shall not be concerned at this stage with questions such as what source is earlier or has influenced the other. For an extensive survey on this subject, see Carsten Vang, "God's Love according to Hosea and Deuteronomy," *TynBul* 62 (2011): 173–194, and bibliography cited there.

102. For example,. Deut 5:7; 6:5; 7:9; 10:12; 11:1, 13, 22; 13:4; 19:9; 30:6, 16, 20]; Hos 2:7, 9, 12, 14, 15; 3:1b; 4:18; 9:1, 10.

demanded which is intimately attached with fear and reverence, and which must be expressed "in loyalty, in service, and in unqualified obedience to the demands of the Law."[103] In contrast, Hosea, Moran asserts, speaks only of Yahweh's parental or conjugal אהב (cf. Hos 3:1; 11:1) but never of Israel's "love" for Yahweh.[104] However, such a dichotomic depiction is simplistic because Deuteronomy's demand of love from Israel is more subtle than this. Barker argues that Deuteronomy expects Israel to fail and Israel's ability to love Yahweh lies with Yahweh's action, not Israel.[105] Ackerman also sees the אהב in Deuteronomy as one-sided love, and it "never describes the people or their ancestors as actually offering Yahweh this love."[106] This observation allows us to construe that Deuteronomy and Hosea, despite their respective differences in emphasis, demand neither blind covenantal fealty (which Israel has never met) nor vague emotional response to the true relationship between Yahweh and Israel. In fact, Sakenfeld argues that the verb אהב can be used interchangeably with חסד which is a dominant theme in Hosea.[107] At any rate, both books demand fidelity from the people and also assume Yahweh's inexplicable forgiveness to continue until the true nature of relationship has been consummated.

In summary, the biblical concept of covenant and the marriage contract of Israel and of the ancient Near East are closely related ideas. The

---

103. William L. Moran, "The Ancient Near Eastern Background of the Love of God in Deuteronomy," *CBQ* 25 (1963): 77–87, 78. Thompson also notes that אהב implies the concept of covenant fealty, and a vague emotional response was unacceptable to the true nature of covenant between Yahweh and Israel. Thompson, "Israel's 'Lovers'," 481.

104. Moran, "The Love of God in Deuteronomy," 77. Several works dealing with the same theme subsequent to Moran include: Dennis J. McCarthy, "Notes on the Love of God in Deuteronomy and on the Father-Son Relationship between Yahweh and Israel," *CBQ* 27 (1965): 144–147; J. W. McKay, "Man's love for God in Deuteronomy and the Father/Teacher – Son/Pupil Relationship," *VT* 22 (1972): 426–435; J. A. Thompson, "The Significance of the verb *Love* in the David-Jonathan Narratives in 1 Samuel," *VT* 24 (1974): 334–338; P. R. Ackroyd, "The Verb Love – אהב in the David Jonathan Narratives – A footnote," *VT* 25 (1975): 213–214.

105. Paul Barker, *The Triumph of Grace in Deuteronomy: Faithless Israel, Faithful Yahweh in Deuteronomy* (Carlisle: Paternoster, 2004), 160–163.

106. Ackerman, "The Personal in Political," 445.

107. Katharine D. Sakenfeld, "Loyalty and Love: The Language of Human Interconnections in the Hebrew Bible," *MQR* 22 (1983): 190–204; reprinted in *Backgrounds for the Bible*, eds. D. N. Freedman and M. P. O'Connor (Winona Lake: Eisenbrauns, 1987), 215–230.

terminological and conceptual links are too obvious to be unnoticed. Hosea sees his marriage as a bond relationship which symbolises Yahweh's relation to his people. As a husband takes the initiative in acquiring a bride or family, so Yahweh first chooses Israel. As the subordinate members of the family owe fidelity to the father, so Israelites (Yahweh's household) owe allegiance to Yahweh. As the stronger partner assumes love and responsibility for the weaker partner, Yahweh fulfils his paternal and marital obligations towards Israel. Just as Hosea loves his licentious wife, Yahweh loves his adulterous people, Israel. The contrasting images in the first few verses of Hosea are clearly visible: Hosea/Yahweh remains faithful to relationships whereas Gomer/Israel has thus far failed her commitment of fidelity to relationships. The consequence of this failure is chastisement in the form of the suspension of the support and care that were otherwise expected. It is to this theme we now turn.

Chastisements (1:4–9 [2–5]; 2:8–15 [6–13]; 3:3–4)

Having set Hosea's marriage metaphor in a relational context we can now move on to the subject of irresponsibility and its attendant chastisements. The theme of judgment is our proposed second component of God's relational justice in the book of Hosea. This aspect has been well perceived by scholars. What is yet to be observed, however, is that the message of judgment in Hosea is an essential part of God's righteousness that perpetuates his relationship with his people. Elsewhere we have argued that the sole aim of צדק is to perpetuate a right relationship which embraces both God's gracious faithfulness to his promises by forgiving the unforgivable and his corrective judgement of unfaithfulness to the demands of relationship.[108]

---

108. John Piper, "The Righteousness of God in Romans 3:1–8," *TZ* 36 (1980): 3–16, argues that God's righteousness does not rule out all judgment. Rather, his righteousness includes both his unwavering commitment to preserve his covenant people in salvation and in judgment.

Embryonic Names for Chastisement (1:4–9)

As noted earlier, there are four divine commands in 1:2–9. We have noted that the first command (v. 2) does not contain a threat but an accusation of relational irresponsibility. The three divine remaining commands (vv. 4, 6, 9), concerning the births and naming of Hosea's children, however, are attached to judgment. These names are pregnant words, what Buss calls "one-word or one-phrase oracles."[109] Having been told that Gomer's children are the ילדי זנונים, we can anticipate that the names will carry only a negative message. The name of the first child is Jezreel (יזרעאל) which means "God sows."[110] This term is generally understood in terms of faithfulness and productivity. It is a recognised name of the fertile valley in the heartland of the Northern Kingdom. This agricultural bounty of the land is a gift of Yahweh to Israel, which can be taken back by Yahweh as an act of judgement.[111] Interestingly, יִזְרְעֶאל is grammatically and phonetically similar to [112]יִשְׂרָאֵל which suggests a pun that draws attention to a prior "bloodshed (דמים)" committed by Jehu at Jezreel (v. 4). The references to Jezreel and Jehu reflect the Elijah narrative where Ahab is charged with crimes of murder, land seizure and false worship and with Jehu for repeating the same errors. Accordingly, the "sowing" here means the scattering of judgment on the people for violating their neighbour, the land and Yahweh through bloodshed and false worship. The second child, a daughter named Lo-Ruhamah (לא רחמה) means "unpitied/shown no compassion."[113] The reason why she shall be called לא רחמה is explained in the verse "For Yahweh will no longer have mercy on Israel" (v. 6). Yahweh will have no love or feeling for her.[114] The name anticipates Yahweh's disciplinary measures that will come upon Israel and no forgiveness will be at hand. The Lord will now withdraw his fatherly love and protection from the people. The name of the third child, Lo-Ammi (לא עמי), means "not my people." As noted elsewhere, the name expresses the termination of the covenant

---

109. Buss, *Word of Hosea*, 29.
110. *BDB*: 281.
111. Braaten, "God Sows," in Redditt, *Thematic Threads*, 109.
112. See Dearman, *Hosea*, 92.
113. *BDB*: 283.
114. Fensham, "The Marriage Metaphor in Hosea," 74.

between Yahweh and his people. Like the name of the second child, לא עמי cancels a previous relationship. With her current status and nature, Israel could never remain the people of Yahweh (cf. Exod 19:5–6).

Reaction from a Spurned Husband (2:8–15)

The next passage that deals with chastisement is 2:8–15. Having stated the case against the adulterous wife in 2:4–7 [2–5], Hosea/Yahweh now announces the impending measures expressed in the words of an aggrieved husband. At this point, it would be helpful to keep in mind that reality sometimes "intrudes" into the metaphor.[115] In addition, as Gordis has shown, there is a process of "identification" in chapter 2 in which the paradigmatic pair has been replaced by the Yahweh/Israel image.[116] The transition-point from the human to a cosmic plane, Gordis claims, starts with 2:5e "I will slay her with thirst" (והמתיה בצמא) and the complete transition comes in verse 6, (ואת־בניה לא ארחם כי־בני זנונים המה).[117] This is to say that the "children" in this context are not Hosea's offspring in 1:2, but rather his co-inhabiting Israelites addressed in 1:9. Once this transition has been affected, the personal lot of Gomer is no longer of interest in the chapter.[118] It bears noting that there are three realities that intrude into the metaphor: Hosea's marital experience, Baal worship and Yahweh's ownership. The language of the case against adultery and its imposed sanctions are grounded on Hosea's marriage, reflecting the culture known then to Hosea's audience. However, this gives way to Yahweh's ownership of Israel and "the threat of divorce ceases to be a contingency and becomes instead a plan of future action."[119]

What must be stressed in analysing the passage is that in his entire attempt, Hosea/Yahweh aims to win the deviant partner back. Despite imposing the threat of harsh punishments, Hosea/Yahweh will not give up the adulterous wife Gomer/Israel. Weems rightly warns against the danger of

---

115. Greenberg, *Ezekiel 1–20*, 287–288.
116. Robert Gordis, "Hosea's Marriage and Message: A New Approach," *HUCA* 25 (1954): 9–35 (19–23).
117. Ibid., 21–22.
118. Ibid., 23.
119. Westbrook, "Adultery," 578.

an obsession with the detail of the metaphor that disregards the *dissimilarities* between Yahweh's covenantal relation with Israel and Hosea's marriage relationship with Gomer. This sort of deduction, she cautions, could suggest the notion of divine retribution. Nevertheless, when the punishment in Hosea is viewed as part of the husband's (either Hosea or Yahweh) restorative actions, the idea of retribution ceases to dictate the metaphor.[120] As for now, Yahweh/Hosea claims grounds as a wronged husband. Here the reality of ANE ethos intrudes, suggesting that the husband has every right to punish his adulterous wife, "Lest I strip her naked" (פן־אפשיטנה ערמה) and she could be humiliated by exposing her nakedness in the sight of her paramour or lover (v. 5).[121] If the wife will not remove her נאפופים, the husband in return will remove her clothing, food and water so that she dies exposed.[122] Also he will no longer have compassion on the children, the Israelites, because they, too, are prostituting themselves (כי־בני זנונים, v. 6). They are tainted by the waywardness of their mother, sharing in the punishment that will be hers.[123] The promiscuous wife who is obsessed with her lovers (אלכה אחרי מאהבי, v. 7) has forced the husband to make a drastic resolution. Thus, he resolves to "obstruct her path" and "wall her in," keeping her out of the reach of her "lovers" (v. 8). When every attempt to find her lovers proves futile, she would come to her senses and return to reconcile with her husband (v. 9).[124]

Additional evidence against the faithless wife is exposed in verse 10. This set of chastisements is marked by an inclusio, as Mays rightly notes, "The opening 'But she does not acknowledge that it was I . . .' is echoed in

---

120. Weems, "Gomer: Victim of Violence?," 88.
121. The threat to "strip" Israel "naked" reflects the divorce proceeding and the curse language of Ancient Near Eastern treaties. See Delbert R. Hillers, *Treaty-Curses and the Old Testament Prophets* (Rome: Pontifical Biblical Institute, 1964), 58–60.
122. It is important to remember that marriage relationship in ancient patriarchal social structure was not symmetrical. A man can send his wife (who belongs to him only) away (but not vice versa).
123. Macintosh, *Hosea*, 46.
124. Remarriage after divorce in certain circumstances is forbidden by the law of divorce (Deut 24:1–3). It must be remembered, however, that there has been no mention in the text that Gomer has actually divorced her husband, nor officially married another man. Further, as Westbrook notes, the husband's action at this point has no legal content as he is identified with Yahweh. Westbrook, "Adultery," 579.

the climatic anguish of 'But me she forgot' at the end of verse 13 [15]."[125] The husband explains his right to take his marital gifts and supports, and claims that he has been the real provider. The mother/Israel preferred to attribute such blessing to her lovers, the fertility and plenty of the land. Israel's thoughtlessness and forgetfulness once again forces Yahweh to suspend his support because it was Yahweh who has given her the grain, the new wine, and the oil (v. 10).[126] Because of wrongly crediting the Baals with the economic prosperity of the days' "silver and gold," Yahweh, the husband of the metaphor, will withdraw his support of agricultural bounty from Israel (v. 11). He will humiliate her in the sight of her lovers (v. 12). The withdrawal of agricultural products by the husband will bring her festivities to an end (v. 13) and her arable lands will be overgrown (v. 14). Yahweh will finally punish his wayward wife, Israel, for her dalliance with the Baals, for her false worship and her rejection, all of which have resulted in her forgetting her covenant Lord (v. 15).

Hosea's Stricture to his Wife (3:3–4)

The third passage that deals with the chastisement includes 3:3–4. As in chapter 2, the message of judgment oscillates between the metaphor's source domain and target domain. Hosea's stricture to his wife in verse 3 stands in strict parallel to Yahweh's judgment of Israel in verse 4.[127] The phrase "You shall stay (ישב) with me for many days" is all but identical to "For the sons of Israel will remain (ישב) many days." The spurned husband will now restrict the activities of his wayward wife. She is first to remain legally owned by him, forbidden to engage in further prostitution or have relations with anybody else. This is followed by three pairs of parallel negations, describing Israel's basic institutions which would suffer deprivation. Israel would remain for many days without king and prince (devoid of socio-political independence); without sacrifice and sacred pillar (deprived of

---

125. Mays, *Hosea*, 40.
126. Stuart points out that the three words, "grain, wine and olive oil" are a synecdoche for the full range of agricultural blessings given to Israel by Yahweh (Deut 7:13; 11:14; 12:17; 14:23; 18:4 and 28:51) which Israel attributes them to the powers of Baal in the final years of Jeroboam II. Stuart, *Hosea–Jonah*, 50.
127. Silva, *A Literary Analysis*, 221–222.

religious institution); and without household idols (deprived of devotion and worship of the Baals). Gomer's restrictions are intended to purify her from vice, and by analogy, Israel's lack of her socio-political and religious institutions represents the purification from corrupt social apparatuses that have debilitated the people and led them astray.[128] As Hosea would not allow Gomer's adulterous behaviour to flourish, Yahweh would not let Israel's current social functioning to continue. Israel must go through a process of chastisement in preparation for a better time to come.

In brief, Hosea's proclamation, following Buss, can be branded as a negation of the negation. In its entirety, Israel's relational faithlessness negates Yahweh's relational faithfulness. The metaphorical presentation of Gomer and the children is a prosecution of Israel. The household father, Hosea, has been exasperated by the perfidy of his wife and children, and this frustration represents an aggrieved Yahweh. In response to the rejection, the spurned husband Yahweh pronounces harsh measures upon Israel, but fascinatingly, the threat of divorce becomes a part of the roadmap towards inseparable relationship between Yahweh and his people, Israel.

Restoration (2:1–3 [1:10–2:1]; 2:16–25 [14–23]; 3:5)

Reversals of Ill-omened Names (2:1–3)

We have discussed that there are three sections of judgment oracles in chapters 1–3 and each declaration of judgment has been followed by a reversal of prophecy. The first restorative proclamation includes 2:1–3 [1:10–2:1]. The salvific predictions in this unit are a reversal of severe punishment depicted in 1:4–9. The transition from negative to positive speech is abrupt, and this leads many scholars to question the placement and authenticity of 2:1–3.[129] However, as the overall structure of this study shows, an abrupt

---

128. Dearman, *Hosea*, 137.
129. Harper, *Amos and Hosea*, 245, and Ward, *Hosea*, 24, treat the unit as a later piece. Wolff, *Hosea*, 25–26, considers this section Hosean in origin, but he proposes that the oracle to be placed alongside another authentic oracle at the end of 2:4–25.

transition from one theme to another is classically Hosean.[130] The denial of authenticity or its transference to another place "disrupts the intrinsic structure of the chapters 1–3."[131]

The linkages between 1:2–9 and 2:1–3 and their interdependence are strong.[132] This has been demonstrated by the new application of the names of Hosea's children, namely: Jezreel (1:4–5, 2:2), Lo-Ammi (1:9; 2:1, 3) and Lo-Ruhamah (1:6; 2:3). Put simply, these judgment names are transformed to salvation names. We have observed elsewhere that the name Jezreel designates a place where Yahweh would scatter malediction because the house of Jehu had repeated the same apostasy of the Omrides (2 Kgs 10:31; 13:1).[133] Opinions are divided over the interpretation of the ambiguous reference to "in the place [במקום]" (2:1).[134] Perhaps the identification of any specific location seems less important than the new meanings carried by the converted names. It is evident from the passage as a whole that each name with negative connotation will be changed to delightful ones. The negative connotation initially given to Jezreel is now reversed with the affirmation of God's future "sowing." On that day the children (בני) of Israel and Judah will be reunited and will flourish (2:2).[135] Jezreel now means a place where Yahweh dwells among the people of Israel and Judah and intimately relates with them. The reinterpretation of the name Lo-Ammi has radically reversed two negative names, the "Children of whoredom" (1:2) and the "Not God's people" (1:9). The Lo-Ehyeh "Not Your I AM" (1:9) has been linked to the expression אל־חי "the living God" (2:1). The people are now called the בני אל־חי "Sons of the living God" (2:1) and "My people" (2:3). The name Lo-Ruhamah "No Compassion"

---

130. Andersen and Freedman, *Hosea*, 199, maintain that, "Hosea often sets the most opposite ideas side by side in striking contrast."
131. Wyrtzen, "The Theological Center," 316–317.
132. Stuart, *Hosea*, 36, sees seven affinities between the two passages under consideration.
133. Garrett, *Hosea, Joel*, 57.
134. Wolff, *Hosea*, 27, suggests that the expression במקום אשר (literally, "in the place where") means "instead of." This interpretation also is followed by Garrett, *Hosea*, 72. Mays, *Hosea* 32, is in favour of the valley of Jezreel while Andersen and Freedman, *Hosea*, 203, suggest the wilderness where Israel would return to Yahweh.
135. Two different days are presupposed: one a day of defeat ("in that day I will break" [1:5]) and another day for restoration ("great is the day of Jezreel" [2:2]).

(1:6) is also reinterpreted positively as "Compassion" (2:3). Needless to say, the proleptic reapplication of names primarily suggests that the severed relationship will be amended. All the family members (the people) have regained their status and are now acknowledged by the household father (Yahweh) as his own.

The prophecy is characterised by familial terms and inter-possessive expressions, such as "You are my people" (2:1), "[You are] children *of* the living God" (2:1), "Your brothers" (2:3), and "Your sisters" (2:3). The plural number is used throughout 2:1–3. The plural imperative ([אמרו] "say to your brothers…") in 2:3 may suggest that the whole nation is in perspective. Admittedly, in the day of restoration the citizens of the united Israel and Judah will greet each other in warm and loving relationship, and this ideal of a future Israel contrasts with present realities. In other words, this ideal future apparently is meant to shape the present community. In this light, Wolff's interpretation of the verse as a prophetic plea to end the hostility between Judah and Israel in the years following Syro-Ephraimite war could be considered as a valid application of the prophetic words.[136] However, this reading must be regarded only as a partial answer to Hosea's overall message since the hostility between the two nations is not the major issue in the book. More important than this is the fact that the divine command applies to the Israelites, including Judeans, requiring them to address their fellow citizens with such delightful designations. That is, the "brothers" and "sisters" are fellow Israelites.[137] They are to say to each other, "You belong to me" or "I belong to you" and "I love you" and so on. Given the importance of what precedes and what follows, Hosea probably indirectly intends to emphasise the social-relational aspect of the time.

Images of Faithful Relationship (2:16–25)

The next passage that brings the message of restoration includes 2:16–25. Once again, the transition is abrupt and the same pattern of the previous engagement is maintained. Just as the negative language in terms of ominous names of 1:4–9 is followed by the promise of restoration in 2:1–3, so

---

136. Wolff, *Hosea*, 28–29; Macintosh, *Hosea*, 37;
137. Stuart, *Hosea–Jonah*, 40.

the language of disciplinary measures of 2:5–15 is followed by the restorative commitment of 2:16–25. The section opens with the third "therefore" (לכן, v. 16) in the chapter. The first two usages of לכן (vv. 8, 11) introduce Yahweh's engagement with Israel by means of chastisement whereas the לכן in this verse introduces the process of the restoration of Israel. Perhaps the best translation of לכן here is "even so" or "nevertheless"[138] as it signals a process of reconciliation. Despite Israel's grave transgression, Yahweh's relational commitment will still continue. In fact, the judgment scene in the previous section has not guaranteed that Israel has come to her senses, only that Yahweh's relentless pursuit, with a changed approach, will eventually overcome the wayward Israel.

The trend of moving from negative to positive continues in this unit. The "wilderness" used as a threat to Gomer (2:5) has now become a place for reconsolidation (v. 16). The expression "in that day" (vv. 18, 20) not only frames the structure of this unit but also emphasises a new dawn is at hand.[139] The valley of "trouble"[140] becomes the "door of hope" (v. 17). The word of renunciation, "I am not her husband" (v. 4), is replaced by a word of acceptance, "you will call me 'my husband'" (v. 18). Hosea's paradigmatic "taking" of Gomer gives way to Yahweh's collective "taking" of Israel (vv. 21–22).[141] The three names Jezreel, Lo-ruhamah and Lo-ammi now reappear with positive connotations (vv. 24–25).

The initial imagery is that of a *wooing* deity.[142] Its striking feature is that Yahweh always takes the initiative. The first person expression, reflecting commitment, occurs twelve times in this unit. Yahweh speaks seductively and romantically to his wife (v. 16; cf. Gen 34:3; Exod 22:16; Judg 14:15; 16:5). The purpose of leading Israel into the wilderness is to stir Israel's recognition of Yahweh as husband which is expressed in binary similes: "Like

---

138. Dearman, *Hosea*, 199. "Israel has transgressed, therefore, I will punish them," but the logic of the link is "Israel has transgressed, even so, I will. . . ."
139. Most commentators regard the expression "In that day" as an eschatological formula. See Wolff, *Hosea*, 47–49; Mays, *Hosea*, 46; Andersen and Freedman, *Hosea*, 277; Stuart, *Hosea–Jonah*, 57.
140. Literally it is rendered "Achor" (cf. Josh 7:26).
141. Though this oracle is built on the marriage imagery, Hosea and Gomer have receded into the background. All that remains are the feminine pronouns.
142. Nwaoru, *Imagery*, 59.

the days of her youth, like the day when she came up from the land of Egypt" (v. 17). He will now let the suspended marital provision flow once again (cf. vv. 10–11). Yahweh will erase all traces of Israel's transgression and will approach her as if the past did not exist. As a result, Israel for the first time would acknowledge Yahweh as her husband (v. 18). She would address him as "my husband" (אישי), not my "master" (בעלי), since the latter could have a negative connotation at least in this context.[143] Yahweh will then restore Israel's security by making tame all destructive wild animals (v. 14) so that the vines and figs produce enough provision for her (v. 20). Instead of breaking Israel's bow (1:5), he will destroy Israel's invading armies and eradicate war from the land (v. 20). Yahweh's restoration, or the eternal peace, covers not only human beings but also the world of animals.[144]

The husband is ready to ratify a renewed relationship with his wife in terms of betrothal (vv. 21–22).[145] It should be noted that some key words and new themes are introduced for the first time in the oracles.[146] In verse 21 the verb ארש "to betroth" is used three times for marriage (cf. 2 Sam 3:14). This renewed marriage presupposes settlement between the prospective families which would seal the commitment as binding. The Hebrew term מהר is not employed in Hosea, but is implied in the context. There are five metaphorical bridal gifts made available for the wife: משפט, צדקה, חסד, רחם, and אמונה (vv. 21–22).[147] The words צדקה, משפט and חסד appear for the first time and anticipate further links while the remaining two themes, on the other hand, maintain continuity with the preceding unit.[148] For Rudolph, the five qualities cannot be understood as human attributes (qualities of Israel) since the gifts are the groom's payment.[149] However, it is plausible in this instance that "Yahweh will give these qualities to Israel

---

143. The term "husband" and "master" could be used interchangeably (see 2 Sam 11:26).
144. Akio Tsukimoto, "Peace in the Book of Hosea: Hos 2:20a in the Biblical Context," *AJBI* 30/31 (2004/5): 23–29 (28–29).
145. Hosea is the only prophet who speaks of marriage imagery in terms of betrothal. See Baumann, *Love and Violence*, 93.
146. Nwaoru, *Imagery*, 60.
147. See our earlier conceptual analysis of these themes, pp. 128–29.
148. Nwaoru, *Imagery*, 60.
149. Rudolph, *Hosea*, 81.

as 'things' to possess, rather than doing on her behalf."¹⁵⁰ For Tsukimoto, חסד, אמת, and דעת אלהים constitute the basic elements of human morality. By reading 2:20–22 against the background 4:1–3, those basic features of human morality, once lost from among the people (4:1), will be recovered again on Yahweh's initiative on the last day (2:21–22: משפט, צדקה, אמונה, רחם, חסד and ידעת את־יהוה).¹⁵¹ The execution of such magnificent gifts will bring about the hoped for recognition of the husband by the wife: Israel (the bride) will know (ידע) Yahweh (v. 22). The play on words with the verb ידע "to know," on the one hand connotes a sexual intimacy between husband and wife (e.g. Gen 4:1; 38:26) and on the other, a relationship in covenantal context (e.g. Exod 6:2–7; Jer 16:21).¹⁵² Admittedly, it is used here in its relational sense wherein Israel would recognise or relate to Yahweh as her Lord and husband, reflecting the deepest relationship. Such a recognition required fidelity demonstrated concretely through obedience to Yahweh's commands (cf. Isa 1:2; Amos 3:10; Mic 6:3–8). "Knowing" Yahweh here precisely means implementing משפט, חסד, צדקה, רחם, and אמונה in the community.

As a result of this reconciliation, the withdrawn marital provisions of grain, wine and oil (vv. 10–11) would be restored to their original standing by the husband (vv. 23–24). Note that the metaphor of marriage now shifts to agriculture imagery. As Nwaoru puts it, "Yahweh is no more the 'husband' but the farmer. Israel, the spouse now becomes the seed: 'I will sow her for myself in the land' (v. 25)."¹⁵³ Yahweh will command the life-giving rain to fall on the soil. The soil will then respond to the crops, which in turn respond to Jezreel (likely being used here as a name for Israel) by providing Israel with the staples of life. Like the first cycle, this unit concludes the reapplication of the names of Hosea's children to mark the final reconciliation. Essentially, three elements that were withdrawn will now be

---

150. Sakenfeld, *The Meaning of Hesed,* 182.
151. Tsukimoto, "Peace in the Book of Hosea," 27.
152. Rosengren, "Knowledge of God According to Hosea the Ripper," 125, argues that דעת יהוה in verse 22 specifically implies sexual intercourse. Andersen and Freedman, *Hosea,* 283–284, maintain that the idiom in this context does not describe sexual intercourse because the subject is male.
153. Nwaoru, *Imagery,* 60.

restored. Yahweh will replant Israel in a fertile land suggesting agricultural bounty (v. 24). He will have compassion on the "uncompassionate" and will accept those who were not "God's people" as his. The exchange dialogue confesses with thanksgiving that "Yahweh is my God" (v. 25).

Chastised but Restored (3:5)

The third passage that records Yahweh's restorative commitment is 3:5. Like the previous two restorative oracles (2:1–3 [1:10–2:1] and 2:16–25 [14–23]), Yahweh promises Israel's future reconciliation "in the latter days." The same pattern of the previous cycles continues. Just as the language that is pregnant with judgment in 1:4–9 and 2:8–15 is followed by the promised reconciliation of 2:1–3 and 2:16–25, Yahweh's disciplinary restriction in 3:3–4 is followed by the declaration of the renewed blessings of 3:5. Having been delivered and chastised by Yahweh, the people of Israel will come to their senses and will seek (בקש) Yahweh's favour. The people of Israel were once to remain without socio-political independence, without religious institution and without worship (v. 4). These three elements that have been withdrawn from them will now be restored to them. They would seek Yahweh their God, recognise the Davidic king as their divinely chosen ruler and be in awe before not Baals but Yahweh (v. 5).

In summary, the restorative oracles noted thus far have clearly predicted a time of reconciliation, a renewal of relationship between Hosea/Gomer and Yahweh/Israel. The message that had initially begun with a charge of irresponsibility evolved into chastisement that, in turn, has been supplanted by reconciliation. The dynamic of Israel's transformation lies in Yahweh, the one who initiates relationship, mends it when fractured and brings restoration that is undeserved. Israel, Yahweh's human household, shall be ultimately restored and hence be the pinnacle of justice.

Before drawing our overall conclusions to close this chapter, it would be worth considering the social aspect of Hosea's message. It is clear that Hosea sees the present direction of the Northern Kingdom as doomed to failure. Nevertheless, one needs to ask whether Hosea's message only deals with future restoration or does it have implications for the crises of his own community? Before we answer this question, we must remember that Hosea's line of proclamation is often to pinpoint what is "missing" in a given situation. We have noted that Hosea urges the Israelites to address each other with the delightful words "my brothers" and "my sisters" (2:3). Such a relational justice is the antidote for the society plagued with hostility. Interestingly, he points out five fundamentals that will seal the restored relationship between Yahweh and his people: "righteousness" (צדקה), "justice" (משפט), "unfailing fidelity" (חסד), "compassion" (רחם) and "faithfulness" (אמונה, 2:21–22). Arguably, these qualities of Yahweh are intentionally placed here to suggest what is required from the Israelites for their relationship to Yahweh and to their fellow human beings as these qualities "are the basic building blocks of a covenant community."[154] They are the primary threads that knit the people together, creating a relationship of concord in the community. These are the "lost realities" in the community and the final restoration will not come without these qualities. Thus, this ideal, future reality is meant to shape the present Israelite community. Perfect, just relationships are a hope for the nation, but the hope for future perfection does not deny its demands in the present. Hosea does not go on explaining these individual concepts probably because they are crystal clear to his audience, and modern readers, too, can depend on the biblical notions of these concepts. As our earlier analysis has shown, the biblical concept of צדק connotes faithful actions performed in the community in conformity to norms of conduct arising from relationship, aiming to perpetuate right relationships. The primary demand of משפט, whether legal, ethical or religious, involves commitment to sustain right relationships between God and his people and between humans and their fellow human beings. חסד expresses mutual, friendly, brotherly, dutiful, loyal and loving actions towards others, as well as a compassionate, generous and merciful disposition to maintain right relationships between humans and their neighbours and God and his people. רחמים emphasises a loving sensitivity towards the needs of humankind grounded on an enduring devotedness, motivated by sympathy. אמונה underlines the truly divine reliability and dependability of that intimate, living community that has been established.[155] This evidence confirms our argument that Hosea does indeed address the social aspect of

---

154. Dearman, *Hosea*, 127.
155. G. Quell, "ἀλήθεια, ἀληθής, ἀληθινός, ἀληθεύω" *TDNT*: 1, 233; Wolff, *Hosea*, 53.

the people's broken relationships with Yahweh and their fellow Israelites. Though chapters 1–3 do not explore the themes comprehensively, they pave the way for a more detailed exploration of those in what follows.

Summary Assessment

We have explored the structure, content and message of Hosea 1–3. We have contended with the idea that treats the structure of the book in general and chapters 1–3 in particular simply as a formless mass collection. Instead, this study postulates three cyclical relational patterns in the first three chapters. In analysing the content, we have identified three leitmotifs – responsibility, chastisement and restoration – which not only characterise the text, but run through the chapters.

The first component of each "responsibility" cycle lays the ground on which justice can be tested. On the one hand, it portrays what it means by "just" relationship and on the other exposes what it means by "unjust" relationship. Hosea by his prophetic symbolic action depicts what a just person would do, whereas Gomer's adulterous behaviour represents the opposite. This normative relationship serves as a baseline by which every relationship shall be judged – to Yahweh and fellow human beings. In order to enhance our comprehension of what the text (metaphor) is speaking about, we have scrutinised the idea conveyed by the literal meanings of the words used metaphorically. In so doing, we have explored ancient family structure in the context of Hosea as a patrilineal father who stands true to his marriage relationship with Gomer and so, by analogy, Yahweh to his covenantal relationship with Israel. In contrast, Gomer and Israel, whom she represents, stand uncommitted to maintain and sustain relationship. If our thesis is correct, which contends that justice is necessarily a matter of justice in relationship, then, a breakdown in relationship is injustice. There is injustice when one party is hurt in any given relationship. Israel, standing in relationship to Yahweh, is accountable for her actions to her wronged partner. This paradigmatic relationship also stands true with regard to their relationship to other fellow human beings.

As has been argued, relational justice assumes mutual trust and loyalty as an original position in relationship. This relationship demands responsibility which, in turn, entails accountability and obligation. Unaccountability and irresponsibility to the obligation necessarily incur chastisement in order to reinstate the original position. As the entire conduct of Gomer/Israel negates the relational correctness of Hosea/Yahweh, Gomer/Israel must tread the path of correction and purification. It is crucial, however, to note that the various disciplinary measures pronounced in Hosea are not mere retributive judgment. It is clear from our analysis that Hosea could have legally opted for "divorce" or "stoning to death" in response to the rejection of Gomer, his wife. Instead, Hosea/Yahweh pronounces judgment to set a new platform to re-establish a better relationship.

Relational justice not only embraces chastisement as a pathway that leads to reconciliation, but also essentially involves forgiving the unforgivable. In other words, though relational justice incorporates distributive punishment for violation of norms, it goes beyond the legal notion of giving everyone their just due. Gomer/Israel deserves the termination of relationship (divorce or death) from Hosea/Yahweh. However, as our analysis of the restorative oracles has shown, there would be a time of reconciliation promised by Yahweh. It would be absolutely certain that Israel, his household, would be restored to him, the rightful owner. A fracture in relationship will be mended and a true and just relationship will be re-established. If we consider the loss of right relationship as the source of injustice in eighth-century Israel, right relationship with God and right relationship with one another, therefore, is justice.

CHAPTER SEVEN

Yahweh and His People (4:1—6:3)

By using marriage imagery (chs. 1–3), Hosea depicts a relationship and its attendant mutual responsibilities. What is sinful and unjust according to him is primarily unfaithfulness to relationship. This basic tenet is found through the chapters that follow. What is called for (relational justice) and what is denounced (relational unjustice) in Hosea 1–3 continue to be the dominant theme in Hosea 4–11. By this time, the signifiers Hosea/Gomer are placed in the background and give way to the signified Yahweh/Israel. The image of Yahweh as a responsible father has shifted to Yahweh, the prosecutor, laying out his charges against the accused, the Israelites. The people's failure to keep just relationship with Yahweh has begun to have wider moral and social consequences. The focus now is not just confined to Israel's vertical relationship with Yahweh, but expands towards the horizontal aspects of the moral and social political state of the nation. Before commencing this discussion, it is necessary to sketch the content of the proposed structure.

Structural Analysis of Hosea 4–11

As noted in the preceding chapter, interpreters have been perplexed by a series of Hosea's isolated oracles in chapters 4–14, leading many to concede that the orderly arrangement in chapters 1–3 is lost in chapters that follow.[1]

---

1. For instance, Rudolph, *Hosea*, 26, concedes that it is difficult to see any regulatory principle in these chapters. For Mays, *Hosea*, 15, chapters 4–14 lack the clear plan of chapters 1–3. Similarly, Andersen and Freedman, *Hosea*, 69, 321, state that the major

To overcome this sort of obstacle, some venture towards a possible redactional solution.² Scholars' opinions with respect to this puzzle are by no means misdirected, but reflect the multi-layered nature of Hosea's oracles.³ Other scholars such as Childs, however, take more of a constructive attitude, approaching a given prophetic book, even with its stark incongruity, as intentionally arranged and theologically fashioned.⁴ Accordingly, Childs suggests that Hosea 1–3 "provides the exegetical key in the framework from which the entire book is to be read."⁵ Yet how exactly does it serve as the exegetical key to read the entire book? For this study, perhaps this operates in two significant ways. First, it provides key words that will be repeated and reinterpreted in what follows.⁶ Second and more importantly, it presents operational themes – responsibility-chastisement-restoration – under which those key words find their place and even new subjects are introduced.

---

literary problem encountered in chapters 4–14 is its apparent incoherence and the pattern in the previous section not being followed.

2. Classic modern representative works include, Emmerson, *Hosea: An Israelite Prophet;* Yee, *Composition and Tradition in the Book of Hosea;* Naumann, *Hoseas Erben;* Rudnig-Zelt, *Hoseastudien.* More than half a century ago, Martin Buber, *The Prophetic Faith,* trans. C. Witton-Davies; 1949; repr. (New York: Harper & Row, 1960), 111, concluded that there is no conscious structure in Hosea and "only a few remnants of the original corpus saved from the destruction of Samaria . . . and are bound up together."

3. For example, the cohesive dialogue, dealing with Hosea's marital and family strife in the first three chapters, evaporates in chapters that follow. The flow of narration in 1–3 gives way to the isolated oracles of 4–14.

4. Brevard S. Childs, "The Canonical Shape of the Prophetic Literature," *Int* 32 (1978): 46–55. Along this line, Yee, *Composition and Tradition,* 44, pays attention to the final form of the book of Hosea. For her, the redactor is a type of the author who has crafted "a new tradition out of the old." She regards the selection and placement of the traditions preserved in the book as conscious and deliberate.

5. Childs, *Introduction to the Old Testament as Scripture,* 281. The same conclusion was earlier made by J. Lindblom, *Prophecy in Ancient Israel* (Philadelphia: Muhlenberg, 1962), 242, when he writes, "There is nothing to suggest the man who collected the revelations of Hosea contained in iv–xiv was not also the collector of the various units in i–iii, who placed them as an introduction at the head of the whole collection."

6. Morris, *Prophecy,* 111. According to Morris, the idea of incongruity or incoherency in Hosea lies in scholars' inappropriate approach to poetic text with rhetorical standards. Rhetoric, he argues, in order to persuade with clarity, requires coherence and logical transition which is not the case in poetry. If Hosea is read as poetry, he contends, the sharpest disjunctions become insignificant (*Prophecy,* 108–109).

Yahweh and His People (4:1–6:3)

While delimiting the structure within Hosea 4–14 is no easy matter, there seems to be a larger structural unity of chapters 4–11.[7] The complex, as Wolff notes, is demarcated by a proclamation formula שמעו דבר־יהוה in 4:1 and concludes with the formula of divine utterance נאם־יהוה in 11:11.[8] As in chapters 1–3, the contents of the prophetic oracles in this complex largely orbit around the themes of responsibility, chastisement and restoration. Given the importance of this cyclical interplay, there are two further internal panels based on our proposed cyclical movement. The first panel (Cycle 4) includes the lengthy prophetic collections of accusation of irresponsibility (4:1–5:7),[9] chastisement (5:8–5:15a) and an exhortation of repentance (5:15b–6:3).[10] The second panel (Cycle 5) includes accusation of irresponsibility (6:4–8:14),[11] chastisement oracles (9:1–10:15) and Yahweh's promise of restoration (11:1–11).

The boundary of the fourth cycle (4:1–6:3) starts with the collection of the accusation of Israel's irresponsibility. It begins with Yahweh's ריב (4:1) against all Israel: the people (vv. 1–3), the priesthood and false cult (vv. 4–19)[12] and the national leaders (5:1–7).[13] A clear break for the theme of chastisement comes with the alarms of war (v. 8).[14] Israel's rejection of

---

7. Most commentators assume the unity of this larger section. See Harper, *Amos and Hosea*, 360; Wolff, *Hosea*, 196–197; Ward, *Hosea*, 194; Rudolph, *Hosea*, 212; Mays, *Hosea*, 151; Buss, *Prophetic Word*, 33; Morris, *Prophecy*, 115; Dearman, *Hosea*, 18, 145.

8. Wolff, *Hosea*, 40–41, 193–197. For a similar position see Andersen and Freedman, *Hosea*, 331.

9. *Pace* Silva, *A Literary Analysis*, 230–243.

10. It must be remarked, following Silva, that identification of the concluding restorative unit is not as conclusive as the units in the other cycles. Although there is a lack of consensus among commentators regarding its interpretation, the message of 5:15b–6:3 nonetheless falls under the theme of restoration. We will return to this issue over the course of this study.

11. *Pace* Wyrtzen, "The Theological Center," 315–329.

12. Wolff, *Hosea*, 74, divides chapter 4 into 4:1–3 and 4:4–19. Stuart, *Hosea–Jonah*, 72–74, segments chapter 4 into four sections 4:1–3, 4:4–10, 4:11–14, and 4:15–19. Elizabeth Achtemeier, *Minor Prophets I*, eds. R. L. Hubbard and R. K. Johnston; NIBC (Peabody: Hendrickson, 1996), 34, argues for a division of 4:1–10 and 4:11–19.

13. Andersen and Freedman, *Hosea*, 317, treats 4:1–5:7 as a large unit, composed of three sections (4:1–3; 4–19 and 5:1–7).

14. Most interpreters agree that 5:8 begins a new section. For example, Wolff, *Hosea*, 108; Andersen and Freedman, *Hosea*, 399; Stuart, *Hosea–Jonah*, 99; Macintosh, *Hosea*, 193; Dearman, *Hosea*, 179.

relational faithfulness and her rebellion against Yahweh must be chastised (vv. 9–11). Yahweh will now be like pus to Ephraim and rottenness to the house of Judah (vv. 12–13). He will be like a lion to Ephraim and like a young lion to Judah (vv. 14–15a). The collections of Yahweh's assessment of Israel's fidelity and the imposed chastisement for unfaithfulness come to an end when a note of exhortation to return to Yahweh closes the cycle in 6:1–2 and expresses the certainty of Yahweh's commitment to relationship (v. 3).

The beginning of the fifth cycle (6:4–11:11) is marked by Yahweh's assessment of responsibility (6:4–8:14). Yahweh declares that Ephraim and Judah have failed the fidelity test (6:4–6). Israel's unfaithfulness results in national defilement as crime follows after crime (6:7–7:2). This is followed by Yahweh's criticism of Israel's national and international politics which have been plagued by corruption (7:3–12) because they have wandered away from Yahweh (vv. 13–16). Israel has broken her covenant with Yahweh (8:1–6) but associates herself with Egypt and Assyria (vv. 7–14).

A graphic feature of the chastisement section (9:1–10:15) commences at the direct address in 9:1 with a brief baseline accusation of promiscuity (vv. 1–2 [cf. 1:2, 4:12]) that is then followed by a series of chastisements.[15] Captivity will replace Israel's feasting (vv. 3–6) and the days of punishment will come for her deep corruption (vv. 7–9). Luxuriant Ephraim will bear no fruit (vv. 10–14) and the people of Israel will be cast out of the house of Yahweh (vv. 15–17).[16] The final demise of the cult, king and capital will come (10:1–8). Ephraim, a trained heifer who is characterised by lies, will be punished and the king of Israel will be completely cut off (vv. 10–15). A dramatic shift of theme from judgment to restoration comes in 11:1–11.[17] The spirit of the passage now offers a hope of restoration. With a retrospective reiteration of failure (vv. 1–4) and with the recognition of chastisement

---

15. Again, most commentators agree chapter 9 begins a new scene. See Wolff, *Hosea*, 151; Mays, *Hosea*, 125; Andersen and Freedman, *Hosea*, 515; Stuart, *Hosea–Jonah*, 140; Macintosh, *Hosea*, 335; Dearman, *Hosea*, 235.

16. Wolff takes 9:10–17 as a "transmission unit," having two-part parallel structure (*Hosea*, 162).

17. Wolff, *Hosea*, 193, takes chapter 11 as a homogeneous unit. Andersen and Freedman, *Hosea*, 575, divides the chapter into two principal parts (vv. 1–4 and 5–11). Stuart, *Hosea–Jonah*, 175–176 and Dearman, *Hosea*, 274, also treat the chapter as a new pericope.

(vv. 5–7), the Holy One resolves not to annihilate Israel (vv. 8–11). The surprise verdict is comparable to that of 2:16–17 and 14:2–10 [1–9]. A new theme of responsibility begins with 12:1 [11:12] which shows that 11:1–11 concludes this cycle.

The suggested structure is as follows. Again, each cycle has three subunits.

Cycle	Responsibility	Chastisement	Restoration
4	4:1–5:7	5:8–5:15a	5:15b–6:3
5	6:4–8:14	9:1–10:15	11:1–11

Having made this suggestion, it is essential to go on at once to remark that the boundaries of the cycles are determined by the general flow of the text rather than its minute individual oracles. In a book with diverse oracles in which poetic devices of varying types of wordplay have such a pivotal role, one may not expect a clean or larger linear arrangement based on the proposed themes.[18] Nevertheless, the careful reader can recognise that the individual poetic oracles alternate between accusation of irresponsibility and pronouncement of chastisement and restoration. As such, the demarcation lines particularly between the accusation of irresponsibility and chastisement oracles are thin and at times overlapping. To build logical arguments, the accusations of irresponsibility have often been interspersed with laconic declarations of chastisement, and so the sections on chastisement, too, are speckled with terse statements of accusation, and even with the promise of restoration.[19] This will become clearer in the course of the study.

Responsibility (4:1–5:7)

It has been argued that any given relationship necessitates responsibility in terms of answerability and commitment. Justice occurs when two entities

---

18. Morris, *Prophecy*, 78.
19. This point is well illustrated by Silva's analysis of Hosea 10:9–15. See Silva, *A Literary Analysis*, 271–272.

exercise their reciprocal duties and rights. Yahweh, who himself is just, requires justice of his people. Hosea's prophetic call in 4:1–5:7 reflects this demand. The Israelites are to demonstrate that they are Yahweh's people by keeping just and true relationship with their God, their fellow Israelites and Yahweh's gift of land. Our interest at this point is to uncover Hosea's social message by asking two key questions. What are the points of reference for irresponsibility? Who are the addressees? Hosea begins to disclose the answers to these questions in 4:1–3. If the claim that this passage serves as an introduction to the rest of the collections in chapters 4–14[20] is true or if it functions as the "programmatic statement" for what follows,[21] then it is indeed worth dwelling on to examine Hosea's message closely.

Yahweh's Controversy against the People (4:1–3)

Hosea 4:1–3

¹ שִׁמְע֥וּ דְבַר־יְהוָ֖ה בְּנֵ֣י יִשְׂרָאֵ֑ל כִּ֣י רִ֤יב לַֽיהוָה֙ עִם־יוֹשְׁבֵ֣י הָאָ֔רֶץ כִּ֠י אֵין־אֱמֶ֧ת וְאֵֽין־חֶ֛סֶד וְאֵין־דַּ֥עַת אֱלֹהִ֖ים בָּאָֽרֶץ׃

² אָלֹ֣ה וְכַחֵ֔שׁ וְרָצֹ֥חַ וְגָנֹ֖ב וְנָאֹ֑ף פָּרָ֕צוּ וְדָמִ֥ים בְּדָמִ֖ים נָגָֽעוּ׃

³ עַל־כֵּ֣ן ׀ תֶּאֱבַ֣ל הָאָ֗רֶץ וְאֻמְלַל֙ כָּל־יוֹשֵׁ֣ב בָּ֔הּ בְּחַיַּ֥ת הַשָּׂדֶ֖ה וּבְע֣וֹף הַשָּׁמָ֑יִם וְגַם־דְּגֵ֥י הַיָּ֖ם יֵאָסֵֽפוּ׃

The prophetic speech begins with an introductory proclamation formula שמעו דבר־יהוה (4:1a) which not only stresses divine authority but also legitimates Hosea as a prophet.[22] The call to attention explicitly identifies the addressee as Israel (בני ישראל). The use of parallelism in the verse suggests that the בני ישראל and the יושבי הארץ (v. 1b) are the same.[23] This overt identification of the addressee at this time makes explicit what is implicit in 1:2 where the personified land represents the people of Israel.[24]

---

20. Andersen and Freedman, *Hosea*, 332.
21. Brueggemann, *Tradition for Crisis*, 38.
22. Stuart, *Hosea–Jonah*, 75.
23. Andersen and Freedman, *Hosea*, 333.
24. Dearman, *Hosea*, 147.

The prophet's accusation of the people (עַם־יוֹשְׁבֵי הָאָרֶץ) with a רִיב-pattern prophetic speech has been well studied.[25] Some commentators such as Wolff and Mays argue that 4:3 concludes the speech unit (vv. 1–3), interpreting the verbs in verse 3, תֶּאֱבַל ("she shall mourn") and וְאֻמְלַל ("he shall languish") as referring to the future.[26] Others, however, are of the opinion that the unit continues into 4:4, interpreting the verbs to refer to the present habitual action ("she mourns" and "he languishes").[27] The present study adopts the latter possibility which suggests that 4:3 is *not* a statement of an impending divine judgement and thus does not conclude the unit.

Although scholars such as Huffmon, Brueggemann, and Nielsen[28] have all observed that the noun רִיב in 4:1 means "lawsuit," they also acknowledge that the basic components of Hosea 4:1–3 do not contain the majority of the constituent elements of the prophetic lawsuit.[29] Huffmon, for instance, notes that "it lacks the appeal to the covenant witnesses and omits the historical prologue."[30] Brueggemann remarks that "there is no 'announcement formulae' as in the other prophets."[31] Nielsen also admits that "the defence speech is missing."[32] Accordingly, Westermann treats Hosea 4:1–3 as a variant formulation of the prophetic speech.[33] For further modifications, Achtemeier treats Hosea 4:1–10 as a lawsuit[34] whereas

---

25. For more details see Claus Westermann, *Basic Forms of Prophetic Speech*, trans. Hugh C. White (Philadelphia: Westminster Press, 1967).

26. Wolff, *Hosea*, 65–67; Mays, *Hosea*, 62.

27. For instance, Jared J. Jackson, "Yahweh v. Cohen et al.: God's Lawsuit with Priest and People – Hosea 4," *PPer* 7 (1966): 38–32, analyses vv. 1–3 within the limit of chapter 4. Other proponents may include Harper, *Amos and Hosea*, 248; Andersen and Freedman, *Hosea*, 321; Stuart, *Hosea–Jonah*, 72–74; Dearman, *Hosea*, 146.

28. Huffmon, "The Covenant Lawsuit," 285–295; Brueggemann, *Tradition for Crisis*, 71; Kirsten Nielsen, *Yahweh as Prosecutor and Judge: An Investigation of the Prophetic Lawsuit (Rîb-Pattern)* (JSOTSup 9; Sheffield: University of Sheffield, 1978), 32–34;

29. For a description of the complete form of a prophetic lawsuit, see Huffmon, "Lawsuit in the Prophets," 285.

30. Huffmon, "Lawsuit in the Prophets," 294.

31. Brueggemann, *Tradition for Crisis*, 63.

32. Nielsen, *Yahweh as Prosecutor and Judge*, 42.

33. Westermann, *Basic Forms of Prophetic Speech*, 199.

34. Elizabeth Achtemeier, *Minor Prophets I*, eds. R. L. Hubbard and R. K. Johnston; NIBC (Peabody: Hendrickson, 1996), 34–38.

Jackson argues that 4:1–3 is the preface to the lawsuit of 4:1–19.³⁵ Heading in another direction, the lack of detailed correspondence leads some scholars to concentrate on the limits of portraying Yahweh as both plaintiff and judge in a legal proceeding³⁶ while others challenge the existence of prophetic lawsuit as a literary genre altogether.³⁷ These considerations allow us to infer that Hosea 4:1–3 or Hosea 4 represents an adaptation of the lawsuit to the particular situation which Hosea faced in Northern Israel. It must be noted that the language of the law court is not maintained which means that the accusation of irresponsibility need not be strictly judicial. What is at issue for us is to see the significance of its presence. Simply, Yahweh has a "complaint against"³⁸ all the inhabitants of the land which includes the populace, the priests and the political leaders. As noted earlier, Hosea employs the ריב-pattern discourse to declare that there is something wrong with Israel's relationships with Yahweh and their fellow human beings. Gemser conveys this point well:

> The ריב-phraseology [sic] reveals the decidedly ethical, normative conception of God and the religious relation. The controversy is exponent [sic] of the feeling that there is something wrong in the relations of the entities concerned, that there is a hitch somewhere that something is out of joint. This presupposes that there is an order of things which cannot be disturbed with impunity. This is the צדקה, the "justice", the God-maintained moral order in world – and national – and individual affairs.³⁹

---

35. Jackson, "Yahweh v. Cohen et al," 29.
36. For instance, Michael DeRoche, "The Reversal of Creation in Hosea," *VT* 31 (1981): 400–409; idem, "Yahweh's *Rîb* against Israel: A Reassessment of the So-Called 'Prophetic Lawsuit' in the Preexilic Prophets," *JBL* 102 (1983): 563–574.
37. Dwight R. Daniels, "Is there a 'Prophetic Lawsuit' Genre?," *ZAW* 99 (1987): 339–360.
38. James Limburg, "Root ריב and the Prophetic Lawsuit Speeches," *JBL* 88 (1969): 291–304 (301).
39. Gemser, "The *Rîb* or Controversy-Pattern," 136.

Hosea spells out the points of reference for Israel's irresponsibility by outlining three social virtues that are absent from the society (4:1b). The next verse goes on to catalogue the six social vices that have created a social vacuum of the time (4:2). The former group is compacted in three non-verbal clauses with a triad of terms אמת, חסד, and דעת אלהים. The first list of crimes of the latter group uses five infinitive absolutes (אָלֹה "swearing," כַּחֵשׁ "lying," רָצֹחַ "murdering," גָּנֹב "stealing," and נָאֹף "committing adultery") which function like nouns whereas the last clause lists a sixth transgression דמים בדמים נגעו "bloodshed follows bloodshed" (4:2).

The Disappearing Social Virtues (4:1b)

The irresponsibility of Israel to which Yahweh levels his controversy is first depicted by means of listing "sins of omission" and it is this breakdown at the personal level that grieves Hosea most.[40] The active social virtues, אמת, חסד, and דעת אלהים, by which the society should live have all disappeared from sight. The negative particles (אין), which are deliberately placed before each term, accentuate "the complete absence of these essential qualities in Israel's life."[41] Most interpreters come to an understanding that these qualities are social virtues that should brand the social relationship of Israelites to their covenant God and their fellow covenant partners. However, mere acknowledgement with just a few lines of observation would not do justice to Hosea's social message. Since these virtues are listed distinctly, each aspect deserves a separate, closer examination.

The Lack of אמת

The first virtue that is lacking in the land is אמת. Earlier in chapter 3, we have hinted that אמת basically refers to a good deed and the reliability of a person on whom another party can rely. In Exodus 18:21, the people of Israel are to select men of אמת who fear God and hate bribes. Rahab asks for a sure sign (אמת) on which she can rely (Josh 2:2). Proverbs 11:18 refers to a reward (אמת) of which a person can be certain. These passages refer to something which not only guarantees the present but also proves to

---

40. Mays, *Hosea*, 13, 62.
41. Bosma, "Creation in Jeopardy," 91.

be true in the future. The term often appears in a hendiadys with חסד (Josh 2: 14; 2 Sam 2:6; Prov 3:3; Mic 7:20), שׁלום (Esth 9:3) and in parallelism with חכמה (Prov 23:23). As אמת belongs to the heart (cf. Prov 3:3), it denotes the innermost quality of a person.[42] Essentially, אמת denotes "the nature of the man who is said to be faithful to his neighbour, true in his speech, and reliable and constant in his actions."[43] Thus, to accuse people of being without אמת is "to say that they are all living a lie and thus are without moral integrity."[44] While the absence of such a quality is mourned by Hosea, Isaiah laments its demise in public squares, despite the time difference (Isa 59:14). Interestingly, Isaiah's presentation is also accompanied by a series of infinitive absolutes, describing social crimes (vv. 13–15). The fall of אמת necessarily means the emergence of injustice. Both prophets bewail the absence of אמת because they know that it is the prerequisite for true relationships where justice and righteousness characterise a society.

The Absence of חסד

The second virtue that is missing in the land is חסד. Since we have done an analysis specifically on this concept elsewhere, we will only reiterate the essence of the reflection at this point.[45] We concluded earlier that the biblical understanding of חסד essentially entails an inward temperament of love and outward expression of responsibility. It has a strong relational flavour that lies in the domain of interpersonal relations and can only be defined by a cluster of words. It is an active social virtue that, together with אמת, knits individuals together, and its life-blood is to preserve and promote life. It is a humane willingness to be there for others especially those who are in need. However, Hosea finds that this essential quality is missing in Israelite society and calls for its reimplementation.

We have observed that חסד consist of the inner nature of commitment and the outward expression of dutiful action and this can be applied to both God and people. Strikingly, of the eleven examples of חסד in the

---

42. Jepsen, "אמן, … אמת," 312.
43. Ibid., 313.
44. Garrett, *Hosea, Joel,* 110.
45. [[See pp. 87–96.]]

prophetic literature in which the noun is applied to human beings, six are found in Hosea (Hos 2:21; 4:1; 6:4, 6; 10:12; and 12:7).[46] The fact that Hosea 4:1 is followed by the series of sins of commission strongly suggests that the חסד in this context is directed to one's neighbours.[47] As such, חסד is applied to right behaviour towards each other in a community on the one hand, and to faithfulness before Yahweh on the other.

The use of the term in Zechariah 7:9–10 also associates חסד with the concern for justice in society. Recalling the message of earlier prophets, Zechariah stresses the requirement to practice חסד and רחם to one another (v. 9). The path for this, of course, is not to oppress the widow or the orphans and the alien or the poor (v. 10). Similarly, Psalm 109:16 describes the absence of the חסד in a person resulting in the persecution and killing of the poor and needy. Though Hosea does not single out the socially underprovided people by name, his call for חסד clearly advocates justice not only for the community as a whole but also justice for the poor in particular. It is sensible to suppose that Hosea's message in respect to this would have been clear to his audience. Sakenfeld's remark is telling: "The absence of חסד is the wholesale abandonment of the stipulations of the Decalogue; it is the absence of justice and righteousness within the Israelite society."[48]

The Deficiency of דעת אלהים

The third virtue that is wanting in the land is דעת אלהים. The term דעת appears elsewhere in 4:6 "knowledge" and in 6:6 "knowledge of God." The meaning of דעת אלהים has been the object of discussion as the root verb ידע and the noun דעת have a wide range of meanings. The two primary nuances of the term as a relational concept should be noted. First, as discussed in the previous chapter, the verb ידע can connote a physical intimacy based upon the analogy of marriage relationship in 2:21–22 [19–20]. However, it does not mean mere natural erotic love but an intimate, conjugal relationship of the people with Yahweh,[49] suggesting "a proper

---

46. Sakenfeld, *The Meaning of Hesed*, 169.
47. Ibid., 173.
48. Ibid., 175.
49. This aspect is underscored by Eberhard Bauman, "ידע und seine Derivate," *ZAW* 28 (1908): 22–41; idem, "'Wissen um Gott' bei Hosea als Urform von Theologie?," *EvTh* 15

attitude of the people to their God."⁵⁰ Second, the term can also refer to the reciprocal recognition between Yahweh as suzerain and Israel as the vassal,⁵¹ referring to Israel's recognition of Yahweh by means of obedience to the treaty stipulations.⁵² On the basis of these considerations, it can be said that דעת אלהים means an intimate relationship on the one hand and obedience on the other.

Another significant point concerns the placement of the term. The two contexts under discussion have placed דעת alongside other moral qualities, צדק, משפט, חסד, רחם and אמונה in 2:22 and חסד and אמת in 4:1. Moreover, the immediate context following 4:1 clearly shows that the absence of דעת אלהים (with חסד and אמת) result in the avalanche of crimes in 4:2. In this light, it seems legitimate to infer that the דעת אלהים in Hosea's usage signifies a moral quality rather than a mere intellectual apprehension. McKenzie argues that Hosea's use of the דעת אלהים in 4:1–6 is "the knowledge of traditional Hebrew morality, understanding knowledge in the dynamic Hebrew sense, therefore the practice of traditional Hebrew morality, moral integrity."⁵³ Wolff also describes that דעת אלהים is not a different kind of "religious" sphere in addition to "ethical." Rather, דעת אלהים means knowledge of Yahweh's "teachings as the source of a harmonious community life within Israel."⁵⁴ In a similar vein, Macintosh takes the phrase to refer to the fundamental requirements of morality which recognises Yahweh's character and accepts his demands.⁵⁵ In Isaiah 5:8–13, the lack of דעת for which the people go to exile, is associated with injustices in the community. Israel's failure to recognise the deeds of Yahweh in history result in the increase of deadly vices.

A key text for verifying this meaning is 4:6, which functions as a prophetic accusation against the priests who were responsible for teaching תורה.

(1955): 416–425.

50. Eichrodt, "The Holy One in Your Midst," 264.

51. Herbert Huffmon, "The Treaty Background of Hebrew Yādaʿ," *ASOR* 181 (1966): 31–37.

52. For this aspect, see Hans Walter Wolff, ""Wissen um Gott" bei Hosea als Urform von Theologie," *EvTh* 12 (1953): 533–554.

53 John L. McKenzie, "Knowledge of God in Hosea," *JBL* 74 (1955): 22–27 (27).

54. Wolff, *Hosea*, 67.

55. Macintosh, *Hosea*, 128.

נָדְמוּ עַמִּי מִבְּלִי הַדָּעַת כִּי־אַתָּה הַדַּעַת מָאַסְתָּ
וְאֶמְאָסְאךָ מִכַּהֵן לִי וַתִּשְׁכַּח תּוֹרַת אֱלֹהֶיךָ אֶשְׁכַּח בָּנֶיךָ גַּם־אָנִי:

The context suggests that the דעת for want of which the people perish (4:6a) and the דעת rejected by the priest (4:6b) are the same as they look back on דעת אלהים which is absent from the land (4:1).[56] This is evident from the fact that the definite article is used with the noun which "refers to a knowledge which is defined, either in the mind of the speaker or by a previous reference."[57] Clearly, "Hosea is referring to a well-known concept, and this can only be the knowledge of God."[58]

The דעת is paralleled with תורה אלהים which directs us to the issue of the content of the knowledge of God. Largely, interpreters agree that the content of תורה includes cultic laws as well as legal and moral laws. According to Pedersen, "the priestly instruction is called *tora* (Deut 17:11; 33:10), the common term for the law, the standard of Israelite conduct. The prophets bear witness in their speeches that the responsibility of communicating it rests with the priests."[59] Östborn also sees the close connection between תורה and דעת when he writes: "*Tōrā* was imparted by the priests in the guise of 'instruction' – chiefly in respect of cult and ritual, but also with reference to Yahweh's 'law' in general. The prophets delivered *tōrā* primarily in the form of ethico-religious 'instruction', while the *tōrā* of the Wise men consisted in 'Wisdom doctrines'."[60] In light of these considerations, it is possible that Hosea employs תורה in its ethical sense but without being restricted only to it. Hosea has the ethical basis of תורה in view, especially the moral precepts which were a part of Hebrew tradition.[61] Both the prophets and priests have responsibility to the people to instruct

---

56. See Wolff, *Hosea*, 79.
57. McKenzie, "Knowledge of God in Hosea," 26.
58. Dwight R. Daniels, *Hosea and Salvation History: The Early Traditions of Israel in the Prophecy of Hosea* (BZAW 191; Berlin: Walter de Gruyter, 1990), 112.
59. Johannes Pedersen, *Israel: Its Life and Culture III–IV*, trans. Annie I. Fausbøll; 1940; repr. (London: Oxford University Press, 1954), 161.
60. Gunnar Östborn, *Tōrā in the Old Testament: A Semantic Study*, trans. Cedric Hentschel (Lund: Håkan Ohlssons Boktryckeri, 1945), 179.
61. McKenzie, "Knowledge of God in Hosea," 26.

morality, but the priests' failure to execute this office as they should, result in Yahweh's rejection.

If this line of reasoning is correct, we can now understand that Hosea employs key terms such as אמת, חסד and דעת אלהים, not as abstract concepts nebulous to his audience, but as dynamic moral concerns known to all walks of life. This is evident from the sins of commission enumerated in 4:2 and to which we shall now turn.

The Rampant Social Vices (4:2)

Most commentators who deal with Hosea 4:2 accept the close association of Hosea's list of five social crimes with the apodictic law, which is Israelite in origin commanded by divine authority.[62] Though the wordings do not precisely correspond with the Decalogue, it reflects a free presentation of the substance of a number of the Ten Words. The table below compares the crimes in Hosea to apodictic law.[63]

Hosea 4:2	Apodictic Law	Exodus 20
אלה, "cursing"	Exod 21:17; 22:27; Lev 19:14; 20:9	20:7 (3rd?)
כחש, "lying"	Exod 20:1–3, 6–9; Lev 19:11; Deut 5:20	20:16 (9th?)
רצח, "murdering"	Exod 21:12, 14; Deut 5:17; 27:24	20:13 (6th)
גנב, "stealing"	Exod 20:17; Lev 19:11; Deut 5:19	20:15 (8th)
נאף, "committing adultery"	Lev 20:10; Deut 5:18	20:14 (7th)

The specific connections to the Decalogue for the first two offences are more tenuous than the last three. Yet as the table shows, all the five crimes are forbidden by apodictic law. A similar free grouping of social crimes

---

62. Albrecht Alt, "The Origins of Israelite Law," in *Essays on Old Testament History and Religion*, trans. R. A. Wilson (New York: Doubleday, 1967). For a different account of apodictic law, see Erhard Gerstenberger, "Covenant and Commandment," *JBL* 84 (1965): 38–51.
63. Wolff, *Hosea*, 67–68. Stuart, *Hosea–Jonah*, 76, lists six crimes instead of five. Following Dahood, he interprets דמים as "idols" which violates the second commandment of the Decalogue.

occurs in Jeremiah 7:9, sharing the three core offences of Hosea and of Exodus, but using a different sequence:[64]

Exodus 20	Hosea 4	Jeremiah 7
רצח	רצח	גנב
נאף	גנב	רצח
גנב	נאף	נאף

The above table shows Hosea's list of crimes coming from the apodictic materials or the Decalogue. Grounding his accusation on this, Hosea intends to establish the guilt of the covenant people by offering "a bill of particulars showing precisely and in what ways Israel has sinned and broken covenant."[65] These crimes "are not simply breaches of general morality; they are acts prohibited by the normative tradition of Israel which summarises the will of Yahweh under the covenant."[66] They are those that ruin human community on the one hand and are an affront to Yahweh on the other.[67] What is interesting is that Hosea "lists primarily the social crimes of the Decalogue rather than the more theological evils (worshiping other gods, making idols, or Sabbath breaking) or the more domestic or private sins (failure to honour parents and coveting)."[68] It must be stressed that these five social crimes are pivotal to interpreting Hosea's subsequent prophetic words as they all reappear in the later chapters.[69]

The proliferation of such crimes potentially shows that the northern state had drifted into a chaotic situation and Hosea had no other alternative but to confront the people of his time. Contextually, the listing

---

64. Andersen and Freedman, *Hosea*, 337, suggest that the Masoretic placement of *zāqēp qāṭōn* separates the first two sins from the rest, to reflect that the following offenses are based directly on the Decalogue. Harper, *Amos–Hosea*, 250, interprets the first two infinitive absolutes as a *hendiadys* which means perjury which stands in contrast to אמת.
65. Brueggemann, *Tradition for Crisis*, 57.
66. Mays, *Hosea*, 64.
67. Dearman, *Hosea*, 148.
68. Despite noting this fact, Garrett refuses to explore Hosea's social message in its own right but simply focuses on Israel's religious apostasy. Garrett, *Hosea, Joel*, 111–112.
69. אלה (10:1), כחש (7:3; 10:13; 12:1; cf. 9:2; 12:8), רצח 6:8–9, גנב (7:1) and נאף (2:4; 3:1; 4:13, 14; 7:4). Wolff, *Hosea*, 67–68; Morris, *Prophecy*, 114.

of social vices points back to the moral-social nature of חסד, אמת and דעת אלהים because their absence in society leads to a consequent rise in crimes of human against human. The juxtaposition of sins of omission and sins of commission suggests the inextricable dependency of social ethics and theological orthodoxy.[70] Mays's description is telling: "An Israelite was faithless to God in acting against the rights of his brother. And in maintaining the fabric of the social order an Israelite was showing faithfulness, devotion and the knowledge of God."[71]

This compelling evidence shows that Hosea, like his fellow prophets, has deep concern about the lack of responsibility among those who live together in the land. As in the case of Amos, Hosea's sweeping accusation depicts the hideous realities as an aftermath of the prosperity of Israel under Jeroboam II. This is reflected by the verb פרצו ("they have broken out") which is associated with the list of crimes. Cursing, lying, killing, stealing and adultery "break out" in the land, filling the vacuum created by the dearth of the social virtues אמת, חסד and דעת אלהים. The last transgression of the list, "bloodshed follows bloodshed" (דמים בדמים נגעו) depicts "the societal dissolution as a result of the vices listed previously."[72] As social violence dictates all areas of life, "no moment is left free of their crime as one bloody deed follows another."[73]

Hosea's holistic perspective is unfolding in 4:3. The irresponsible deeds of humans not only result in dysfunctional human relationships but also ruin the non-human inhabitants of the land. The social crimes of verse 2 are linked to their consequences in verse 3 by על־כן. Jeremias suggests that there is a syntactical difference between לכן and על־כן. He points out that unlike לכן, which typically links the announcement of divine judgement, the conjunction על־כן introduces the statement of a *fact*, rather than a *declaration*.[74] For him, על־כן indicates "die (notwendige) Folge einer Tat."[75]

---

70. Mays, *Hosea*, 64.
71. Ibid., 65.
72. Dearman, *Hosea*, 149.
73. Mays, *Hosea*, 65.
74. *BDB*: 486–487.
75. Jeremias, *Hosea*, 33. In fact, this argument goes back to Gelderen, *Het Boek Hosea* (COT; Kampen: Kok, 1953) and Rudolph, *Hosea*, 101, before him. See fuller analysis on

Hence it indicates the necessary consequences of crimes committed by irresponsible Israelites. If Koch's claim is correct, the "concept of actions with built-in consequences is at work" here.[76] Since there is no אמת, חסד and דעת אלהים *in* the land (בארץ, v. 1), the personified land, therefore, *mourns* (אבל, v. 3). Because of the moral crimes of *(human) inhabitants* of the land (יושבי בארץ, v. 1), *all* those who live in it (כל־יושבי), including non-human, *languish* (אמל) and the animals of the field, the birds of the air and fish of the sea "are swept away"[77] (יאספו, v. 3).

The land, which can also mean Earth,[78] is presented as a victim, suffering for the sins of her human inhabitants.[79] On the other hand, the land is also an active agent of Yahweh in bringing about the consequences of the indictment upon Israel.[80] The prophet envisages nothing other than the reversal of creation and its good order.[81] When the inhabitants of the earth fail to maintain the proper order of their lives, the entire natural world suffers. Against this backdrop, it is not difficult to see Hosea's holistic thinking. In a nutshell, the social crimes committed by the people of Israel have three levels of irresponsibility. They are crimes against Yahweh, fellow human beings and creation.

---

this Carl J. Bosma, "Creation in Jeopardy: A Warning to Priests (Hosea 4:1–3)," *CTJ* 34 (1999): 64–116 (70).

76. Klaus Koch, "Is There a Doctrine of Retribution in the Old Testament?," in *Theodicy in the Old Testament*, ed. James L. Crenshaw (London: SPCK, 1983), 57–87 (69). The article first appeared in *ZTK* 52 (1955): 1–40. Translated by Thomas H. Trapp.

77. Andersen and Freedman, *Hosea*, 340.

78. Walter Brueggemann, "The Uninflected Therefore of Hosea 4:1–3," in *Reading from this Place, vol 1: Social Location and Biblical Interpretation in the United States*, eds. Fernando F. Segovia and Mary Ann Tolbert (Minneapolis: Fortress Press, 1995): 231–249 (241).

79. Laurie J. Braaten, "Earth Community in Hosea 2," in *The Earth Bible: The Earth Story in the Psalms and the Prophets*, ed. Norman C. Habel (Sheffield: Sheffield Academic, 2001), 184–203; idem, "God Sows," in Redditt, *Thematic Threads*, 104–132.

80. Katherine M. Hayes, *"The Earth Mourns": Prophetic Metaphor and Oral Aesthetic* (AcBib 8; Atlanta: SBL, 2002).

81. DeRoche, "The Reversal of Creation in Hosea," 400–409; Bosma, "Creation in Jeopardy," 101–108; Melissa T. Loya, "'Therefore the Earth Mourns': The Grievance of the Earth in Hosea 4:1–3," in *Exploring Ecological Hermeneutics*, eds. N. C. Habel and P. L. Trudinger; SBLSymS 46 (Atlanta: SBL, 2008): 53–62.

The Irresponsible Priests, People and Rulers (4:4–19)

We have noted that Yahweh's controversy in 4:1 is explicitly addressed to all individual Israelites. The grounds for accusation are set forth in 4:1–2 and the debilitating influence of the crimes is stated in 4:3. This initial charge is elaborated in 4:4–19 and 5:1–7. The prophet singles out three classes of people who are ultimately responsible for the moral catastrophe: the priests (4:4–10), the people (4:11–19) and the leaders (5:1–7).

The Unreliable Priests (4:4–10)

By narrowing down his focus and by maintaining the language of accusation, the prophet traces the ultimate responsibility for the social chaos to the priests (4:4). The terminology employed in verse 4, especially the final clause, is extremely problematic. Commentators are hard pressed to understand the phrase ועמך כמריבי כהן (v. 4b).[82] One of the emendations proposed in *BHS* ("And with you my controversy, O priest"), perhaps, serves the context best. The verse may be rendered: "If no one makes any case, or no one reproves; surely, my accusation is with you, O priest."[83] Given the moral sickness of the society in perspective, someone has to stand up in protest at the "moral anarchy of the people."[84] But then a desire to put justice in place in society is entirely absent. The blasphemers, liars, murderers, thieves, and adulterers fill all corners of the land, yet there is no conscientious objection to them at all. Hosea points the finger of blame at the priests whose chief functions are to guard knowledge, and teach justice and the law of God.[85]

The accusation is amplified in verses 5–6. As noted elsewhere, the דעת אלהים mentioned in 4:1 is the same as הדעת in 4:6.[86] Society is doomed through lack of knowledge for which the priests are held responsible. The

---

82. Wolff, *Hosea*, 70, opts for a major reconstruction which reads וְעַמְּךָ רִיבִי כֹהֵן. See the extended discussion in Andersen and Freedman, *Hosea*, 346–350. For another approach see Jack R. Lundbom, "Contentious Priests and Contentious People in Hosea IV 1–10," *VT* 36 (1986): 52–72.
83. After Macintosh, *Hosea*, 134 and Dearman, *Hosea*, 155.
84. Macintosh, *Hosea*, 135.
85. Cf. Deut 17:8–13; Jer 2:8; Ezek 7:26; Mal 2:6–9.
86. According to Mays, *Hosea*, 69, "the knowledge" is an abbreviated form of the expression "the knowledge of God/Yahweh".

(false) prophets who are jointly responsible to teach Yahweh's words will also stumble (כשל) with them (4:5; cf. Jer 23:11). A similar criticism comes from Micah. He blames the priests for giving instruction for payment and accuses the prophets of doing the same thing (Mic 3:11). For Hosea, to say that the society lacks הדעת is equivalent to saying perversions are present in the sanctuaries and moral sickness reigns over the nation. The priests have destroyed the people by "rejecting" (מאס) knowledge and "forgetting" (שכח) the law of God (v. 6). To "forget" something in this context means "to ignore its significance, so that it no longer guides a person to the proper response."[87] Their transgressions determine the consequences. Yahweh will "reject" (מאס) them from his priestly service and will "forget" their families[88] (cf. אם, v. 5 and בן, v. 6) or their associates in priestly service.[89]

Hosea's further blow against the wickedness of the priests comes in verses 7–10.[90] It is remarkable that the prophet brands them as wealthy (כרבם).[91] "The richer they became the more they sinned (חטאו) against me" (v. 7). This echoes a scenario of eighth-century Israel discussed in an earlier chapter.[92] The economic growth and political stability during the time of Jeroboam II also benefited the priests. Stuart describes that "Their [the priests'] uncritical support of the upper classes and indulgence of syncretism and materialism earned them (and probably the cult prophets) wealth and prestige from a grateful populace, via tithes and donations."[93] Instead of leading the people along the pathway of being righteous and just, they feed (אכל) themselves on the sin of the people (v. 8). That is, they encourage the people to sin in order to benefit from the abundance of sin offerings. The phrase נשׂא נפשׁ ("to lift the appetite" v. 8b) suggests that "the

---

87. Dearman, *Hosea*, 159.
88. Stuart, *Hosea*, 78.
89. Dearman, *Hosea*, 159.
90. There is a sudden change of speech from collective second singular (vv. 4–6) to third person plural (vv. 7–10). However, the changes of form are not significant as both passages deal with the same content. Besides, Hosea's conflict throughout this text is with the whole priesthood and not with any individual (*contra* Andersen and Freedman, *Hosea* 344). See Macintosh, *Hosea*, 141.
91. The word רבב can indicate to increase either "in riches" or "in number" or "in greatness and power." See Stuart, *Hosea–Jonah*, 72 and Macintosh, *Hosea*, 141.
92. See chapter 5, pp. 108–120.
93. Stuart, *Hosea–Jonah*, 79.

charge is godlessness and greed in the guise of religious practice."[94] They apparently celebrate sacrifices so as "to obscure the moral requirements which were prior in importance"[95] (cf. Amos 4:4f). Punishment is self-incurred and the evil doers will get what they deserve and will be punished according to their "ways" (דרך) and "deeds" (מעלל) (vv. 9–10).

The Misguided People (4:11–19)

The prophetic confrontation concludes with the irresponsibility of the people as a whole (vv. 11–19). In fact, it is the mutual contribution of the priests and the people which has dragged the nation down to a level of chaos. Though Yahweh places primary responsibility on the priests, this does not necessarily excuse the sins of the people because they have allowed themselves to be misled.

The main concern of Yahweh's polemic against the people is their indifference to injustices in the society (v. 4). The priest feed on their sin (v. 8).[96] They are now the object of accusation for irresponsibility. Subdued by the power of the רוח זנונים (4:12; 5:4), sex and drunkenness have taken their hearts (v. 11), and dominated their worship (vv. 12–13).[97] The spirit of whoredom then spreads from cult to town and home, infecting the younger generation (v. 13b).[98] Yahweh's response to the sexual promiscuity of Israel's daughters and daughters-in-law by withholding their punishment is initially surprising (v. 14), but this is not surprising when the earlier incident is taken into account. In verse 4, the ultimate responsibility for social

---

94. Dearman, *Hosea*, 161.
95. Macintosh, *Hosea*, 144.
96. Ibid., 146.
97. Most scholars recognise the charge against whoredom as not only being metaphorical for Israel's infidelity towards Yahweh or in the act of giving love to other gods, but also as being literal, in the acts of sacred prostitution or sexual rites for fertility under trees and on hill tops or various Canaanite shrines. This line of consideration has been challenged by some scholars in recent years. For the former, see Wolff, *Hosea*, 14, 86–87. For the latter, see Keefe, *Women's Body*, 10–11, 36–103. While caution must be applied in handling Hosea's allusive presentation, his criticism in this passage nonetheless seems to focus on the sexual activities behind the syncretistic cult of the time. A similar critique comes from Amos. As noted elsewhere, Amos vehemently attacks Israel for their "drink" and "feast" loving culture (4:1; 6:4–7). He denounces the behaviour of men who "resort to the same girl" as their sons (2:7b).
98. Mays, *Hosea*, 74.

crimes is laid at the door of the priests, so here responsibility for the contagious harlotry and adultery is held to be that of their seniors (הם, "they" [i.e. men, males] v. 14).[99] The charge of harlotry applies to the people as a whole in verses 15–19. Israel is without hope (v. 16) and is warned against further liability regarding Judah (vv. 15, 17). Ephraim is also captive to harlotry and wine (vv. 18–19).

The Failing Rulers (5:1–7)

Hosea 5:1–7 is generally understood as a unit which depicts the apostasy of the nation in general and of the leaders in particular. Having identified the first two addressees in 4:1–19, a new target is introduced in 5:1, בית המלך ("the house of the King"). Perhaps the climactic position of בית המלך among the three groups addressed here accentuates the total failure of Israel as a nation.[100] The specific identity of בית ישראל is debated. For Wolff, the phrase, in view of Micah 3:1, 9; 1 Samuel 11:3; 1 Kings 21:8; Deuteronomy 19:12, means the "elders [or chieftains] of the house of Israel."[101] Others, however, take בית ישראל to mean "its leadership collectively,"[102] or "a reference to the nation as a whole."[103] In context, it is more likely a reference to a cluster of representative leaders (cf. Mic 3:1 "heads," ראש), which include elders in the city gate, judges in the royal court and officials who associate with the royal house and priestly service. The point is plain nonetheless. The בית ישראל, כהנים and בית המלך are indicted as having "responsibility of just and good order in society."[104] Hosea tells them their common responsibility: "For you are accountable for justice" (לכם המשפט, v. 1b).[105]

---

99. Macintosh, *Hosea*, 159. The point that these women would be excused from punishment is more rhetorical than literal as no one would be spared when Israel falls to Assyria. Garrett, *Hosea, Joel*, 125.

100. Andersen and Freedman, *Hosea*, 383, argue that there are only two groups addressed – priestly and royal. The middle term בית ישראל describes both.

101. Wolff, *Hosea*, 97.

102. Stuart, *Hosea–Jonah*, 91.

103. Dearman, *Hosea*, 171.

104. Macintosh, *Hosea*, 176.

105. Wolff, *Hosea*, 97–98. Stuart, *Hosea–Jonah*, 88, recognises that the term משפט is used here with a sarcastic double entendre. It can mean either, "this judgment is against you" or "justice is entrusted to you." The latter sense serves the context better.

As discussed in an earlier chapter, the biblical concept of משפט represents a range of different ideas from moral, legal and religious domains. However, we have argued that the core meaning of משפט, which is engrained in all the diverse meanings, is its relational aspect. In essence, משפט denotes an action that preserves relationships and restores the disturbed order and hurt of individuals in the community.[106] This ethos is entirely absent in the eighth-century Israelite society. "The leaders, all of them, having failed to do what they should have done, have done what they should not have done."[107]

As hinted above, the climactic position of בית המלך is intended to depict the ailing condition of the society on the one hand, and the failure of the royal court to maintain justice on the other. In early Israel, leaders at any level were called to be active in doing justice (Deut 1:10–20). Judges functioned both as judicial arbitrators and military deliverers, restoring a person or Israel as a whole from oppression (1 Sam 7:15–17; Judg 4:5). The priests, by using sacred lots, Urim and Thummim, were to assist in bringing justice in society (Deut 17:8–13). The kings were also responsible for establishing a just society (2 Sam 8:15; 1 Kgs 10:9; 2 Chr 19:4–11; Jer 22:2–5).[108] Though Hosea's laconic statement does not explain the judicial structure of the Northern Kingdom, yet it places the responsibility of just and good order in society at the door of the בית המלך.

In contrast, the rulers and leaders, abducted by the רוח זנונים (v. 4), have become a trap at Mizpah, a net spread over Tabor and a pit at Shittim (v. 1b). All of them are, as Macintosh lucidly notes, "perverse, flawed in their ethical stance, who have delved into the hidden depths of corruption. It is in the sphere of justice that their wickedness obtrudes" (v. 2).[109]

---

106. [[See pp. 104–106.]]
107. Macintosh, *Hosea*, 176.
108. On the subject of Israel's judicial system, see Ludwig Köhler, "Justice in the Gate," in *Hebrew Man* (Nashville: Abingdon Press, 1956), 149–175; Donald A. McKenzie, "Judicial Procedure at the Town Gate," *VT* 14 (1964): 100–104; Keith W. Whitelam, *The Just King* (Sheffield: JSOT Press, 1979); Robert R. Wilson, "Israel's Judicial System in the Preexilic Period," *JQR* 74 (1983): 229–248; idem, "Enforcing the Covenant: The Mechanisms of Judicial authority in Early Israel," in *The Quest for the Kingdom of God*, eds. H. B. Huffmon, et.al. (Winona Lake: Eisenbrauns, 1983), 59–76.
109. Macintosh, *Hosea*, 181. The translation of 5:2a is difficult. Macintosh, *Hosea*, 178, translates the expression ושחטה שטים העמיקו as "These perverse men have delved deep

The corrupt nation, deprived of rulers of integrity, which has behaved promiscuously and polluted by wicked deeds, is not hidden (לֹא־נִכְחַד) from all-seeing Yahweh (v. 3). Yahweh will certainly discipline (מוּסָר) all those who are responsible for trashing the community with cursers, deceivers, killers, stealers and fornicators (v. 2; cf. 4:2). The people, whose treacherous deeds (מַעַלְלִים) do not permit them to return to their God, no longer know (יָדַע) Yahweh (v. 4) simply because they have become entirely forgetful of Yahweh's character and requirements of אֱמֶת, חֶסֶד and מִשְׁפָּט (cf. 4:6; 5:1). In other words, for a person so engrossed with corruption, the possibility of repentance or return to the God of אֱמֶת, חֶסֶד and מִשְׁפָּט becomes a practical impossibility (cf. Isa 59:2; Jer 13:23).[110] The "pride of Israel" (גְּאוֹן־יִשְׂרָאֵל), which "refers to the arrogant rebellion of the people against Yahweh's law by their false cult and social injustice," becomes her own condemnation (v. 5).[111] Though they seek (בָּקַשׁ) Yahweh, they will not find him (v. 6) because "it is not in sacrificial feasts that Yahweh is found but in integrity and recognition of his ethical nature and demands (cf. 6:6)."[112] Misguided by the leaders of the nation, the people have betrayed (בָּגְדוּ) Yahweh. The evidence is the bastards (בָּנִים זָרִים) born to them (v. 7; cf. 2:4f.; Jer 2:27). Their infidelity determines their fate and its inevitable result is home-grown. A חֹדֶשׁ ("new moon" or "month")[113] will overtake and destroy the entire nation. Their erroneous cultic practices will become their final demise.

In summary, we are now in a position to answer the questions posed earlier. By employing a prophetic רִיב-pattern discourse, Hosea declares that Israel's relationships with Yahweh and her neighbours are totally wrong. He accuses the Israelites of discarding three social virtues אֱמֶת, חֶסֶד, and דַּעַת אֱלֹהִים and for replacing those qualities with social crimes such as cursing, lying, murder, stealing and adultery. The prophet charges them with

---

into corruption."
110. Garrett, *Hosea, Joel*, 145.
111. Stuart, *Hosea–Jonah*, 93.
112. Macintosh, *Hosea*, 188.
113. The exact meaning of this term is obscure. Scholars have proposed a wide range of meanings. For examples: "the locust" (Wolff, *Hosea*, 101); "someone else" (Andersen and Freedman, *Hosea*, 397); "a new people" (Stuart, *Hosea–Jonah*, 94); "a time of misfortune" (Macintosh, *Hosea*, 189–90).

having failed their responsibility towards Yahweh, fellow human beings and creation. The culprits for this social disaster are the priests who have failed to act upon their duty, the rulers who have failed their responsibility to establish justice and good order in society, and the people who have not only allowed themselves to be misled by their leaders but also have indulged in flawed cultic practices. In light of this analysis, it is plausible to conclude that Hosea's soft but strong voice reflects a real social concern for the nation of his time. Hence contrary to what has often been assumed, Hosea 4:1—5:7 is not so much about judgment but a prophetic critique of social irresponsibility. As a result of their irresponsibility, the prophet has more to offer in the way of stringent response to the traitorous people. This will now be addressed.

Chastisement (5:8–15)

Hosea 5:8–15 constitutes a new section. As noted elsewhere, this is evident due to a clear shift to a theme of chastisement, initiated by a warning signal of wars in 5:8 and then another shift to a theme of reconciliation in 6:1.[114] The flow of progression in 4:1–5:7 reaches its climax in this speech in two ways. First, the mode of chastisement threatened in the preceding verses (cf. 4:10, 19; 5:2) is going to be fulfilled in history. In other words, the notion of chastisement that has received only a passing reference in previous verses becomes graphic in this text as Israel's actual crimes recede to the background. Second, Judah, who was cautioned not to imitate Ephraim (4:15), has subsequently stumbled with Ephraim (5:5) and is now considered to receive the same discipline for identical crimes.

Alt has proposed that Hosea 5:8—6:6 is to be taken as a unit and its setting should be found in the so-called Syro-Ephraimite war and Judah's

---

114. Wolff, *Hosea,* 108–10, sees no new beginning comparable to 5:8 until 8:1. He argues that the whole piece of 5:8–7:16 is a "kerygmatic unit" which is syntactically, stylistically, and thematically linked together. Mays, *Hosea,* 87, following Alt (see below), considers 5:8–6:6 as a unit on the basis of literary and thematic interdependence as well as common setting. Against these views Davies, *Hosea,* 149–150, argues that a break should be made at 6:4, which, "with its opening rhetorical questions, has all the appearance of being the beginning of a new unit."

political muddle with Assyria around 733 BC.[115] Good, however, argues for the cultic setting to explain the text (5:8–6:6).[116] In contrast to Alt who takes 5:8 as a warning of Judah's countermove against Israel, Arnold also proposes that 5:8 is actually the prophetic warning to the Benjaminite cities, reflecting the prophet's opposition to the Syro-Ephraimite forces moving south to invade Judah.[117]

Many subsequent scholars accept that the Syro-Ephraimite war and its immediate aftermath functions as a reference point to this unit.[118] However, other scholars are concerned whether this theory solves all problems. For Andersen and Freedman, the heuristic questions of both Alt and Good are not capable of handling Hosea's literary material with "archaic motifs which go back to disputation in the old tribal league and which no longer reflect political realities of the day."[119] Garrett and Sweeney point out several difficulties with this scenario. First, while Hosea pictures Judah as the aggressor (5:10), Judah in the Syro-Ephraimite war was on the defensive. Besides, there is no substantial evidence from either Assyrian or biblical sources, which suggests Judah has ever attacked Israel during the war. Second, in the Syro-Ephraimite war setup, it was Judah that appealed to Assyria for help against Israel, whereas Hosea 5:13 envisages a situation in which Israel turned to Assyria for help.[120] It is more likely that "this passage refers in general to political events of the latter half of the eighth century, but not especially to the events of this particular war."[121] After all, Hosea's dispute throughout is that Israel should turn to Yahweh alone by eradicat-

---

115. Albrecht Alt, "Hosea 5:8–6:6. Ein Krieg und seine Folgen in prophetischer Beleuchtung," in *Kleine Schriften zur Geschichte des Volkes Israel* (Band II; München: Beck, 1959): 163–187.

116. Edwin M. Good, "Hosea 5:8–6:6: An Alternative to Alt," *JBL* 85 (1966): 273–286. Good, however, does not deny the possibility of actual military campaigns. Good, "Hosea 5:8–6:6," 282.

117. Patrick M. Arnold, "Hosea and the Sin of Gibeah," *CBQ* 51 (1989): 447–460 (458–459).

118. For instance, Alt's theory has its bearing on the historical reconstructions of Wolff, *Hosea*, 110–112; Mays, *Hosea*, 86; Andersen and Freedman, *Hosea*, 402–405; Macintosh, *Hosea*, 194–198.

119. Andersen and Freedman, *Hosea*, 402.

120. Garrett, *Hosea, Joel*, 149; Sweeney, *Twelve Prophets*, 61.

121. Garrett, *Hosea, Joel*, 149.

ing social crimes and fallacious cultic observances from the community, and by staying away from foreign political reliance altogether. The central issue, with whatever associated menace, is that Yahweh's chastisement is in motion in the historical process because of Israel's irresponsibility to her mandate as the people of God.

An Urgent Warning of War (5:8)

The passage begins with an urgent warning of war directed to three principal towns (Gibeah, Ramah and Bethaven) in the territory of Benjamin.

8:5 תִּקְעוּ שׁוֹפָר֙ בַּגִּבְעָ֔ה חֲצֹצְרָ֖ה בָּרָמָ֑ה הָרִ֙יעוּ֙ בֵּ֣ית אָ֔וֶן אַחֲרֶ֖יךָ בִּנְיָמִֽין׃

Most commentators agree on the strategic importance of these sites as they controlled the route through the north from Jerusalem into the heart of the hill country of Ephraim.[122] The blowing of שׁופר and חצצרה primarily signals the danger of the attack from the enemy (Num 19:9; Judg 3:27; 6:34; Jer 4:5; Joel 2:1; Zeph 1:16). The instruments were also used to call the people into cultic observances (Lev 25:9; Ps 81:3; 98:6; 1 Chr 15:28; 2 Chr 15:14). The phrase אחריך בנימין ("behind you O Benjamin") seems to refer to the threat against Benjamin posed by Judah. However, as noted above, it is not entirely clear whether this is the only possibility. What seems clear in the context, however, is that two brother nations are turning against each other and are also looking to foreign powers for protection. Whether one understands "the blowing" of שׁופר and חצצרה and "the raising of shouts in alarm" (רוע) against the setting of "war cries" or "liturgical shouts," the primary intention remains the same. That is, Hosea's use of them is sarcastic.[123] Yahweh's chastisement is underway and an exploitative enemy, Assyria, is encroaching. Both Judah and Ephraim are at fault as they have sought their security in relying not on obedience to Yahweh by means of doing justice but on weaponry. Both will suffer (cf. 8:12) the results of their internecine strife and faithlessness.

---

122. For detail analysis of these sites, see Arnold, "The Sin of Gibeah," 448–454; Davies, *Hosea*, 152–153; Macintosh, *Hosea*, 194–195; Sweeney, *Twelve Prophets*, 63.
123. Garrett, *Hosea, Joel*, 150.

In verse 9, the prophet provides the reason for the war alarm of verse 8, affirming the certainty of Ephraim's impending destruction through the Assyrian domination. The land would be plundered, presumably by foreign armies. The devastation of Ephraim may be understood to constitute the chastisement of Yahweh levelled against a nation which has not only initiated the Syro-Ephraimite war but has also dragged the society into social vacuum and religious idolatry (cf. 4:1–5:7). Yet Hosea's portrayal of divine judgment with the expression יום תוכחה is interesting. Wolff thinks that "Hosea chose this word to give the destruction the positive sense of Israel's 'correction'."[124] Another term deliberately employed is שבטי ישראל.[125] The prophet appears to have in view the reminiscent days of the old tribal league "when all tribes were held together by the common bond of being the 'children of Israel'."[126] It is likely that Hosea alludes to the ideal tribal society, which was grounded in communal solidarity, as normative[127] and in such a context Judah, too, is liable to chastisement for transgression (cf. v. 10).[128] Since Yahweh's justice is revealed in the context of the entire covenant people, both Ephraim and Judah are indicted to suffer destruction at the hands of foreigners.

The Culpability of Judah and Ephraim (5:10–11)

In 5:10–11, both Judah and Ephraim appear to have transgressed Yahweh's relational norms for his people. Judah's crime is compared with the malicious deeds of those who move boundaries (כמסיגי גבול, v. 10a). In its simplest terms, the expression means "the appropriation of another's property."[129] Such behaviour against the weaker neighbour is strictly forbidden by both legal and wisdom texts (Deut 19:14; 27:17; Prov 22:28; 23:10; cf. Job 24:2), simply because it breaches relationships and hurts another party. It is possible that the accusation refers to the literal annexation of the

---

124. Wolff, *Hosea*, 113.
125. It must be noted that in this scene the term "Israel" is not used when Hosea means the Northern Kingdom. Instead, "Ephraim" is employed throughout. Wolff, *Hosea*, 113.
126. Garrett, *Hosea, Joel*, 151.
127. Blenkinsopp, *Prophecy in Israel*, 90.
128. Macintosh, *Hosea*, 200.
129. Hong, *Illness and Healing in Hosea*, 146.

Bejaminite territory in Judah's countermove against Israel as a result of the Syro-Ephraimite war. If this is the case, it may imply Yahweh's displeasure over a lack of unity between the brother tribes. It may also be rhetorical rather than indicating a particular military endeavour to charge Judah with being treacherous in that they are *like* (היה) such criminals.[130] As such, "the princes (שרים) of Judah have violated canons of human rights to advance their causes."[131] Another possibility is "a petty, furtive, and cowardly means of stealing" parcels of land, by the officials or leaders of Judah.[132] This view would fit well with the condition of economic injustices condemned by Isaiah (5:8) and Micah (2:2) in Judah.

Whether the expression refers to a large-scale territorial expansion or minor land-grabbing or a rhetorical charge against treacherous behaviour, of most significance is Judah's action. Hosea declares that the deeds of the leaders of Judah have betrayed the relational fidelity and hurt fellow covenant brothers. The result of such action is Yahweh's wrath that will be poured out like water. The Assyrians will plunder the land.

Yahweh turns his attention back to Ephraim in verse 11, laying a charge against the northern nation. He declares that עשוק אפרים רצוץ משפט ("Ephraim is oppressed, justice is crushed"). The MT is supported by the presence of an identical word pair (עשק and רצץ) in Deuteronomy 28:33. Along this line, scholars relate this verse to the aftermath of the Assyrian onslaught as a covenant curse on Israel in 733/732 BC.[133] However, it is more reasonable to follow LXX[134] that reads עשק and רצץ as active, "furnishing another charge in the indictment against Ephraim for which the punishment is coming."[135] It bears noting that what is initially at stake in Judah and Ephraim is the place of משפט in domestic policies. The occurrences of the root עשק "to oppress," particularly in the prophets, refer to

---

130. Dearman, *Hosea*, 184.
131. McComiskey, "Hosea," in *The Minor Prophets*, 82.
132. Garrett, *Hosea, Joel*, 146.
133. See Wolff, *Hosea*, 144; Stuart, *Hosea Joel*, 104; Macintosh, *Hosea*, 205; Dearman, *Hosea*, 185.
134. LXX makes the two verbs, עשק and רצץ, active, "κατεδυνάστευσεν Εφραιμ τὸν ἀντίδικον αὐτοῦ κατεπάτησεν κρίμα" ("Ephraim has oppressed his opponent, he has trampled justice under foot").
135. Harper, *Amos and Hosea*, 276.

the exploitation of the underprivileged classes by the privileged (Jer 7:6; Amos 4:1; Mic 2:2; Zech 7:10; 3:5). The root רצץ "to crush" is also employed in the context of social exploitation of the weak (1 Sam 12:3; Job 20:19; 4:1). Taking into account Hosea's predilection for allusions and his penchant to confront the upper class (cf. 4:14; 5:1), it is appropriate to suppose that the charge turns against the ruling elite of the northerners in the midst of crises.[136] The personified משפט, which should dictate the nation's social relations and politics, is crushed.[137] All hope for משפט is gone for Ephraim as a result of their deviation from the relational principles of the covenant by chasing after futility (צו), foreign gods and foreign counsel.

Yahweh as Illness and Ferocious Lion (5:12–15a)

This passage describes the awful consequences of Ephraim and Judah's irresponsible actions. With imagery drawn from physical disease and ferocious animals, Hosea portrays Yahweh's relation to Ephraim and Judah.

In 5:12, Yahweh compares himself to "pus" (עש)[138] and "rottenness" (רקב) to clearly state that Yahweh is the source of illness. As a result, the two nations have to remain "metaphorically morbid, injured and hurt from Yahweh's affliction."[139] Perhaps the metaphor of illness here constitutes two elements. First, illness is associated with Yahweh's visitation upon Ephraim and Judah through the historical reality of foreign invasion as a result of their misguided political actions. Though this seems a self-inflicted judgment, it is Yahweh who has willed it. Hence Yahweh is the source of the disease. Second, illness involves their broken relationship with Yahweh by seeking after other deities and the disturbed social relationships among covenant brothers (cf. 4:1–5:7). The prophet depicts this relational brokenness in physical terms as an illness.

In verse 13, the prophet describes that Ephraim and Judah finally have become aware of their sickness. They begin to see their military deficiency and social upheaval. What they do not perceive is the ultimate source of

---

136. Perhaps, the text suggests that just as the socially underprivileged were oppressed, so the ruling elites will also experience oppression that already hangs over the nation.
137. Nwaoru, *Imagery*, 72.
138. Wolff, *Hosea*, 115.
139. Nwaoru, *Imagery*, 72.

their illness and healing. Instead of viewing Yahweh as the true cause of their illness and healing, they wrongly turned to Assyria and its great king for assistance.[140] Judah may be assumed to be the subject of "sent to the great king" (מלך ירב), "since Ephraim and Judah are so regularly paired in alternating lines in the sequence."[141] Both kingdoms are "no curable patients" for Assyrians.[142] To cure their sickness (חלי) and heal their wound (מזור), Ephraim and Judah must turn to Yahweh who is the hidden cause of their ailments. Healing in this sense would mean removing their dependence on other deities and foreign powers, restoring them to fidelity in social relationships with sole dependence on Yahweh, and then granting them the blessing promised in the covenant.[143]

The next similes in verses 14–15a amplify Yahweh as the real cause of woundedness. He is like a lion and a young lion to Ephraim and Judah respectively. The intensity of the metaphors is made evident by the fact that Yahweh abandons any comparison but directly identifies himself as the wild animals.[144] Moreover, the repeated first person pronoun, אני, stresses the certainty of Yahweh's actions and depicts him as a foe who tears to pieces (טרף), departs (הלך), carries away (נשא) and returns (שוב) to his place.[145] Having been attacked via internal (disease) and external (ferocious animal) means, Ephraim and Judah will not escape Yahweh's judgment. As Landy notes, the similes are representative of "two extremes of destructiveness among the creatures, of subversion from within and aggression from without."[146] A day of chastisement (תוכחה), which Yahweh declares

---

140. Hong, *Illness and Healing in Hosea*, 148.
141. Mays, *Hosea*, 91.
142. It is impossible to identify the exact historical event Hosea has in mind. In all probability, the reference would fit 732/731, when both states, under Hoshea and Ahaz, were made Assyrian vassals.
143. Dearman, *Hosea*, 186.
144. Nwaoru, *Imagery*, 72.
145. Yahweh's withdrawal of his presence from Ephraim and Judah probably functions as the harshest means of chastisement. As already noted in 2:8–15 [6–13], the final chastisement upon the wayward wife comes with the withdrawal of agricultural products by the husband. Yahweh's withdrawal here will result in Ephraim and Judah being captured and carried away into exile by Assyrians and Babylonians in 722 and 586 BC respectively (2 Kgs 17:3–6; 25:1–30).
146. Landy, *Hosea*, 78.

to bring it about (v. 9), has indeed come upon them. Yahweh's drastic actions preclude all other options but the only escape offered is to return to a relationship with him.

In sum, this passage (vv. 8–15a) presents a notion of divine chastisement that is reserved for those who are unfaithful to relationships. The discourse, moving a step further from the concept of actions with built-in consequences, presents Yahweh's active engagement in bringing chastisement upon Ephraim and Judah for their relational infidelity. In so doing, however, the prophet highlights that chastisement is not mere retaliation, nor an end in itself, but a means to inculcate obedience and return. Yahweh, the discipliner (מוסר, 5:2) and chastiser (תוכחה, 5:9), desires only the return of the people in right relationship with him and with fellow covenant members. "I am your teacher and I wish to correct you and not to punish you, to save you and not to lose you."[147]

Restoration (5:15b–6:3)

As has been argued, chastisement is a component of the divine relational justice. Ephraim and Judah cannot avoid Yahweh's loving chastisement that is meant to produce a desirable outcome – reconciliation. Yahweh, who has initiated relationship with his people, will not give them up despite their many follies. They may be battered and chastened, but they are not obliterated.[148] The path of restoration offered to them is described in 6:1–3, while 5:15 functions as a bridge from one theme to the next. That is, the judgment speech of 5:8–14 gives way to the "glimmer of hope for restoration in the invitation song of 6:1–3."[149]

The positive intention of judgment is displayed in 5:15 by an expression of Yahweh's willingness for and anticipation of the people's return. The exact identity of the "place" (מקום), to which Yahweh withdraws himself, is

---

147. Jerome cited in Macintosh, *Hosea*, 181.
148. Andersen and Freedman, *Hosea*, 328.
149. Stuart, *Hosea–Jonah*, 106.

obscure.[150] However, the point is clear that the absence of Yahweh, which results in Israel's affliction (צר), is meant to produce contrition within the people so that they seek (בקש) him (5:15b). Israel's unfaithfulness towards Yahweh has fractured their relationship such that they have become separated by a seemingly inaccessible chasm. Even searches and offerings are ineffective (5:6; 6:6). The journey to restoring their relationship will only begin when they recognise and acknowledge Yahweh's rightful place and seek with contrite, earnest hearts (ידע, 6:3). This ידע, needless to say, entails fidelity to relationships and recognition of his ethical nature and demands. They will be compelled to do this due to the distress (צר) they endure as Yahweh hides his face (5:15b).

The form and function of 6:1–3 have prompted much discussion.[151] The divergent interpretations are primarily offshoots of the assumption that Yahweh's renewed accusation of Ephraim and Judah of 6:4ff about the fickleness of their חסד is related to these preceding verses.[152] Some interpreters regard 6:1–3 as sham repentance on the part of the people. Accordingly, Wolff classifies 6:1–3 as a "penitential song" sung by the priests to invite the people to repent in times of danger. Similarly, Mays identifies 6:1–3 as a liturgical "song of penitence in times of national crisis," while Hubbard labels it as a "song of feeble penitence" to urge the people to return to Yahweh.[153] However, other scholars such as Andersen and Freedman and Garrett contend that 6:1–3 depict a sincere "statement of faith," not a "pseudo-return."[154]

However, such considerations are deemed unnecessary. As Davies cogently notes, "Hosea 6:1–3 is not itself a song of repentance but an

---

150. In light of the lion metaphor, some scholars take מקום to be "lair," (Wolff, *Hosea*, 116, Andersen and Freedman, *Hosea*, 415). For others, it may mean a "heavenly palace" (Mays, *Hosea*, 92–93 and Sweeney, *Twelve Prophets*, 68), or even the "wilderness" based on Hosea 2:14 (Davies, *Hosea*, 158).

151. For a more detailed analysis of the differing explanations proposed by various interpreters, see Davies, *Hosea*, 150–151.

152. Davies, *Hosea*, 150.

153. See Wolff, *Hosea*, 116–117; Mays, *Hosea*, 93; Hubbard, *Hosea*, 126.

154. See Andersen and Freedman, *Hosea*, 329–330 and Garrett, *Hosea, Joel*, 159. Stuart, *Hosea–Jonah*, 107, also argues that 6:1–3 "represents a faithful presentation of covenant teaching, because its orientation is eschatological, not immediate."

exhortation designed to call one forth."[155] It is a call addressed by Hosea in the name of Yahweh to the people, in hope of true repentance.[156] In other words, 6:1–3 is the prophet's composition of what Yahweh would like to hear from the people. As such, the concern of the words at this stage is not to outline whether the people sincerely express guilt or not. Rather, the voice highlights the fact that Yahweh's offer of reconciliation is on the table and affirms the certainty of his disposition to reconcile with his people. Hence the prior concern of the passage is restoration.

Exhortation to Return to Yahweh (6:1–2)

The opening verse (6:1) grows out of the previous units, as evident from the connection of thought and repetition of key vocabulary.[157] The imagery of Yahweh as the chastiser and healer, and of Ephraim and Judah as the wounded and sick, continues. The first person plural cohortatives *let us return* (v. 1) and *let us know* (v. 2) represent Hosea's utterance of calling the people to renew their relationship with Yahweh. The notion of "returning" to Yahweh is a major theme of Hosea.[158] The verb שוב in 6:1 may imply "turning from an action or attitude and embracing Yahweh himself and his covenant ethos."[159] Holladay has credibly argued that "שוב in its covenantal usage expresses *a change of loyalty on the part of Israel or God, each for the other.*"[160] The first step of the task required by the people is to renew their loyalty to Yahweh. The שוב here underscores the restoration of relationship at a personal level, although this would be naturally followed by obedience to instructions and proper sacrifices and offerings. The return would primarily reverse the punishments described in 4:8–15. For a reversal of the lion metaphor in 5:14, Yahweh will heal (רפא) what he has torn to

---

155. Davies, *Hosea*, 151.
156. Carl F. Keil, *The Twelve Minor Prophets, vol. 1*, eds. C. F. Keil and F. Deitzsch; Biblical Commentary on the Old Testament (Grand Rapids: Eerdmans, 1954), 94.
157. Such connections include: הלך (5:11, 13, 14, 15; 6:1), שוב (5:15; 6:1) טרף (5:14; 6:1) and רפא (5:13; 6:1). Macintosh, *Hosea*, 217; Nwaoru, *Imagery*, 72.
158. See p. 315.
159. Dearman, *Hosea*, 190.
160. William L. Holladay, *The Root Šûbh in the Old Testament: With Particular Reference to Its Usages in Covenantal Contexts* (Leiden: E. J. Brill, 1958), 116–125 (116).

pieces. To reverse the physical illness metaphor of 5:12, Yahweh will bandage (חבש) the injuries of Israel.

In verse 2, the motif of healing and renewal continues with the promise to restore life (חיה). The expression יחינו מימים ביום חשלישי יקמנו ("He will revive us after two days, on the third day he will raise us up") has been the source of much discussion. While some interpreters relate the statement to the cult of a dying and rising god, others think that it is more natural to understand it in terms of healing from physical sickness.[161] Barré argues that the notion of two or three days, in light of Akkadian medical omen texts, strongly suggests a short period of time.[162] Still other interpreters are inclined to connect the expression with the notion of resurrection after death.[163] However, given the importance of relationships in Hosea, it is most reasonable to understand 6:2 in the setting of Israel's covenant thinking. The expression "to revive" and "on the third day," as Wijngaards has argued, can be best understood as Yahweh's renewal of his covenant with the people.[164] This consideration is substantiated by the presence of other relational concepts in what precedes (שוב, v. 1) and what follows (ידע, v. 3 and חסד, v.4). As such, the emphasis is that Israel can certainly expect Yahweh to renew relationship with them. Their "returning" to Yahweh and Yahweh's "reviving" and "raising up" of them will bring blessing and national security which is inherent in covenantal relations.

A Pathway to Return (6:3)

The prophet's second exhortation to the people comes with an invitation, "Let us strive to know Yahweh" (ונדעה נרדפה לדעת את־יחוה). The phrase seems to be carefully designed to form a parallel to the initial invitation, "Let us return to Yahweh" (v. 1).[165] Interestingly, each exhortation has its

---

161. For the former, see Else K. Holt, *Prophesying the Past: the use of Israel's History in the Book of Hosea* (JSOTSup 194; Sheffield: Academic Press, 1995), 83–84. For the latter, see Wolff, *Hosea*, 118–119; Michael L. Barré, "New Light on the Interpretation of Hosea VI 2," *VT* 28 (1978): 129–141.

162. Barré, "Hosea VI 2", 139–140.

163. See Andersen and Freedman, *Hosea,* 420 and Garrett, *Hosea, Joel,* 158.

164. Johannes Wijngaards, "Death and Resurrection in a Covenantal Context (Hos VI 2)," *VT* 17 (1967): 226–239.

165. Stuart, *Hosea–Jonah,* 108.

respective objective: "living in his presence" (ונחיה לפניו, v. 2) and "knowing him" (לדעת את־יהוה, v. 3). Perhaps the two objectives are one and the same, that to live in his presence is to know him. By knowing Yahweh Israel must become totally loyal to their relationship with him and to his ethical demands. The notion of vigorous striving (רדף) to know Yahweh on the part of Israel probably alludes, by way of contrast, to mother Israel's futile pursuit of her lovers (2:9 [7]), the nation's passionate and futile pursuit of her lovers (i.e. Baals [2:7; 5:11]).[166] As discussed elsewhere, knowledge of Yahweh indicates resolute fidelity to him and his ethical nature.[167] It bears noting that the verb רדף expresses a deliberate effort and that the term is used elsewhere often in relation to other relational terms such as צדק (Deut 16:20; Isa 51:1; Prov 15:9), טוב (Ps 38:21), שלום (Ps 34:15), חסד (Ps 23:6; Prov 21:21).[168] By stressing the importance of seeking the knowledge of Yahweh, Hosea presents it as the pathway for their return to relationship.

As Israel's "return" is followed by Yahweh's healing and bandaging in verses 1–2, so Israel's striving to know Yahweh is followed by the reliability of Yahweh's benevolent action portrayed through cosmic imagery of "dawn" and "rain." His appearance (i.e. his "going forth" [מוצאו] and "coming" [בוא]) is as sure as the dawn, which implies the daily appearance of the sun, and also the spring rain, which refreshes dry land every single year. Once again, the emphasis here is the certainty of Yahweh's inherent nature in restoring his people. Hence the restoration of relationship will reverse the vicious wind (4:19) and devouring moon (5:7), but give birth to the harmonious relationship with nature (cf. 2:22–25). In sum, the prophet, whose task involves decreeing Yahweh's relational will to reconcile with his people, has done his part. The dissolution can come only through Israel's inability to comprehend such "knowledge."

---

166. See Davies, *Hosea*, 162, Macintosh, *Hosea*, 226 and Nwaoru, *Imagery*, 74.
167. [[See pp. 223–226.]]
168. Macintosh, *Hosea*, 226.

Summary Assessment

This chapter has explored Hosea's message in 4:1–6:3. In the course of this analysis, we have examined the texts based on our proposed three strands of the book: responsibility, chastisement and restoration.

Our exploration of 4:1–5:7 has shown that Hosea's prophetic message primarily concerns Israel's relational irresponsibility. Hosea declares that Israel's relationships with Yahweh and her neighbours are essentially wrong. The people have made grave errors of judgment by discarding social virtues such as אמת, חסד, and דעת אלהים and for replacing those qualities with social vices such as cursing, lying, murder, stealing and adultery. Their irresponsible actions are abhorrent to the prophet and to Yahweh simply because they hurt others with whom they stand in inseparable relationships – their God, their fellow humans and creation. Their deplorable deeds, of course, do not happen in a vacuum, but come as a result of the priests' failure to act according to their responsibility to impart knowledge, the rulers' failure to set משפט in the society, and the populace who have indulged in flawed cultic practices and social crimes. Indeed, every strata of Israelite society has become corrupt.

Our analysis of 5:8–15a has demonstrated that relational justice not only demands responsibility but embraces chastisement as a pathway to restoration. In other words, inseparable relationship necessitates correction brought about by the divine chastisement that is used as a means to bring relationally disloyal Israel (i.e. Ephraim and Judah) back to right relationship with Yahweh. Yahweh himself is active in bringing affliction upon Israel, and as a result, foreigners will plunder the land. However, it is noteworthy that the prophet, amid pronouncement of judgment, stresses the fact that chastisement is not mere retaliation, nor an end in itself, but rather a means to inculcate obedience and return.

Relational justice not only holds chastisement as a pathway to reunion, but also, fundamentally, involves forgiving the unforgivable as presented in 5:15b–6:3. Despite Ephraim's lack of sincere remorse and in spite of Judah's many failures, Yahweh will not obliterate them entirely. Treading beyond the legal notion of giving everyone their just due, the prophet exposes Yahweh's readiness to reconcile with his undeserving people. Yahweh is prepared to heal their relational brokenness. He is waiting to be sought and, in fact, could found through "knowledge." He wants Israel to live in his presence and to know him. Whether Israel has comprehended this, or has actually returned to Yahweh and right relationship with sincere remorse, will become clearer when we examine Hosea's subsequent prophetic oracles.

CHAPTER EIGHT

Yahweh and His People (6:4–11:11)

We have already examined the demarcations and basic literary structure of this section in the preceding chapter. Once again, the cycle comprises a sizable collection of accusations of irresponsibility on the part of Israel and Judah (6:4–8:14), followed by chastisement oracles (9:1–10:15) and Yahweh's promise of restoration (11:1–11). Earlier, we have also stated that the demarcation lines, particularly between the accusation of irresponsibility and chastisement oracles are thin and, at times, overlapping. Nevertheless, one can be sure that the theme of accusation for irresponsibility is dominant in 6:4–8:14, whereas chastisement is prominent in 9:1–10:15.

Responsibility (6:4–8:14)

As in the previous responsibility-chastisement-restoration cycle (4:1–6:3), this phase begins with Yahweh's assessment of Ephraim and Judah's accountability (6:4–8:14). This can be outlined as follows:

6:4–6	A lament for Israel's ephemeral relational virtues
6:7–7:2	Israel is defiled: horrible deeds encompass her
7:3–7	Debauchery and perfidy within the royal court
7:8–16	Ephraim is like an unturned cake, a fooled dove and a faulty bow
8:1–14	Israel is rebellious, rejecting what is relationally good

Following this basic structure, we will highlight that the central issue in this section is disloyalty in relationships.

The Fleeting Relational Virtues (6:4–6)

We have argued that 6:1–3 represents Hosea's composition of what Yahweh would like to hear from his people as well as the affirmation of Yahweh's nature to reconcile with his people. In this light, we do not need to interpret 6:4–6 as Yahweh's response to the people's sham repentance in 6:1–3. In fact, there is neither a confession of sin, nor a return to Yahweh which is implemented by the people. Put differently, the restorative message in 6:1–3 remains one-sided affair, which in due course serves a rhetorical purpose for further accusations. To ultimately restore the harmonious relationship with Yahweh, Israel is still lacking something. The prophet, therefore, has yet to condemn Israel's irresponsibility in the subsequent discourses.

The discourse in 6:4–7:2 has a close resemblance to 4:1–3. The prophet addresses Ephraim and Judah once again by pinpointing the sins of omission and the sins of commission. A progression of discourse from previous texts is also noticeable when Judah is brought down to Israel's level of depravity. They are now on the same footing (v. 4). Accordingly, 6:4–6 is bound together by the subject of the sins of omission: the "two desiderata of Hosea,"[1] חסד and דעת אלהים.[2] The prophet's soliloquy, "What shall I do with you?" (מה אעשה־לך, v. 4), in relation to both Ephraim and Judah, suggests Yahweh's frustration or "theodicy"[3] with the transitory חסד of the people. Every tactic used by Yahweh to win the people back has failed so far. Wealth leads them to ignore him (4:7), and catastrophe causes them to turn to others for a help, which ultimately cannot be delivered (5:13). Neither the threatened chastisement (cf. 1:4–9; 2:8–15; 3:3–4; 5:8–15), nor the promised restoration (cf. 2:1–3; 2:16–25; 3:5; 5:15b–6:3) has actually resulted in their return to Yahweh.

As has been argued, the dearth of חסד is like a slap in the face for Yahweh as the term refers primarily to a relationship with God and fellow

---

1. Garrett, *Hosea, Joel*, 161.
2. On the meaning and significance of these terms see chapters 2 and 5.
3. Macintosh, *Hosea*, 229, understands vv. 4–6 as a theodicy rather than a divine decree or answer.

human beings. Over and again, חסד represents, as Robinson notes, the "mingling of duty and love which springs directly from the conception of common ties, and expands to include and regulate the conception of Yahweh's relation to Israel."[4] A genuine חסד of sorts may once have existed in Israel, but the simile that qualifies the term mitigates against its validity, particularly in the eighth-century Israelite context. The חסד that disappears (הלך) as quickly as morning mist (ענן) and early dew (טל), is tantamount to saying there is no חסד at all.[5] The evanescent חסד (and דעת אלהים, v. 6) of Israel and Judah is intolerable for Yahweh, and this is the simple reason why he has hewn (חצב) them by his prophets and slain (הרג) them by his fearsome words (v. 5). The use of משפט in plural form (v. 5b) perhaps indicates Yahweh's corrective chastisements as being repetitive.[6] On the other hand, the משפט here, as Wolff notes, denotes "right relationships within the community," and is thus intended to compare the constancy and superiority of Yahweh's משפט over and against Israel's חסד (v. 4).[7]

The חסד and דעת אלהים are contrasted with sacrifice (זבח) and burnt offering (עלה) respectively (v. 6). The stative verb "I desire" (חפצתי) expresses the universal validity of Yahweh's will. There is worship and so sacrifice, but חסד and דעת אלהים which give worship its value is lacking.[8] Sacrificial worship, rightly understood, is a gift to the covenant community, and is intended as a means to a greater end.[9] The essential fault of the people, however, is the priority placed on the means in place of the ends, and on the peripheral in place of the fundamentals. In fact, the reformative period depicted in 3:4 has already suggested that there are essentials more important than sacrifice. These include the disposition and deeds which unfailingly maintain a given relationship and the unqualified response to Yahweh in obedience to his demands.[10] In a nutshell, חסד, which

---

4. H. Wheeler Robinson, *Corporate Personality in Ancient Israel* (rev. ed.; Philadelphia: Fortress Press, 1980), 43–44.
5. Stuart, *Hosea–Jonah*, 111.
6. Dearman, *Hosea*, 196.
7. Wolff, *Hosea*, 120.
8. Nwaoru, *Imagery*, 74.
9. Dearman, *Hosea*, 197.
10. See Mays, *Hosea*, 98.

denotes faithfulness in relationship with Yahweh, and its parallel concept, דעת אלהים, which displays this relationship to God, are the foundations of everything for Israel.[11]

Horrible Deeds Encompass the Entire House of Israel (6:7–7:2)

In this unit, the prophet elaborates on his accusation of the people's irresponsibility by featuring the sins of commission. The employment of the terms אדם and ברית in 6:7 has attracted attention. Some scholars have interpreted כאדם (lit. "like Adam") as a personal name and thus as a reference to Genesis 3 and the disobedience in the garden.[12] But most commentators have understood the term to be the name of a city.[13] This view seems to be supported by the particle שׁם in the same verse, and also by the paralleled names: "Gilead" and "Shechem" in verses 8–9. What one can be sure of, however, is that Hosea has made a pun on the names of the town and the original transgressor,[14] depicting Israel as having broken her covenant relationship with Yahweh.

In addition, interpreters debate the specific identity of ברית in Hosea.[15] Perlitt interprets ברית in 6:7 as referring to a political treaty rather than to the covenant with Yahweh.[16] However, scholars such as McCarthy and others have credibly argued that the ברית in this text connotes Yahweh's

---

11. See Wolff, *Hosea*, 120.
12. For instance, McComiskey, "Hosea," 95. Following M. J. Dahood, Dennis J. McCarthy, "*berît* in Old Testament History and Theology," *Bib* 53 (1972): 110–121 and Stuart, *Hosea–Jonah*, 98, however, opt for a translation, "Behold, they have walked over the covenant like dirt, lo they have betrayed me." The existence of words אדם "dirt" and שׁם "lo" in Biblical Hebrew is highly dubious.
13. See Wolff, *Hosea*, 121; Mays, *Hosea*, 100; Andersen and Freedman, *Hosea*, 439; Macintosh, *Hosea*, 326–237; Garrett, *Hosea, Joel*, 162.
14. Garrett, *Hosea, Joel*, 163.
15. For a detailed survey of scholarship on this concept of ברית, see Ernest W. Nicholson, *God and His People: Covenant and Theology in the Old Testament* (Oxford: Clarendon Press, 1986), 83–116.
16. Lothar Perlitt, *Bundestheologie im Alten Testament* (WMANT 36; Neukirchen Vluyn: Neukirchener Verlag, 1969), 141–144. Perlitt's argument is basically grounded on the assumption that ברית is a Deuteronomic *theologoumenon*. Accordingly, he concludes that the covenant as a theological concept did not exist prior to the Deuteronomic movement.

covenantal relationship with Israel.[17] It is Yahweh's "demand for exclusivity" (*Ausschließlichkeitsanspruch*),[18] which Holt calls "the essential feature of the theology of the book of Hosea."[19] This consideration is substantiated contextually by other covenantal terms such as חסד and דעת אלהים in 6:6 and by the phrase "they deal faithlessly with me" (v. 7). Hosea's fondness and usage of such relational terms and the parallelism of ברית and מורה in 8:1 (cf. 4:6; 8:12) naturally suggest that the ברית is another way of illustrating the relation between Yahweh and Israel. In fact, we have discussed at length in an earlier chapter that Hosea's marriage is presented as a bond relationship, symbolising the relationship between Yahweh and his people Israel.[20] That is, the metaphors of marriage (Hosea 1–3) and of ברית (6:7; 8:1) both signal the solemn commitment of Yahweh to Israel and of Israel to Yahweh.[21] As such, the ברית refers to the exclusive faithfulness to Yahweh and to "the loyal conduct within the community designated by משפט in verse 5 and חסד and דעת אלהים in verse 6."[22]

As in 4:2, 6:7–9 catalogues the crimes of three specific places to indict the whole nation.[23] The crimes consist of violation of the covenant and treachery in Adam (6:7), bloodshed in Gilead (6:8) and premeditated murder on the way to Shechem (6:9). The perpetrators include the priests (v. 9) and the people (6:10–7:2). Though the incidents that are notorious in Hosea's time are unspecified, the crimes sorted in context are reminiscent of Israel's lack of חסד and דעת אלהים in 6:6. We have noted elsewhere that the disappearance of such social virtues from sight necessarily means the appearance of social evils. The one certainty about the

---

17. McCarthy, "*bᵉrît* in Old Testament history," 110–121; Nicholson, *God and His People*, 179–186; John Day, "Pre-Deuteronomic Allusions to the Covenant in Hosea and Psalm 78," *VT* 36 (1986): 1–12.

18. Walther Zimmerli, "Das Gottesrecht bei den Propheten Amos, Hosea und Jesaja," in *Werden und Wirken des Alten Testaments,* ed. R. Albertz (Göttingen: Vandenhoeck, 1980), 216–235.

19. Holt, *Prophesying the Past,* 56–57; idem, " דעת אלהים and חסד im Buche Hosea," *SJOT* 1 (1987): 87–103.

20. [[See pp.145–151.]]

21. See Nicholson, *God and his People,* 184–185.

22. Wolff, *Hosea,* 121.

23. Mays, *Hosea,* 99, describes this unit as a mini guidebook to the geography of sin in Israel.

absence of חסד and דעת אלהים is that it leaves a train wreck in its wake. Accordingly, transgression (עבר) and faithlessness (בגד) in relations have literally become Israel's societal norms (v. 7). As the evildoers (פעלי און) and murderers or raiding parties (גדוד) are in control, bloody foot prints (עקבה מדם) and atrocities (זמה) become their hallmarks (vv. 8–9). It must be admitted that the characterisations of the crimes is so all-encompassing that it is impossible to recover anything specific from the words which were spoken by the prophet. The summary statement in verse 10, with the phrases "horrible thing" (שעריריה) and "harlotry" (זנות), too, is inclusive. Yet it indicates that the earlier charges are directed to the whole בית ישראל. Yahweh personally perceives (ראתי) his people (cf. עמי v. 11b) unfit to be his people because Israel is defiled (טמא). It is perhaps for the same reason that קציר ("harvest") is set for Judah (v. 11a), suggesting that Judah, too, would reap the results of irresponsibility.[24]

As in verse 4, 6:11b–7:2 also depict the dilemma of Yahweh, describing "the impasse between Yahweh's willingness to restore his people and their total identification with evil."[25] Yahweh's image as restorer and healer has exposed the misdeeds of Samaria (7:1). The crimes exposed include fraud (שקר), thieving (גנב) and banditry (פשט). Fraud is a common means by which the ruling class exploit the peasant majority. It echoes the vicious marketplace depicted in 12:7, where the vulnerable have been cheated with "adulterated grain and dishonest scales" (cf. Amos 5:11; 85). "Thieving inside" (גנב יבוא) and "banditry outside" (פשט גדוד בחוץ) are "a synecdoche for civil and social injustices in general."[26] Their evil deeds encompass them and are right in front of Yahweh (7:2). The concluding phrase with "their transgressions" (מעלליהם) indicates the general trend of relational infidelity, underlying the sense of failure to live up to the expected responsibilities to Yahweh and fellow human beings. All that Yahweh can see, from whatever angle, is their irresponsibility towards right relationships.

---

24. A number of commentators regard 6:11a as a gloss (e.g. Mays, *Hosea,* 102). However, Andersen and Freedman, *Hosea,* 443, note that the verse hardly follows a "conventional gloss."

25. Mays, *Hosea,* 100.

26. Stuart, *Hosea–Jonah,* 118.

Debauchery and Perfidy within the Royal Court (7:3–7)

The preceding discourse focuses on the society's indifference to crimes of all sorts, whereas 7:3–7 pays attention to the national leadership. The scene shifts to describe the conditions within the palace of Samaria, underlining the growing relational breakdown through political conspiracy and regicide. Hence humans are offending against each other. Yet it is difficult to determine whether the passage points to one specific historical event.[27] The setting is best related more broadly to the internal chaos of kingship that took place after the death of Jeroboam II.[28] Out of six Israel's final kings, four were assassinated within a matter of twelve years (2 Kgs 15:8–30). The statement כל־מלכיהם נפלו (v. 7) perhaps indicates a retrospective remark from the time of Hoshea.[29]

There are three similes that run through the verses: "adultery" (נאף, v. 4), "hot oven" (תנור בערה, vv. 4, 6–7) and "heat" (חמה, v. 5). These images primarily relate to the predatory passions of the conspirators. The theme of "wickedness" (רעה, vv. 2, 3), to which "lies" (כחשים) is added, also remains dominant.[30] The oven is a simile for the conspirators' regicidal fury (תנור), whose burning heat remains constant for the fire is allowed to die down for only a few hours before it is stirred up again. The few short hours that the baker allows the heated oven to rest (v. 4) correspond to the dormant rage of the conspirators for a little while (v. 6). Equally, the activity of the stirring up of the fire in the morning corresponds to their renewed nefarious intrigues.[31]

Who, then, are the conspirators? It has not been easy to establish the identity of the unidentified plural subjects "they" in verse 3 and "all of them" (כלם) in verses 4 and 7. It is difficult to limit these to the king and

---

27. For Wolff, *Hosea*, 111 and Stuart, *Hosea–Jonah*, 117, Hoshea's assassination of Pekah constitutes the point of reference. However, Menahem's assassination of Shallum or Pekah's assassination of Pekaiah are potential candidates as well. See Sweeney, *Twelve Prophets*, 78.
28. See chapter 4, section I, particularly pp. 98–104.
29. Mays, *Hosea*, 104; Dearman, *Hosea*, 201.
30. Nwaoru, *Imagery*, 75.
31. See Shalom M. Paul, "The Image of Oven and the Cake in Hosea VII 4–10," *VT* 18 (1968): 114–120 (115–116).

court officials[32] or to the priests just because they are mentioned previously.[33] The ill-defined subjects perhaps are best understood as plotters who include the people, priests, king and princes.[34] It is worth noting that four kings in this context are assassins who have overthrown their predecessors and so, too, become plotters themselves. The successive regicides could never have happened without the support of their circles – officials, priests and the people. In this prevailing situation, a just and true relationship is out of the question. In contrast, the national leaders "gladden" (שמח) each other with רעה and כחשים (v. 3). A king in Israel should rejoice in justice and righteousness, but here are ones whose joy is the fruit of violent evil.[35] Appallingly, the practical norms of the society are "lies" and "wickedness," which stand in a stark contrast to the desired relational norms, חסד and דעת אלהים (6:6), and the משפט which denotes right relationships within the community (6:5). It must be noted that Hosea's prophetic accusation of the conspirators' malicious schemes to topple the monarchs is neither to back kings despite their flaws, nor to defend them simply because kingship is a divinely ordained institution. His concern, rather, is the ongoing hostile environment of killing and plotting that is gravely detrimental to social bonds based on just and true relationships.

The conspirators are also identified as "adulterers" (מנאפים, v. 4), whose adulterous passion is likened to a "heated oven." This term metaphorically portrays the treacherous deeds of the conspirators who are trying to seize throne, power, privilege and wealth through political intrigue and treachery (cf. v 6).[36] On the other hand, the possibility of literal adultery cannot be dismissed altogether.[37] The expression, "on the day of our king" (יום מלכנו, v. 5),[38] indicates the kind of indulgent lifestyle that goes on at

---

32. See Wolff, *Hosea*, 124; Mays, *Hosea*, 105.
33. See Andersen and Freedman, *Hosea*, 455.
34. See Nwaoru, *Imagery*, 75, footnote 279.
35. Mays, *Hosea*, 105.
36. Hong, *The Metaphor of Illness*, 159.
37. See Premnath, *Eighth Century Prophets*, 143.
38. Most commentators take the reference, "the day of our (their?) king," to denote a coronation or some other day of royal significance and public celebration (Wolff, *Hosea*, 125; Macintosh, *Hosea*, 261; Dearman, *Hosea*, 204).

the centre of power.³⁹ Similarly, the saying, "the princes are sick with the heat of wine," describes the effects of overconsumption that is a euphemism for being "very drunk".⁴⁰ Given this context, the scene reflects the feast-loving culture and decadent lifestyle of the upper-class characterised by מרזח, which was vehemently attacked by Amos (cf. Amos 6:4:7).⁴¹ In this light, it is not unreasonable to suppose that Hosea alludes to the sexual immorality of the time (cf. Hos 4:14). The phrase משך ידו את־לצצים, "he stretched out his hand with mockers" (v. 5), probably indicates the king (Shallum? Pekaiah? or Pekah?), or usurper's ignorance by embracing those who intend to kill him.⁴² The ferocious conspiracy of those mockers (i.e. the intoxicated princes or court officials) is portrayed through the hot-oven simile in verse 6. The concern here is apparently to expose the rupture of relationships. It can be imagined that relationships everywhere have virtually become sham relations as all "hearts" lie in wait to grasp the opportunity to exterminate others (v. 6; cf. Mic 2:1). The ones who ought to assist destroy instead.

The oracle reaches its climax in verse 7, summarising the net results of such vulture-like inter-human relations as a result of political machinations. Outbreaks of revolution and counter-revolution victimise kings one after another in a way that strikes at the foundations of the nation. The summary statements, אכלו את־שפטיהם "they consume their judges" (v. 7a) and כל־מלכיהם נפלו "all their kings have fallen" (v. 7b), depict the nation's downward spiralling in an irreversible process. As discussed in an earlier chapter, a שפט is someone in administrative authority, whether as a military leader, or political leader or one in judicial affairs. The central mandate of the judges (or rulers) is to regulate the social relationships within the community and to lead the people with a view to saving those whose rights have been violated or taken. They are to exercise their authority with relational and social commitment in decisive action.⁴³ It is possible that the prophet alludes to the fact that the people swiftly depose the guarantors

---

39. See Eidevall, *Grapes in the Desert*, 110.
40. Yee, "The Book of Hosea," 257.
41. See pages 106–109.
42. Sweeney, *Twelve Prophets*, 80.
43. See pages 89–90.

of justice from the central power. The fundamental mistake is the failure to cry out to Yahweh (בהם אלי אין־קרא, v. 7b), who alone can restore and heal the nation. In sum, the discourse (7:3–7) remains an accusation of irresponsibility at the level of national leadership. The governance that is based on lust and arrogance must give way to right relationships with fellow rulers, and with faith placed in Yahweh alone.

Ephraim is like an Unturned Cake, a Fooled Dove and a Faulty Bow (7:8–16)

This passage deals with Israel's entanglement in international politics, reflecting the struggle for survival during the last two decades of national existence. The unit (vv. 8–16) is demarcated by the closure at 7:7 and by the new beginning at 8:1.[44] Besides, the shift from domestic affairs to external ones (אפרים בעמים, v. 8a) gives this section its unified character.[45] As observed elsewhere, the Northern Kingdom during the period 738–732 BC was characterised by Samaria's vacillating alliances with great powers, namely Assyria and Egypt.[46]

Two metaphors are featured in the first sub-units: the unturned cake (vv. 8–10) and the senseless dove (vv. 11–12). The first simile compares Ephraim's openness to foreign influences with an "unturned cake" (v. 8b).[47] The phrase "unturned" indicates that the bread is "half raw", "burnt on one side and undone on the other,"[48] and is virtually useless and inedible. A half-baked cake that is "of no savour to anyone"[49] illustrates the worthlessness of Ephraim among other nations (cf. 8:8b). Ephraim's foreign policy – its pride (גאון) and the source of its rebellion (v. 10a; cf. 5:5) – becomes the source of its emasculation. "Foreigners are eating up his strength" (אכלו זרים כחו, v. 9a). The expression could mean the forfeiture of material resources (cf. 2 Kgs 15:20). This tragic dimension is portrayed in the imagery of the grey hairs: גם־שיבה זרקה בו (v. 9b) for which two

---

44. Andersen and Freedman, *Hosea*, 463.
45. Nwaoru, *Imagery*, 77.
46. See pages 102–104.
47. As in most modern commentaries.
48. Mays, *Hosea*, 108.
49. Davies, *Hosea*, 187.

different readings have been offered: a man with grey hair,[50] or mouldy bread.[51] Whichever alternative one might take, the image depicts a state of decay.[52] Simply, Ephraim is old, and death is near. Of special interest for us is to stress the climactic accusation of Hosea's central themes of "knowing," "returning" and "seeking". In verse 9, Ephraim is found twice ignorant, lacking ידע (והוא לא ידע, v. 9ab).[53] In verse 10, the people, despite their entire predicament, fail to return (שוב) and seek (בקש) Yahweh. It is worth noting that in 5:5–6 the people seek Yahweh without finding him because they seek him through sacrifices. But in 7:10b, the people do not even seek him.[54]

The next simile likens Ephraim to a silly (פתה) and senseless (אין לב) dove (vv. 11–12) on account of its foreign policy which alternates between loyalties to Assyria and Egypt. The verb פתה is used to describe those who are easily deceived (Deut 11:16; Job 31:27). The prophet perhaps regards the dove as the silliest bird and able to be trapped easily, in order to belittle the nation's diplomatic manoeuvring. It is impossible to relate the imagery to a specific historical incident.[55] Yet it reflects the habitual behaviour of the leadership and the situation of the final stage of Israel's monarchy. The basic folly of Ephraim is the failure to recognise their dependence on and relationship with Yahweh. Yahweh's actions, in response to Ephraim's foolish attempts, depict him as a "fowler" and "chastiser" (v. 12). He will spread his net to bring his people down on its way to the nations, and to their senses so that they will turn away from their evil ways.[56]

---

50. This reading presupposes that the gaining of grey hair was seen as something negative. See Wolff, *Hosea*, 126; Mays, *Hosea*, 108–109; Davies, *Hosea*, 187; Macintosh, *Hosea*, 217.

51. In light of Prov 16:31; 20:29 in which grey hair is highly regarded, and with extrabiblical support, this reading suggests that שיבה can be translated as "mould." See Paul, "The Oven and the Cake in Hosea," 119; Andersen and Freedman, *Hosea*, 467; Garrett, *Hosea*, 170.

52. Stuart, *Hosea–Jonah*, 121. The reading of "grey hair" seems a more plausible alternative.

53. Nwaoru, *Imagery*, 77.

54. Eidevall, *Grapes in the Desert*, 118.

55. Wolff, *Hosea*, 127, isolates this text to the year 733 BC.

56. Paul A. Kruger, "The Divine Net in Hosea 7:12," *ETL* 68 (1992): 132–136 (135).

The subunit (vv. 13–16) separates itself from the previous ones, not only with a "woe" (אוֹי) oracle, which begins at verse 13, but also with its emotional content. The divine speech relates Ephraim's offences specifically against Yahweh. That is, the victim of the people's horrible deeds that encompass the entire house of Israel (6:7—7:2), the rapacious plotting against others (vv. 3–7), and the leaders' misdirected political actions (vv. 8–12), is none other than Yahweh himself. The emphatic pronouns אנכי and המה point to the contrast between Yahweh's willingness to restore his people and their defiance of him.[57] Once again, the speech reflects Hosea's typical prophetic accusation, listing the sins of commission and of omission (cf. 4:1–3; 6:4–6).[58]

7:	13b	For *they* **have strayed** *from me*	כי־נדדו ממני
	13d	For *they* **have rebelled** *against me*	כי־פשעו בי
	13f	*They* **speak lies** *against me*	והמה דברו עלי כזבים
	14d	*They* **turn away** *from me*	יסורו בי
	15c	*They* **plot evil** *against me*	ואלי יחשבו־רע
7:	14a	*They* **do not cry out** *to me* from their hearts	ולא־זעקו אלי בלבם

The verbs employed to describe Ephraim's offences against Yahweh are broad in scope. Therefore, it is difficult to specify which historical wrong was the focus of the prophet. However, each of the individual concepts reflects Yahweh's demand of justice and righteousness in all areas of life. Though Yahweh longs to redeem (פדה) them, they wilfully "flee away" (נדד) from him and disobediently "rebel" (פשע) against him (v. 13). The use of פשע in this context may have a political nuance, underlining Ephraim's rebellion against her overlord, Yahweh.[59] The people "do not cry out" (זעק) to Yahweh from their hearts but "turn away" (סור) from him and "speak lies" (דבר כזבים) against him. Again, the context of verses 13–14 clearly indicates that the point at issue is religious, denoting Ephraim's breaking of

---

57. Davies, *Hosea*, 189.
58. See Nwaoru, *Imagery*, 78.
59. Wolff, *Hosea*, 127; Dearman, *Hosea*, 212.

faith. Like a wisdom teacher or like responsible parents, Yahweh disciplines (יסר) his people, but they devise (חשב) evil against him (v. 15). It is best to suppose that the figure of "strengthening the arms" (חזק זרועתם) has to do with education in morality (cf. Job 4:3).[60] Surprisingly, Hosea's holistic perspective is clarifying. For Ephraim to remain true to Yahweh, her social, political and religious life must reflect the character of Yahweh. Yet the people's unreliability and their refusal of Yahweh's offer of a new relationship remain constant. Instead, they turn to "Not High" (לא על), a term presumably for a Canaanite deity.[61] Hence Ephraim is compared to a slack bow, קשת רמיה (v. 16b), indicating the uselessness of the nation. The rulers who have been the architects of the royal assassinations shall fall by the sword. The victory of the exodus will be reversed because their defeat will bring derision from the Egyptians whose help they alternately sought and spurned.[62]

Israel is Rebellious, Rejecting what is Relationally Good (8:1–14)

The command to sound the alarm (אל־חכך שפר) at 8:1a, which indicates the looming danger, possibly through the Assyrian army, marks a new unit.[63] This is followed by a series of accusations of Israel's (and Judah's [v. 14]) faithlessness. Interpreters have offered a wide variety of proposals for the literary structure and yet without consensus.[64] The issues addressed are more or less a further elaboration of themes from previous discourses. As argued elsewhere, Yahweh's covenantal lordship demands exclusive fidelity on the part of Israel, extending over all areas of life. Israel's moral life (vv.

---

60. Wolff, *Hosea*, 128, cites Job 4:3 to suggest that the figure "strengthening the arms" has to do with education in ethical matters. Similarly Andersen and Freedman, *Hosea*, 476.
61. Wolff, *Hosea*, 108; Davies, *Hosea*, 192.
62. Mays, *Hosea*, 113.
63. The addressee who is to blow the שופר is unidentified. It could be the prophet himself (Rudolph), or the commander of Israel's army (Wolff), or the nation as a corporate person (Mays).
64. For examples: 1–3, 4–14 (Wolff); 1–3, 4, 5–6, 7, 8–10, 11–13, 14 (Mays); 1–3, 4–10, 11–13, 14 (Davies); 1–3, 4–7, 8–10, 11–13, 14 (Rudolph); 1–8, 9–14 (Andersen and Freedman); 1–3, 4–6, 7–8, 9–10, 11–13, 14 (Stuart); 1–14 (Macintosh); 1–2, 3–6, 7, 8–10, 11–14 (Yee); 1–4, 5–13, 14 (Sweeney); 1–6, 7–14 (Dearman). I find Mays' division most persuasive.

1–3, 14a?), political values (vv. 4a, 8–10) and religious worship (vv. 4b–6, 11–13) must mirror her covenantal relationship with Yahweh.

The first oracle (vv. 1–3) sets the scene, depicting Israel's failure of moral obligation to the one with whom she stands in relationship. The core problem is faithlessness. Israel's fundamental sin includes violation of ברית and rebellion against the תורה (8:1b). This obvious charge makes explicit what is implicit in 6:7 and 4:6. Earlier, we have observed that Hosea uses ברית (6:7) to represent the solemn commitment of Yahweh to Israel and of Israel to Yahweh.[65] We have also noted that Hosea, like other prophets, delivers תורה (4:6) in the form of ethico-religious instruction.[66] As Mays notes, instruction (תורה, in parallel with ברית) represents the policy which Yahweh has promulgated as the covenant's stipulation.[67] Although Hosea knows of a written tradition of תורה (v. 12), his use of the term always implies more than simply individual instructions. On the one hand, תורה describes the attitude and conduct of חסד, and yet mediates the entire דעת אלהים (4:6).[68] The people, the family members of Yahweh (בית יהוה),[69] are to incorporate with ברית and תורה. But they have revolted (פשע) against his תורה and walk away (עבר) from his ברית instead.

The people's cry in verse 2, לי יזעקו, at first sight contradicts the censure of the people for not calling upon Yahweh in 7:14a. However, 7:14b makes it clear that their appeal is only for food and protection. Their words and deeds are in direct contradiction. Though they say אלהי they break his ברית, and though they claim ידענו they rebel against his תורה.[70] Simply, this contradiction is between orthopraxis and orthodoxy. In other words, "to know Yahweh is both to have a right view of him and to enjoy a close relationship with him."[71] Their claim appears to be superficial and ridiculous. In fact, what Yahweh knows is that Israel does not know him (cf.

---

65. [[See pp. 210–211.]]
66. [[See pp. 181–182.]]
67. Mays, *Hosea*, 116.
68. Wolff, *Hosea*, 138.
69. Some regard this as a reference to Yahweh's temple in Samaria or Jerusalem. For the former see Eidevall, *Grapes in the Desert*, 127. For the latter see Yee, *Composition and Tradition*, 288.
70. Mays, *Hosea*, 116.
71. Davies, *Hosea*, 198.

5:3–4).⁷² Israel's lack of commitment to right relationships is demonstrated by her rejection of the "good" (טוב) in verse 3. The meaning of טוב is broad in scope, but the context denotes conduct in conformity with the ברית and תורה mentioned in verse 1b.⁷³ It bears noting that Amos uses טוב not only as a surrogate for Yahweh, but equates טוב with משפט (Amos 4:15), while Micah associates טוב in parallel with משפט and חסד (Micah 6:8). Perhaps Hosea uses the term in its broadest sense, which includes goodness of life under the covenant (3:5; 2:8; cf. Deut 5:33; 6:24; 10:12; 26:11). On the other hand, it could be that Hosea chooses to concentrate on the source – right relationship with Yahweh – of which the ultimate offshoot is justice in relations towards fellow humans. When Yahweh is no more a friend⁷⁴ or covenant lord, in effect he becomes a foe of Israel. An enemy, possibly the Assyrians, will pursue them to their doom (v. 3b), the rod of Yahweh's chastisement.

Israel's relational faithlessness is elucidated in verse 4 in two directions. The first concerns Israel's monarchy, whereas the second deals with her cult. The nation's rejection of the טוב, ברית and תורה has left them with "man-made governments and gods."⁷⁵ Yahweh distances himself from the royal court of Samaria whose succession of coups has been dictated by lies and treachery (7:3). The expressions, לא ממני and לא ידעתי, accentuate the disruption of relational dynamics between Yahweh and Israel. Yahweh's rebuff, however, is not of kingship *per se*, but of the mechanisms for running the palace independent of Yahweh. The theme resumes in verses 8–10, where Israel is assessed in the sphere of international politics (cf. 7:8–16).⁷⁶ Here Israel is likened to a useless vessel (ככלי אין־חפץ בו) which has no value to the nations (v. 8). The nation's expedition for alliance with Assyria is further portrayed as a wild ass wandering alone (פרא בודד), searching for lovers (v. 9). Most interpreters suggest that the figure depicts the stubborn-

---

72. Landy, *Hosea*, 102.

73. Wolff, *Hosea*, 138; Sweeney, *Twelve Prophets*, 87.

74. In treaty terminology, as Moran has shown, טוב can mean "friendship, good relations." William L. Moran, "A Note on the Treaty Terminology of the Sefire Stelas," *JNES* 22 (1963): 173–176 (174).

75. Mays, *Hosea*, 117.

76. The historical events probably relate to the period of Hoshea's rule. See Hayes and Kuan, "The Final Years," 179–181. See also our discussion on pp. 102–103.

ness of Israel (who wilfully departs the covenant relationship with Yahweh in favour of independence) and the miserable, forlorn condition of the nation.[77] This observation has more weight when viewed from a relational perspective. Desiring independence, wandering away from Yahweh, and looking for the company of others is gravely negative.

The second direction of Israel's relational disloyalty concerns the man-made gods (vv. 5–6). The statement of verse 4b, "with their silver and gold, they made idols for themselves," echoes "silver I lavished upon her and gold which they made into a Baal (2:10)."[78] The concern of verses 5–6 is particularly with Samaria's bull image, whereas verses 11–13 concentrates on Israel's syncretistic altars and sacrifices. Yahweh laments "Israel's inability to live in innocence, free of the deeds that disqualify for relation to God."[79] Ephraim's many altars to expiate sin become altars for sinning (v. 11), leading the people to shun the law of Yahweh (v. 12). Both oracles are rounded off by Yahweh's chastisement. The calf in Samaria will be smashed (v. 6b) and their guilt will cost them a return to Egypt (v. 13b), once again reversing the exodus event.

The two proverbial sayings in verse 7 summarise Israel's foolish and self-destructive course of action. By one's action or behaviour, one creates a domain with built-in consequences of fortune as well as misfortune. In place of "sowing" seed, Israel has sown the "wind" (רוח). As a result, they will be "reaping" an increased wind-force of storm or whirlwind (סופה) (v. 7a).[80] The word רוח can mean "an empty, vain thing" (cf. 12:2; Ps. 78:39; Isa 41:29) which is conveyed in the second simile, reinforcing the metaphor of sowing and reaping. "Standing grain without bud (צמח) will produce no flour (קמח)" (v. 7b). Rudolph succinctly puts the main point

---

77. So Harper, *Amos and Hosea*, 318; Mays, *Hosea*, 121; Andersen and Freedman, *Hosea*, 505. For an alternative interpretation, see Stuart A. Irvine, "Politics and Prophetic Commentary in Hosea 8:8–10," *JBL* 114 (1995): 292–294.
78. As observed by Yee, *Composition and Tradition*, 190.
79. Mays, *Hosea*, 119.
80. Andersen and Freedman, *Hosea*, 481, 497, Stuart, *Hosea–Jonah*, 127, 133 and Garrett, *Hosea, Joel*, 184, see the metaphor of "sowing wind" as quite unnatural, and offer the translation: "They sow in a wind and they reap in a storm." However, this suggestion undercuts the force of the metaphor. As Eidevall, *Grapes in the Desert*, 130, notes, "the utterance becomes quite pointless."

thus: "aus Nichts wird Nichts."[81] What fails in the beginning denies the possibility of success at the end. Israel's relational faithlessness makes the success of the nation's politics and cult a practical impossibility.

A concomitant issue that must be addressed for the purposes of this study is the social aspect of verse 14a. The topic shifts from politics and altars to palaces (היכלות) and fortified cities (ערים בצרות). Many consider this verse to be a redactional addition, particularly on account of the reference to Judah and its close resemblance to Amos 1:3–2:5.[82] Yet there is no compelling reason to regard the text as "secondary" or to disqualify it as a fitting conclusion to the section 8:1–13.[83] In fact, the verse links well to parts of 8:1–13.[84] Most likely, the building activity reflects the social reality during the reigns of Jeroboam II in the north and Uzziah in the south.[85] As Premnath has shown, to the prophets (cf. Amos 3:9–11; 6:1–3), "cities symbolised the malady that afflicted the society. They were painfully aware of the effects of the urban paraphernalia on the lives of the poor."[86] Under the guise of national security, Israel and Judah have proliferated palaces and walled cities. These palatial dwellings are classic examples of the elite's indulgence to provide for their political security.[87] The fortresses (ארמון) are residential quarters of special strength, which belonged to the richer citizens or the king.[88] Prophets recognise the adverse effects of such undertakings, "the exploitation of the work force and the infringement of citizen's rights."[89] For Hosea, such recourse to building operations means not only relational faithlessness to Yahweh but also injustice to fellow citizens. Such self-delusive defence purposes are doomed to destruction by the fire of

---

81. Rudolph, *Hosea*, 165.
82. Harper, *Amos and Hosea*, 324; Knight, *Hosea*, 93; Emmerson, *Hosea*, 74–77.
83. Wolff, *Hosea*, 136, 146; Mays, *Hosea*, 124; Sweeney, *Twelve Prophets*, 92.
84. Israel's forgetfulness (v. 14a) contrasts with divine remembrance (v. 13b) while the theme of "eating/devouring" (אכל) provides a link between vv. 13a and 14b. See Eidevall, *Grapes in the Desert*, 138. Moreover, the occurrence of the root עשה in v. 14a ("his Maker") recalls vv. 4b ("they made") and 6a ("a workman made"). See Yee, *Composition and Tradition*, 190–191.
85. See Andersen and Freedman, *Hosea*, 196–197 and Macintosh, *Hosea*, 333.
86. Premnath, "Amos and Hosea," 120. See p. 107 of this study.
87. Premnath, *Eighth Century Prophets*, 123.
88. Davies, *Hosea*, 221.
89. Andersen and Freedman, *Hosea*, 512.

Yahweh. This suggests that Israel's relational failure extends over all spheres of life: moral, social, political and religious.

To sum up what has been discussed so far, the central issue in 6:4–8:14 is irresponsibility in relationships. In 6:4–6, Yahweh laments Israel and Judah's fleeting relational virtues חסד and דעת אלהים. Both concepts primarily denote faithfulness in relationship with Yahweh and fellow humans. Worship is there and so are sacrifices, but the qualities that give worship its value are lacking. With the theme of ברית, the prophet recapitulates the people's relational faithlessness in 6:7–7:2. The covenant refers to the exclusive faithfulness to Yahweh and loyal conduct within the community. Again, the people have failed to live up to this expected responsibility. In 7:3–7, the prophet exposes the ruptured and hostile relationships in the national leadership whereas 7:8–16 discloses Israel's disloyal actions in international politics. Indeed, Ephraim fails to remain true to Yahweh, her social, political and religious lives totally negate the character of Yahweh. The discourse in 8:1–14 reiterates the people's relational faithlessness by elaborating on themes from previous discourses. The people who must keep the ברית violate it. The ones who are meant to incorporate תורה have revolted against it. The nation which should enjoy a close relationship with Yahweh has walked away from it. This is the prophet's dilemma and so, too, what hurts Yahweh the most.

Chastisement (9:1–10:15)

There is scholarly consensus that chapter 9 begins a new scene. The dominant feature of this section (9:1–10:15) is Yahweh's looming chastisement described in various ways. We have argued that the dominant theme in the previous section (6:4–8:14) is Yahweh's accusation of Israel's irresponsibility interspersed with laconic statements of threatened judgment. Now the reverse is noticeable in the way that the diverse descriptions of chastisement are interspersed with concise baseline accusations of irresponsibility. The graphic image of chastisements, however, has been superseded by the theme of restoration in 11:1–11. In agreement with the majority of exegetes,⁹⁰ the passages 9:1–9; 9:10–17; 10:1–8; 10:9–15 will be treated as sub-units within the larger section 9:1–10:15. Following this basic structure, we will argue that the core reason that brings Yahweh's chastisement is injustice or disloyalty in relationships.

From Days of Celebrations to Days of Dispersion (9:1–9)

Yahweh's speech in chapter 8 ends with prediction of judgment (8:14). The prophetic discourse in 9:1–9, which presents a case against the people in Yahweh's name, proceeds to and ends with pronouncements of chastisement. A divine speech in the first person resumes at verse 10 with a retrospective style.⁹¹ As the train of thought of this subunit reflects a flashback to the themes of earlier discourses (especially Hos 1–4) it may be wise to tie together the two lines in our analysis of the passage.

Hosea, first of all, employs one of his staple criticisms of the people – "harlotry against God" – as a reference point for the impending chastisement. The expression כי זנית מעל אלהיך (v. 2) strongly echoes 1:2 and 4:12.⁹² Relational faithlessness remains intact as Hosea's central charge.

1:2	the (feminine) land (of Israel) commits harlotry	מאחרי יהוה
4:12	the people commit harlotry	מתחת אלהיהם
9:1	the (corporate) Israel commits harlotry	מעל אלהיך

The land (and Gomer), people and Israel, in whatever roles, have all abandoned their relationships with Yahweh. "Harlotry" is necessarily conceived of as a generic notion for disloyalty in relationship and hence punishment is justified for their failure to maintain it.

The next important intratextual connection, in the second place, comes with the terminology of "harlotry" and "wages." The expression, "you have loved a harlot's wage (אתנן), on every threshing floor (כל־גרנות)

---

90. So Wolff, *Hosea*, 149–189; Andersen and Freedman, *Hosea*, 515–573; Jeremias, *Hosea*, 119–138; Davies, *Hosea*, 211–250; Stuart, *Hosea–Jonah*, 138–172; Macintosh, *Hosea*, 335–435; Garrett, *Hosea, Joel*, 177.
91. Stuart, *Hosea–Jonah*, 140.
92. See Dearman, *Hosea*, 236.

[you have loved] grain (דגן)" (9:1b), strongly echoes Israel's passionate concern for commodities portrayed by the wayward wife in 2:7, 14. The contents of gifts from Gomer's lovers (2:14) are food and water, wool and flax, oil and drink (2:7). In this light, it is not difficult to see Hosea's point which draws the connection between commodity concerns and harlotry. Threshing floors were places where harvest reached its final stage and were normally built on higher ground in order to facilitate the wind's action in winnowing.[93] They are often associated with achievement and cheerfulness (cf. Ruth 3; Judg 21:16–24). Hosea's negative assessment, however, suggests otherwise. It is possible that the threshing floor, to the prophet, serves as a place for injustice. As such, the "harlot's hire" in the context of harvest can be read "as the share of agricultural product given to the landowners as rent in kind."[94] Given the deep moral sickness of the society, it is not unreasonable to suppose that Hosea's polemic is primarily levelled against the landowners (possibly the royalty, elite administrators and leading priests), who love to exact shares from every threshing floor (cf. Amos 5:11).

Israel's cultic celebration is branded as being on the same level as that of other nations (v. 1a) because it adores Yahweh as though he were Baal.[95] As Harvey has shown, Hosea does not reject "joy and gladness" (שמח and גיל) in the mighty acts of God as such (cf Joel 1:16–17; 2:21–27; Isa 42:10–13; 48:20; 54:1). Yet שמח and גיל, with any form of ritual that compels God's action or forces his favour, is condemned.[96] Thus, their exuberant rejoicing, which nurtures the carefree preoccupation with immediate self-indulgence, must now be put to an end. This anti-celebration theme, as a third link, leads us to one of Hosea's lines of attack, namely, negation of the negation. Israel's behaviour that negates just relationship with Yahweh will be bitterly negated. Strikingly, the discourse contains a series of negatives:[97]

---

93. Macintosh, *Hosea*, 338–339.
94. Premnath, *Eighth Century Prophets*, 136.
95. Mays, *Hosea*, 126.
96. See Dorothea W. Harvey, "Rejoice not, O Israel," in *Israel's Prophetic Heritage: essays in honor of James Muilenburg*, eds. B. Anderson and W. Harrelson (London: SCM Press, 1962): 116–127.
97. As observed by Landy, *Hosea*, 111.

9:	1a	"do *not* rejoice"	אל־תשמח
	2a	". . . will *not* sustain them"	לא ירעם
	3a	"they will *not* dwell"	לא ישבו
	4a	"they will *not* pour out"	לא־יסכו
	4a	"their sacrifices will *not* be sweet"	לא יערבו
	4b	"it will *not* enter"	לא יבוא

These powerful, repetitive "nots," in essence, represent the termination of relationship (cf. 1:4, 6, 9; 2:4, 6; 3:4). Hosea seems to allude to the festival of Yahweh and its attendant feast of סכות (Booths/Tabernacles). The יום מועד (Exod 23:15; Lev 23:2) and the חג־יהוה יום (Lev 23:39) are means by which Israel expresses her sound relation to Yahweh, which should be cherished with utmost joyfulness (Lev 23:40; Deut 16:14). However, the prophet's rhetorical question, מה־תעשו ליום מועד וליום הג־יהוה (v. 5), only intends to highlight the reversal of the scenario. In other words, the point is to turn a proclamation of joy into a lamentation. Landy has plausibly observed that Hosea is developing an anti-festival/anti-pilgrimage theme. The הג־יהוה and חג־הסכות are the moments of rejoicing over the products of the land (Deut 16:10–15).

> But this is an anti-festival, when joy is turned to mourning, libations are not poured out, sacrifices are not sweet, and the harvest is not brought into the house of Yahweh. . . . This is an anti-pilgrimage; instead of dwelling in the Yahweh's land, Israel returns to Egypt and goes to Assyria, where it eats 'defiled' bread. Sacred history is reversed: if Egypt is the antonym of Yahweh's land, then the return, marked by a wordplay between 'dwell'(ישבו) and 'return'(שב), results in a parody.[98]

For the purposes of this study, it suffices to identify a chain of chastisements described in verses 2–6. First, Yahweh, the divine rightful owner (cf. 2:10), will suspend the products of the personified גרן and יקב that people

---

98. Landy, *Hosea*, 111.

sought as their "harlot's wage." They will not "befriend" them (רעה),⁹⁹ but will deceive (כחש) them instead (v. 2). A failed harvest is in view. Second, Yahweh, the owner of the land (cf. Lev 25:23), will expel them from the land (cf. 2:10). Third, the expulsion necessarily entails exile in foreign lands. Those who are unfit for residence in the holy land have no other choice but to eat defiled food in Egypt and Assyria. The sacrifice that has characterised Israel's existence alongside Yahweh will finally cease (v. 4). The fourth and final disaster depicts a state of being gathered for burial (v. 6a). Destruction (שד) ravages their land. It is highly unlikely that the people will escape their coming defeat and exile (v. 3), but even if (כי) they do, their flight will be an escape to death.¹⁰⁰ The terse, threatened judgment of 8:13b will come to reality in reversing salvation history. A place treated with disdain by their ancestors to entomb their bones (cf. Gen 47:29; Exod 13:19) will become their only lot as Egypt will collect them (תקבצם), and Memphis will bury them (תקברם) (v. 6a). The shrine or idols made with silver (cf. 2:10; 8:4; 13:2) and festival "tents" will be inherited by "thorns" and "thistles" (cf. 2:5b, 8, 14), instead of their children (v. 6b).

Though the text of verses 7–9 is difficult,¹⁰¹ the primary concern is detectable, and that is the prophet-people relationship. By making use of the opposition he experiences, the prophet ushers in further assertion of chastisement. In so doing, Hosea reaffirms two things. First, the divine judgment is surely on its way. The second concerns the depravity of Israel. Interestingly, the theme of judgment frames this unit. The punishment (פקדה) and recompense (שלום) in verse 7a correspond to the remembrance (זכר) of wickedness (עון) and visitation (פקד) of sins (חטאת) in verse 9b.

---

99. Wolff, *Hosea*, 149. Two translations are possible with the verb רעה. רעה I means "to pasture", "graze" (of flocks). רעה II means "to associate with", or "to accompany" someone (*BDB*, 444–445). See Helmut Utzschneider, *Hosea Prophet vor dem Ende* (OBO 41; Göttingen: Vandenhoeck & Ruprecht, 1980), 155–156, who discusses different options. Given Hosea's concern about relationship, the latter sense seems to serve the context 9:2 best. Hosea's point is that Israel's trust is misplaced and her miscalculation is bound to end in disappointment. See also Eidevall, *Grapes in the Desert,* 140–141.

100. Mays, *Hosea*, 128; Hubbard, *Hosea*, 158; Sweeney, *Twelve Prophets,* 96.

101. Many critics express this frustration. For instance, Margaret S. Odell, "Who were the Prophets in Hosea?," *HBT* 18 (1996): 78–95, 83, declares that this passage is "the most difficult in the entire book of Hosea." Harper, *Hosea,* 332, also expresses that it is "almost hopelessly confused." Wolff, *Hosea,* 156, too, concedes that 9:8a is "one of the most difficult passages in Hosea."

The *days* of visitation/recompense also contrasts the joyful repetitive *day* of festivals in verse 5. Simply, God's judgement is inescapable. Instead of joyful days, there will only be terrifying days of judgement.

The phrase אויל הנביא משגע איש הרוח in verse 7b is best understood, with most commentators, as a quotation of a derogatory remark by the people (or some group of addressees) in response to Hosea's verdict of divine judgment in verse 7a.[102] The point is clarified by the ensuing response by the prophet (v. 7c). With the recurrent themes of "iniquity" (עון) and "hostility" (משטמה) (cf. v. 9b and v. 8b respectively), which Hosea has personally seen or experienced, he affirms his earlier accusation of the people and justifies their verdict (vv. 7a and 9b). It is likely that Hosea, a prophetic watchman over Israel with God (v. 8a), is here portrayed as a hunted bird (v. 8b).[103] To seek a refuge even at the holy place (or land) is impossible for him because the בית אלהיו is described as an arena for hatred (v. 8b).[104]

Verse 9 summarises the whole speech by comparing the depth of moral sickness of the time to Israel's darkest hour in history. Apparently, the phrase כימי הגבעה alludes to the grisly story told in Judges 19–21 where the entire episode is characterised by rape and murder.[105] The expression "they have sunk deep into corruption" (העמיקו־שחתו v. 9a)[106] condenses Israel's wickedness and relational injustice. As in 5:2, the emphasis is on moral perversion which intends to bring harm (שחת) to others. The people who have a horrible history of attacking the Levite are now against the prophet.[107] It is possible that Hosea also has in mind the internecine strife addressed in previous discourses (7:3–7). The moral bankruptcy and depravity of Ephraim cannot and should not go on simply because it is not

---

102. For example,. Wolff, *Hosea*, 156–157. Other alternatives have been suggested. For instance, Odell, "Who were the Prophets?" 83–84, reads it as the people's outburst in frustration against the prophets who have misled them, whereas Dearman, *Hosea*, 248, interprets it as a charge by Hosea against prophets who mislead the people. Still others even think that it is the prophet himself who claims to be mad and senseless because of the people's sin and the disaster he foresees (Landy, *Hosea*, 115 and Garrett, *Hosea, Joel*, 196).

103. As with most commentators.

104. Eidevall, *Grapes in the Desert*, 143.

105. Again with most commentators.

106. After Macintosh, *Hosea*, 357. Literally: "they have made deep, they have corrupted."

107. Wolff, *Hosea*, 158.

able to be ignored by the all-seeing Yahweh. He surely remembers their guilt and will call them to account for their sins (v. 9b; cf. 8:13).

From Grapes in the Desert to Barrenness (9:10–17)

The divine speech that begins at 9:10 demarcates a new discourse (vv. 10–17). One way to analyse the text is to see the subunit as having a two-part parallel structure, each divine speech followed by prophetic interjection: verses 10–14 and 15–17.[108] Another approach is to trace an elaborate chiastic structure (A-B-C-D-E-D'-C'-B'-A') in the discourse.[109] With either of the approaches employed, the message is another depiction of Israel's faithlessness and the coming judgement in the strongest terms possible. The passage is primarily characterised by two lines of contrasting features: election (v. 10a) and rejection (v. 17), apostasy (vv. 10b, 15) and judgement (vv. 11–13, 16).

The two evocative similes in verse 10a, "like grapes in the desert" and "like early figs on the fig tree," set a baseline of accusation for the people. The first simile appears to be a paradox, something impossible for which various attempts have been made to find a possible solution.[110] Yet the paradox, as Eidevall argues, needs no solution, for "the election of Israel is presented as a miracle."[111] Simply, it describes Yahweh's perspective, suggesting that there existed in the past an ideal relationship between Yahweh and his people with unreserved satisfaction and delight (cf. 2:16–25).[112]

Significantly, Eidevall has pointed out that it is the "quality" of the people's ancestors that is likened to delectable fruits. In light of Jeremiah 8:13, Isaiah 5:1–7 and Micah 7:1–2, he plausibly argues that "grapes" and "figs" stand figuratively for desirable acts and attitudes – the idea of righteousness, or for a righteous person. Eidevall substantiates his argument with the Hittite document, *Telepinus myth*, where the sweet contents of

---

108. For example, Wolff, *Hosea*, 162; Heinz-Dieter Neef, *Die Heilstraditionen Israels in der Verkündigung des Propheten Hosea* (BZAW 169; Berlin: Walter de Gruyter, 1987), 68–69.
109. For example, Andersen and Freedman, *Hosea*, 539; Garrett, *Hosea, Joel*, 198.
110. See Rudolph, *Hosea*, 185; Andersen and Freedman, *Hosea*, 539–540; Davies, *Hosea*, 226.
111. Eidevall, *Grapes in the Desert*, 149.
112. Macintosh, *Hosea*, 363.

figs, olives and grapes are compared with the attitude of faithfulness towards a divine king.[113] If this line of thought is correct, Yahweh's "finding" (מצא) and "seeing" (ראה) of Israel as delectable fruits denotes a people meant to be faithful and upright.

The brief nostalgic element of Israel's idyllic past, however, is quickly eclipsed by the divine dismay over Israel's immorality, first embraced at Baal-Peor (v. 10b; cf. Num 25).[114] Faithlessness to Yahweh involves commitment to something else: "they consecrated themselves to Shame" (וינזרו לבשת v. 10b). Hosea's choice of the verb נזר is probably ironic, alluding to a Nazirite who whole-heartedly consecrates himself to the uncompromising service of Yahweh (Num 6:1–21).[115] In contrast, the object of Israel's devotion is Shame, a polemical slur on the Baal of Peor.[116]

The horrific transformation from being delectable to abominable (שקוצים) fruits has serious consequences. Ephraim's glory (כבודם) is envisaged flying away like a bird (v. 11a). The כבוד can signify wealth and success in the first half of the eighth century BC (4:7; 10:5). It could also signify the gift of children (vv. 11b–12a),[117] and the divine presence ("I depart"[118] v. 12b).[119] As has been argued, Yahweh's withdrawal from his people is closely connected with defeat, starvation and exile, but here with sterility and bereavement: "no birth, no pregnancy and no conception," and "even if (כי אם) they rear children, I will bereave them of each one" (vv. 11b–12a). The pseudo-sorites (a train of thought which does not seem logical)[120] underscores the seriousness of the situation.[121]

The translation of verse 13a (אפרים כאשר־ראיתי לצור שתולה בנוה) is extremely difficult. Various emendations have been proposed, but without

---

113. Eidevall, *Grapes in the Desert*, 150–151; (*ANET*, 127).
114. Discussion of the site and any specific event or tradition is beyond the scope of this study.
115. Rudolph, *Hosea*, 185; Davies, *Hosea*, 227.
116. Macintosh, *Hosea*, 360; Dearman, *Hosea*, 252.
117. Mays, *Hosea*, 133; Jeremias, *Hosea*, 123; Andersen and Freedman, *Hosea*, 542.
118. The MT has בשורי. It is understood as a variant spelling of the verb סור ("depart").
119. See M. Weinfeld, "כָּבוֹד *kābôd*," *TDOT* 7: 22–37.
120. Andersen and Freedman, *Hosea*, 393.
121. See Richard D. Patterson, "An Overlooked Scriptural Paradox: The Pseudosorites," *JETS* 53 (2010): 19–36 (33).

any real justification.¹²² By drawing contextual support on verses 10–14, however, it is possible that verse 13a paints an idyllic picture. As 9:10 contrasts delectable fruit with distasteful fruit, so 9:13a counterpoints between a pleasant planting and the death of children.¹²³ Verse 13b and verse 14 elaborate on the refrain of verses 11–12, the demise of the future generation. The peculiar prophetic prayer in verse 14 brings about a reversal of Israel's fertility blessings (Deut 28:4, 11; Exod 23:36). Instead of "blessings of the breasts (שׁדים) and the womb (רחם)" (Gen 49:25), Yahweh will give the people a "miscarrying womb and dry breasts."¹²⁴

Verses 15–17 reiterate the themes and form of verses 10–14. The expression "all evil" (כל־רעתם) in verse 15 is comprehensive. As to what exactly is referred to in Gilgal, we can no longer speak with certainty. It could refer to Israel's rebellion in the distant past (cf. 1 Sam 11:14–15), or socio-political violence (cf. 5:1–7; 6:7–11), or cultic impurity (cf. 4:15 and 12:11) in the recent past.¹²⁵ The vocabulary of "hate" (שׂנא) and "love" (אהב) in juxtaposition to שׂרים indicates Israel's rebellion (סרר) against the supremacy of Yahweh.¹²⁶ The rejection is that of the sovereign for the vassal. On the other hand, the language, in light of "I will drive them out of my house" (cf. Deut 24:3), "I will love them no more," (cf. 1:6), may also be understood as referring to a failed marriage.¹²⁷ The household metaphor seems at work as Yahweh is a driving out family member from the house.¹²⁸ In either case, the point offers grounds for judgment.

---

122. For a summary of options, see Macintosh, *Hosea*, 370–372. See also Thomas E. McComiskey, "Hos 9:13 and the Integrity of the Masoretic Tradition in the Prophecy of Hosea," *JETS* 33 (1990): 155–160.

123. Dearman, *Hosea*, 254.

124. Stuart, *Hosea–Jonah*, 153. See also Deborah Krause, "A Blessing Cursed: The Prophet's Prayer for Barren Womb and Dry Breasts in Hosea 9," in *Reading between Texts: Intertextuality and the Hebrew Bible*, ed. D. N. Fewell (Louisville: Westminster/John Knox, 1992), 191–202.

125. Discussions for options, see Wolff, *Hosea*, 167; Mays, *Hosea*, 137; Davies, *Hosea*, 230; Macintosh, *Hosea*, 376; Dearman, *Hosea*, 255.

126. See Norbert Lohfink, "Hate and love in Osee 9:15," *CBQ* 25 (1963): 417. In this case "my house" is a metaphor for the land.

127. Macintosh, *Hosea*, 377; Sweeney, *Twelve Prophets*, 101–102.

128. Dearman, *Hosea*, 257.

In verse 16, the speech returns to a fertility image, depicting Ephraim as a tree which has been struck down (נכה), whose roots wither away (יבש) and are put to death (מות). The topic of the metaphor hence is barrenness (v. 16b).[129] Simply, there will be no reproduction. It is highly unlikely that the blighted nation has the ability to have children. "Even if" (גם כי) the women manage to give birth to descendants, those "precious offspring of their wombs" will be killed by Yahweh. Israel's election (cf. v. 10) evolves into rejection (מאס v. 17). Their state of wandering among the nations as a result of Yahweh's rejection contrasts with Yahweh's finding them like grapes in the desert.

From Luxuriant Vines to Poisonous Weeds (10:1–8)

A shift of focus from Gilgal to Samaria, a designation from Ephraim to Israel and a divine speech to a third-person prophetical speech indicates a new literary unit that begins at 10:1. While Rudolph treats 10:1–8 as a collection of miscellaneous sayings,[130] Jeremias sees it as a well-planned symmetrical composition: verses 1–2 and 8 deal with altars and sacred pillars, verses 3–4 and 7 with the king, and verses 5–6 with the calf image.[131] As will be noted below, the structure adopted by Jeremias features the theme of chastisement very well, as the wrath of Yahweh falls upon all significant institutions of Israel: "altar and pillar, king and capital, idol and high place."[132] On the other hand, the unity of the passage could also be maintained, as Wolff has suggested, with accusation predominating in verses 1–2a, 3–5 and threat in verses 2b, 6–8.[133] For the purposes of this study, it would be worth exploring the two specific accusations in verses 1–4.

This section begins with a depiction of Israel's recent flourishing situation with a view to exposing its negative influence on the present. Israel

---

129. Eidevall, *Grapes in the Desert*, 154.
130. Rudolph, *Hosea*, 190, sees three originally separate units in the passage: 1–2, 3–4 and 5–8.
131. See Jeremias, *Hosea*, 127.
132. Mays, *Hosea*, 138.
133. Wolff, *Hosea*, 172.

is now represented as a "luxuriant" or "prolific"[134] vine that produces fruit only for itself (10:1a). Perhaps the text alludes to the period of prosperity under Jeroboam II.[135] It is clear that the prosperity in itself is not the object of the criticism, but the misuse of it. In verse 1, the growth of wealth (כרב לפריו) is paralleled by the multiplication (רבה) of adorned altars (מזבחות). The better the land produces, the better sacred pillars (מצבות) are built. In fact, 8:11 has already described the proliferation of מזבח as a source of increasing sinfulness. Hence the utterance in verse 1 is an implicit accusation against Israel's "fruitfulness" in terms of syncretistic and idolatrous cult.

A more explicit accusation comes in verse 2 with the expression "their heart is false" (חלק לבם). The people have not given their hearts to Yahweh in moral uprightness. The antithesis to חלק "false," "divided" may be אמת "faithfulness," אמנה "trustworthiness" and חסד "loyalty" (2:21f; 4:1; 6:6; 10:4).[136] Along this line, the statements in verse 3 are best understood as the prophet representing the people speaking,[137] rather than as words Hosea expects the people to speak in the future as a result of judgment.[138] The prophet could accurately decipher the actual or imagined words of the people (cf. 2:7; 4:4; 8:2; 9:7; 13:10) based on the socio-political situation at hand. Accordingly, the statement אין מלך לנו כי לא יראנו את־יהוה conceivably reflects the dynastic instability and social chaos during Hosea's day, particularly depicting the king's impotence in installing a just society.[139] The theme of verse 2aα ("false heart") is resumed in verse 4. What the nation desperately needs is a strong government that offers protection and

---

134. This translation is based on the LXX (ἄμπελος εὐκληματοῦσα) and Arabic cognate *bqq*. The MT בוקק means "to empty" or "lay waste." Most interpreters, in light of the theme of "multiplying," feel that the rendering "lay waste" is impossible in this context.
135. Davies, *Hosea*, 233.
136. Wolff, *Hosea*, 174.
137. Dearman, *Hosea*, 262.
138. Wolff, *Hosea*, 175.
139. It is conceivable that "we have no king" (אין מלך לנו) refers to the death of one king in Samaria, while the rhetorical question "what can he do for us?" (מה־יעשה־לנו) anticipates the enthronement of another. See Utzschneider, *Hosea*, 122. It is also possible that the former phrase can be perceived as hyperbole that conveys the sense "it is as if we have no king," indicating the king's ineffective power, whereas the latter phrase can be seen to be a variant of the first. See Macintosh, *Hosea*, 393.

justice. Yet what the people get is what appears to be superficial justice: speaking (fine) words (דברו דברים), swearing emptily (אלות שוא) and making covenants (כרת ברית).[140] The משפט "justice" in verse 4b (cf. 5:1, 11; 6:5) refers to the erosion of the administration of justice and order.[141]

The משפט that the king is supposed to have provided has actually turned out to be deceit. "Poisonous weeds" (ראש) – in this case injustice – sprouts (פרח) luxuriantly in a food-producing field. As Fleischer has shown, the simile of deadly weed stresses two aspects of the perverted justice: its sweeping diffusion among the people and its physical as well as psychological harmfulness.[142] This line of reading is supported by Amos's condemnation of the Israelites for "turning justice into a poisonous plant (ראש)" (Amos 6:12). Further, the "Song of the Vineyard" provides another example. In Isaiah 5:1–7, Yahweh's looking for "grapes" from his vineyard but getting "wild grapes" is paralleled with his seeking of "justice" (משפט) and "righteousness" (צדקה) but finding only "bloodshed" (משפח) and "outcry" (צעקה). The core message of Hosea is simple: Israel worships her calf instead of promoting fidelity and justice, that is, faithlessness to God and to fellow humans. It suffices to say that Hosea's social concern is indeed far from less than his fellow prophets who have been well known for their candid quest of justice.

As a result of religious apostasy and moral depravity, each significant institution in Israel will come to an end. The total destruction of altars and pillars will come when Yahweh's chastisement breaks (ערף) and destroys (שדד) them all (v. 2b). The verb ערף ("break the neck") describes the devastation in terms of killing animals. The places of animal sacrifice will now be treated as animals bound for slaughter.[143] Though the residents of Samaria lament (גור "be afraid") its disappearance, and though the priests "bewail" (אבל) its departure, the calf statue of Beth-aven will be deported (vv. 5–6).

---

140. Stuart, *Hosea–Jonah*, 161.
141. Wolff, *Hosea*, 175; Andersen and Freedman, *Hosea*, 554; Davies, *Hosea*, 237; Macintosh, *Hosea*, 397; Dearman, *Hosea*, 264–265. There are other interpreters who read v. 4b as a prediction of coming divine judgment, e.g. Harper, *Hosea*, 346; Rudolph, *Hosea*, 193–195. However, with regard to the immediate context and with the intertextual support, the suggested reading is preferable.
142. G. Fleischer, "ראש *rōʾš* II," *TDOT* 13: 262–263.
143. Eidevall, *Grapes in the Desert*, 156.

The grim fate of the king is likened to foam on the surface of the water (v. 6). Royalty will not withstand the strong current of divine wrath by means of invading armies (v. 7).[144] All hope and expectation of securing good harvests and renewal of life are gone. The masses of thorns and thistles will invade sacred altars (v. 8; cf. 9:6). In their distress, those participating in the cultic practices invite the personified mountains and hills to consummate their longing for death: "Cover us!", "Fall over us!"

A Trained Heifer who Ploughs for Wickedness (10:9–15)

Yahweh's direct speech, the reappearance of "the days of Gibeah" as a point of contact and the internal literary unity, indicate that 10:8–15 is a separate unit. There is little dispute among scholars with regard to the division of the sub-units. The use of a war motif in 10:9–10 and 10:13b–15 forms an inclusio, framing an agricultural imagery in 10:11–13a.[145] This A-B-A pattern is reinforced by the catchword "war" (מלחמה) that occurs in verses 9 and 14.[146] More plainly, the enclosing passages (10:9–10 and 10:13b–15) are characterised by chastisements, whereas the centre (10:11–13a) could be seen as a depiction of Israel's ideal past to serve as criticism of her present depravity.

In fact, all the three oracles, as Holt has observed, have the identical point of reference, (i.e. either the distant or the most recent past). The first and final speeches, which share the theme of chastisement, can be matched as follows.[147]

9a	The sin of Gibeah and now		13b	The sins of the past
9b	War is on the way		14a	War has started
10a	The kind of war		14b	The kind of war
10b	The cause of war		15	The cause of war and its result

---

144. Jeremias, *Hosea*, 131.
145. Andersen and Freedman, *Hosea*, 563 and Davies, *Hosea*, 241.
146. Wolff, *Hosea*, 182 and Stuart, *Hosea*, 167.
147. Holt, *Prophesying the Past*, 77.

The text of verses 9–10 with a reference to Gibeah is difficult to follow. However, the intratextual support in 9:9 suggests an allusion to the events of Judges 19–21.[148] If so, Hosea's reference is related to the horror of sexual injustice and resulting civil war. Though much more cannot be said with any certainty, the verdict "Israel, you have sinned" (חטאת ישראל v. 9a)[149] provides a point (whatever events are in mind) in confirming Israel's ongoing sin in a familiar pattern.[150] The ensuing line "there they stood" (עמדו שם) asserts that Israel has maintained the Gibeah mind-set (v. 9a).[151] The closing phrase, בני עלוה (cf. עלוה v. 13),[152] "the sons of unrighteousness" (LXX τὰ τέκνα ἀδικίας), not only validates the war declared against the culprits in Gibeah, but also by analogy, relates to Israel's current perversity. If such is the case, the "double iniquity" (עון; Qere) refers to the past and present history tainted with injustice and violence.[153] As war was declared against the reprobates in Gibeah, so Yahweh has come to chastise (יסר) the perverse Israel (v. 10).

The judgment motif is elaborated more graphically in verses 13b–15. Israel's misplaced trust in military power results in the alarm of war which will demolish (שדד, cf. 7:13; 9:6; 10:2) all Samaria's fortifications (vv. 13b–14a). The identification of Shalman[154] and Beth-arbel,[155] and the specific events referred to in verse 14b are obscure. What had actually happened nonetheless appears to be clear in the mind of Hosea's audience. The prophet's point is to paint the looming judgment in the blackest terms

---

148. Rudolph, *Hosea*, 199–100, believes that the text alludes to the events in Judges 19–21 but this can be neither proved nor dismissed. Sweeney, *Twelve Prophets*, 107–108, provides a comprehensive analysis to correlate 10:9 with Judges 19–21.
149. LXX reads ἥμαρτεν Ισραηλ which seems more consistent with the literary form of vv. 9–11. Davies, *Hosea*, 244.
150. Dearman, *Hosea*, 268.
151. Garrett, *Hosea, Joel*, 215.
152. The term עלוה is probably a copyist's error for עולה as in 9:13 which means "injustice," "unrighteousness," "perversity," or "wickedness." See Dearman, *Hosea*, 269.
153. Thus Pentiuc, *Long-suffering Love*, 135.
154. Possible candidates include Shalmaneser III, the ninth-century Assyrian ruler, or Shalmaneser V (727–722) who conquered Samaria, or a Moabite ruler named Salamanu. See major commentaries.
155. Most scholars regard Beth-arbel to be a Galilean city where the modern Irbid is now located. See Davies, *Hosea*, 249; Garrett, *Hosea, Joel*, 217; Dearman, *Hosea*, 273.

possible. Mothers will be dashed in pieces alongside their children (v. 14b). The heart of Israel's darkness, Bethel, will be eradicated. The king will also be gone when chastisement rolls through the land (v. 15). In short, what the prophet projects is a war that is totally destructive.

At first sight, the oracle in verses 11–13a, which in itself does not deal with judgment, hardly fits the flow of the larger passage. However, the placement and choice of images appear to be intentional. As such, as Holt notes, "it illustrates the kind of sin [עולה] that called down Yahweh's punishment."[156] If this observation is correct, this passage is about Yahweh's election of Israel so as to disclose Israel's infidelity in maintaining justice in interpersonal relationships.

The metaphor in verse 11 has become a well-recognised image of the disobedience of the chosen nation.[157] The expression "a trained heifer who loves to thresh" (v. 11aα) depicts the nation as an animal which is obedient to the guidance of the farmer, Yahweh. The phrase, ואני עברתי על־טוב צוארה "I passed by the beauty of her neck"[158] (v. 11aβ) reflects Yahweh's discovery of something valuable.[159] The next line, Ephraim is harnessed to thresh, Judah[160] ploughs, Jacob tills (v. 11b), reflects the related steps of preparation for the actual cultivation, perhaps, to underline the people's weighty moral responsibility.[161] Noticeably, the topic of the metaphor is Israel's election as a call to service.[162] The task is spelled out in verse 12 with exhortations to

---

156. Holt, *Prophesying the Past*, 78. In fact, Mays, *Hosea*, 145, understands the term עולה in vv. 9 and 13 as a catch word.

157. See most commentaries.

158. Wolff, *Hosea*, 179, Jeremias, *Hosea*, 132 and Dearman, *Hosea*, 269. With small textual emendations, other scholars have arrived at a reading: "I laid a yoke on her fair neck." See Mays, *Hosea*, 144, Andersen and Freeman, *Hosea*, 560 and Stuart, *Hosea–Jonah*, 165.

159. Wolff, *Hosea*, 185 and Eidevall, *Grapes in the Desert*, 160.

160. Many scholars (e.g. Mays, *Hosea*, 145 and Emmerson, *Hosea*, 85–86) hold that Judah is an editorial insertion for an original "Israel." However, as Dearman, *Hosea*, 272, points out, if the horizon of the metaphor (from Hosea's point of view) constitutes the broad tribal kingdom before its division, both Judah and Jacob are appropriate referents. See also Wolff, *Hosea*, 185.

161. Eidevall, *Grapes in the Desert*, 162.

162. Wolff, *Hosea*, 185, Macintosh, *Hosea*, 420 and Holt, *Prophesying the Past*, 89–90. Holt, however, argues that what Hosea wants to tell is not *when* the people were called, but *that* they were called to service for Yahweh.

the people to fulfil their responsibilities of sowing, reaping and tilling. They are to "sow" (זרע) the seed of "righteousness" (צדקה) and "reap" (קצר) the fruit of "devoted fidelity" (חסד) by the transformation of breaking up their untilled ground (v. 12a). As such, Israel's election is in the service of צדקה and חסד. As pointed out elsewhere, צדקה and חסד constitute the essence of covenant ethos (4:1; 6:6).

Our analysis of the biblical concept in an earlier chapter has shown that צדקה/צדק is used with an ethical, forensic and or religious meaning.[163] However, it is essentially a relational term that denotes faithful action performed through and beyond the norms of conduct necessitated by right relationships. A righteous person preserves the peace and prosperity of the community and fulfils the demands of that communal relationship, whereas the unrighteous person does otherwise. The antitheses to צדק, among others, include רשע ("wrong," "injustice," or "wickedness") and עולה ("unrighteousness," "injustice," or "wickedness"), whereas its common parallels include אמן, חסד, and שלום, which designate the general condition of positive communal relationships.[164] צדק is precisely paralleled with חסד in verse 12a while it is contrasted with רשע and עולה (cf. v. 9) in verse 13a. This compelling contextual evidence allows us to infer the metaphor of 10:11–13a as a depiction of Hosea's moral concern. In fact, Reiterer has argued that צדקה/צדק in this text belongs to the group of concepts: משפט, חסד, אמונה, רחמים, and דעת (Hos 2:21–22). It denotes "the behaviour (as deed and/or as attitude) of the people" within interpersonal relationships. The people should treat each other decently and properly so that Yahweh would send his צדק (v. 12b).[165] However, Israel, who is called to sow the seed of righteousness, plants injustice instead. The one who is supposed to reap the fruit of fidelity secures wickedness, and so eats the fruit of deception (v. 13a). This conspicuously illustrates that, for Hosea, failure to maintain justice in communal relationships is exactly the kind of evil that has called down Yahweh's chastisement.

---

163. [[See pp. 76–88.]]
164. Johnson, "צָדֵק," *TDOT* 12: 246, 250 and J. Schreiner, "עֲוֹל, עַלְוָה," *TDOT* 10: 522–530 (525).
165. Friedrich V. Reiterer, *Gerechtigkeit als Heil: SDQ bei Deuterojesaja. Aussage und Vergleich mit der alttestamentlichen Tradition* (Graz: Akademische Druck, 1976), 151–153.

To sum up, the section (9:1–10:15) is dominated by Yahweh's various chastisements upon Israel because of her relational unfaithfulness. Largely, 9:1–9 deals with the chastisement of dispersion, while 9:10–17 concerns the judgment of infertility. Yahweh has withdrawn from the people and from their worship because they do not reflect that of his own. The withdrawal of his presence will leave the people with a failed harvest, a cessation of sacrifice, an expulsion from the land and death in a foreign land. As a result of evolving from delectable fruits to detestable fruits, Israel will face rejection, bereavement and sterility. The ensuing passages (10:1–8 and 10:9–15) depict a total destruction of both the sacred and political institutions of Israel. The misuse of wealth and the failure to serve the purpose of election bring about war that destroys everything. Importantly, there are two threads of accusation running through the passage which have actually called down Yahweh's chastisement, namely, religious infidelity and moral depravity. It is a failure to keep right relationship with God in terms of true worship, and a failure to keep right relationship with fellow humans in terms of maintaining justice and righteousness in the society.

Restoration (11:1–11)

There is a broad consensus that 11:1 marks a new pericope which is rounded off by a typical concluding formula נאם־יהוה in 11:11.[166] With regard to the internal division, some scholars argue for a twofold structure.[167] Others see four discernible smaller units: 1–4, 5–7, 8–9 and 10–11,[168] which can

---

166. See most modern commentaries. See also Ernst R. Wendland, *The Discourse Analysis of Hebrew Prophetic Literature: Determining the Larger Textual Units of Hosea and Joel* (MBPS 40; New York: Mellen Biblical Press, 1995), 111–112.
167. Wolff (*Hosea*, 193–196) sees a break at v. 8. While Jeremias, *Hosea*, 139–140, draws the line between v. 6 and v. 7, Andersen and Freedman, *Hosea*, 575, argue for a division of vv. 1–4 and vv. 5–11.
168. Yee, *Composition and Tradition*, 217–218; Eidevall, *Grapes in the Desert*, 166–167; Pentiuc, *Long-suffering Love*, 139. Cf. similarly Mays, *Hosea*, 151–152; Ben Zvi, *Hosea*, 228. Macintosh, *Hosea*, 436 and Kakkanattu, *God's Enduring Love*, 32, opt for a division of vv. 1–4, 5–6, 7, 8–9 and 10–11.

be read either to form a chiastic structure[169] or a sequential structure[170] (see below). Thematically, however, the same composition can be viewed as a having threefold structure in which verses 1–4 deals with the theme of responsibility, whereas verses 5–7 and 8–11 concern the chastisement and restoration respectively.[171] These observations can be summed up as follows.

Inclusio Structure	*Sequential Structure*	*Thematic Structure*
v. 1 out of Egypt	vv. 1–4 past	vv. 1–4 responsibility
v. 2 walk away from Yahweh	vv. 5–7 present/future	vv. 5–7 chastisement
v. 5 back to Egypt	vv. 8–9 interlude: divine deliberations	vv. 8–11 restoration
v. 10 walk behind Yahweh	vv. 10–11 future	
v. 11 out of Egypt		

The proposed thematic reading above exhibits the presence of Hosea's cyclical presentation of responsibility-chastisement-restoration within chapter 11. The retrospective element in verses 1–4 is not itself new in Hosea, but the presentation this time has a double purpose. On the one hand, the accusation of irresponsibility (vv. 2, 3b) lays the ground for chastisement of verses 5–7. On the other hand, the description of the divine unilateral affectionate deeds (vv. 1, 3a, 4) towards Israel forms the basis for the new element of restoration in verses 8–11.[172] Here the divine soliloquy leads to the total termination of Yahweh's relationship with his people.

Before moving to our study of this unit, it is necessary to comment briefly on the logical connection between the themes of chastisement and

---

169. Yee, *Composition and Tradition*, 217.
170. Eidevall, *Grapes in the Desert*, 167. Cf. similarly, Stuart, *Hosea–Joel*, 176. Yee, *Composition and Tradition*, 227 also speaks of a "three-part journey."
171. Cf. similarly Davies, *Hosea*, 250–251. James D. Nogalski, *The Book of the Twelve: Hosea–Jonah* (Macon, Georgia: Smyth & Helwys Publishing, 2011), 155, also reads this unit as having three movements.
172. See Davies, *Hosea*, 251.

restoration. Our analysis of the preceding section has concentrated on Yahweh's harsh censures, which have fallen upon Israel. Those chastisements are meant neither for annihilation, nor for the sake of retaliation. Yahweh's express intention is to chastise or correct Israel: "In my desire I will chastise them" (10:10a; cf. 5:2; 7:12). Hence chastisement [or judgment] is *not* used as a means to announce Israel's total eradication, but to channel a new relationship. Besides, it is not Hosea's final word to describe Yahweh's actions towards Israel. Rather, chastisement anticipates restorative words to come (cf. 2:25; 6:1; 11:9; 14:5).[173] So too, Yahweh's restorative action assumes chastisement as evident from 11:10–11 that exile has not been eliminated (cf. 2:17; 3:4–5; 6:1). What has been annulled is its perpetuity.

Yahweh's Consistent Unilateral Love (11:1–4)

The retrospective utterance in 11:1–4 contrasts Yahweh's consistent love with Israel's consistent lack of love. As in the husband-wife metaphor, the parent-child[174] metaphor here exhibits "what a relationally faithful person [Yahweh] does" in contrast with "what a relationally faithless person [Israel] does." Once again, the covenantal relationship between Yahweh and Israel is depicted as a close familial parent-child relationship.[175]

---

173. George Farr, "The Concept of Grace in the Book of Hosea," *ZAW* 70 (1958): 98–107 (100).

174. Most commentators describe Hosea 11:1–4 as a metaphor of a loving father (Yahweh) and his disobedient son (Israel), and at v. 4, the parental metaphor shifts to complementary imagery of a good farmer and his trained animals (e.g. Wolff, *Hosea*, 197–204; Mays, *Hosea*, 150–159; Jeremias, *Hosea*, 139–142; Macintosh, *Hosea*, 437–448; Dearman, *Hosea*, 282–283). Helen Schüngel-Straumann, "God as Mother in Hosea in Hosea 11," in *A Feminist Companion to the Latter Prophets*, ed. Athalya Brenner (Sheffield: Sheffield Academic Press, 1995), 194–218; originally published as "Gott als Mutter in Hosea 11," *TQ* 166 (1986): 119–134, challenges this established scholarly view by pointing out that the metaphor of a father lacks textual support and argues that Yahweh is represented as a mother taking care of her child. Yet the proposed alternative is convincingly refuted by Siegfried Kreuzer, "Gott als Mutter in Hosea 11?," *TQ* 169 (1989): 123–132. Eidevall, *Grapes in the Desert*, 17–171, sees several metaphors: Parent-child metaphor in v. 1, shepherd metaphor in v. 3 and farming/animal in v. 4. Other interpreters such as Seifert, *Metaphorisches Reden*, 183–198, Nwaoru, *Imagery*, 147–150 and Kakkanattu, *God's Enduring Love*, 57–63, find parental imagery is stronger throughout.

175. Several scholars hold that what lies behind the parent-son metaphor is the concept of covenant. See F. C. Fensham, "Father and Son as Terminology for Treaty and Covenant," in *Near Eastern Studies in Honor of William Foxwell Albright*, ed. Hans Goedicke

As with some of the preceding speeches, this oracle looks back at Israel's idyllic beginning that, this time, refers to the exodus tradition (v. 1).[176] The metaphor is grounded on two factors: Yahweh's love (אהבהו) and his call (קראתי). As in 3:1 where the term was used to describe a familial (husband-wife) relationship, the verb אהב is used to indicate Yahweh's parental love for his son, Israel.[177] The depth of Yahweh's אהב is expressed in the call of Israel (v. 1b) and the קרא is the initial manifestation of Yahweh's אהב which forms the basis of his subsequent care and guidance.[178]

The fact that Yahweh is said to have loved Israel when it was young (כי נער) defines the nature of אהב. The term נער can mean "child," "lad," "youth," "servant," or "slave."[179] Perhaps the paralleled construction between נער and בני "my son" favours the notion of a "child,"[180] underlining the state of helplessness. The verb קרא with Yahweh as subject means "to commission," which underlines an intensive relationship between the "caller" and the "called one."[181] That is to say, Yahweh's love of Israel, which had initiated relationship, began long ago when it was totally helpless.[182] It is likely that the incapability of any free action of a mere child represents Israel's slavery in Egypt.[183] The emphasis is on Yahweh's free choice and love of Israel to be his own (Exod 4:22–23), which can only be explained by the concept of "election." Hosea does not use the term, but he "stands fully in the stream of the exodus tradition (i.e. the election)."[184] Yahweh's אהב precedes Israel's existence as a nation and his קרא makes her as a people.[185]

(Baltimore: Johns Hopkins Press, 1971), 121–135; McCarthy, "Father-Son Relationship between Yahweh and Israel," 144–147; Moran, "The Love of God in Deuteronomy," 77.

176. Daniels, *Salvation History*, 67
177. Kakkanattu, *God's Enduring Love*, 38.
178. Nwaoru, *Imagery*, 148.
179. See H. F. Fuhs, "נַעַר na'ar," *TDOT* 9: 479–483; V. P. Hamilton, "נַעַר," *NIDOTTE* 3: 125.
180. Nwaoru, *Imagery*, 148 and Kakkanattu, *God's Enduring Love*, 33.
181. C. J. Labuschagne, "קרא qr' to call," *TLOT* 3: 1161.
182. Thus Holt, *Prophesying the Past*, 60.
183. Rudolph, *Hosea*, 214; Macintosh, *Hosea*, 437.
184. Dietrich Ritschl, "God's Conversion," *Int* 15 (1961): 286–303 (295).
185. Mays, *Hosea*, 153, notes that קרא is an election verb. Other terms for election in Hosea include: פתה "allure/entice" (2:16–17), לקח "take" (2:1; 3:1), מצא "find" and ידע "know" (13:5). See Dearman, *Hosea*, 369–370.

Verse 3a expounds the image of Yahweh's endearing parental love towards Israel, his son: teaching him to walk and holding him in embrace. The mentioning of "Ephraim" is possibly deliberate to represent the contemporary or, at least, northern Israelites.[186] The primary parental responsibility is to rear the נער to full maturity. The mention of "Yahweh's arms" (cf. Exod 19:4; Isa 63:12; Ps 89:22) depicts the protection needed by a child to reach adulthood, which signifies the providential leading and guidance for Israel to attain nationhood in the wilderness (cf. Deut 1:31; 32:11).

The next parental duty is described as nursing a sick child back to health.[187] As discussed elsewhere, Hosea uses רפא "healing" in the context of relationships (5:13; 6:1; 7:1; 14:5).[188] In essence, the רפא in 5:13 and 6:1 means a return to and dependence on Yahweh, whereas 7:1 describes Yahweh's attempt to relate to his people as a restorer and healer that exposes their crimes. The instance in 14:5, too, anticipates the idea of renewal of relationship. Thus, it is likely that the רפא here, on the one hand, denotes Yahweh's initiation of relationship in history, and on the other hand, his bringing out of his people from Egypt and the ensuing interaction with them as a healing process. The notion of קרא in context also supports this consideration.

As noted above, interpreters are divided over the interpretation of verse 4, especially the second half. Some exegetes have construed that the logic of a gentle father image continues. In so doing, they resort to a slight emendation of עֹל (v. 4bα) to עוּל, "infant" or "suckling."[189] This option depicts Yahweh as lifting up the small child and bowing down in order to feed the child, which assumes the role of a tender mother.[190] The idioms

---

186. H. F. van Rooy, "The Names of Israel, Ephraim and Jacob in the Book of Hosea," *OTE* 6 (1993): 135–149.

187. See discussion in D. F. O'Kennedy, "Healing as/or Forgiveness? The use of the term רפא in the Book of Hosea," *OTE* 14 (2001): 458–474, especially 464.

188. [[See pp. 199–201.]] Norbert Lohfink, "Ich bin Jahwe, dein Arzt," in *"Ich will euer Gott werden": Beispiele biblischen Redens von Gott*, eds. Norbert Lohfink et al.; SBS 100 (Stuttgart: Verlag Katholisches Bibelwerk, 1981), 46–47, has already argued that the core sickness of Israel, in the latter prophets, is the broken relationship.

189. Wolff, *Hosea*, 199–200; Schüngel-Straumann "God as Mother," 124–125; Seifert, *Metaphorisches Reden*, 286–288; Nwaoru, *Imagery*, 149 and Kakkanattu, *God's Enduring Love*, 57–63.

190. Nwaoru, *Imagery*, 149; Sweeney, *Twelve Prophets*, 114.

בחבלי אדם and בעבתות אהבה are understood to feature Yahweh's wooing love, which leads Israel to her destined goal and binds the people to himself.

Other interpreters, however, have seen a shift from the parental imagery to the image of a farmer and his cattle.[191] This retains the MT vocalisation of עֹל "yoke." This image likens Yahweh as "those [farmers] who lift up the yoke [that binds a pair of oxen together] over their [animals'] jaws" [in order to facilitate their feeding]. Having removed the yoke, the farmer feeds the oxen (v. 4bβ). Yahweh "drawing" (משך) the "cords" and "bands," which are used in training, is deemed suitable for the tasks of animal husbandry. With either of the readings adopted, the topic of the metaphor in verses 1–4 is easily grasped. It is Yahweh's paradigmatic providential care of and graciousness to his people. The prophet presents the election in the exodus and subsequent wilderness experience as a unilateral act of love in favour of Israel.[192]

Corrective Measures for Rebellious Ephraim (11:5–7)

Another thin line that runs parallel to the metaphor of Yahweh as the ideal father is the accusation of Israel's classic ungratefulness. The prophet charges the people for two breaches: "walking away" (הלכו) from Yahweh (v. 2) and "not knowing" (לא ידעו) him (v. 3b). The contrast between Yahweh's loving election and Israel's maleficent ingratitude is presented with the "call" (קרא) of the divine "I" (אנכי) and the rejection of the "they" (הם). In any event, the anticipated response of Israel to the gracious "call" of Yahweh is to "walk" in his presence and his ways.[193] It is difficult to ascertain whether the קרא in verse 2 refers to a one-time event or Yahweh's continuous call in Israelite history.[194] In context, it is likely that the term refers

---

191. Rudolph, *Hosea*, 215–216; Mays, *Hosea*, 154; Jeremias, *Hosea*, 142; Andersen and Freedman, *Hosea*, 581; Eidevall, *Grapes in the Desert*, 172–173; Macintosh, *Hosea*, 446–447; Dearman, *Hosea*, 282–283.
192. Thus Macintosh, *Hosea*, 449 and Kakkanattu, *God's Enduring Love*, 63.
193. F. J. Helfmeyer, "הָלַךְ hālakh," *TDOT* 3: 392–400.
194. The MT (קראו להם כן הלכו מפניהם) presupposes the former while the LXX (καθὼς μετεκάλεσα αὐτούς οὕτως ἀπῴχοντο ἐκ προσώπου μου) presupposes the latter. With good reason, the LXX's rendering must be preferred. So, Davies, *Hosea*, 255; Dearman, *Hosea*, 280; Kakkanattu, *God's Enduring Love*, 46.

to an ongoing relationship between Yahweh and his people with a view to highlight Ephraim's persistent idolatry (v. 2b). Despite Yahweh's efforts, Ephraim refuses to recognise Yahweh's initiation of relationship and chooses "not to know" that it is Yahweh who provides protection, and has finally lost contact (v. 3a). The lot that awaits Israel on account of their irresponsible behaviour is Yahweh's corrective measures described in what follows.

Yahweh's speech in verses 5–7 focuses on the theme of chastisement. Verse 5 makes use of the references to Egypt and Assyria as a means of connecting the period of slavery in Egypt to the impending exile to Assyria.[195] The circumstances in this passage possibly reflect the situation during the reign of King Hoshea. Interpreters have discussed whether the MT particle לא should be treated as a negating element ("He shall not return to the land Egypt")[196] or as an emphatic ("He shall indeed return to the land of Egypt").[197] Whichever interpretation is adopted, the next phrase אשור הוא מלכו clarifies that a literal return to Egypt is not meant. The prophet skilfully uses the notion "return to Egypt," which is used only in the context of judgment oracles (7:16; 8:13; 9:3, 6), and associates it with subjugation to the Assyrians. So the verse depicts, as Kakkanattu notes, "the reversal of the exodus and revocation of Israel's election, which, in Hosea's view, has its historical realisation in the altered situation in the deportation to Assyria."[198] The reason given concisely for this chastisement is Ephraim's consistent refusal to repent/return (שוב) to Yahweh (cf. 5:4; 7:10).

Verse 6 elaborates on the consequences of Israel's defection from Yahweh. While the threat of a "return to Egypt" in verse 5 alludes to deportation, verse 6 spells out the notion in terms of its violent military invasion.[199] The opening line, וחלה חרב בעריו, reflects fierce fighting. The personified sword perhaps poetically portrays the fury of the Assyrian army who swing the sword through the cities.[200] While other possibilities exist for translation, the next line is best understood as "it will destroy and de-

---

195. Nogalski, *Hosea–Jonah*, 158.
196. For example, Macintosh, *Hosea*, 450–451; Garrett, *Hosea, Joel*, 225.
197. For example, Mays, *Hosea*, 150; Kakkanattu, *God's Enduring Love*, 63.
198. Kakkanattu, *God's Enduring Love*, 68.
199. Davies, *Hosea*, 258.
200. Garrett, *Hosea, Joel*, 226.

vour the bars of his gates (בדיו)."²⁰¹ Warfare and besiegement is in view. The rationale for this chastisement, as in verse 5b, is that they sought counsels (מועצה) of others, which "refers to considered, purposeful conduct" against Yahweh (v. 6b).²⁰²

Despite the textual uncertainty, the summary statement in verse 7 reflects the termination of relationship between Yahweh and his people. It also constitutes a transition between what precedes (accusation/judgment) it and what follows (restoration).²⁰³ As in 1:9, the relational phrase, "*But* my people," underlines the contrast between Yahweh's faithfulness and Israel's inflexible stubbornness. They "hang up" (תלא) or are addicted to "apostasy" (משובה) (v. 7a).²⁰⁴ Israel is entangled by her misdeeds from which she alone is incapable of escaping.²⁰⁵ The one (אל־על [God on high])²⁰⁶ she relied on is incapable of raising her up (v. 7b). Pentiuc notes two ironies here: first, Yahweh "calls" Israel repeatedly, but the people ignore him. This time they "call" Baal but he gives no answer. Second, Yahweh "lifts" his child [or the "yoke"] in love for Israel while Baal is incapable of such a genuine love towards Israel.²⁰⁷ Simply, the Yahweh-Israel relationship has reached a stalemate. Whether Yahweh abandons this relationship in ruins or not is the subject of what follows.

---

201. The various renderings for בד include: "bars (of the city)," "fortification," "villages," "warriors," "strong men," "braggarts," "oracle-priests/diviners." Kakkanattu, *God's Enduring Love*, 24.
202. McComiskey, *The Minor Prophets*, 188.
203. Macintosh, *Hosea*, 457; Kakkanattu, *God's Enduring Love*, 73.
204. See Kakkanattu, *God's Enduring Love*, 26, for various proposals for the meaning of תלא.
205. Ibid., 75.
206. The term על "high" already appeared oddly at 7:16. Here, a good number of interpreters understand it either as an epithet for Baal or as a defective form of בעל. For example, Wolff, *Hosea*, 192; Daniels, *Hosea and Salvation History*, 65; Seifert, *Metaphorisches*, 184. Other take על as a corrupted form or one synonymous with עליון which refers to Yahweh (as "Most High"). For example, Andersen and Freedman, *Hosea*, 587; Dearman, *Hosea*, 276. According to H. J. Zobel, "עֶלְיוֹן *'elyôn*," *TDOT* 11: 129–130, the term in Hosea 7:16 and 11:7 refers to "the god Baal, against whom Hosea is campaigning. The Northern Israelites thus gave the title 'the Exalted,' 'Most High,' to the storm God." This is the name rejected by Yahweh and is considered to be the name of another god (i.e. Baal). See Garrett, *Hosea, Joel*, 227.
207. Pentiuc, *Long-Suffering Love*, 142.

A Compassion that Thwarts Human Logic (11:8–11)

Though many scholars have described 11:8–9 as the high point of the book of Hosea,[208] it is more correct to call the passage one of its turning points, since the restoration theme has already been dealt with in other passages.[209] As has been argued, the shift of gears from chastisement to reconciliation is typically Hosean, and occurs more conspicuously in 2:16–25, 6:1–3 and 14:5–9. Readers are invited, once again, to see Yahweh's emotional and existential struggle in keeping intact his relationship with his people. The tension is a tug of war between the idea of giving up on them and his restorative inclinations.

Several interpreters have argued that verses 8–9 should be taken as words of doom.[210] However, the majority of modern scholars have abandoned this interpretation in favour of an oracle which affirms Yahweh's refusal to eradicate his people.[211] Yet the nature of the divine self-questioning ("How [אֵיךְ] can I…?") in verse 8a has been debated. Some interpreters understand it as a rhetorical question, which assumes the answer is "impossible."[212] Others, however, understand it as an existential question which implies "a not yet-completely-determinate, directional possibility" in which the questioner's self has become the solution.[213] Understood in this sense, Yahweh's answer to the self-question determines the future of the Yahweh-Israel covenant relationship.[214]

---

208. Gerhard von Rad, *Old Testament Theology, II*, trans. D. M. G Stalker; Munich: Christian Kaiser Verlag, 1960; repr. (London: SCM Press, 1965), 145, labels the passage as "an utterance whose daring is unparalleled in the whole prophecy," while Jeremias, *Hosea*, 143, calls it "den theologischen Höhepunkt" within the book. For Rudolph, *Hosea*, 218, "Hier ist Evangelium in Alten Testament."

209. Cf. similarly, Davies, *Hosea*, 261.

210. For example, Andersen and Freedman, *Hosea*, 590. Their predecessors include H. S. Nyberg, *Studien zum Hoseabuche* (Uppsala, 1933); S. Mowinckel, *Det Gamle Testamente* (Oslo 1944), cited in Geir Hoaas, "Passion and Compassion of God in the Old Testament: A Theological Survey of Hos 11, 8–9; Jer 31, 20 and Isa 63, 9+15," *SJOT* 11 (1987): 138–159 (146); J. L. McKenzie, "Divine Passion in Osee," *CBQ* 17 (1955): 287–299.

211. With most recent commentaries. See also J. Gerald Janzen, "Metaphor and Reality in Hosea 11," *Semeia* 24 (1982): 7–44; Reider B. Bjornard, "Hosea 11:8–9, God's Word or Man's Insight?," *BR* 27 (1982): 16–25; Hoaas, "Passion and Compassion," 138–159.

212. Hoaas, "Passion and Compassion of God," 146.

213. Janzen, "Metaphor and Reality," 12, 14.

214. Kakkanattu, *God's Enduring Love*, 77.

It is well recognised that the statement in verse 8aβ alludes to the Sodom and Gomorrah tradition (Gen 10:19; 14: 2, 8; Deut 29:22). The question why Admah and Zeboiim are referred to rather than their better-known neighbours is difficult to answer, but it is not difficult to see that the two cities stand "as paradigms for what could happen to Israel if she disobeyed the covenant."[215] The interpretation of the phrase נחפך עלי לבי (v. 8bα) is difficult. It could either suggest the internal struggle of love against wrath[216] or represent the intra-mutual transformation *within* Yahweh, or the emotional *upheaval* of God himself.[217] Along these lines, the former consideration understands נחומים in verse 8bβ as "remorse," denoting the dynamic that holds back Yahweh's wrath,[218] while the latter takes the "change of mind" to suggest God's essence is in change.[219] Perhaps it is best to take נחומים in its abstract sense to denote "compassion" (cf. Isa 57:18; Zech 1:13) which stands in "synonymous parallelism"[220] with לבי "my heart." Together they express the idea of Yahweh's inner tension. If one places the emphasis on Yahweh's refusal to efface the apostate, then it involves a change of mind. However, if the tension is understood as Yahweh's desperate salvific attempt at keeping intact his relationship with Israel, then it does not bring any change of mind. Instead, it exhibits the resolve of Yahweh to remain true to his love of Israel.[221]

The self-questioning of verse 8 is followed by self-expression in verse 9, describing Yahweh's solemn decision *not* to terminate his relationship with Israel.[222] In answering the existential questions of verse 8, Yahweh declares: "I will not execute my fierce anger; I will not return to [or not again] wipe

---

215. Stuart, *Hosea–Jonah*, 181.
216. For example, Wolff, *Hosea*, 202. In this case, the verb חפך in understood in the sense of Yahweh's *overthrowing* his own heart in place of annihilating the wicked Israel.
217. For the former, see Janzen, "Metaphor and Reality," 11 and the latter, Hoaas, "Passion and Compassion," 146–147.
218. Wolff, *Hosea*, 201; Jeremias, *Hosea*, 145.
219. Janzen, "Metaphor and Reality," 29–30.
220. James L. Mays, "Response to Janzen: 'Metaphor and Reality in Hosea 11," *Semeia* 24 (1982): 42–51 (47).
221. See Kakkanattu, *God's Enduring Love*, 84.
222. Those who regard vv. 8–9 to be an oracle of threat understand the negative particles לא as asseveratives. See Andersen and Freedman, *Hosea*, 589–590.

out Ephraim" (v. 9a). The divine wrath (חרון אף) presupposes Israel's relational faithlessness in previous verses. The function of the שוב "return" and בוא "come" (v. 9c) is best understood in light of the account of destroying the wicked cities, Admah and Zeboiim.[223] Within this context, what Yahweh refuses to do is to "turn" in execution of, or to "enter" the city with the full vent of his divine fury in annihilating Israel, as he did with Sodom. Importantly, this "not" of Yahweh is not to annul chastisement as such but only to cancel retributive judgment that will break off the relationship.[224] The uniqueness of the declaration is that it pronounces "continuation" for the Yahweh-Israel relationship in place of its "termination." This thwarts human logic in two ways. First, a human point of view expects punishment of the guilty. Second, a traditional understanding assumes repentance as the prerequisite of pardon.[225] Yet Yahweh, the Holy One (קדוש) in the midst of Israel, is free of such bounds. He could afford to do this because he is God (אל), not human (v. 9bβ). No perpetual divorce is tolerable from his side and the future Yahweh-Israel relationship solely rests on himself.

The message of Yahweh's self-interrogation (v. 8) and self-expression (v. 9) is clear: Yahweh, who is true to his holy nature, who remains faithful to his relationships, intends no destruction, but a new future for Israel. His compassionate resolve of heart takes effect in verses 10–11. As regards verse 10, many interpreters have suggested it as a later redaction,[226] but the thought is Hosean[227] and the shift from first person to third person is not unusual in Hosea.[228] Besides, the canonical form of verses 10–11 perfectly illustrates "the meaning of Yahweh's not carrying out his fierce anger in a concrete situation."[229]

---

223. Cf. Garrett, *Hosea, Joel*, 228–229.
224. Cf. Mays, *Hosea*, 158.
225. As Bovati has shown, the cessation of divine wrath is equivalent to "pardon." See Pietro Bovati, *Re-Establishing Justice: Legal Terms, Concepts and Procedures in the Hebrew Bible*, trans. Michal J. Smith; JSOTSup 105 (Sheffield: JSOT Press, 1994), 152.
226. For example, Wolff, *Hosea*, 195; Jeremias, *Hosea*, 147; Emmerson, *Hosea*, 41; Mays, *Hosea*, 158. For a good summary of views, see Macintosh, *Hosea*, 466–471.
227. Dearman, *Hosea*, 293.
228. See Janzen, "Metaphor and Reality," 41–42.
229. Kakkanattu, *God's Enduring Love*, 93.

The metaphors chosen include a roaring lion in verse 10 and birds returning to their nests in verse 11. The people are depicted as children and as fowl. In 5:14 and 13:7 the terms שחל and כפיר are employed to depict Yahweh as a ferocious "lion" to indicate the severity of Yahweh's chastisement. Here אריה is used to carry a positive connotation,[230] not simply because of its new vocabulary, but also on account of its context. It not only promises a future (vv. 8–9) but also declares it (vv. 10–11). In contrast to previous usages, the simile of Yahweh as a lion in verse 10 is "ascribed to Yahweh"[231] and the point of reference is "not the fierce nature of a lion but its roaring."[232] "Like a lion he shall roar (שאג)" (v. 10aβ) echoes Amos 1:2; 3:8; Jeremiah 25:30; and Joel 4:16. However, the roaring here symbolises "Yahweh's summons to his scattered people to come home. It scares the enemy and ensures safe return for Yahweh's people."[233] With a change of attitude the people will walk after (הלך אחרי) Yahweh, trembling (חרד) with awe and joyful hope from their dispersion that extends to the farthest reaches of the earth (מִיָּם, literally "from the sea").[234]

As noted, the restoration does not cancel the chastisement of exile. Verse 11 specifies Egypt and Assyria as the place from which the people (cf. v. 7) will come in reversal of the judgment pronounced in verse 5. As the portrayal of Yahweh in verse 10 reverses the images in 5:14 and 13:7–8, the paired bird similes for the people, ספור and יונה, can be seen as a reversal of the utterance in 7:11.[235] The political leaders in 7:11 lost their ways, but the dove and sparrow (?) in 11:11, by contrast, find their ways. A return from Egypt and Assyria indicates a renewed Yahweh-Israel relationship. They will be resettled in their homes. There is no restorative language clearer than contained in this passage.

---

230. Stuart, *Hosea–Jonah*, 182.
231. Nwaoru, *Imagery*, 154.
232. Kakkanattu, *God's Enduring Love*, 95.
233. Nwaoru, *Imagery*, 154.
234. Sweeney, *Twelve Prophets*, 117.
235. Emmerson, *Hosea*, 1984; Eidevall, *Grape in the Desert*, 181.

Summary Assessment

This chapter has examined Hosea's message in 6:4–11:11. Our examination has shown that a fruitful way of reading Hosea is to pay attention to the suggested three threads found throughout the book: responsibility, chastisement and restoration.

The first section of our analysis has demonstrated that the central message of Hosea in 6:4–8:14 is his criticism against Israel's irresponsibility in relationships. The relational virtues חסד and דעת אלהים, which tie together Yahweh and his people, and Israel and fellow Israelites, have vanished from the land (6:4–6). The people destined to keep exclusive ברית faithfulness to Yahweh violate it and utterly fail to maintain loyal conduct within the community (6:7–7:2). The prophet's ingenious oracle exposes the relational rupture within Israel's domestic politics (7:3–7) and her disloyal actions in the international arena (7:8–16). By rejecting what is relationally good, Ephraim fails to emulate the character of Yahweh in her social, political and religious life (8:1–14).

The substantial collection of the prophet in 9:1–10:15 deals with Yahweh's various chastisements upon relationally faithless Israel. Dispersion is clearly projected in 9:1–9, while 9:10–19 pictures infertility. Yahweh's withdrawing from his people has resulted in failed harvest, cessation of sacrifice, expulsion from the land and death in a foreign land. The delectable fruits have become detestable fruits and the chosen one has become the rejected. Every important institution will come to an end and their only lot is war that destroys everything (10:1–15).

Nevertheless, judgment is not the last word in Hosea, for Yahweh's desire is only to chastise Israel with a grand noble purpose to channel a new relationship. This aspiration is described by Yahweh's dramatic restorative actions in Hosea 11. Yahweh's free choice, and unilateral love and the call of Israel, make them a people. However, Ephraim remains rebellious towards the one who chooses, cares and sustains her, but walks away from him instead (11:1–4). Ephraim will indeed be chastised (11:5–7). Yet despite Israel's consistent infidelity and stubbornness, Yahweh, who is true to himself, remains faithful to relationship and he will not and cannot let Israel go (11:8–11).

This analysis has confirmed the general trend of Hosean studies as well as countering it at several points. It confirms that Hosea is indeed a prophet of God's love. It also confirms that the dominant themes include judgment and restoration. Contrary to what has often been assumed, however, Hosea is not merely a prophetic figure who addresses only cultic problems. In fact, the bulk of his prophetic collection comprises accusations of irresponsibility dealing with social issues, chiefly relational problems. For Hosea, there is no justice as long as there are no right and true relationships between humans and between humans and God. As such, his concern for the social brokenness of his time is deeper than that of other prophets, which brands him a prophet of justice in his own right. Moreover, Hosea does not have a message filled only with doom. He does not preach justice that retaliates or annihilates but only that which chastises and restores.

CHAPTER NINE

Yahweh and His People (12:1–14:10 [11:12–14:9])

Structural Analysis of Hosea 12–14

As noted in chapter 4, this study adopts a tripartite division of the book in which Hosea 12:1–14:9 [11:12–14:8] constitutes the third and final major section. The reading of the book proposed here is to follow Hosea's cyclical presentation of responsibility-chastisement-restoration, which can also be established in this final section. As such, the call for relational justice and the denunciation of relational unjustice of chapters 1–3 and 4–11 continues to characterise chapters 12–14.

The sixth cyclical presentation in Hosea 12–14 is demarcated by several criteria. First, the thematic shift from the promised restoration in 11:8–11 to Yahweh's accusation of Ephraim-Israel's relational irresponsibility in 12:1 marks a new scene.[1] As 4:1–3 introduces the second major section, 12:1–3 begins another programmatic charge against Ephraim's present behaviour in the final section.[2] The unifying theme of this discourse unit (12:1–15

---

[1]. With major commentaries. For example, Wolff, *Hosea*, 207–209; Andersen and Freedman, *Hosea*, 593–597; Jeremias, *Hosea*, 148–151; Davies, *Hosea*, 267–268; Macintosh, *Hosea*, 475; Dearman, *Hosea*, 294.

[2]. Each of the three major sections includes a ריב–statement oracle (2:3; 4:1; 12:3), which begins either the section as a whole, or a significant part of that section. Observed by Morris, *Prophecy*, 116.

[11:12–12:14])³ is deception,⁴ or better, relational faithlessness. Second, though the line between 12:15 and 13:1 is admittedly thin, the theme of judgment is clearly dominant in the next unit (13:1–14:1 [13:1–16]) where death and destruction can be seen as a unifying topic.⁵ Third, as always, the cycle is concluded by Yahweh's restorative disposition to heal apostate Israel and to love them freely in 14:2–9 [14:1–8]. Finally, the proverbial saying in the epilogue (14:10 [9]) concludes the book.⁶ Again, the suggested structure can be established as follows.⁷

Cycle	Responsibility	Chastisement	Restoration
6	12:1–15 [11:12–12:14]	13:1–14:1 [13:1–16]	14:2–9 [14:1–8]

Responsibility (12:1–15 [11:12–12:14])⁸

Although there is little dispute among scholars that Hosea 12:1–15 forms a literary unit, there is no consensus regarding its internal division.⁹ It is possible to find eight smaller units within the discourse: verses 1–2, 3, 4–6, 7, 8–9, 10–12, 13–14, 15. However, the complexity and syntactical independence of these units create interpretive difficulties.¹⁰ Thus, the unity of the pericope is better sustained by the intratextual links (the interplay of accusation, illustration, word play and allusion) than by its rhetorical structure.

---

3. Again, all interpreters noted above take Hosea 12:1–15 as a literary unit.
4. Several scholars regard מרמה "deception," "treachery" as the catchword of Hosea 12. See Wolff, *Hosea*, 207–208; Naumann, *Hoseas Erben*, 101; Eidevall, *Grapes in the Desert*, 187.
5. Eidevall, *Grapes in the Desert*, 193. Landy, *Hosea*, 156, also takes "death" as the major theme of the chapter.
6. With most commentaries. See also Silva, *A Literary Analysis*, 284.
7. Ben Zvi, *Hosea*, 241, also advocates a tripartite "reading" (12:1–15, 3:1–14:1 and 14:2–9) although his division is not derived from its thematic flow.
8. To avoid unnecessary repetition, this study follows MT versification.
9. Numerous divisions into smaller units have been proposed to the point that almost every commentator comes up with another division. In addition to commentaries, see Good, "The Composition of Hosea," 49–50; Holt, *Prophesying the Past*, 30.
10. Nogalski, *Hosea–Jonah*, 165.

In fact, as Andersen and Freedman note, each verse is associated in some way with something else within the chapter.[11] For instance, the term מרמה ("deceit" or "treachery") in verse 1a not only reappears in verse 8a ("treacherous scales") but also is echoed in תמרורים ("bitterness") in verse 15a. The "multiplication" (רבה) of lies (כזב) and violence (שד) in verse 2aβ corresponds to the "accumulation" (מצא/ עשר) of wealth in verse 9a. The idea of "trickery" (עקב) and "contention" (שרה) in verse 4 perhaps matches the "oppression" (עשק) in verse 8 of betrayal of close relationship. There is a play on words with שוב in verses 7, 10 and און and עון in verse 9. The motif of שמר ("observance") runs through verses 7, 13, 14.

Not surprisingly, the unifying theme of this discourse unit is Yahweh's accusation against irresponsible Ephraim (vv. 1a, 2, 4, 8, 12a, 13, 15a), whose deceitful behaviour is dealt with in various ways.[12] Andersen and Freedman point out that there are no "fewer than fifteen words to refer to sins or sinful attitudes of various kinds."[13] While the subject is grounded on Yahweh's controversy against the people in verse 3, the references to the Jacob/exodus traditions (vv. 4–6, 13 and 10, 14) and the prophets (v. 11) reinforce the prophetic charge. The fundamental call to the people is to come to the table to reconsider the terms and conditions of relationship (v. 7). The threats (vv. 3b, 15b) that envelop the unit accentuate the gravity of Israel's accountability. Most importantly, Hosea's three specific accusations shape the discourse. Ephraim is accused of socio-political irresponsibility (12:1–2), socio-economic/ethical violations (12:7–8) and socio-religious infidelity (12:12).[14]

Ephraim's Socio-political Irresponsibility (12:1–3, 4–6)

As hinted above, Hosea 12:1–3 introduces the section as a whole (12:1–14:10) as well as the first discourse (12:4–15).[15] The first person pronominal suffix (v. 1a), which assumes "Yahweh" in verse 3a, indicates that the

---

11. Andersen and Freedman, *Hosea*, 595–596; cf. Morris, *Prophecy*, 87–88.
12. Wolff, *Hosea*, 208; Eidevall, *Grapes in the Desert*, 186; Pentiuc, *Long-Suffering Love*, 186.
13. Andersen and Freeman, *Hosea*, 596.
14. Thus Stuart, *Hosea–Jonah*, 189; Nogalski, *Hosea–Jonah*, 165.
15. See Holt, *Prophesying the Past*, 49; Ben Zvi, *Hosea*, 245–246.

accuser is Yahweh rather than the prophet.[16] The accused is referred to as Ephraim-the house of Israel-Judah. Judah's attitude (v. 1b) contrasts with that of Ephraim (v. 1a) for a time, but immediately becomes the object of Yahweh's dispute (ריב) regarding her "ways" (דרך) and "deeds" (מעלל) (v. 3). This suggests that the accusation is levelled against the people or leaders corporately, even though the inhabitants of the Northern Kingdom remain as the immediate focus.[17] The national identity is placed in the context of the ancestor Jacob/Israel.[18]

The divine lament, "Ephraim surrounds (סבב) me," depicts the people as Yahweh's vilest enemies whose weapons include כחש, מרמה (v. 1a), כזב and שד (v. 2).[19] Interpreters usually understand the accusation in light of Ephraim's vacillating attitude between Assyria and Egypt. However, the text's focus is on Ephraim's dishonesty relative to Yahweh, even though her political action is denounced. The image of Ephraim's herding (רעה I)[20] or befriending with (רעה II; cf. 9:2)[21] the wind, and pursuing (רדף) the east

---

16. With most interpreters; *contra* Wolff, *Hosea*, 209.

17. Interpreters have split over the interpretations of Judah's description in 12:1b, whether to understand it as negative (NIV, NAS) or positive (NRSV, RSV), and of the originality of the name "Judah" in 12:1b and 12:3a. Concerning the former, the negative sense is, for example, preferred by (with textual emendations) Rudolph, *Hosea*, 221; Andersen and Freedman, *Hosea*, 601–603; Stuart *Hosea–Jonah*, 185–189; Garrett, *Hosea, Joel*, 230. However, a positive sense is adopted by Wolff, *Hosea*, 209–210; Sweeney, *Twelve Prophets*, 118; Dearman, *Hosea*, 295–197. There are others who read v. 1b in its positive sense, but regard it as representing a later Judean addition (e.g. Mays, *Hosea*, 159–160; Emmerson, *Hosea*, 113–114; Davies, *Hosea*, 270; Macintosh, *Hosea*, 473–476). As regards the latter, many scholars take the name "Judah" in v. 1b and v. 3a as a substitution for "Ephraim" or "Israel" (e.g. Wolff; Mays; Macintosh; Daniels, *Salvation History*, 34), whereas others retain the MT reading of "Judah," (e.g. Stuart, Garrett, Hubbard, and Dearman). The interpretation adopted in this study follows the plain meaning of the MT that the text in v. 1b presents Judah as constant and faithful to "the Holy One," a possible momentary exception (cf. 1:7, 11), as well as another culpable who is subjected to Yahweh's accusation in v. 3. The citation of Judah notionally communicates a sense of totality (cf. Landy, *Hosea*, 147). In fact, intertextual evidence shows that Judah is often paired with Ephraim (5:5; 6:4, 10–11; 8:14; 10:11). In the present context, both Ephraim and Judah are subsumed under Jacob/Israel (Ben Zvi, *Hosea*, 247). In other words, the criticism includes both Judah and Ephraim as members of the disobedient covenant community (cf. Dearman, *Hosea*, 299).

18. Dearman, *Hosea*, 301.

19. Cf. Wolff, *Hosea*, 209; Andersen and Freedman, *Hosea*, 600.

20. See Andersen and Freedman, *Hosea*, 593; Garrett, *Hosea, Joel*, 235; Dearman, *Hosea*, 295.

21. See Wolff, *Hosea*, 211; Rudolph, *Hosea*, 221; Jeremias, *Hosea*, 148; Mays, *Hosea*, 159.

wind (קדים), depicts the political behaviour of Ephraim/Israel/Jacob/Judah both as a knave and as a fool.[22] As in 8:7, the word wind (רוח) not only implies futility, but alludes to a threatening danger, a scorching sirocco ("east wind" v. 2 [cf. "whirlwind" in 8:7]).[23] Every move of Ephraim is probably portrayed as that of a "suicidal fool."[24]

Of interest to us is to press for further meaning from those conceptual words noted above. The term מרמה is best understood in the sense of "treason against one's master" (cf. 2 Kgs 9:23).[25] For a nation, having alliance with external powers is not unusual, but for Israel companionship (ברית) with foreign powers (v. 2bα) means a treacherous move against Yahweh. As noted elsewhere, the use of כחש concerns relationships in socio-political contexts.[26] Ephraim has a ghastly habit of lying through her teeth against her neighbour (4:2), and indeed her internal political system is built on lies (7:3). As Freedman and Welch have shown, although the term שד generally occurs in prophetic literature in the context of war caused by external enemies (which is the case in 7:13; 9:6; 10:4), it also describes the condition in which havoc emerges from the act-consequence nexus (e.g. Amos 3:10; Jer 6:7; Ezek 45:9; Isa 59:7).[27] Interestingly, these passages employ שד to condemn the internal social chaos. What the prophets long to see are true and just interpersonal relationships in society. For Hosea, Ephraim's multiplying of lies and violence creates social oppression from within, as well as her final downfall from without. The delivery of oil to Egypt (v. 2bβ)[28] may refer to the tribute paid in kind for political appeasement or for export in commerce. Yet Hosea's point is easily understood: this heavy undertaking has been done at the expense of the peasantry.[29]

---

22. Cf. Harold L. Ginsberg, "Hosea's Ephraim, more Fool than Knave: a New Interpretation of Hosea 12:1–14," *JBL* 80 (1961): 339–347.
23. Eidevall, *Grapes in the Desert,* 188.
24. Stuart, *Hosea–Jonah,* 189.
25. Ben Zvi, *Hosea,* 248.
26. See our discussion on pp. 209–210, 241–242.
27. D. N. Freedman and A. Welch, "שָׁדַד *šādad*;שֹׁד *šōd* ," *TDOT* 14: 412–418 (416).
28. On this see, D. J. McCarthy, "Hosea XII 2: Covenant by Oil," *VT* 14 (1964): 215–221.
29. See Premnath, *Eighth Century Prophets,* 124–125.

As discussed in earlier chapters, the employment of the ריב-pattern discourse (v. 3a), which represents an adapted lawsuit speech,[30] essentially indicates that there is a breach in relationship (cf. 2:4 [2]; 4:1). That is, Yahweh has a complaint against his people because there is something wrong with Ephraim/Judah's relationships with him and with their fellow Israelites. The ריב also intends to lead to a call for conversion (v. 7) as well as to lay the ground for chastisement (v. 15). The characterisation of Jacob's [Judah/Ephraim] misconduct, "his ways" and "his deeds" (v. 3b), is comprehensive. This sweeping statement precisely accentuates Israel's broken relationships in all walks of life. At this point, several exegetes take Yahweh's words, in a formula very similar to 4:9, "to visit (פקד) Jacob according to his ways and repay (שוב) his deeds" (v. 3b, also v. 15), as refering to divine retribution.[31] However, it is more appropriate to understand that the people are given over by Yahweh to experience the consequences of their actions and hence there is no retributive judgment as such.[32]

Interpreters in the last decades have debated whether the portrayal of patriarch Jacob in 12:4–6 is positive (a role model to emulate)[33] or negative (an example to avoid).[34] Subsequent investigations have understood the depiction of Jacob as an ambiguous or a double-faced figure in Hosea's presentation, for the text (vv. 4–6) provides no critical appraisal but it simply portrays Jacob with his mistakes and virtues.[35] Given the limited scope of this study, the issues relating to the relationship between Hosea and Jacob/Israel in Genesis 25–35 have to be left aside.[36] It suffices to note that the

---

30. [[See pp. 169, 201–202.]]
31. Wolff, *Hosea*, 217; Eidevall, *Grapes in the Desert*, 189.
32. Thus Koch, "Is there a Doctrine of Retribution," 65.
33. For example, Peter R. Ackroyd, "Hosea and Jacob," *VT* 13 (1963): 245–259 and Neef, *Die Heilstraditionen Israels*, 15–49.
34. For example, Wolff, *Hosea*, 211–212; Davies, *Hosea*, 272–273; Edwin M. Good, "Hosea and the Jacob Tradition," *VT* 16 (1966): 137–151; William L. Holladay, "Chiasmus, the Key to Hosea xii 3–6," *VT* 16 (1966): 53–64; Robert B. Coote, "Hosea XII," *VT* 21 (1971): 389–402.
35. Steven L. McKenzie, "The Jacob Tradition in Hosea 12:4-5," *VT* 36 (1986): 311–322; Holt, *Prophesying the Past*, 30–51; Eidevall, *Grapes in the Desert*, 187; Pentiuc, *Long Suffering Love*, 187; Dearman, *Hosea*, 294.
36. Beside standard commentaries and works cited above, see W. C. Kaiser, "Inner Biblical Exegesis as a Model for bridging the "Then" and "Now" gap: Hos 12:1–6," *JETS* 28

portrayal of Israel's past (i.e. Jacob's life) is neutral, while the application made to the present situation is primarily negative. It is likely that Hosea presents the fact that Israel/Judah has inherited Jacob's deceitful genes, but unlike the eponymous ancestor, the present Israelites have no appetite to return to Yahweh to attend to their covenant responsibilities.[37] As such, the Jacob story reinforces the accusation of the people's continuous rebellion against Yahweh (vv. 1–3), and also serves as a means for a call to return to implement חסד and משפט in society (vv. 7–8).

Ephraim's Socio-economic/Ethical Violations (12:7, 8–10)

The discourse turns attention back to the contemporary Israelites, calling them to return: "you should return (שוב) to your God" (v. 7a).[38] This appeal arguably constitutes the fundamental goal of Hosea's accusation and his portrayal of Jacob/Israel.[39] Perhaps the ancestor Jacob is the model in mind here (cf. Gen 28:15, 20).[40] The return, however, could only be realised through the keeping (שמר, imperative) of חסד and משפט, and by placing hope/trust (קוה, imperative) in God (v. 7b).

The only way forward to reunion is a שוב that results in חסד and משפט, simply because "they are an antidote to deceit, lies and violence with which Israel has been charged."[41] As has been argued, חסד and משפט are essential to personal relationships and social order. חסד underlines social, political and religious fidelity, whereas משפט stresses fundamental justice and lawful action towards others. They are two of the five attributes by which Yahweh has betrothed Israel (2:21–22). חסד is one of the three virtues that is lacking in the land (4:1). It is Yahweh's sole desire to see חסד, which has vanished far too quickly from the land (6:4, 6). In 5:1, 11, the leaders of Israel are censured for failing in their responsibility to install

---

(1985): 33–46; Daniels, *Salvation History*, 33–52; W. D. Whitt, "The Jacob Traditions in Hosea and their Relation to Genesis," *ZAW* 103 (1991): 18–43.

37. Cf. Stuart, *Hosea–Jonah*, 197.

38. The verb תשוב is imperfect which could be rendered "you shall return." However, the imperatives that follow in v. 7b indicate that this is not a prediction of the future, but a call by the prophet for a change of direction. Sweeney, *Twelve Prophets*, 122.

39. Sweeney, *Twelve Prophets*, 123.

40. Dearman, *Hosea*, 308.

41. Ibid., 309.

justice (משפט) in society. In 10:4, Yahweh charges the people with eroding the administration of justice. In 10:12, the personified Jacob is urged to cultivate חסד and צדקה in social and sacred relations. The term שמר has occurred also in 4:10b, where it refers to the priests' abandonment of their responsibility to "keep" or "guard" Yahweh. Keeping Yahweh is equivalent to keeping חסד and משפט.[42] Accordingly, "placing hope/trust continually" (v. 7bβ) indicates that חסד and משפט can be attained only in a continuous relationship with Yahweh. Hosea's statement, as always, is economical, but one can notice that the socio-ethical dimension takes a central position in his message.[43]

The dereliction of responsibility addressed in 12:1–3 and many times elsewhere in Hosea, is illustrated in verses 8–9. Ephraim is charged with social oppression, compared to a merchant in whose hands are deceitful scales (v. 8). At this point, scholars are reluctant to explore Hosea's social message because of a supposition that there is very little consciousness in Hosea of oppression or exploitation. It is claimed that unlike Amos, he is not primarily a social critic,[44] and the poor simply do not figure in Hosea's thinking.[45] In response, it is plausible to suggest that Amos pays more attention to the rights of the oppressed while Hosea is concerned with injustice in any given relationship. Hosea focuses on the guilt of oppression and the oppressors themselves: the conspirators, priests, judges and rulers. Besides, a genius poet like Hosea need not sing the same tune as his fellow contemporary prophet who immediately precedes him in preaching justice, but could afford another way to address the same issue.

The nation (Ephraim v. 9a) is charged not only with active involvement in social exploitation (v. 8), but also with denial of wrongdoing (v. 9). Ephraim is portrayed as a dishonest trader (כנען),[46] using deceptive

---

42. Observed by Landy, *Hosea*, 149.
43. Interestingly, Micah 6:8 has the same tripartite concept חסד and משפט and walking (הלך) with God. Nogalski observes that Hosea12:7 conceivably serves as the anchor text for Micah 6:8. See Nogalski, *Hosea–Jonah*, 169. If this consideration is correct, and if scholars regard Micah as a prophet of justice *par excellence*, far more so would be Hosea.
44. See Utzschneider, *Hosea*, 212–216.
45. See Landy, *Hosea*, 151.
46. Most commentators understand the noun כנען to be a derogatory double entendre for Ephraim. The term could not only refer to the native inhabitants of Canaan, but

scales and loving to oppress (v. 8). The verb עשק "oppress" or "extort" is a well-established term for social injustice and oppression of the downtrodden.⁴⁷ The "deceptive scales" (מאזני מרמה) in the hands (Prov 11:1; Deut 25:13; Amos 8:5) depict loathsome greediness in commercial practices.⁴⁸ This defines the meaning of מרמה in verse 1. The prophet's parting shot is his portrayal of Ephraim as the personified trader who *loves* to oppress. The people who are called to love Yahweh (Deut 6:5) and neighbour (Lev 18:19) prefer to *love* oppression. Though we hear nothing about the oppressed, the topic of this metaphor is the social injustice and economic fraud against the poor within the nation.⁴⁹

A rich Ephraim sees neither "wrongdoing" (עון) nor "sin" (חטא) in her making of wealth (אשר/און, v. 9). Ephraim's boastful attitude indicates the continued rebellion against Yahweh as well as the failure to acknowledge him as the provider. The people had mistakenly understood the prosperity under Jeroboam II as a divine favour which contributed to their moral decay.⁵⁰ Verse 9 quotes Ephraim, who claims to be honest in his acquisition (יגעי) of wealth, but the rhetorical context clarifies the claim to be illusory, for Ephraim indulges in immorality, religious infidelity and in the oppression of others. The pun of און and עון indicates that Ephraim's wealth is inseparable from his iniquity. Ephraim has found (מצא) fortune instead of finding (מצא) the God of Bethel (cf. v. 5).

The self-presentation (the divine "I," אנכי) in verses 10–11 intends to put the identity of Israel into a right perspective. Yahweh's association with Ephraim precedes national life in Canaan (cf. 11:1). The covenant LORD is the one who brought the ancestors from Egypt (v. 10a; cf. Exod 20:2; Deut 5:6). It is Yahweh who communicates and instructs his people through his prophets (v. 11). Ephraim's wealth comes from his only benefactor, Yahweh (cf. 2:10). The Yahweh-Ephraim relationship now requires

---

also a "trader" or a "merchant". Hosea compares Ephraim either with the unscrupulous mercantile or unethical original Canaanites. Cf. Wolff, *Hosea*, 214; Andersen and Freedman, *Hosea*, 615; Stuart, *Hosea–Jonah*, 192–193; Davies, *Hosea*, 278.

47. Lev 19:13; Deut 24:14; Ps 72:4; Prov 14:31; Amos 4:1; Mic 2:2; Jer 7:6; 21:12; Mal 3:5.
48. See Premnath, *The Eighth Century Prophets*, 161.
49. Cf. Eidevall, *Grapes in the Desert*, 189.
50. Macintosh, *Hosea*, 497.

a new start. Yahweh will discipline his people in pursuit of their unreserved return. As a result, the economic disparity will be equalised and those who are arrogant about their ill-gotten wealth will be made to dwell in tents (v. 10b).[51] It must be remarked, however, that threats and chastisements in Hosea are devised to prompt the people to return/repent, and that "on the other side of destitution is the possibility of restoration."[52]

Ephraim's Socio-religious Infidelity (12:12, 13–15)

The accusation of the ריב-discourse, generally interspersed with evidence and verdict sentences, continues in verse 12.[53] The criticism is about Gilead and Gilgal and the reporting of sin of each place and its resultant chastisement. The text is difficult. As in 6:8, the reference of Gilead apparently alludes to then-known crimes to make the point. The city is labelled simply as "evil" (און) in both occurrences. The word און is used to describe Bethel in 4:15. Gilgal is also mentioned in two places in the context of its failures. In 4:15, it is a shrine city like Bethel (Beth-Aven) that leads people into apostasy (cf. Amos 4:5; 55). In 9:15, it stands as the paradigm of everything that is evil in Israel.[54] The general tendency among interpreters is to view the subject of this verse as cultic evil,[55] whereas others have attempted to illuminate the passage with the Jacob story to illustrate the moral wickedness of Hosea's contemporaries.[56] It is best to take the charge of verse 12 as being levelled against Ephraim's religious apostasy as well as its moral failure to meet covenant responsibilities.[57] Because of

---

51. Interpreters debate the interpretation of the statement in 12:10b: "I will cause you to dwell in tents again, as in the days of solemn feast." The majority of scholars understand this to be a threat of punishment (Wolff, *Hosea*, 215; Mays, *Hosea*, 165; Stuart, *Hosea–Jonah*, 193; Davies, *Hosea*, 279–280; Garrett, *Hosea, Joel*, 243). Other commentators take the statement as a promise of redemption (Andersen and Freedman, *Hosea*, 618; Jeremias, *Hosea*, 155–156), a promise of new beginning (Holt, *Prophesying the Past*, 63), Yahweh's care for Israel (Sweeney, *The Book of the Twelve*, 124), or both punishment and restoration (Landy, *Hosea*, 152; Macintosh, *Hosea*, 501).
52. Landy, *Hosea*, 152.
53. Stuart, *Hosea–Jonah*, 194.
54. Cf. Garrett, *Hosea, Joel*, 245.
55. Wolff, *Hosea*, 215; Mays, *Hosea*, 168; Stuart, *Hosea–Jonah*, 194.
56. For example, Macintosh, *Hosea*, 506–507; Sweeney, *The Book of the Twelve*, 126–127.
57. Thus Garrett, *Hosea, Joel*, 244–145.

its treacherous enterprise, the people of Gilead are designated "worthless" (שוא). As a result of its many altars, like useless heaps of stones in a furrow which must be cleared by farmers, Gilgal becomes an impediment to a true harvest of חסד and משפט.

Most interpreters have understood that the two sayings in verses 13–14 allude to different strands of tradition, namely Jacob (Genesis 28–29) and the exodus/prophet.[58] There are, as Dearman notes, three connections between the two verses: a shared verb, a geographical analogy and the marriage metaphor. The first link is the verb שמר ("keep," "preserve," "guard"). Israel[59] "kept" (שמר) his flocks, so Israel was "kept" by Yahweh's prophet (Moses?).[60] Second, Jacob fled to serve and subsequently returned to the land, so Israel served in Egypt and returned to the land. Third, Jacob served for his spouses, so Yahweh redeemed his spouse, Israel.[61] It is likely that the comparison in the context of accusation constitutes both a motivation and warning. Yahweh's care for the people is meant to be a motivation for their potential return to him.[62] By placing Hosea as a prophet in line with Moses (cf. Amos 2:10–12), the oracle warns that the people will not survive unless they take heed of the prophetic warning, acknowledge their failure and return to Yahweh. Rejecting Hosea is tantamount to rejecting Moses.[63] Yet Ephraim shows no signs of transformation, but has continued to provoke (כעס) Yahweh (v. 15a). The path to a reunion offered as a transformative possibility in verse 7 hangs there simply as a proposal.[64] As a result, the only way forward is to resort to an act-consequence chastisement continuum (v.

---

58. See in addition to commentaries and articles cited above, Roman Vielhauer, *Das Werden des Buches Hosea: eine redaktionsgeschichtliche Untersuchung* (Berlin: W. de Gruyter, 2007), 178–179; Konrad Schmid, *Genesis and the Moses Story: Israel's Dual Origins in the Hebrew Bible*, trans. James Nogalski; Siphrut 3 (Winona Lake: Eisenbrauns, 2010), 74–75.
59. The deliberate employment of "Israel" instead of Jacob in relation to the winning of Rachel is to link the patriarch Jacob and his descendants (the contemporary Israel). Cf. Macintosh, *Hosea*, 509.
60. For a discussion and the prophetic office, see Daniels, *Salvation History*, 49.
61. Dearman, *Hosea*, 313; cf. Coote, "Hosea XII," 401.
62. Sweeney, *Twelve Prophets*, 128.
63. Garrett, *Hosea, Joel*, 245.
64. Dearman, *Hosea*, 315.

15b). Ephraim's guilt will not be removed by her Lord (אדניו). Instead, her master will turn (ישיב) Ephraim's insult (חרפה) against Yahweh.

In sum, the underlying theme that binds the utterances in 12:1–15 together is the prophetic accusation against the relational irresponsibility of the nation. Ephraim's lies, violence and self-destructive ways and deeds are characterised as personal attack on, or injury to Yahweh (12:1, 3). The people are accused of chasing illusions instead of keeping their covenant responsibility (12:2). They are accused of walking a suicidal political path (12:2). The nation is charged with treason against her master and Lord (12:2, 15). The people are accused of social oppression against fellow citizens (12:8). They are accused of relying on ill-gotten wealth in places of doing justice (12:9) and seeking Yahweh (12:10–11). They are accused of worshiping strange gods (12:12). Hence the answerability of the nation extends to all spheres of life: political, economic, ethical and religious. The prophet asks the people for a commitment: a return that results in חסד and משפט. Remarkably, Hosea's holistic perspective is well presented in this section.

Chastisement (13:1–14:1 [13:1–16])

Most interpreters have recognised that a new discourse unit begins at 13:1.[65] It is clearly noticeable that another break for the theme of restoration comes at 14:2, delimiting 13:1–14:1 as a self-contained rhetorical unit. Yet the internal division of the resulting unit is complex. While other alternatives for the inner structure exist,[66] it is possible to see a trifold structure (vv. 1–3, 4–9, 13:10–14:1) in this section. Though the lines of accusation of 12:1–15 make their way to 13:1–14:1, they are employed primarily to

---

65. As with most commentaries.
66. A number of scholars divide the text into four: vv. 1–3, 4–8, 9–11, 13:12–14:1. See Wolff, *Hosea*, 222–224; Mays, *Hosea*, 171–183; Davies, *Hosea*, 284; Silva, *A Literary Analysis*, 290–291; Dearman, *Hosea*, 316. Buss, *Prophetic Word*, 24–26, divides the text into two: 13:1–11, 13:12–14:1, whereas Hubbard, *Hosea*, 213 and Pentiuc, *Long-suffering Love*, 194–201, find five sub-units: vv. 1–3, 4–8, 9–11, 12–13, 13:14–14:1. Eidevall, *Grapes in the Desert*, 193 and Ben Zvi, *Hosea*, 267, advocate for two major divisions 13:1–8/9, 13:9–14:1 but they also see four possible sub-sections in the discourse.

Yahweh and His People (12:1–14:10 [11:12–14:9])

lead to the climactic message of chastisement. In other words, this discourse unit complements the previous one by stressing the announcements of judgment.[67] Therefore, the unifying theme of the discourse is Yahweh's chastisement upon relationally faithless Israel.

This consideration is supported by two features of the passage. First, the discourse, which is replete with dreadful images, aims to paint a picture of the impending chastisement in the darkest terms possible.[68] It is well received that guilt and death (13:1, 14:1) frame the section.[69] The similes of mist and dew, which depict Israel's evanescent social virtues in 6:4, here portray the swiftness of Ephraim's punishment (13:3). The sword that destroys their cities (11:6), as well as by which their leaders fall (7:16), reappears to describe the final demise of Samaria (14:1). The imagery of wild beasts, which denies any escape to Ephraim and Judah from judgment in 5:14, is elaborated upon in 13:7–8. The saviour (ישׁע) (13:4) and helper (עזר) (13:9), Yahweh, is metamorphosed into an attacker (13:8) and destroyer (13:9) of Ephraim. Moreover, the usage of appalling terms such as "death" (מות) (13:1, 14), "grave" (שׁאול) (13:14), "pangs of childbirth," (חבלי יולדה) (13:13), "little ones being dashed to pieces," and "pregnant women being ripped open" (14:1), all depict the looming dark hours of chastisement. Second, as Nogalski has observed, the trifold chronological discourse, in which each movement interweaves the past/present irresponsibility with future punishment,[70] underlines the climatic position of chastisement. Both the intertextual formulation and its sequential movement suggest that judgment is the unifying subject.

---

67. Hubbard, *Hosea*, 212.

68. Several interpreters have regarded "death" as a unifying factor of the utterances. See Jeremias, *Hosea*, 160; Davies, *Hosea*, 284; Landy, *Hosea*, 156; Eidevall, *Grapes in the Desert*, 193–194.

69. See Andersen and Freedman, *Hosea*, 626; Jeremias, *Hosea*, 160; Davies, *Hosea*, 285; Eidevall, *Grapes in the Desert*, 193; Dearman, *Hosea*, 315.

70. Nogalski, *Hosea–Jonah*, 177, has observed a trifold chronological movement (13:1–3; 13:4–10; 13:11–14:1), each having three sub-sections. First movement: past (13:1), present (13:2) and future (13:3). Second: past (13:4–6), future (13:7–9), and present (13:10). Third: past (13:11), present (13:12–14), and future (13:15–14:1). While arguments for such a neat division, especially the second and third movements, are difficult to establish, it is significant for this study as each movement leads to the climatic message of Ephraim's chastisement.

Having established the theme of the section, our analysis in what follows will treat the text as comprising of three judgment speeches, "each of which is reinforced by literary devices that intensify the indictments or sharpen the threats."[71] Arguably, cultic infidelity is foregrounded in the first speech (13:1–3), whereas the second (13:4–10) and third (13:11–14:1) speeches focus on moral and political issues respectively. Ephraim's infidelities in these spheres have created a breach in her relationship with Yahweh, and therefore justify chastisement.

Ephraim's Chastisement for Illegitimate Cult (13:1–3)

Hosea 13:1–3 forms a typical structured judgment speech,[72] assessing the problem of past actions (v. 1), present guilt with idolatry (v. 2) and inevitable future chastisement (v. 3).[73] The text of verse 1a, with Ephraim's speaking (דבר) and lifting up (נשא) of voice in pride that causes terror (רתת) in Israel, seems relatively clear. Yet the text provides no clues to what specific historical events are in mind.[74] Scholars generally take the line (v. 1a) that this alludes to (the tradition of) Ephraim's glorious past as a leading tribe within Israel (cf. Gen 48:8–20; 49:24–26; Josh 24:30),[75] or as a political entity (cf. 1 Kgs 11:26; 12:20).[76] It could also be a reference to the recent economic success of Ephraim (cf. 12:8).[77] However, the prophet's assessment, "but he became guilty (ויאשם) through Baal and died" (v. 1b), immediately cuts short Ephraim's glory, whatever it may be. Yet the sense in which Ephraim then dies is not entirely clear. Among the several options

---

71. Hubbard, *Hosea*, 212.
72. Cf. Eugene March, "Prophecy" in *Old Testament Form Criticism,* ed. John H. Hayes (San Antonio: Trinity University Press, 1974), 159–160.
73. For example, Wolff, *Hosea,* 222; Mays, *Hosea,* 172; Dearman, *Hosea,* 321.
74. Andersen and Freedman, *Hosea,* 624, 629, argue that it is the decree of Yahweh that causes the terror (רתת). This interpretation is adopted by Stuart, *Hosea–Jonah,* 186–187 and Yee, *Composition and Tradition,* 249.
75. Mays, *Hosea,* 172; Eidevall, *Grapes in the Desert,* 194; Pentiuc, *Long-Suffering Love,* 195.
76. According to Wolff, *Hosea,* 225, "Ephraim" here refers to the contemporary leaders from the royal residence of Samaria.
77. Garrett, *Hosea, Joel,* 248.

advanced by scholars,[78] it is likely that verse 1 constitutes the scenario of the formation of a separate kingdom under Jeroboam I, accompanied by the setting up of the two calves in Dan and Bethel (1 Kgs 12:16ff).[79] At any rate, the terseness of the oracle cannot confirm any suggestion with certainty. What is clear, though, is that the addressees are told that Ephraim's previous acts of worshipping Baal have brought about their downfall. For Hosea, Ephraim is "as good as dead."[80]

The accusation against Ephraim's idolatry continues in verse 2 (cf. 2:10, 15, 18, 19; 9:10; 11:12). The people have not learned from history. The fate, which has brought the nation down into a rump state ruled by Hoshea after 733 BC, will be repeated on a greater scale because of their continuing dalliance with idols: "now (עתה) they add (יוספו) to their sinning" (v. 2aα). Hosea's sarcastic criticism, which specifies the idolatrous practices of the nation (v. 2aβγ), indicates the people see the covenant at Sinai only as "a quaint historical fact, not a living relationship."[81] The bull worship that is also addressed in 8:5–6 and 10:5–6 appears to be the primary focus of Hosea's invective, for such practices violate the first two commandments of the national covenant (Exod 20:3–6; Deut 5:7–10).[82] The MT of verse 2b could be read as referring to human sacrifice.[83] This reading with such a gruesome practice cannot be dismissed for it was known in the

---

78. For instance, Kelle, *Hosea*, 162, takes the reference as an allusion to the encounter with the Baal of Peor in Transjordan (Num 25), while Sweeney, *Twelve Prophets*, 129–30, thinks that it alludes to the golden calf episode in Exodus 32–34. Another possibility proposed by Wolff, *Hosea*, 225, is that it refers to Ephraim's military disaster through the assaults by Tiglath-pileser III in 733–732 BC.

79. Macintosh, *Hosea*, 220.

80. Dearman, *Hosea*, 319.

81. Stuart, *Hosea–Jonah*, 202.

82. See Mays, *Hosea*, 172 and Stuart, *Hosea–Jonah*, 202.

83. The translation of v. 2b is disputed. The MT reading supported by Wolff, *Hosea*, 219, 225; Andersen and Freedman, *Hosea*, 624, 632; Yee, *Composition*, 249–250; Pentiuc, *Long-Suffering Love*, 195; Nogalski, *Hosea*, 179. Others (e.g. Mays, *Hosea*, 172; Stuart, *Hosea–Jonah*, 198, 202; Davies, *Hosea*, 287; Macintosh, *Hosea*, 522–523; Dearman, *Hosea*, 202) resort to various emendations in order to avoid such an interpretation of human sacrifice. Emmerson's, *Hosea*, 174, remarks summarises this position: it is unlikely that "the prophet would dismiss with such brevity so grave a perversion… as human sacrifice."

ancient world including Israel.[84] Nonetheless, it cannot be overstressed, as the text is somewhat obscure. Though it is not clear whether Hosea's contemporaries practised such a thing or not, the idolatrous practices they had adopted from their neighbours certainly had a history of such a practice.

As in 2:8, 11, the לכן in 13:3 introduces Yahweh's verdict appropriate to Israel's continuing sin.[85] By means of a cluster of four similes, "morning mist" (ענן בקר), "dew" (טל), "chaff" (מץ) and "smoke" (עשׁן), the imminent chastisement is prefigured. Each simile uses an observable ephemeral phenomenon. Unlike 6:4b, the similes of "mist" and "dew" have the force of a verdict, but as there, they depict the fleeting existence of those engaged in idolatrous practices. It is possible that the first two similes underline the rapidity of the nation's demise, whereas the second two "chaff" and "smoke" similes emphasise the irreversibility of the coming disaster. The formulation of metaphors from different domains (weather, agriculture, domestic life) perhaps is intended to reinforce the point that the destruction will be total.[86] Plainly, the Ephraim that once struck terror in the hearts of its neighbours soon will disappear. The nation of Israel as a political entity will irreversibly have gone from the world scene.

Ephraim's Chastisement for Moral Decay (13:4–10)

The second judgment speech begins with Yahweh's introduction of his care and deliverance of Israel (vv. 4–5), as in 11:1–4. The brief sketch of Yahweh's acts in the events of Exodus and the wilderness prepares for the accusation of Israel's proud and arrogant rejection of Yahweh in the present (v. 6). The oracle ends with a depiction of a time when a defender shall become a destroyer – Yahweh as a ravaging beast (vv. 7–9).

The divine self-presentation in verse 4a, which alludes to the Exodus, reiterates the statement in 12:10, but this time an emphasis is placed on Yahweh's election that demands exclusive loyalty: "you know (ידע) no god(s) but me, and there is no saviour except me" (v. 4b). Israel is to *know* no other deity for it was Yahweh who *knew* (ידע) the people in their need

---

84. Cf. Deut 12:31; Josh 6:26; 1 Kgs 16:34; 2 Kgs 3:27; 16:3; 21:6; 23:10; 1 Chr 33:6; Isa 57:5; Mic 6:7; Jer 7:31; 19:5; Ezek 16:20–21, 36; 20:26.
85. As with most commentaries.
86. Eidevall, *Grapes in the Desert*, 195.

(v. 5a).⁸⁷ The repetition of the verb ידע in verses 4–5 ("you know me . . . I knew you") appears to be deliberate (cf. Deut 2:7; 8:2; 9:24). It conveys the notion of Israel's personal relationship with Yahweh (cf. Exod 20:2), and also emphasises the ideal state of reciprocity.⁸⁸ Hosea's contemporary, Amos, conspicuously employs the term in the sense of "choose and enter into a relationship" (Amos 3:2).⁸⁹ The expression, "in the desert" (במדבר, v. 5a), echoing 9:10a, perhaps underlines Yahweh's sustenance of Israel from the time of her formative experience as a nation in the Exodus. It was "in a land of burning heat" (v. 5b) that Yahweh himself (אנוכי and אני) took the initiative in entering into an unwavering and loving relationship with his people.

Yahweh's initiative serves as the basis for the criticism of Israel in verse 6, which depicts Israel as a flock that grazes, but is eventually satiated and forgets Yahweh. Within the framework of a shepherd metaphor,⁹⁰ the assertion "I knew you" can be interpreted as "knowing one's flock" by taking responsibility for them, as a good shepherd would.⁹¹ The result of Yahweh's shepherding (מרעיה) in the cultivated land (v. 6aα) is satiation (שבע) accompanied by "uplifting hearts" (וירם לבם, v. 6aβ). Similar charges are put forward elsewhere in 2:15, 4:6 and 8:14. As there, Israel's self-sufficiency leads to the dismissal of relationship with their divine benefactor: "they forgot me" (v. 6b). Israel's subsequent amnesia stands in stark contrast with the reciprocal "knowing" in verses 4–5⁹² (cf. Deut 6:10–19; 8:10–14). Rhetorically, verse 6 does not limit itself to the past, but challenges the current generation. It is a question of moral failure. The problem it creates is the collapse of relationship. With Macintosh, it can be said that if

---

87. Based on the LXX and Syriac, some scholars emend ידעתיך to רעתיך to arrive at a translation of "I fed/shepherded you." See Wolff, *Hosea*, 220; Rudolph, *Hosea*, 238; Jeremias, *Hosea*, 159; Stuart, *Hosea–Jonah*, 200. For support for the MT reading, see Andersen and Freedman, *Hosea*, 624; McComiskey, "Hosea," 215; Holt, *Prophesying the Past*, 73–75; Macintosh, *Hosea*, 528; Dearman, *Hosea*, 321.
88. See Holt, *Prophesying the Past*, 74 and Macintosh, *Hosea*, 257.
89. Dearman, *Hosea*, 321.
90. Cf. Mays, *Hosea*, 175; Davies, *Hosea*, 289; Holt, *Prophesying the Past*, 73; Eidevall, *Grapes in the Desert*, 196; Pentiuc, *Long-suffering Love*, 196.
91. Eidevall, *Grapes in the Desert*, 196.
92. Thus Holt, *Prophesying the Past*, 74 and Eidevall, *Grapes in the Desert*, 197.

the knowledge of God has an ethical dimension which involves the gifts of justice and kindness, then the forgetting of him implies injustice and unkindness.[93] The charge of a fractured relationship only awaits the fierce threats that follow.

The climatic message of the oracle in verses 7–9 describes Yahweh's future action with the announcement of chastisement, employing metaphors from the animal kingdom. By means of a cluster of five related similes, Yahweh compares himself to four predatory animals: a lion (שחל) and לביא, vv. 7a, 8bα), a leopard (נמר, v. 7b), a she-bear (דב, v. 8a), and a wild beast (חית השדה, v. 8bβ).[94] It is possible that the sequence of the similes is deliberate to reflect a progressive escalation of the violence[95] while the verbs, "become" (היה), "lurk" (שור), "attack" (פגש) "tear apart" (קרע), "devour" (אכל), "rip open" (בקע), appear to express the nature or harshness of the chastisement.[96] Interestingly, the lion simile is used in 5:14 as a threat against Ephraim and Judah primarily because of their strife. Here, too, the threat is prompted by Ephraim's reckless ingratitude and moral irresponsibility.

Clearly, Israel's relational faithlessness has forced Yahweh to change his role: from the shepherd to a predator, from the saviour to a furious destroyer.[97] Yahweh now resorts to a hostile approach in dealing with his irresponsible people: "So I have become like a lion" (v. 7a). Like a leopard, he will get ready for an attack of his people along the road (v. 7b). He will suddenly confront them like a bear bereft of her cubs which furiously assaults a helpless prey (v. 8a). His fury will consume the nation, like a hungry lioness,[98] which jumps upon her prey with a fearsome roar and

---

93. Macintosh, *Hosea*, 531.
94. Four of the five similes are formulated with כ, which is lacking in the fifth simile, but in context, is assumed. Dearman, *Hosea*, 323.
95. Cf. Eidevall, *Grapes in the Desert*, 198.
96. Cf. Nwaoru, *Imagery*, 152.
97. The change of the deity's role has been observed by most scholars.
98. Wolff, *Hosea*, 220, amends כלביא (like a lion, lioness) to כלבים (dogs). However, the MT reading of לביא with the comparative particle כ is supported by most traditions including LXX. See Nwaoru, *Imagery*, 22 n. 104, for further discussion. For Nwaoru, the לביא in this particular context can be identified as lioness, as the lioness is more carnivorous than the male lion (*Imagery*, 153). In either case, v. 8b depicts the final act of

devours the dead victim (v. 8bα). To complete the destruction, the remaining cadavres are left to other (unnamed) wild animals (v. 8bβ). It is well recognised that the main function of the metaphors is to underline that the destruction will be absolute.[99] As elsewhere in Hosea, the aim is to put the coming dark moment of chastisement into perspective. Needless to say, Hosea sees no future except total annihilation for Israel.[100] Perhaps even Amos (5:1–2, 18–19; 8:2–3) is no more severe than this.[101] The statement in verse 9 recaps what has been said in the preceding verses (4–8).[102] The verb שחת "it destroys you" (v. 9a) is difficult to render, but it appears to refer to the devastating assaults in verses 7–8.[103] The fault lies with Israel for turning against Yahweh, their helper (v. 9b), and the chief crime or prime folly of Israel is arrogant self-reliance. It is significant for us to note that the two relational terms frame the oracle: "helper" (עזר) in verse 4 and "saviour" (ישע) in verse 9. Both terms indicate that Yahweh remains relationally faithful. Who would rebel against such a close partner?

Ephraim's Chastisement for Political Folly (13:10–14:1 [13:10–16])

The third judgment speech (13:10–14:1) focuses on political issues. It begins with a taunt in verses 10–11, describing the leadership crisis in Israel. For one more time, judgment (13:14–14:1) is justified by the essential relational faithlessness of Israel, which is represented by the terms *iniquity* (עון) and *sin* (חטאת) (v. 12) and also by Ephraim's lack of wisdom (הוא־בן לא חכם) (v. 13). The discourse concludes with Hosea's last and harshest announcement of Israel's end as a nation (3:14–14:1).

The rhetorical question in verse 10 is addressed to the king (מלך) and high officials (שפטים and שרים). It presupposes a time when they will be

---

the tragedy. The metaphorical emphasis is on the verb: "devouring" (Eidevall, *Grapes in the Desert*, 198).
99. For example, Eidevall, *Grapes in the Desert*, 199
100. Mays, *Hosea*, 176.
101. Davies, *Hosea*, 292.
102. Thus Macintosh, *Hosea*, 537.
103. Thus Garrett, *Hosea*, 260.

helpless in the face of the political crisis.[104] Along with a number of exegetes, the ambiguous term אהי can be understood as a variant interrogatory particle "where" both in verse 10a and in verse 14b,[105] with a view to mocking Samaria's incompetent rulers. As has been argued, the prime responsibility of the rulers (king-judges-officials) in Israel was to set just and good order in society, to save those whose rights have been violated and to secure the nation from external threats (cf. ישׁע, v. 10aβ).[106] The fate of the *people* and *cities* is at stake, but those rulers lack the saving power (v. 10a). The language of "giving" (נתן) and "taking" (לקח) of kings, each marked by Yahweh's anger (אף) and fury (עברה) respectively (v. 11), has been the subject of discussion regarding Hosea's view of monarchy.[107] It may allude to the beginning and ending of the Israelite monarchy.[108] However, in light of intratextual evidence particularly of 7:3–7, 8:4 and 10:3, 7, Hosea's primary concern appears to be the current desperation of the nation regarding leadership and not of the distant past.[109]

A short saying in verse 12 declares Ephraim's "iniquity" (עון) is "bound up" (צרר), whereas his "sin" (חטאת) is "stored" (צפן). The two verbs צרר and צפן seem to carry the nuance that the deity has kept track records of the people's sin. Interpreters take the verbs to depict the image of a document, bound and secured for a future presentation.[110] The personified word pair "iniquity and sin," which appears in 4:8; 8:13; 9:9 and 12:9, is of more

---

104. Perhaps it reflects the time when Hoshea broke his vows to Shalmaneser V and his subsequent capture by the Assyrians (2 Kgs 17:1–4). Macintosh, *Hosea*, 539; Pentiuc, *Long-Suffering Love*, 198; Dearman, *Hosea*, 324.

105. For example, Rudolph, *Hosea*, 238; Davies, *Hosea*, 292; Dearman, *Hosea*, 317. Several scholars take the term as having two levels of meaning. On the primary level, it introduces a rhetorical question: "where is your king…?" On another level, it could be read as an assertion: "I am your king…?" See Eidevall, *Grapes in the Desert*, 199; Yee, *Composition*, 255–256; Sweeney, *Twelve Prophets*, 133.

106. [[See pp. 117, 216–217.]]

107. In addition to major commentaries, see Anthony Gelston, "Kingship in the Book of Hosea," in *Language and Meaning*, ed. James Barr; OtSt 19 (E. J. Leiden: Brill, 1974): 71–85.

108. Most interpreters take the verbs in v. 11 to be past sense. However, as Wolff, *Hosea*, 221 suggests, they would refer to habitual actions that continue into the present, which would mean, "I would give." With the support of Vulgate, Garrett, *Hosea, Joel*, 261, opts to read future in meaning.

109. Thus Garrett, *Hosea, Joel*, 261.

110. With most commentators.

interest. The present context does not define the notions, but simply assumes what has been outlined elsewhere in the book. It is worth noting, albeit briefly, that Hosea employs the word pair essentially in the contexts of relationships. In 4:8, the terms primarily denote the priests' irresponsibility in misguiding the people, whereas 8:13 describes Israel's religious and political faithlessness vis-à-vis Yahweh. Again, in 9:9, the expression denotes Israel's harmful moral perversion. Ephraim's social exploitation is foregrounded in 12:8. The plain message is that Ephraim's repetitive relational breaches are off limits and unforgivable. Perhaps the "binding and keeping in store" has the idea of inextricability, underlining the certainty of judgment.

The mixed metaphor in verse 13 portrays Ephraim[111] as both a writhing woman and a breech baby. As a mother Ephraim is in labour pains (חבלי). As a foetus he is assessed as "unwise," one who does not recognise the time (עת) of its birth (במשבר בנים, cf. Eccl. 8:5).[112] Despite its irregularity,[113] the metaphor aims to portray the judgment and culpability of Ephraim. Most likely, the birth pangs express the potential dangers that the nation is going through, while the unwise child simile underscores its inability to take right actions for its deliverance (cf. 7:9, 11).

The climatic focus of the speech, death and destruction, separates 13:14–14:1 from the previous verses (12–13). The exegetical tradition is divided over the reading of the divine soliloquy in verse 14. The first bicolon (v. 14a) can be rendered as a declaration ("I will … them"),[114] or as

---

111. The pronouns לו and הוא have their antecedents in the "Ephraim" of v. 12.

112. Nwaoru, *Imagery*, 91. It is strange to assess the unborn baby as if wisdom were attainable already in the womb. A possible solution is that perhaps "the metaphor leaves aside technical accuracy" at this point (Stuart, *Hosea–Jonah*, 206), or if "Jacob can be typified in the circumstances of birth (12:4a), so too can Ephraim" (Dearman, *Hosea*, 327).

113. Though the metaphor mentions a woman, there is no mother who gives birth, nor an actual birth of a child. The metaphor is complicated by the use of a feminine participle for masculine pronouns. It is not clear whether the metaphor portrays Ephraim as a writhing woman, or a foetus who is affected by the birth pangs that come upon the mother. For the former option, see Macintosh, *Hosea*, 543; Garrett, *Hosea, Joel*, 262. For the latter, see Wolff, *Hosea*, 228; Andersen and Freedman, *Hosea*, 638.

114. So LXX; KJV; NIV; Andersen and Freedman, *Hosea*, 639–640; Garrett, *Hosea, Joel*, 264–265.

rhetorical questions. With most recent interpreters,[115] the latter is the option offered here, for the present as well as the wider literary contexts are not in favour of a reading of a promise of salvation. Note that the train of thought in this chapter is chastisement. Besides, the concluding clause of the verse (v. 14bγ) declares that Yahweh's *compassion*,[116] which gives rise to the change of mind in 11:8, is not within sight. Its absence in effect "has the full force of unconditional threat."[117] The self-questioning (v. 14a) arguably indicates Yahweh's role: Israel's *ransomer* (פדה) and *redeemer* (גאל). However, the possibility of redemption, a real temptation to a loving God, is only mentioned in order to be denied.[118] The next pair of rhetorical questions (v. 14bαβ) summons death personified and Sheol, apparently as powers in Yahweh's service, to send forth "plagues" and "pestilence" over the people.[119]

The initial clause כי הוא בן אחים יפריא (v. 15a) is difficult. Interpreters have offered two possible readings. By reading בן אחו מפריא in the place of בן אחים יפריא, several scholars have suggested as a translation "he flourishes among the reeds."[120] This view pictures Ephraim as a plant that first flourishes among reeds where there is always water, but then as a withering plant when the "east wind" (קדים) of judgment comes "from the desert" and dries all sources of life-giving moisture (v. 15bαβ). Following MT and LXX, another alternative reads אחים as "brothers" and the verb פרא as a denominative from פֶּרֶא ("a wild ass" cf. 8:9).[121] This line of thought underlines the enmity between brothers within Israel or between Ephraim and Judah. In any case, the purpose of the utterance is to lead to its main point: the coming judgment. Drought as a result of war is clearly projected. It is not accidental that Hosea reuses the simile of *east wind*, which indicates

---

115. For example, Wolff, *Hosea*, 221; Mays, *Hosea*, 181–182; Davies, *Hosea*, 295; Eidevall, *Grapes in the Desert*, 202; Macintosh, *Hosea*, 546; Dearman, *Hosea*, 328.
116. The term נֹחַם is a hapax legomenon and its sense is most probably "pity or compassion."
117. Eidevall, *Grapes in the Desert*, 202.
118. Cf. Davies, *Hosea*, 295 and Macintosh, *Hosea*, 548.
119. After Mays, *Hosea*, 182 and Eidevall, *Grapes in the Desert*, 202.
120. Wolff, *Hosea*, 222; Jeremias, *Hosea*, 160; Mays, *Hosea*, 179; Garrett, *Hosea, Joel*, 266.
121. As advanced by Andersen and Freeman, *Hosea*, 625, 640 and Macintosh, *Hosea*, 550–551.

Israel's faithless pursuit of political alliance with Egypt and Assyria in 12:2, and connects it here to the image of "plundered treasury" (אוצר) with a view to indict Samaria's rulers. If so, the palace's secure storeroom (1 Kgs 7:51; 2 Kgs 12:9; Ezek 28:4) is the primary target. Victors will loot every valuable thing in their storehouse (v. 15bγ).

The concluding verse (14:1) makes this plainer. Now the royal city of "Samaria" is stricken. It is remarkable that Hosea never misses any chance to rehearse his fundamental charge of Israel's relational infidelity. Samaria is declared "guilty" (אשם) exactly so for her rebellion (מרה) against Yahweh, *her God* (v. 14:1a).[122] The consequences of relational faithlessness are tragic and the מלך, שפטים and שרים (vv. 10–11) are incapable of saving the inhabitants of the city from falling to the sword of invading armies (14:1bα). It possibly envisages Samaria's besiegement by Assyrian troops between 724–721 BC (Kgs 17:5). Gruesome cruelties are foreshadowed (14:1b βγ). Their little ones will be "crushed" (cf. 10:4) and pregnant women "ripped up" (cf. 9:16).

In sum, our analysis above has demonstrated that the unifying theme of Hosea 13:1–14:1 is chastisement. The literary effect of the threefold structure is to underscore the climatic message of Yahweh's coming inevitable judgment. The reason for which Ephraim/Samaria is chastised is stated in each section. Israel's guilt consists of her continuous dalliance with idols (v. 1–2), her moral failure in plenteous times (v. 6) and her illusive political actions of self-assistance (v. 10–11). The people *of* God have failed to build a true and right relationship with *their* God. This is the reality of the demise of Samaria. Whether Yahweh has abandoned the people utterly is the subject of what follows. Thankfully, chastisement is not the last word in Hosea.

---

122. Wolff (*Hosea*, 229) surmises that the new word, מרה, which occurs only here in Hosea, is synonymous with סרר (4:16; 9:15). It is used several times in Deuteronomy, and can denote obstinacy (Deut 9:7, 21:20; 31:27; Ps. 78:8).

Restoration (14:2–9 [14:1–8])[123]

The final cyclical presentation in Hosea 12–14 is concluded by a discourse which reflects Yahweh's restorative frame of mind in 14:2–9. The hopeful vision is comparable with the equally hopeful passages in 2:1–3, 16–25, 3:5, 5:15b–6:3, 11:8–11. It represents the culmination of the book as a whole and the discourses in 12:1–14:1 in particular.[124] As has been argued, the heart of Hosea's message is to restore the broken relationship between Yahweh and his people. Hosea 14:2–9 thereby constitutes Hosea's final appeal.

There seems to be an exegetical consensus that divides Hosea 14 into three sub-units: 14:2–4, 5–9, and 10. The first unit (vv. 2–4) is usually treated as the people's penitential prayers (the people's speech), while the second (vv. 5–9) is taken as a response (with the deity's speech).[125] However, as Eidevall has argued, a closer examination has revealed that 14:2–9 is best taken as an open-ended prophetical summons to repentance.[126] The divine statement in verse 5 takes a central position and the surrounding sayings (vv. 2–3 and 6–9) depend upon the declaration of the divine love (v. 5).[127] Within this chiastic structure,[128] this study will treat verses 2–4 as a prophetic call to the people to renew their covenantal relationship with Yahweh, whereas verses 6–9 concerns the potential imports of the restored relationship. Then the third unit follows, being the epilogue of the book (v. 10).

---

123. Unless otherwise indicated, this study follows MT versification.
124. Hosea 14:2–9 with its restorative mood has been treated as a secondary addition to the book from post-exilic times. However, as Eidevall, *Grapes in the Desert*, 208, has noted, more recent scholars have abandoned this position, and are increasingly seeing it as the work of the prophet himself. Cf. Wolff, *Hosea*, 234; Rudolph, *Hosea*, 249–250; Davies, *Hosea*, 300–301; Sweeney, *Twelve Prophets*, 136–137. Argument for a late origin, see Yee, *Composition*, 131–132; P. A. Kruger, "Yahweh's Generous Love: Eschatological Expectations in Hosea 14:2–9," *OTE* 1 (1988): 27–48). For this study, this unit constitutes an essential part of Hosea's overall message. Without it Hosea's relational message in Hosea 12–14 would be inconceivably truncated.
125. For example, Wolff, *Hosea*, 233; Rudolph, *Hosea*, 250; Davies, *Hosea*, 298.
126. See Nogalski, *Hosea–Jonah*, 189.
127. Eidevall, *Grape in the Desert*, 208–209.
128. In essence I follow the structural observations of Yee, *Composition*, 135–136 and Eidevall, *Grapes in the Desert*, 208–209.

A Final Prophetic Call to Return (14:2–4)

As noted above, the rhetorical goal of 14:2–9 is to convince the people of Israel to re-enter a personal communion with Yahweh.[129] The roadmap which is set out entails a return to Yahweh by abandoning all other associations (vv. 2–4). The call is conveyed through the imperative שוב, "return!" of verse 2a and reiterated in verse 3a. Interestingly, the proposed prayer (vv. 3–4)[130] specifies what Israel is to repudiate in terms of her conduct depicted in chapters 12–13. More precisely, Israel now is to renounce her ethical violation (v. 3; cf. 12:7–8; 13:4–10), her idolatrous cult (v. 4b; cf. 12:12; 13:1–3) and her political alliance with other powers (v. 4a; cf. 12:1–2; 13:11–14:1).

As discussed elsewhere, the concept of "re/turning" is a major theme in Hosea.[131] The root, שוב, occurs twenty-five times in Hosea.[132] LeCureux has grouped the different connotations of the term into three main categories: punishment [chastisement] (2:11; 4:9; 5:15;12:3, 15; 8:13; 9:3; 11:5), restoration (3:5; 6:11b; 11:9; 14:5, 8) and repentance (2:9; 5:4; 6:1; 7:10, 16; 11:5; 12:7; 14:2, 3, 5). As in 6:1 and 12:7, the occurrence of שוב in verses 2a and 3a explicitly describes the call to return/repentance,[133] calling for a reversed direction on the part of Israel to turn to Yahweh in loyal relationship.

A changed course always comes with a demand. The object of the exhortation in 6:1–3 is to "know" Yahweh by living in his presence (i.e. to implement his ethical demands). Similarly, the exhortation in 12:7 appeals to Israel to renew a personal relationship by keeping חסד and משפט and by placing their trust in him. Arguably, the call to return to Yahweh in the present context demands that the people of Israel relinquish their relational faithlessness in three spheres of life: their self-righteous morality, their political alliance and their cultic idolatry.

---

129. According to Harold Fisch, *Poetry with a Purpose: Biblical Poetics and Interpretation* (Bloomington: Indiana University Press, 1988) 154, the discourse unit 14:2–9 illustrates the "wished-for dialogue" between the people and Yahweh.

130. After Fisch, *Poetry with a Purpose,* 155. Similarly, Stuart, *Hosea–Jonah,* 212. Contra Rudolph, *Hosea,* 250 and Mays, *Hosea,* 184.

131. [[See pp. 202–203.]]

132. Cf. Garrett, *Hosea,* 270.

133. LeCureux, *The Thematic Unity,* 64.

This contention can be substantiated in several ways. First, Ephraim's boastful attitude and blatant denial of wrongdoing are described in 12:9. Her lifting up of voice in pride and her outright rejection of Yahweh are presented in 13:1 and 13:6 respectively. In this light the suggested prayer "Take (לקח) words with you . . . we may present (שלם)[134] the fruit (פרי)[135] of our lips" (v. 3) can be understood to be a confession coming from contrite hearts (cf. Ps. 51:17), offering genuine spoken promises.[136] Second, a return to Yahweh entails rejection of the Assyrians. By stating publicly that "Assyria will not save us" (v. 4a), the prophet calls upon the people to repudiate publicly their alliance with the Assyrians (12:1) as a part of the process of restoring the relationship with their saviour, Yahweh.[137] Third, Israel is to forswear idolatry. The declaration, "we will no longer say 'Our gods!' to the work of our hands" (v. 4bα), indicates a renunciation of false objects of faith (8:6; 13:2). Instead, like a helpless orphan Israel must put her trust in Yahweh's compassion (v. 4bβ). Finally, much of the criticism of Israel is summed up in verse 2b: "for you have stumbled (כשל) in your iniquity (עון)." The comprehensive terms "stumbling" (cf. 4:5; 5:5; 14:10) and "iniquity" (cf. 4:8; 5:5; 7:1; 8:13; 9:7, 9; 10:10; 12:9; 13:12; 14:3) describe Israel's faithlessness in various contexts. Similarly, Hosea's use of "good" (טוב), too, is broad in scope (cf. 8:3).[138] Here it most likely stands for that which is relationally good, worthy of divine acceptance.[139] Thus, the expression: "Forgive our sins and accept what is *good*" (v. 3b) can be taken as a proposed new step for the commitment of Ephraim to renew a relationship with Yahweh. These compelling reasons suggest that the prophet recaps, for a final time, his holistic message of relational justice, which demands forsaking everything else upon which Israel might depend.

---

134. The Piel of שלם denotes the action of fulfilling a vow or paying what is necessary.
135. Most interpreters read פְרִים in place of פָּרִים. Wolff, *Hosea*, 231, regards the final ם as an "archaic Canaanite case ending." This reading is supported by LXX: καρπὸν χειλέων ἡμῶν. However, other scholars such as Kruger, "Yahweh's Generous Love, 29; McComiskey, "Hosea," in *The Minor Prophets*, 228–230; Sweeney, *Twelve Prophets*, 138, opt for the MT reading.
136. Cf. Nogalski, *Hosea*, 190.
137. Thus Sweeney, *Twelve Prophets*, 139.
138. See our discussion on pp. 221–222.
139. Cf. McComiskey, "Hosea," 229.

Yahweh's Express Will to Restore the Nation (14:5)

Interpreters discuss whether the declaration of restoration in verse 5 should be understood as the basis for the exhortation in verses 2–4,[140] or as a response to the penitential prayers of the people.[141] Since the prophetic summons in verses 2–4 is only a proposed prayer for the people, and since the rhetorical admonition in verse 9a presumes idolatry as an ongoing problem, the divine assertion cannot be taken contextually as a response to the people's repentance. However, the tension between the two is best held together.[142] Reunion between Israel and Yahweh will not happen unless the people return to Yahweh in contrition, nor will it be possible unless Yahweh turns to his people in grace. The oracle with an eschatological tune simply assumes these mutual "turnings" to come together in unison one day.

The salvific promise in verse 5 consists of healing (רפא), love (אהב) and cessation of anger (אף). The two obstacles – Israel's "apostasy" or "turning" (משובה) and Yahweh's anger – are removed (שוב), and all the actions are based on Yahweh's own volition (נדבה). As noted elsewhere, Hosea employs the term רפא in the context of relationships (5:13; 6:1; 7:1). The concept denotes either Israel's return to Yahweh (5:13; 6:1), or Yahweh's attempt to relate to his people as a healer (7:1). Moving a step further, the divine healing here concerns the apostasy, Israel's sickness itself (cf. 7:1). The term משובה has the basic meaning of "turning" or "turning one"[143] and Hosea uses this nuance in 11:7 to describe Israel "turning away" from Yahweh. This subsumes Israel's cultic, political and social relational violations. Once again, the stress is the people's fractured relationship with Yahweh that needs to be healed.[144] The declaration "I will love them freely" (v. 5b), the uncoerced love (cf. 3:1; 11:1), entails a restored relationship which reverses the rejection found elsewhere in Hosea (cf. 1:6; 9:15).

---

140. Wolff, *Hosea*, 233; A. Hunter, *Seek the Lord! A Study of the Meaning and Function of the Exhortations in Amos, Hosea, Isaiah, Micah, and Zephaniah* (Baltimore: St. Mary's Seminary, 1982), 169–174); Jeremias, *Hosea*, 169; Eidevall, *Grapes in the Desert*, 209.
141. Rudolph, *Hosea*, 250–251; Mays, *Hosea*, 184–185; Macintosh, *Hosea*, 569.
142. As with Mays, *Hosea*, 185.
143. Dearman, *Hosea*, 340.
144. O'Kennedy, "Healing as/or Forgiveness," 465.

The Consequences of the Restored Relationship (14:6–9)

The divine promise of restoration of verse 5 is translated into an image of nature. The cluster of botanical similes in verses 6–8 describes the diverse productivity, stability and prosperity that Israel will experience as a result of her restoration in the unspecified future.

14:6–8

6α	He shall blossom like the lily	יפרח כשושנה
6bβ	He shall strike his roots like Lebanon	ויך שרשיו כלבנון :
7a	His shoots shall spread out	ילכו ינקותיו
7bα	His splendour shall be like the olive tree	ויהי כזית הודו
7bβ	His fragrance like Lebanon	וריח לו כלבנון :
8bα	They shall flourish like the vine	ויפרחו כגפן
8bβ	His fame shall be like the wine of Lebanon	זכרו כיין לבנון :

Although the exact identity of the lily (שׁושׁן) elicits discussion, most interpreters agree that it signifies beauty (v. 6bα).[145] Striking deep roots, like Lebanon, it denotes endurance and stability (v. 6bβ), underlining that "the new life and prosperity of the restored Israel will not be short-lived like the flowers of the lily."[146] The image of a tree spreading its shoots (v. 7a) in all directions, perhaps envisages a territorial expansion of the established Israel[147] or her reproductive power.[148] The splendour (הוד) of the olive tree (v. 7bα) probably implies wealth and well being, since olives are a staple of the region, providing food, oil, medicine and commodities for trade.[149] The link of הוד with divine majesty (Ps 96:6; 104:1) and human royalty (Ps

---

145. For example, see M. Zohary, *Plants of the Bible* (Cambridge: Cambridge University Press, 1982), 176; Rudolph, *Hosea*, 248; Davies, *Hosea*, 306; Nwaoru, *Imagery*, 174–175.
146. Nwaoru, *Imagery*, 175.
147. Ibid.
148. Eidevall, *Grapes in the Desert*, 215.
149. Dearman, *Hosea*, 342.

21:5; 45:3) will prepare Israel to partake of future royal splendour.[150] The ensuing simile in verse 7bβ compares Israel's fragrance (ריח) to Lebanon (cf. Song 4:11), denoting "vitality, the capacity for true living."[151] It is possible that "renewed Israel is pictured as a lush garden."[152] The final two similes in verse 8b extol the peak of Israel future glory: "they shall flourish (פרח) like the vine" (v. 8bα). Interestingly, the verb פרח is used to describe Israel's perverted justice in 10:4. It is possible that Israel's flourishing like the lily (v. 6bα) and vine (v. 8bα) accentuate the notion of prosperity where justice marks the health of the growth. The comparison of Israel's fame (זכר) to the wine (יין) of Lebanon (v. 8bβ) stresses the quality of the product that a "high material standard for the nation will be accompanied by equally high moral standards."[153] At the same time, the fame or "reputation" which makes Israel worthy of "remembrance"[154] brings the process of reversal to Yahweh's "recollection" of Israel as evildoer (cf. 7:2; 8:13; 9:9).[155] It is noticeable that the first set of similes (vv. 6b–7a) focus on Israel's inner revived strength and prosperity whereas the second set (vv. 7b–8b) underline her external appearance after the restored relationship.

Significantly, the emphasis of the rhetorical discourse is not simply on Israel's fecundity and prosperity described by the string of plant similes in verses 6–8, but on the life-giving source: Yahweh (vv. 6a, 8aα and 9bα). Arguably, the first chain of similes in verses 6–7 is grounded on Yahweh's declaration, "I will be like the dew (טל) for Israel" (v. 6a),[156] whereas the saying of verse 8aα sets the background of the next cluster of similes in verse 8b. This is more visible when Yahweh compares himself to an evergreen cypress (v. 9bα) from which Israel derives her fruit (v. 9bβ).

The rhetorical question of verse 9aα moves from the realm of promise (vv. 5–8) to the sphere of Israel's current condition. It urges Israel to confess

---

150. Eidevall, *Grapes in the Desert*, 215 and Dearman, *Hosea*, 342.
151. Nwaoru, *Imagery*, 177.
152. Eidevall, *Grapes in the Desert*, 215.
153. Ibid., 216.
154. Cf. Wolff, *Hosea*, 236.
155. Cf. Garrett, *Hosea, Joel*, 277.
156. In contrast to the way it is used in 6:4; 13:3, the simile of v. 6a focuses on the dew's life-giving aspect. The drops of dew are an essential source of life and growth for the flora described in vv. 6–7.

her error of romancing with idols.¹⁵⁷ The next clause affirms that Yahweh – as opposed to the idols – is able to "answer" (ענה) the people and to "watch over" (שׁור) them (v. 9aβ). The verb שׁור is used in 13:7 to depict the leopard's preparedness for its prey. Yahweh's readiness to watch over the people here nicely reverses that image. The final ironic and polemic simile, "I am like the evergreen cypress; your fruit comes from me" (v. 9b), subsumes the series of botanical metaphors of the preceding verses. In the biblical tradition, "green" is often associated with places of worship, especially with the cultic centres where fertility gods were worshipped.¹⁵⁸ It is not clear which of the great trees in Palestine is in mind.¹⁵⁹ Nevertheless, it is the "greenness" of the tree that brings out the full import of the simile,¹⁶⁰ symbolising the permanent and protective character of divine providence.¹⁶¹ Yahweh apparently exploits the Canaanite concept of associating green with fertility to suggest that all of Israel's prosperity comes from him – the true God of fertility, the "Green One." It is no wonder that some interpreters have gone as far as to identify it with the tree of life,¹⁶² recalling the scene where relationship originated.

The Epilogue of the Book: A Wisdom Poem (14:10)

The last verse of the book (v. 10) is generally treated as an editorial piece of advice to unlock the prophecies of Hosea.¹⁶³ It is also possible that the wisdom style and vocabulary come from the prophet himself.¹⁶⁴ According to Seow, the sapiential element ("the foolish people motif") is pervasive

---

157. Cf. Nogalski, *Hosea–Jonah*, 192.
158. Nwaoru, *Imagery*, 173.
159. According to Tångberg, the concept of Yahweh as an ideal king symbolised by a majestic tree sets the background for the simile. See K. Arvid Tångberg, ""I am like an evergreen fir, from me comes your fruit": Notes on Meaning and Symbolism in Hosea 14:9b (MT)," *SJOT* 2 (1989): 81–93 (87–91).
160. Cf. Nwaoru, *Imagery*, 174.
161. Cf. Mays, *Hosea*, 189 and Andersen and Freedman, 647.
162. For example, Wolff, *Hosea*, 237; Mays, *Hosea*, 190; Andersen and Freeman, *Hosea*, 647; Jeremias, *Hosea*, 173; Eidevall, *Grapes in the Desert*, 219.
163. Wolff, *Hosea*, Mays, *Hosea*, 190; Davies, *Hosea*, 310; Macintosh, *Hosea*, 583; Sweeney, *Twelve Prophets*; Dearman, *Hosea*, 345.
164. Stuart, *Hosea–Jonah*, 219; McComiskey, "Hosea," 236–237; Garrett, *Hosea*, 281. Choon L. Seow, "Hosea 14:10 and the Foolish People Motif," *CBQ* 44 (1982): 212–224.

in Hosea.¹⁶⁵ From a scriptural point of view, this self-contained wisdom poem is a fitting conclusion to the book, summarising Hosea's message of relational justice.

The emphasis of the first part of the verse: "Let whoever is wise understand these things, whoever is discerning recognise them" (v. 10a), falls on the difficulty of the prophecies. Admittedly, the oracles are subtle, allusive and elliptical, and at times, obscure.¹⁶⁶ Nevertheless, the "wise" (חכם) and "discerning" (בין) are assumed to grasp the meaning of "these" (אלה) [things/words], and walk in the "ways of Yahweh" (דרכי יהוה), which are "just, straight, correct" (ישר) (v. 10bα).

In the light of our overall analysis of the book, the unspecified "these" is best understood to refer to the prophecy as a whole in general and relational faithfulness in particular. Ephraim is assessed as "unwise" (לא חכים) for her inability to take right actions in relating to Yahweh (13:13). The people who are indifferent to various injustices in society are labelled as a people "without discernment" (לא־יבין) (4:14). Israel's irresponsible "ways" are variously depicted (2:8; 4:9; 10:13; 12:3). Straying away from Yahweh, they "walk/go" after things which are self-destructive (2:7, 15; 5:11; 12:2). Thus, the wise and prudent are those who are faithful (i.e. צדקים) to relationship. Those people walk in "the ways of Yahweh" (v. 10bα), by which is meant his relational demands of fidelity in all spheres of life. In contrast, the rebels (פשעים) who turn away from Yahweh (7:13) and reject his instruction (8:1) "stumble" (כשל) (cf. 4:5; 5:5; 14:1) because "justice is an obstacle for those who navigate through life by means of injustice and self-deception" (v. 10bβ).¹⁶⁷ Hence the key to understanding is not intelligence but submission, not rebellion but discipleship.

In sum, our investigation above has established that the unifying theme of Hosea 14:2–9 is clearly restoration. The first three verses (2–4) constitutes the final prophetic appeal to the apostate to come back to renew their allegiance to Yahweh. In so doing, they specify the steps involved in that renewal process: the people must renounce their ethical violation, their

---

165. See Seow, "Hosea 14:10," 212–214.
166. Cf. Garrett, *Hosea, Joel*, 281.
167. G. T. Sheppard, "The Last Words of Hosea," *Rev Exp* 90 (1993): 191–204, 198.

idolatrous cult and their alliance with political powers. Despite the lack of evidence that the people have taken such actions, Yahweh still declares his unreserved willingness to restore the nation (v. 5), which is followed by prophetic depictions of productivity, stability and prosperity that the nation will experience after their restoration (vv. 6–8). The book concludes with a wisdom poem (v. 9), challenging the "wise" and "prudent" to choose Yahweh's ways: true and just relationship.

Summary Assessment

In this final chapter, we have examined Hosea's message in 12:1–14:10. Once again, it is based on our proposed three strands of the book: responsibility, chastisement and restoration. As it turns out, this has been a profitable way of reading the book.

Our study, contrary to what has often been assumed, has shown that the unifying theme of the section (12:1–15) is a prophetic critique of Ephraim's irresponsibility. That is, it is not so much about judgment. The section forcefully emphasises various accusations of relational breaches, namely, political irresponsibility (12:1–3, 4–6), economic violations (12:7, 8–10) and religious evils (12:12, 13–15). The mission of the chosen nation is to reflect the character of Yahweh in all areas of life, but Israel's actions reflect otherwise. All her political actions have betrayed her master, Yahweh. Those who are called to love and care for their neighbours not only oppress others but even brag of ill-gotten wealth. The people betrothed exclusively to one deity, Yahweh, have acquired strange gods. Significantly, these fundamental lines of accusation run through the next chapters (13–14). They are the reference lines that trigger the announcements of various chastisements in 13:1–14:1. They are the specified things that the people must renounce in order to renew their personal communion with Yahweh (14:2–4).

The trifold literary structure (13:1–3, 13:4–9, 13:10–14:1) with the climatic message of judgment and the dreadful images that have characterised the intratextual features have all confirmed that the unifying theme of Hosea 13:1–14:1 is chastisement. As has been argued, the sole aim of the divine chastisement of Israel is to repair the breach in relationship with

Yahweh. For that reason, the transformed Yahweh will bring to an end every important institution of Israel. Israel as a religious and political entity will be no more. The projected destruction of Israel is total and irreversible, with no possibility to rebuild the nation.

Nevertheless, as in the previous cycles, chastisement is not the last action of Yahweh in relation to Israel. The final section, 14:2–10, which represents the culmination of the book, describes Yahweh's express will to restore his people. Disappointingly, the book of Hosea has not witnessed Israel's return to Yahweh despite the manifold prophetic calls. Nor has it testified that chastisement, in itself, has brought about the hoped-for renewal of relationship. Therefore, as in 2:1–3; 2:16–25; 3:5; 11:8–9, Yahweh's love has to transcend chastisement as well as Israel's sinfulness. By his own volition, Yahweh will heal Israel's apostasy, love his people freely and withdraw his anger from them (14:5). Divine love, in this way, transcends the demands of justice that have insisted on punishing a people who have abandoned their relational responsibility. Paradoxically, however, in this same way, Yahweh's love fulfils justice by forgiving the unforgivable because what matters most to the God of Israel is to build "true and right relationship" with his people, Israel. Hence justice means right relationship.

CHAPTER TEN

Conclusions

This thesis has offered an in-depth analysis of Hosea's message on justice. The study has argued that the traditional characterisation of the eighth-century BC prophets (Amos, Micah and Isaiah) as prophets of justice as opposed to Hosea as a prophet of love is an oversimplification.[1] Hosea delivers, contrary to what has often been assumed, a social critique on his own terms and in his own style. Every aspect of his profound metaphors and sayings is wed vividly to the political, social, religious and relational faithlessness of his contemporaries, and this evidence brands him a prophet of justice in his own right – a preacher of relational justice. His message is not simply to expose Israel's guilt in terms of the Canaanite fertility cult,[2] nor can it be confined exclusively to the historical and economic crisis.[3] Rather, the message of Hosea is to call corporate Israel to maintain true and right relationships with their God and with their fellow Israelites.

Relational Justice and Hosea

Before we draw out our conclusions on the book of Hosea, it is necessary to redirect attention to our argument that *justice* is essentially *relational*. Our discussions of the concept of "justice" in the secular sphere and of the biblical understanding have both confirmed that *justice* is necessarily a matter of

---

1. Blenkinsopp, *A History of Prophecy*, 90.
2. Wolff, *Hosea*, xxii.
3. Keefe, *Woman's Body*, 11.

justice in relationship. The underlining principle of commutative and social justice is the exercise of reciprocal rights between individuals, and between individuals and their larger society. The protection of rights can only occur when individuals live up to "just living" in relation to other individuals. It is a right not to be harmed as well as a right to act justly towards others. The notion of distributive justice with its miscellaneous emphases of egalitarian, needs-based, libertarian and merit-based justice aims to create a relational context where individuals get their just due. Retributive justice, as outlined in this study, not only aims to punish guilty person in proportion to the offence, but more importantly to reform the delinquent and reduce broken relationships in the society. Restorative justice aims to restore the communal relationships between the transgressors, victims and the community, which have been harmed by the crime. A crucial underlying principle of all the different types of justice is a relational aspect. The intrinsic goal of justice is to promote harmony in the society by delivering equal distribution, maximising utility, assisting the disadvantaged and respecting the rights of the individuals. So justice in effect means just relationships.

We have argued that the biblical concept of justice and many secular conceptions of justice are complementary. However, it is appropriate at this point to indicate some specific biblical emphases. Though the biblical notion of justice accommodates the different types of justice, it appears to have certain issues in the foreground. Arguably, the biblical teaching of justice places its emphasis on the social responsibility of the people to bring about justice in the community. For instance, the biblical understanding of justice puts more weight on the duty to act justly towards others than the right not to be harmed. It places more emphasis on communal responsibility, fulfilling the duty to look after the disadvantaged, than on the inherent rights of the poor themselves. Biblical justice does not negate a secular notion of freedom (or a free society) but locates liberty in a relationship with Yahweh. Moreover, the biblical notion of justice goes further than many philosophical ideas of justice. For example, biblical justice, which is inherently associated with inexplicable divine mercy, does not simply aim to give people what is due to them in terms of distributing fair shares, but is willing to give more than their due in terms of forgiveness. Biblical justice carries both the sense of retribution and restoration.[4] Its innate aim is not merely to punish the guilty in proportion to the seriousness of their crime, but to give the perpetrators the opportunity to turn away from evil, and enter into right relations with their victims and with their God.[5] Thus it can be rightly considered as including restorative punishment as an essential component.[6] Needless to say, biblical justice, dictated by *agape* love, aims to bring the distorted relationship back to its normal state. Hence the biblical concept of justice is fundamentally relational. It demands right living in all areas of life – not a particular type of justice – to preserve right relationship. In brief, relational justice demands, penalises [chastises] and restores.

In order to establish that the biblical concept of justice is relational, we have analysed three main biblical terms צדקה, חסד and משפט. Beyond doubt, these words are well-recognised biblical terms to examining the idea of justice in the Old Testament. צדקה, is used with social, ethical, forensic and religious meanings. However, our analysis has concluded that the underlining notion of צדקה refers to a condition of a person who is relationally faithful. צדקה is a highly relational term which fulfils the claims arising out of actual relationship between two entities: between humans and between humans and God. It refers to a behaviour in accord with some implied norms as well as a unique fidelity to relationship that goes beyond the call of duty. Its core aim is to perpetuate a persistent, right relationship.

We have examined the biblical concept of חסד. Like צדקה, the conceptual term חסד is comprehensive and has a strong relational aspect, which can only be defined by a cluster of several words. The fundamental idea of חסד in the Scriptures involves a voluntary action of one person to (and for) another. It consists of an inward disposition of love (right motives) and an outward expression of love (right actions). In other words, it refers to a moral and ethical behaviour corresponding to a mutual relationship as well as a compassionate deed, which is grounded on divine חסד, aiming to maintain true and right relationships.

---

4. Cf. Burch, "Justice," 641.
5. Cf. Donahue, "Biblical Perspectives of Justice," 72.
6. Cf. Marshall, *Beyond Retribution*, 134.

The most significant term in exploring the biblical concept of justice is משפט. The term represents a range of different ideas and meanings from moral, legal and religious domains. Our study, contrary to what has been customarily assumed, has shown that the underlining essence of the concept is its relational aspect. Even in a forensic context, the primary aim of משפט is not so much about fair play in terms of judicial procedure, but rather about protection and sustaining a relationship for coexistence. Essentially, it refers to an action of any given authority that preserves relations and restores the disturbed order and hurt individuals in the community. It includes the legal demand but goes beyond it. Its key aim is to regulate a right relationship in a particular circumstance. Unlike the modern notion of justice, which is based on *iustitia distributiva*, the biblical concept of justice (משפט) is *iustitia salutifera*. In this, משפט is closely associated with other relational concepts such צדקה, חסד and רחם. Like those concepts, משפט demands a commitment, whether legal, ethical or religious, to sustain right relationships between God and his people and between people and their fellow human beings.

It is now clearly visible that the ultimate concern of all notions of justice, whether secular or biblical, is justice in relationship. Injustice, therefore, is the loss of right relationship. Yet how does this relational justice work? What does it entail? What are the unifying constituents? How does it relate to the message of Hosea?

This study has adopted the idea that human life is always life-lived-with-others. Humans exist as selves in relationship to others.[7] The undergirding body of that relationship is justice, and therefore, justice basically means "right relationship." Its ultimate goal is to maintain and perpetuate that right relationship. Conceivably, the first element of right relationship or relational justice is responsibility which comes with accountability and obligation. Justice, in this sense, assumes mutual trust and loyalty as an original (just) position and aims to build and sustain right relationships. In the life-lived-with-others, every human person is responsible for their actions and thus what justice demands is responsibility from the responsible selves. Noticeably, the philosophical discussions on the significance

---

7. Cf. Raines, "A Relational Theory of Justice," 131; Niebuhr, *The Responsible Self,* 71.

of shared responsibility under the rubrics of commutative, social and distributive justice fall within this category.

The second component of relational justice involves a correction when the assumed right relationship is thwarted or distorted. It comes by means of imposing a penalty with a view to reconstructing the right relationship of the original position. Justice, in this sense, which carries both the sense of retribution and restoration, denounces anything that disturbs the relational equilibrium by imposing punishment on the perpetrator and by asserting the victim's right and therefore includes the notion of retributive justice, especially with its biblical flavour. As its aim is to restore right relationships, retributive justice is better rendered or understood as chastisement.

The final component of relational justice is that it aims to build a new relationship from that which has been distorted or destroyed. Obviously, restorative justice resides in this category. Justice, in this sense, assumes a commitment based on a bond relationship in which a break in the chain is inexcusable. Restorative justice, particularly with its biblical sense, does not only assert the victim's right but also withholds, at times, due punishment of the perpetrator in the hope for restoring right relationship. It moves to a situation where the irresponsible selves are absolved. By transcending human logic, it provides forgiveness to the unforgivable, the pinnacle of relational justice. In a nutshell, relational justice demands (responsibility), chastises (the irresponsible) but restores (even the irresponsible).

Hosea belongs to the group of eighth-century prophets, namely, Amos, Micah and Isaiah who are renowned for their quest for justice. These classical prophets speak on behalf of values central to society and on behalf of Yahweh who sanctions the moral structure of society.[8] Their ministry is no longer confined to the king and his court as in the case of the earlier prophets, but includes the entire people.[9] The social world, which has occasioned their prophetic activities, can be called the "Golden Age" in terms of prosperity and territorial expansion. But it can also be called the "Dark Age" in terms of social and moral sickness. The prosperity, profligacy, exploitation and syncretism of the time have lit the fire of their social criticisms.

---

8. Cf. Petersen, *Israel's Prophets*, 68.
9. Cf. Holladay, "Assyrian Statecraft," 37.

Having come from such a social world and having shared the message of the prophetic corpus, it is unimaginable that the remaining classical prophet, Hosea, would walk away from criticism of the injustices of his time. Not surprisingly, he did not shy away from it. Contrary to popular opinion, this study has argued that the prophet does address the socio-economic, political and religious injustices of his day. We will outline our conclusions on these specific issues later, but for now, it is important to explore the shape of Hosea's overall message. We have suggested that relational justice demands, corrects and restores. Interestingly, this study has demonstrated that these ideas form the three constituting mechanisms of Hosea's prophetic words. His prophetic proclamation always begins with Hosea's/Yahweh's call for responsibility or an accusation for irresponsibility on the part of Israel to maintain right relationship. This is, in turn, always followed by a message of chastisement with a view to reconstructing the lost right relationship. Finally, Hosea's prophetic proclamation is eventually culminated by the divine reconciliatory act even when Israel does not call for a right relationship. Other eighth-century prophets may well be emphasising a particular type of justice (e.g. social justice for Amos), but Hosea chooses to deal with the source of injustice – the loss of right relationship. Put differently, his prophetic oracles in relation to specific types of justice are incorporated under the rubric of relational justice. Based on this theoretical framework, this study has argued for six cycles of responsibility-chastisement-restoration in the book. The proposed structure can be outlined as follows.

Cycle	Responsibility	Chastisement	Restoration
1	1:2b–3	1:4–9	2:1–3 [1:10–2:1]
2	2:4–7 [2–5]	2:8–15 [6–13]	2:16–25 [14–23]
3	3:1–2	3:3–4	3:5
4	4:1–5:7	5:8–5:15a	5:15b–6:3
5	6:4–8:14	9:1–10:15	11:1–11
6	12:1–15 [11:12–12:14]	13:1–14:1 [13:1–16]	14:2–9 [14:1–8]

This thematic reading is guided by the internal message of the book. It demarcates the boundaries of the cycles based on their general flow, and on the unifying themes of each section rather than their minute individual oracles. While arguments for such a division may appear too neat, it is observed that the oracles alternate between the accusation of *irresponsibility* and pronouncement of *chastisement* and *restoration* – the underpinning principles of relational justice.

The first component of Hosea's message – responsibility – is particularly significant for this study, for this has been the neglected feature in Hosean scholarship in favour of the themes of judgment and restoration.[10] That is to say that the message of Hosea is not simply the pronouncement of judgment and restoration. Evidently, the call for responsibility or the accusation of irresponsibility is where Hosea grounds his message of judgment, and his proclamation of restoration is also closely related to the call for responsibility. This study has proposed that a proper exegetical analysis of this aspect is not only central to the overall relational message of Hosea, but it also provides a platform by which to draw more from his specific messages concerning social issues.

Relational Justice in Hosea 1–3

This study has contended that the book of Hosea is all about Hosea's/Yahweh's hard-fought combat against the threatening challenges to right relationships. The ultimate goal is to restore the distorted relationships between Yahweh and his people, and between the people and fellow covenant members. Fascinatingly, in the opening chapters of the book, Hosea sets this relational context in terms of marriage and family which reflect the deepest relationships of all. Perhaps the prophet knows no better way to describe the true relationship of Yahweh to Israel than depicting it in terms of love, marriage, betrothal and having children.[11] Clearly, Israel stands in relationship to Yahweh, and this requires responsibility in terms of accountability and obligation.

---

10. This trend is represented by Wolff, *Hosea*, xxxi; Rudolph, *Hosea*, 35; Wyrtzen, "The Theological Center," 316; Silva, *A Literary Analysis*, 190.
11. Cf. Koch, *The Prophets*, 88.

Based on our proposed three components that run through the book, we have explored the structure, content and message of Hosea 1–3. In so doing, we have discerned three cyclical movements of the three strands that characterise the first three chapters. As one would expect, the first element – responsibility – of each cycle (1:2b–3; 2:4–7; 3:1–2) lays the ground on which relational justice can be tested. The relational context is set by Yahweh's command to Hosea to marry a wife in 1:2: "Go, take to yourself a woman of harlotry and *have* children of harlotry . . . and he went and took Gomer the daughter of Diblaim and she conceived and bore to him a son (1:2b), and the second command to do the same thing in 3:1: "Go again, love a woman who is loved *by her* friend, yet an adulteress . . . and I bought her to me for fifteen *shekels* of silver" (3:1a, 2a). The command appears to be easily understood that Hosea is to "marry" (לקח) and "love" his wife and have a family. But the laconic description of Yahweh's command with Hosea's compliance constitutes a pivotal moral trajectory. It defines what it means to be a just person (faithful to a relationship) in order to mirror what it means to be an unjust person (unfaithful to a relationship). Hosea by his prophetic symbolic action portrays what a just person would do. What the text presents to us is one who as a husband and father is fully responsible in regard to these relationships. In order to enhance our comprehension of the metaphor, we have explored ancient family structure in the context of Hosea as a patrilineal father who stands true to his marriage relationship with his wife and so, by analogy, Yahweh to his covenantal relationship with Israel.

In contrast, Gomer's adulterous behaviour represents the opposite – infidelity to right relationship. Appallingly, Hosea is commanded to have "a woman of *harlotry* and have children of *harlotry*, for the land commits fragrant *harlotry* forsaking Yahweh" (1:2b). Our analysis has suggested that "harlotry" (cf. 2:4, נאף and זנה) is conceived of as a generic description for disloyalty in relationships which can be associated with variety of relational infidelities against Yahweh and his demands. The text presents to us a woman who is a wife and mother who is utterly irresponsible in keeping right relationship. This relational breach is presented in 2:4–7 by means of a well-known ריב-pattern proclamation, which indicates that there is something essentially wrong in the relationship between Hosea and his wife. Gomer's lack of commitment to maintain and sustain her marriage relationship creates the central problem. Again, by analogy, there is something fundamentally wrong in the religious and ethical relation and conduct of the land/Israel, which she represents. This normative relationship witnessed in both Hosea and Gomer serves as a baseline from which every relationship shall be assessed. If justice is a matter of justice in relationship, a breakdown in relationship is injustice. There is injustice when a partner is hurt in any given relationship. Israel, standing in a covenantal relationship to Yahweh, is accountable for her actions to her wronged partner. This paradigmatic relationship stands true with regard to their relationship to other fellow humans.

The theme of chastisement is our second proposed component of relational justice in Hosea. It must be recalled that relational justice assumes mutual trust and loyalty as the original position, demanding responsibility which entails accountability and obligation. As a result, unaccountability and irresponsibility towards the obligation to sustain right relationship necessarily incur chastisement in order to re-establish the original position. As shown in the chart above, the theme of chastisement in the first three cycles of the book is presented in 1:4–9, 2:8–15 and 3:3–4. As a consequence of the faithless conduct of Gomer/Israel, which negates the relationally loyal conduct of Hosea/Yahweh, Gomer/Israel must pass through the path of correction and purification.

In 1:4–9, the message of chastisement is conveyed through pregnant words that can be called "one phrase oracles."[12] The names of Hosea's children, Jezreel, Lo-Ruhamah and Lo-Ammi, are attached to judgment, anticipating Yahweh's disciplinary measures that will come upon Israel. As a result of Gomer's adulterous action in 2:4–7, Hosea/Yahweh announces the impending measures in the words of an aggrieved husband in 2:8–15. Along these lines, 3:3–4 describes how the spurned husband will now restrict the activities of his wayward wife. Israel's basic institutions will suffer deprivation. They will be without socio-political independence, without religious institutions and without worship. Yet relational justice does not incur judgment for the sake of mere retributive judgment. It penalises but

---

12. Cf. Buss, *Word of Hosea*, 29.

it does so for correction. Conceivably, Hosea's/Yahweh's strictures and deprivations imposed upon Gomer/Israel have in fact evolved into a plan of future action. Clearly, Hosea could have chosen a termination of relationship by means of "divorce" or "stoning to death," which would legally be allowed him, in response to the adultery of Gomer, his wife. Hosea/Yahweh nonetheless pronounces chastisement to stage a new platform to re-establish a better relationship.

The three sections on the theme of responsibility (1:2b–3; 2:4–7; 3:1–2) in Hosea 1–3, are followed by three other sections of judgment oracles (1:4–9, 2:8–15 and 3:3–4). Interestingly, each declaration of chastisement is followed by a reversal of prophecy, which comes at 2:1–3, 2:16–25 and 3:5. It is clearly noticeable that what Gomer/Israel deserves from Hosea/Yahweh is only the termination of relationship (divorce or death). Surprisingly, Hosea/Yahweh announces reconciliation in place of termination. It is not so shocking, however, if the default position of relational justice is taken into account. Relational justice not only embraces chastisement as a pathway that leads to reunion, but also involves forgiving the unforgivable. The salvific predictions in 2:1–3 are a reversal of the severe punishment depicted in 1:4–9. The judgment names (Jezreel [1:4–5], Lo-Ruhamah [1:6] and Lo-Ammi [1:9]) are transformed into salvation names, suggesting the severed relationship will be restored. Yahweh will now dwell (Jezreel, 2:2) among the people of Israel and Judah. The "not God's people" (Lo-Ammi) will be called "sons of the living God" (2:1) and "my people" (2:3). The name "no compassion" (Lo-Ruhamah) is reinterpreted positively as "compassion" (2:3).

In the same vein, the next passage in 2:16–25 reverses the language of accusation and disciplinary measures of 2:4–18. Despite Israel's/Gomer's grave transgression, Yahweh's/Hosea's relational commitment endures. The "wilderness" used as a threat to Gomer (2:5) has transformed into a place for reconsolidation (2:16). The word of renunciation "I am not her husband" (2:4) is replaced by a word of acceptance "you will call me 'my husband'" (2:18). Hosea's paradigmatic "taking" of Gomer gives way to Yahweh's collective "taking" of Israel (2:21–22). Yahweh has become a wooing deity (2:16) and will let the suspended marital provisions of grain, wine and oil (2:10–11) flow once again (2:17). The new commitment will be sealed with the gifts of צדקה, משפט, חסד, רחם, and אמונה (2:21–22). The three names Jezreel, Lo-Ruhamah and Lo-Ammi now reappear with positive connotations (2:24–25).

The third passage that reports Yahweh's restorative commitment is 3:5. As in 2:1–3 and 2:16–25, this restorative oracle describes Yahweh's promise of Israel's future reconciliation. The three specific things that have been withdrawn from the nation will be restored to them (cf. 3:4). They will seek Yahweh, their God, will recognise the Davidic divine king as their ruler, and come in trembling awe to Yahweh. Surprisingly, there is no hint that Israel has come to her senses in returning to Yahweh. Yet he will still erase all traces of Israel's transgression and will treat her as if the past did not exist. Certainly, Yahweh's relentless pursuit will eventually overcome the wayward Israel.

In brief, the proclamation of Hosea (Hosea 1–3) that has begun with a charge of irresponsibility (1:2b–3; 2:4–7; 3:1–2) has evolved into chastisement (1:4–9, 2:8–15 and 3:3–4), and this has been consummated by the message of restoration (2:1–3, 2:16–25, 3:5). The people/land/Gomer/Israel are charged and chastised but will be restored. Clearly, this is the central message of Hosea's relational justice. Accordingly, this study has argued that the marriage/family metaphor used in Hosea 1–3 provides the exegetical framework from which the entire book is to be read.[13]

Relational Justice in Hosea 4:1–6:3

Within the parameters of the framework outlined above, we have explored the prophetic words of Hosea in 4:1–6:3. It is argued that this panel is best analysed by exploring our suggested three strands: responsibility, chastisement and restoration, forming a fourth cyclical presentation in the book. The first three chapters primarily describe the relational faithlessness by means of a generic term "harlotry," which can be taken as Israel's *religious apostasy* in terms of their vertical relationship with Yahweh as well as her *socio-ethical failure* in terms of their horizontal relationship with fellow human beings – Yahweh's demands. Based on this normative basis, Hosea makes his message of justice more explicit in 4:1–6:3, by unpacking Israel's

---

13. Cf. Childs, *Old Testament as Scripture*, 281.

infidelity to relationships in various socio-political contexts of the time. That is, the woman of fornications (Hosea 1–3) also signifies the pressing socio-political crisis of Hosea's time.[14]

As in chapters 1–3, the prophetic oracles in 4:1–6:3 revolve around the themes of responsibility (4:1–5:7), chastisement (5:8–5:15a) and restoration (5:15a–6:3). Contrary to what has often been understood, this study has argued that Hosea 4:1–5:7 is not primarily about judgment.[15] Rather, the unifying theme of the discourses is a prophetic critique of Israel's relational irresponsibility. Hosea's criticism is grounded on Yahweh's controversy against all Israel: the people (4:1–3), the priesthood and false cult (4:4–19) and the national leaders (5:1–7). By means of a prophetic ריב-pattern discourse (4:1), Hosea declares that Israel's religious relationship to Yahweh and the ethical relationships and conduct to her neighbours are entirely wrong. More exactly, the prophet accuses them of discarding the three social virtues אמת, חסד, and דעת אלהים and replacing those qualities with social crimes such as cursing, lying, murder, stealing and adultery. The prophet alleges that they have totally failed their relational responsibility towards Yahweh, their fellow human beings and creation (4:1–3). The culprits for social disaster are the priests who have failed to act upon their duty (4:4–10), the rulers who have failed their responsibility to set a just and good order (משפט) in the society (5:1–7), and the people, who are captive to harlotry and wine and have indulged in flawed cultic practices and social crimes (4:11–19). In this light, it is plausible to conclude that Hosea's soft but strong prophetic voice reflects a real social concern for the nation of his time. To interpret the metaphor and message of Hosea exclusively to Baalism and the monarchy with its foreign policy as public concrete sins[16] is indeed an oversimplification for they are only expressions of the socio-economic injustices of the time.[17]

Every irresponsible deed of Israel is utterly opposed by the prophet precisely because it hurts others with whom they stand in inseparable

---

14. Cf. Keefe, *Woman's Body*, 10–11
15. *Contra* Wyrtzen, "The Theological Center," 315–329 and Silva, *A Literary Analysis*, 230–243.
16. Cf. Wolff, *Hosea*, xxii; Mays, *Hosea*, 13; Brueggemann, *Tradition for Crisis*, 120.
17. Cf. Yee, *Poor Banished Children of Eve*, 81–83.

relationships – their God and their fellow humans and creation. It must be remembered that relational justice not only demands responsibility but embraces chastisement as a pathway to restoration.

It has been argued that the notion of judgment, which has received only a passing reference in previous verses (4:10, 19; 5:2), is displayed more vividly in 5:8–15a. The passage stresses Yahweh's active engagement in bringing judgment upon Ephraim and Judah for their relational infidelity. Yahweh's chastisement, which is enacted by means of Israel's encroaching enemy, Assyria, is signalled by the sarcastic war alarms of 5:8. The land would be plundered by foreign armies (5:9) because the leaders of Judah have abandoned relational fidelity with fellow covenant members (5:10). The personified מִשְׁפָּט, which should dictate Ephraim's social relations and politics, is crushed (5:11). As a result, Yahweh, the source of their healing, has evolved into "pus" and "rottenness" to the nation, the source of their illness (5:12). Moreover, as a consequence of their relational faithlessness, Yahweh has become the cause of their woundedness. He will attack Ephraim and Judah like a ferocious "lion" and a "young lion" respectively (5:14–15a). Yahweh's affliction, via internal (disease) and external (ferocious animal) means will make the two nations metaphorically morbid, injured and hurt and they will not escape Yahweh's judgment. Clearly, the unifying theme of this section is chastisement and this has been noted by many interpreters. What has not been observed is that chastisement in Hosea is not mere retaliation, nor an end in itself, but rather a means to instil obedience and return. The ultimate aim of Yahweh, the discipliner (5:2) and chastiser (5:9), is the return of the people in right relationship with him and with fellow covenant members.

The judgment speech of 5:8–14 gives way to the glimmer of hope for restoration in 6:1–3. The expression of Yahweh's expectation of the people's return in 5:15 functions as a bridge from one theme to the next. Our analysis has maintained that the form and function of Hosea 6:1–3 is best taken as exhortation designed to call for a response. It is a call addressed by the prophet in the name of Yahweh to the people, in hope of repentance (6:1–2). The imagery of Yahweh, as the source of illness and healing and of Ephraim and Judah as the wounded and sick, continues. Repentance and healing in this context primarily denote a restoration of relationship between Yahweh and the people at a personal level, which would be naturally accompanied by obedience on the part of Israel. Importantly, the proposed pathway for Israel's return to relationship is דעת אלהים, which denotes resolute fidelity to Yahweh and his ethical nature (6:3). Remarkably, Israel's return/repentance is assumed rather than expressed. There is neither a confession of sin, nor a return implemented by the people. Yet the passage declares Yahweh's one-sided confidence and willingness for Israel's return. Since relational justice not only holds chastisement as a path to reunion but also involves forgiving the unforgivable, it is not difficult to recognise the train of thought of this passage. Israel's return will reverse the lion metaphor in 5:14. Yahweh will heal what he has torn to pieces. In reversing the physical illness metaphor of 5:12, Yahweh will bandage the injuries of Israel. In brief, Israel is accused (4:1–5:7) and chastened (5:8–15) but will also be restored (6:1–3).

Relational Justice in Hosea 6:4–11:11

Based on our suggested three trends, we have explored the structural content and message of Hosea 6:4–11:11. We have argued that the central theme in 6:4–8:14 is a prophetic charge against Israel's *irresponsibility* in relationships, whereas Yahweh's various *chastisements* predominantly feature in the next section (9:1–10:15). This is followed, as one would anticipate, by Yahweh's promise of *restoration* in 11:1–11. As such, the proposed thematic threads form another cycle of the book.

In 6:4–6, Yahweh declares that Ephraim and Judah have failed the fidelity test. Yahweh laments (6:4) their fleeting relational virtues, חסד and דעת אלהים (6:4, 6). We have observed that both of these concepts primarily denote faithfulness in right relationships with Yahweh and fellow humans. These relational virtues, which bind together the people with Yahweh, and with fellow Israelites, have vanished from sight (6:4). Worship and sacrifices are present, but the qualities that give worship its value – חסד and דעת אלהים – are lacking (6:6). Israel's relational disloyalty has resulted in national defilement (6:10) as crime follows after crime (6:8–9). As in 4:1–3, the prophet catalogues the sins of omission (6:4–6) and the sins of commission (6:7–7:2). The nation destined to keep exclusive ברית fidelity to Yahweh has violated it, and has utterly failed to maintain loyal conduct within the community (6:7). In a stark contrast, social evils such as bloodshed (6:8), premeditated murder, robbery and raiding (6:9) prevail in the land. Yahweh's attempt to relate with the people as a restorer and healer has exposed their civil and social crimes of fraud, thieving and banditry (7:1). The all-seeing Yahweh can only perceive their "evil deeds" and "transgressions," which primarily suggest their irresponsibility to right relationships (7:2).

In 7:3–7, the prophet condemns the ruptured and hostile relationships within Israel's domestic politics. The people, priests, king and princes, whose tasks involve national leadership, conspire against one another (7:3–7). They "gladden" each other with "lies" (7:3–4). The rulers who should rejoice in justice and righteousness rejoice in "wickedness" (7:3) by becoming captives of wine and the spirit of conspiracy (7:5). All "hearts" lie in wait to grasp the opportunity to seize throne, power, privilege and wealth through political intrigue and treachery (7:6). Their judges, who might stand up for justice, have swiftly been terminated (7:7). Successive "regicides" (7:7), "lies" and "wickedness" (7:3) all have in effect become the practical societal norms. Worst of all, they have failed to turn to Yahweh, who alone can heal the nation (7:7). Given this prevailing situation, it is implausible to doubt that Hosea addresses justice. His main concern clearly is the absence of right relationships in the society of his day.

The next prophetic speech (7:8–16) deals with Israel's entanglement in international politics. The nation is likened to an unturned cake (7:8), a fooled dove (7:11) and a faulty bow (7:16). We have observed that the image of a half-baked cake primarily depicts worthlessness and the simile of "grey hair" (7:9b) illustrates a state of decay. Foreigners have eaten up the nation's strength because it lacks "knowledge" (7:9a). Despite their entire predicament, the people fail to return and seek Yahweh (7:10). The simile of a senseless dove depicts Ephraim's failure to recognise their dependence on Yahweh (7:11–12), whereas the metaphor of a slack bow indicates the nation's uselessness (7:16). Ephraim's offenses are related to Yahweh because they "strayed from," "rebelled against," "speak lies against" (7:13), "turned away from" (7:14) and "plot evil against" him (7:15). At the worst, the people "do not cry out" to Yahweh with contrite hearts (7:14). For Israel to remain true to Yahweh, her social, political and religious life must reflect his character (7:13–14). To the contrary, Israel's refusal to build a new and right relationship with Yahweh remains constant.

The next series of prophetic speeches in 8:1–14 elaborates the accusations of Israel's faithlessness. The charge of irresponsibility extends over Israel's moral life (8:1–3, 14), political values (8:4a, 8–10) and religious worship (8:4b–6, 11–13). Israel's fundamental sin involves violation of ברית and rebellion against the תורה (8:1b). It is argued that Hosea uses ברית (6:7) to represent Israel's solemn commitment to Yahweh, as well as the communal loyal conduct designated by משפט (6:5), חסד and דעת אלהים (6:6.). Though Israel cries "my God" they break his ברית. Though they claim "we know you," they rebel against him (8:2). Their moral decay is reflected by the fact that their words and deeds are in direct contradiction with each other. Moreover, Israel's lack of commitment to right relationships is demonstrated by her rejection of the טוב (8:3), which in context suggests a conduct in conformity with the ברית and תורה (8:1b). Their outright rejection of the טוב, ברית and תורה has left them with man-made governments and gods.[18] Yahweh declares that he has nothing to do with the royal establishment of Samaria, which is branded by wickedness, lies and treachery (8:4a, cf. 7:3). Like a wild ass, they search for independence from Yahweh by means of an alliance with Assyria (8:8–10). They make idols that will lead to their own destruction (8:4–6) and are used to increase their sinning (8:11–13). In place of "sowing" seed, Israel has sown the "wind" (8:7). Once again, the unifying theme of the discourses in 6:4–8:14 is not about judgment. Rather, as in 4:1–5:7, it is Hosea's prophetic critique of relational irresponsibility.

The next sizable set of prophetic discourses in 9:1–10:15 describes Yahweh's various chastisements upon Israel. Though the lines of accusation from previous discourses continue, they are now primarily employed to bring the message of chastisement. Hosea, for one last time, uses the term "harlotry" as a reference point for the impending chastisement (9:1a). It is argued that harlotry in this context suggests Israel's passionate concern for commodities at the expense of their relationship to Yahweh (9:1b; cf. 2:7, 14). In response, Yahweh, the divine rightful owner (cf. 2:10), will suspend

---

18. Cf. Mays, *Hosea*, 117.

the products of the land. The personified threshing floor and winepress will then deceive them by means of a failed harvest (9:2). They will be eventually expelled from the land to eat defiled food in Egypt and Assyria (9:3). The sacrifice that symbolises their existence alongside Yahweh will finally cease (9:4). Destruction will ravage the land and those who escape destruction, if there are any, will be collected by Egypt and Memphis will bury their bones. Their shrines or idols made with silver (cf. 2:10; 8:4; 13:2) and festival "tents" will be inherited by "thorns" and "thistles" (cf. 2:5b, 8, 14; 9:5–6). Yahweh's chastisement in response to their moral previrsion is inevitable. Instead of joyful days, there will only be terrifying days of judgment (9:7–9).

Yahweh's "finding" and "seeing" Israel as delectable fruit, which denotes election, in 9:10a sets a baseline of accusation against the people. The nostalgic element of Israel's past is quickly eclipsed by the divine dismay over Israel's immorality (9:10b). The horrific transformation from being delectable fruit to becoming abominable has led to Ephraim being sterile and bereaved. The divine presence, departing like a bird, leaves Israel with no birth, no pregnancy, and no conception (9:11). In case someone could manage to rear children, Yahweh will bereave them of each one (9:12). In reversing Israel's fertility blessings (Gen 49:25; Exod 23:36; Deut 28:4, 11), Yahweh will give the people a "miscarrying womb and dry breasts" (9:14), suggesting the total demise of future generation (9:13). In response to their rebellion against him (9:15), Yahweh will give them "barrenness." Even if women of the blighted nation manage to give birth, those "precious offspring of their wombs" will be killed by Yahweh (9:16). Because of their relational faithlessness, Israel's election (9:10) evolves into rejection (9:17).

The ensuing discourses in 10:1–8 continue to feature the chastisement that will fall upon both the sacred and political institutions of Israel. The misuse of prosperity (10:1) and the erosion of the administration of justice and order (10:4) have brought about war that destroys everything. Israel's irresponsibility is twofold: the people worship a calf instead of promoting fidelity and justice. As a result of their religious apostasy and their moral depravity, Yahweh will destroy their altars and pillars (10:2). Though the inhabitants of Samaria lament its departure, the calf statue of Beth-aven will be deported (10:5–6). The royal might of Samaria will not withstand the strong current of divine wrath by means of invading armies (10:7). The fear engendered by total destruction will force them to invite the personified mountains and hills to fulfil their craving for death (10:8).

We have argued that Israel's failure to maintain justice in communal relationships, presented in 10:11–13, is exactly the kind of irresponsibility that has called down Yahweh's punishment in 10:9–10 and 10:14–15. Israel, who is called by Yahweh to "sow" the seed of צדקה, plants "injustice" instead (10:12). The one who is chosen to reap the fruit of חסד secures "wickedness," and eats the fruit of lies (10:13). So Yahweh has come to chastise perverse Israel (10:9–10). All Samaria's fortifications will be demolished. Mothers will be dashed in pieces alongside their children (10:13–14). The heart of the nation's darkness, Bethel, will be eradicated and its monarchy will also be gone when chastisement sweeps through the land (10:15). What the prophet projects is that war will destroy everything. It is now clearly visible that the central theme of Hosea 9:1–10:15 is chastisement. Dispersion is clearly projected in 9:1–9, while 9:10–19 pictures infertility. The demise of every essential institution is depicted in 10:1–15.

As one would expect, judgment is nonetheless not the last word in Hosea. The desire of Yahweh is only to chastise Israel with a noble purpose that will channel a new relationship. It must be remembered that relational justice not only holds chastisement as a path to reunion but also involves embracing the unacceptable as its peak. This reconciliatory mood is executed through Yahweh's dramatic actions in Hosea 11. We have argued that there is a responsibility-chastisement-restoration movement within chapter 11. The purpose of the themes of responsibility in 11:1–4 and chastisement in 11:5–7 is primarily to place the message of restoration in 11:8–11 in its climatic position.

Yahweh's unilateral love (אהב), which not only initiates covenantal relationship in the first place by means of calling (קרא) Israel (11:1) but also sustains that relationship by his providential care of the people (11:3a, 4), is contrasted with Ephraim's consistent lack of love and commitment to relationship (11:2, 3b). Ephraim rebels against the one who chooses, protects and rears her, but walks away from him instead. Her refusal to recognise (ידע) Yahweh's initiation of relationship (11:3b) and her rejection of returning (שוב) are the central issues that not only bring the Yahweh-Israel relationship to a stalemate, but have also prompted Yahweh's corrective measures (11:5b). Israel's only lot is chastisement. Warfare, besiegement and deportation are in perspective (11:5–7).

The climatic message of reconciliation is clearly noticeable in 11:8–11. What Ephraim deserves from Yahweh (as in the case of Gomer) is evidently the termination of relationship. Yet once again, Yahweh announces "continuation" for the Yahweh-Israel relationship in place of its "termination." Yahweh's answer (11:9–11) to the existential self-question (11:8) defines the future of the Yahweh-Israel covenant relationship. Yahweh, who is true to himself, declares that he will not annihilate irresponsible Israel, refusing to execute his divine wrath in favour of his relationship with her (11:9a). He could afford to do this because he is God, not human (11:9b). Yahweh's roaring, like a lion, will summon his scattered people by scaring the enemy and by ensuring safe return for his people (11:10). With a presupposed changed attitude and like birds finding their way, the people will walk after Yahweh in trembling awe and joyful hope from their dispersion in order to be settled in their homes (11:11). Hence the future of the Yahweh-Israel relationship solely rests on Yahweh himself.

In sumary, like the preceding cycles, the bulk of Hosea's proclamation in 6:4–11:11 follows the same trend: Israel is accused (6:4–8:14), chastised (9:1–10:15) and will also be restored (11:1–11). Hosea proclaims a well-balanced message. His critique of Israel's relational problems extends over the moral, social, political and religious domains. For him, there is no justice until and unless there are right and true relationships between humans and between humans and God. His concern for the social brokenness of his time is conceivably deeper than that of other prophets. His proclamation of Yahweh's love transcends human logic. Despite Israel's consistent infidelity and lack of remorseful attitude, Yahweh, who initiates and sustains relationships, refuses to terminate his covenant relationship with her. Hosea preaches no message of doom. This compels us to label him as a prophet of justice as well as a prophet of God's love *par excellence*.

Relational Justice in Hosea 12:1–14:1

Based on the proposed three strands, we have also examined the prophetic words of Hosea in 12:1–14:10. It is argued that Hosea's cyclical proclamation can be established also in this final major section. It is observed that the unifying theme of the discourse in 12:1–15 is primarily the charge against the people's *irresponsibility*, whereas the theme of *chastisement* is clearly dominant in 13:1–14:1. Strikingly, the cycle is concluded by Yahweh's express will to *restore* his people by loving them freely in 14:2–9.

The prophetic oracles in 12:1–15 emphasise various accusations of the relational breaches under the rubrics of Ephraim's political irresponsibility (12:1–3, 4–6), socio-economic/ethical violations (12:7, 8–10) and religious apostasy (12:12, 13–15). Ephraim's lies, violence and self-destructive courses of action are characterised as a personal attacks on Yahweh (12:1–3). The nation is accused of chasing delusions in terms of making covenant with Assyria instead of maintaining their existing relationship with Yahweh (12:2). The nation is charged with treason against its master (12:2, 15). For one last time, the prophet employs the ריב-pattern discourse to complain against Ephraim's and Judah's severed relationships with Yahweh and with fellow Israelites (12:3). The transformative possibility, offered as a path to reunion (i.e. a return that results in חסד and משפט), hangs there simply as a proposal (12:7). The people are accused of social oppression against their fellow covenant members (12:8). They are accused of relying on ill-gotten wealth in place of doing justice (12:9) and seeking Yahweh (12:10–11). What is more, they are accused of worshiping strange gods (12:12). Clearly, the culpability of the nation extends to all spheres of life: political, economic, ethical and religious. Interestingly enough, the holistic perspective of Hosea's message is well-presented in this section: politically, Israel betrays her master, Yahweh; socio-economically, the people exploit and oppress fellow citizens; and religiously, the people betrothed exclusively to Yahweh, have acquired strange gods. Significantly, these central lines of accusation serve as the points of reference that trigger the message of chastisement in 13:1–14:1. By the same token, the lines of accusation outline the demands which the people must renounce in order to renew their relationship with Yahweh (14:2–4).

We have argued that both the effect of the trifold literary structure (13:1–3, 13:4–9, 13:10–14:1, each having a climatic message of judgment), and the intratextual features branded by various awful images, suggest that the unifying theme of Hosea 13:1–14:1 is chastisement. The reason for which Ephraim/Samaria is punished is stated in each section. Israel's culpability consists of her continuous dalliance with idols (13:1–2), her moral failure in plenteous times (13:6) and her illusory political values of self-assistance (13:10–11). As result of the people's religious apostasy (13:2), the nation, which once struck terror in the heart of its neighbour (13:1), will vanish like "morning mist," "dew," "chaff" and "smoke" (13:3). In response to Israel's reckless moral irresponsibility (13:4–6), Yahweh will change his role: from shepherd to predator, from saviour to furious destroyer (13:7–9). Like a leopard, Yahweh will get ready for an attack on his people (13:7). Like a bear he will suddenly assault them, and like a hungry lion, he will devour them (13:8). Because of Israel's political folly (13:10–11) and repetitive relational breaches (13:12), Yahweh's judgment will come upon Ephraim like labour pains (13:13). His compassion, which gives rise to the change of mind in 11:8, is not within sight. Instead, the personified "death" and "Sheol" are summoned to send forth "plagues" and "pestilence" over the people (13:14). Drought as a result of war will ruin Samaria. Victors will loot every valuable thing in their storehouse (13:15). Their little ones will be "crushed" and pregnant women will "ripped up" (14:1). Israel as a religious and political entity will be no more. The projected destruction for Israel is total and irreversible, with no possibility to rebuild the nation.

It is important to stress at this point the positive aspect of judgment. The judgment theme is a well-recognised feature of classical prophets[19] and for which they are labelled as outright preachers of doom. On the other hand, another tendency is to interpret the theme of judgment in terms of covenant curses.[20] However, it is argued that declaration of judgment in Hosea is far from being a concluding point. Yahweh's harsh judgments are corrective measures which function as a means to a greater ends. Again, judgment in Hosea does not retaliate but chastises.

As is to be expected, chastisement in Hosea is not the final word of Yahweh in relation to Israel. Our study has argued that the unifying theme of Hosea 14:2–9 is restoration. In culminating the book, the last section

---

19. Cf. Wolff, "Prophecy," 24 and Mays, "Justice: Perspectives," 16–17.
20. Cf. Stuart, *Hosea–Jonah*, xxxii.

describes Yahweh's express will to restore his people. Its rhetorical goal is to convince the people to re-enter a personal communion with Yahweh. It is observed that 14:2–4 constitutes the final appeal to the apostate to come back and renew their allegiance to Yahweh. The specified steps of that renewal process on the part of the people are to renounce their ethical violation (14:3), their idolatrous cult (14:4b) and their alliance with political powers (14:4a).

Bewilderingly, the book of Hosea has not witnessed the people's return to Yahweh despite the manifold prophetic calls. Nor has it attested that chastisement, in itself, could bring about the hoped-for renewal of relationship.[21] In spite of Israel's inability to comply with his demands, Yahweh, by his volition, declares that he would "heal" Israel's apostasy, "love" his people freely and withdraw his anger from them (14:5).[22] This is followed by a series of metaphorical depictions of productivity, stability and prosperity that the nation will experience after their restoration (14:6–8). Both Israel's internal (14:6–7) and external (14:7–8) strength and prosperity will be revitalised, as Yahweh himself will become the permanent protector of the restored nation (14:9). Divine love, in this way, transcends the demand of justice that insists on retaliation towards the perpetrators. Yet paradoxically, Yahweh's love, in this way, supplements justice by forgiving the unforgivable, for the ultimate goal of Yahweh is to perpetuate a "true and right relationship" with his chosen people, Israel. Hence Yahweh's chastisement with its full reality and his love which expresses his will for restoration is not contradictory.[23]

Once again, like the previous five cycles, Hosea's message in 12:1–14:10 also maintains the suggested trend: Israel is accused (12:1–15), and chastised (13:1–14:1) but will also be restored (14:2–9). Clearly, the lines of accusation of Israel's social, religious and political irresponsibility in 12:1–15 have triggered Yahweh's chastisement in 13:1–14:1, bringing an

---

21. Thus Wolff, "Prophecy," 25.
22. Repentance is called-for and hoped-for in Hosea. But no single instance do we see summons to repentance as a precondition for restoration or forgiveness. For Emmerson, *Hosea*, 39, Hosea's message of Israel's repentance comes as a result of God's saving activity, while Israel's repentance is a precondition in the view of Judean redactor(s).
23. *Contra*, Eichrodt, "The Holy One in Your Midst," 271–272.

end to every significant institution of Israel. However, Yahweh's love, which defines his loyalty to covenant relationship, conquers in the end when irresponsible and unforgivable Israel is absolved and restored.

Concluding Remarks

This study has confirmed the general trend of Hosean studies as well as countered it at some points. It confirms that Hosea is a prophet of God's love. Nevertheless, to categorise Hosea wholly as a prophet of divine love is unattainable. It also confirms that the two dominant themes include judgment and restoration. However, contrary to this popular opinion, our analysis takes the bulk of his prophetic collection as being comprised of accusations of irresponsibility which deal with social issues.[24] Accordingly, this study also sees that Hosea is not merely an anti-cultic maverick who only addresses Israel's religious apostasy. Moreover, Hosea has no message of anything like doom. Nor does he preach justice that retaliates or annihilates. His called-for and hoped-for goal is for right and true relationships between humans and between humans and God. If this thesis is correct, Hosea's sense of justice goes deeper than that of other prophets. Thus, he is indeed a prophet of God's love as well as a prophet of justice *par excellence*.

Hosea's Social Critique

It is now necessary to outline our conclusions relating specifically to Hosea's social critique. This study has argued that Hosea, like other classical prophets, addresses the socio-economic, political and religious injustices of his day, but in his own way. Admittedly, Hosea's invective against the injustices of his time is not as scathing as other prophets especially that of Amos. However, Hosea's soft but strong poetic voice undeniably reflects a real social concern. Essentially, Hosea launches his social criticism with the רִי-pattern discourse, which begins either the relevant section as a whole or a

---

24. Unlike most interpreters, this study reads that accusation of irresponsibility in Hosea predominates over judgment by a slight margin and over promise by a substantial margin.

significant part of that section (2:4; 4:1; 12:3).²⁵ By means of this adapted lawsuit speech, the prophet declares that Israel's religious relationship with Yahweh and their treatment of their fellow citizens are utterly wrong. The latter aspect is of interest at this point. A closer observation of the immediate contexts where the ריב occurs, presents a clearer view of Hosea's social message.

In 2:4, the the ריב-pattern discourse is employed in a familial context, between husband and wife. The context of the metaphor makes it clear that the declaration of divorce comes as a result of the failure of Israel's religious and ethical fibre. It is Israel who has played the harlot. Conceivably, the main hindrance to the marriage is Israel's lack of moral and ethical qualities, which is represented primarily by her passionate concern for commodities (2:7, 14). Interestingly, these qualities are specified in a message of hope where Yahweh declares that he will start over with a clean slate by providing Israel what she had been unable to obtain before: צדק, משפט, חסד, רחם and אמונה (2:21–22). To reiterate what has been stated, צדק suggests a relational faithfulness in and through societal norms, and at times, even in violation of those norms. משפט represents relational integrity in communal life within the reach of legal demand, aiming to regulate right relations in society by restraining vice and protecting the innocent and those who have been hurt. חסד denotes faithfulness to Yahweh and justice in the Israelite society. It entails mutual loyalty, but surpasses mutual obligation by going beyond the call of duty. רחם denotes the tender side of commitment to the well-being of another. It protects the total termination of relationship from happening. אמונה signifies a constancy of commitment to do good deeds to (and for) another. These compelling conceptual observations suggest that the social dimension is on the horizon. These moral qualities constitute the "lost" realities in eighth-century Israel. They are the specific means by which to "recourse" the community's coexistence alongside Yahweh.²⁶ Clearly, the open-ended view of justice in the first

---

25. Cf. Morris, *Prophecy,* 116.
26. Brueggemann, *Tradition for Crisis,* 13, points out the need for Israel to "recourse to tradition" in terms of covenant restoration, but he does not spell out the specified means by which to actually implement the covenant renewal.

chapters of the book paves the way for more detailed exploration of the issue in what follows.

The second ריב-pattern prophetic speech comes at 4:1a in which Hosea declares that Israel's religious relation to Yahweh and her ethical and moral conduct to fellow covenant members are totally wrong. The blatant identification of the addressee, which includes the populace, the priests and the political leaders and the specification of their many crimes (4:1–5:7) make explicit what is implicit in previous chapters (Hosea 1–3). The prophet outlines three social virtues that are absent from the society (4:1b). He goes on to catalogue the six social vices that have created a social vacuum (4:2). The active social virtues, אמת, חסד, and דעת אלהים, by which the society should live have all disappeared from sight. It is observed that אמת primarily denotes the nature of a person who is faithful to neighbour, true in speech, and reliable and constant in actions.[27] As such, the fall of אמת from society means the emergence of injustice. As has been argued, חסד consists of the inner nature of commitment and the outward expression of dutiful action, which can be applied to both God and people. Strikingly, the six occurrences of חסד in Hosea (2:21; 4:1; 6:4, 6; 10:12; and 12:7.) it is applied to human beings. The fact that חסד in 4:1 is followed by a series of sins of commission strongly suggests that the חסד in this particular context is directed to one's neighbours.[28] As such, Hosea's invective is against the absence of justice and righteousness in the community.

We have also argued that דעת אלהים, the third virtue, in Hosea connotes a moral quality rather than a merely intellectual apprehension. It means knowledge of Yahweh's teachings as the source of a harmonious communal life within Israel. It is the recognition of Yahweh's character and the reception of his demands. Markedly, חסד and דעת אלהים are placed together in 6:6. As in the context of 4:1–3, the two desiderata in 6:4–6 are followed by a series of sins of commission (6:7–7:2). That is, by discarding אמת, חסד, and דעת אלהים the Israelites have embraced social crimes such as cursing, lying, killing, stealing, adultery and bloodshed (4:2). By rejecting דעת אלהים (4:6), the corrupt priests indulge in syncretism and materialism

---

27. Cf. Jepsen, "אמן, . . . אמת," 313.
28. Cf. Sakenfeld, *The Meaning of Hesed,* 173.

(4:7). Their godless and greedy actions in the guise of religious observance obscure the weighty moral requirements which are prior in importance (4:8). The failure of the people's ethical fibre has resulted in enslavement to sexual immorality and drunkenness (4: 11, 14, 18). What drives the society is a feast-loving and decadent carefree way of life (7:4–5). The absence of חסד and דעת אלהים necessarily means the presence of bloodshed (6:8) premeditated murder, robbery and raid (6:9). It is observed that thieving inside and banditry outside (7:1) are a synecdoche for civil and social injustices.[29] The increase of palaces and walled cities on the pretext of national security symbolises the malady that has afflicted the poor in society (8:14).[30] Moreover, חסד is paralleled with צדקה in 10:12, whereas it is contrasted with "injustice" and "wickedness" in 10:13. It is argued that צדקה/צדק in this text belongs to the group of concepts: אמונה, רחמים, חסד, משפט and דעת (2:21–22). It denotes the behaviour of the people within the social relationships that they should treat each other decently and justly so that Yahweh would send his צדק upon them (10:12). Clearly, what Hosea condemns is the failure to maintain justice in the community. To say that Hosea bypasses צדקה and משפט emphasised by Amos and Isaiah in favour of אמתם, חסד and דעת אלהים is an oversimplification[31] because Hosea uses them as equivalent terms. This compelling evidence suggests that justice is indeed a real concern of Hosea.

The third ריב-pattern speech comes at 12:3. Like the two previous usages noted above, the present context is characterised by Ephraim-Judah's sinful behaviour such as "treachery," "lies," "violence," and "iniquity" (12:1–2, 8–9, 15). For one more time, Hosea's appeal to the people to "maintain חסד and משפט" in 12:7 constitutes Hosea's social message. As has been noted, חסד denotes religious faithfulness to Yahweh on the one hand and justice in socio-political/economic realm on the other. Again, it is the latter aspect of חסד that we want to pay attention to, and it is only משפט that requires further elaboration here. We have argued that משפט primarily denotes relational fidelity that maintains and restores the

---

29. Cf. Stuart, *Hosea–Jonah*, 118.
30. Cf. Premnath, "Amos and Hosea," 120.
31. Cf. Mays, *Hosea*, 12.

community's existence through legal means. It aims to regulate right relations in society by restraining social vices. It underlines the fundamentals of justice and lawful action towards others. It is argued that all the leaders of Israel are denounced for their failure to install משפט in society (5:1). The personified משפט, which should dictate the nation's social relations and politics, is crushed (5:11). Similarly, Yahweh charges the ruling elite with eroding the administration of justice and order (10:4). The משפט, which the king is supposed to have provided, has turned out to be "poisonous weeds" (ראש) – hence injustice (cf. Amos 6:12; Isa 5:1–7).

Interestingly, these two conceptual terms are placed together intentionally in the context of social exploitation (12:8) and economic injustice (12:9). The absence of חסד and משפט means the presence of social exploitation of various kinds. It is argued that the use of the root עשק "to oppress" or "to extort" (5:11; 12:8) refers to the social injustice and economic exploitation of the underprivileged classes by the privileged. The leaders of Israel are compared to a personified merchant in whose hands are "deceptive scales," which depict loathsome greediness in commercial practices (12:8). It is observed that the "threshing floor" in 9:1 signifies a place for injustice, where the rich and ruling landowners extort shares from every threshing floor. The people who are called to love neighbours have opted instead to *love* oppression (12:8) and even brag about their ill-gotten "wealth" (12:9). The moral collapse of the people is clearly mirrored by their reckless ingratitude in "forgetting" Yahweh, their true benefactor (13:6). Clearly, the people of the north have indulged in immorality and the oppression of others, particularly the peasantry. Though we hear no clear voice about the oppressed, the prophetic words of Hosea, in his own style, address the social and economic injustice against the poor within the nation.[32]

Concluding Remarks

Although Hosea's social message is harder to decipher than that of other classical prophets, his soft but strong prophetic voice nonetheless deals with the social issues of the nation plagued by various injustices. The main

---

32. *Contra* Utzschneider, *Hosea*, 212–216; Landy, *Hosea*, 151; Kelle, *Hosea 2*, 293.

reason that Hosea's social criticism is not as scathing as that of others appears to be that his view of justice is subsumed under a larger theme of relational justice as outlined in this study. That is to say, the lower visibility of Hosea's social message is occasioned by his holistic or balanced prophecy which deals with Israel's crisis from the moral, social, political and religious domains. The crisis consists of false worship of the true God and the seeking of power externally rather than seeking justice in internal affairs. In other words, the book is about Israel's failure to serve Yahweh in terms of their vertical relationship with him and it is about Israel's failure to accomplish Yahweh's purposes in terms of their horizontal relationship with their fellow covenanted members. Therefore, the traditional cultic-religious interpretation and more recent socio-economic interpretation of Hosea must be held together in Hosean scholarship. To focus on any single aspect of Hosea's message is to miss the totality of his proclamation.

Recommendations

Our first recommendation concerns the overall structure and themes of the book. Hosea's strong sense of social responsibility, his firm conviction on the need of chastisement for correction and his confidence in God's saving impulse for reunion constitutes the pillars upon which the entire prophecy is built. In other words, the three constituent themes – responsibility-chastisement-restoration – form a unified whole, and the removal of one makes the others incomprehensible. If this thesis is correct, then there is a particular pattern discernible in the way that the oracles are crafted. Thus, the exegetical tradition that views the structure of Hosea as a formless collection may now be abandoned.[33]

Second, the current biblical scholarship has surmised that the book of Hosea, with its thematic *judgement* and *restoration*, stands as a programmatic statement of the primary issues addressed throughout the Book of the Twelve.[34] If that is the case, it is highly likely that the "responsibility"

---

33. Cf. Mowinckel, *Prophecy and Tradition*, 55–57; Wolff, *Hosea*, 75, Mays, *Hosea*, 5 and Andersen and Freedman, *Hosea*, 69.
34. Cf. Sweeney, *Twelve Prophets*, 3.

theme outlined in this study will also find its way throughout the Book of the Twelve.

Third, judgment in Hosea is far from being annihilation, but a part of the process towards restoration. If this claim that *judgment* in Hosea has a positive implication and hence "chastisement," other prophetic books could be revisited from this perspective. It may be that the other prophets in the Old Testament also do not preach judgment that annihilates or justice that retaliates.

Finally, if our approach using the theme of *relational justice* could unlock a prophecy like that of Hosea it would be worthwhile to reread other prophetic books from this angle, especially the other eighth-century prophets. Traditional scholarship that normally interprets the messages of Amos, Micah and Isaiah primarily in terms of social justice can also be re-evaluated. Nevertheless, these further avenues remain the challenges we may pass on to the next generation of students.

Bibliography

Abma, Richtsje. *Bonds of Love: Methodic Studies of Prophetic Texts with Marriage Imagery, Isaiah 50:1–3 and 54:1–10, Hosea 1–3, Jeremiah 2–3*. SSN 40. Assen: Van Gorcum, 1999.

Achtemeier, Elizabeth R. *Minor Prophets I*. Edited by R. L. Hubbard and R. K. Johnston. NIBC. Peabody: Hendrickson, 1996.

———. "Righteousness in the Old Testament." In *IDB* 4, 80–85. New York: Abingdon Press, 1962.

Ackerman, Susan. "The Personal is Political: Covenantal and affectionate Love (ʾāhēb, ʾahăbâ) in the Hebrew Bible." *VT* 52 (2002): 437–458.

Ackroyd, Peter R. "Hosea and Jacob." *VT* 13 (1963): 245–259.

———. "The Verb Love – אהב in the David Jonathan Narratives – A footnote." *VT* 25 (1975): 213–214.

Ahlström, Gösta W. *The History of Ancient Palestine from the Palaeolithic Period to Alexander's Conquest*. JSOTSup 146. Sheffield: JSOT Press, 1993.

Alt, von Albrecht. "Hosea 5:8–6:6. Ein Krieg und seine Folgen in prophetischer Beleuchtung." Pages 163–187 in *Kleine Schriften zur Geschichte des Volkes Israel*. Edited by von Albrecht Alt. Band II. München: Beck, 1964.

———. "The Origins of Israelite Law." In *Essays on Old Testament History and Religion*, 79–132. Traslated by R. A. Wilson; New York: Doubleday, 1967.

Andersen, Francis I. "Yahweh, the Kind and Sensitive God." In *God Who is Rich in Mercy: Essays presented to Dr. D. B. Knox*, edited by Peter T. O'Brien and David G. Peterson, 41–88. Homebush, NSW: Lancer Books, 1986.

Andersen, Francis I. and David N. Freedman. *Hosea: A New Translation with Introduction and Commentary*. AB 24. New York: Doubleday, 1980.

———. *Amos: A New Translation with Introduction and Commentary*. The Anchor Bible 24A. New York: Doubleday, 1989.

Anderson, Arnold A. *Psalms, I*. NCBC. London: Marshall, Morgan & Scott, 1972.

Aristotle. *The Ethics of Aristotle: The Nicomachean Ethics Translated*. Translated by J. A. K. Thomson. 1956. Repr., Harmondsworth: Penguin Books, 1969.

———. "Justice." In *Justice: Selected Readings*, edited by Joel Feinberg and Hyman Gross, 16–27. Encino: Dickenson Publishing Company, 1977.

Arnold, Patrick M. "Hosea and the Sin of Gibeah." *CBQ* 51 (1989): 447–460.

Astour, Michael C. "841 BC: The First Assyrian Invasion of Israel." *JAOS* 91 (1971): 383–389.

Atkinson, David. *To Have and to Hold: The Marriage Covenant and the Discipline of Divorce*. London: Collins, 1979.

Baer, D. A. and R. P. Gordon. "Ḥsd." In *NIDOTTE* 2, ed. Willem Van Gemeren, 210–218. Grand Rapids: Zondervan, 1997).

Balz-Cochois, Helgard. *Der Höhenkult Israels im Selbstverständnis der Volksfrömmigkeit*. Frankfurt am Main: Peter Lang, 1982.

Barker, Paul. *The Triumph of Grace in Deuteronomy: Faithless Israel, Faithful Yahweh in Deuteronomy*. Carlisle: Paternoster, 2004.

Barr, James. "Some Semantics Notes on the Covenant." In *Beiträge zur alttestamentlichen Theologie: Festschrift für Walther Zimmerli zum 70 Geburtstag*, edited by Herbert Donner et al., 23–38. Göttingen: Vandenhoeck & Ruprecht, 1977.

———. "The Synchronic, the Diachronic and the Historical: A Triangular Relationship." In *Synchronic or Diachronic? A debate on Method in Old Testament Exegesis*, edited by Johannes C. de Moor, 1–14. OtSt 34. Leiden: E. J. Brill, 1995.

Barré, Michael L. "New Light on the Interpretation of Hosea VI 2." *VT* 28 (1978): 129–141.

Barstad, Hans M. *The Religious Polemics of Amos: Studies in the Preaching of Am 2, 7B–8; 4,1–13; 5,1–27; 6,4–7; 8,14*. Leiden: E. J. Brill, 1984.

Batten, Loring W. "The use of מִשְׁפָּט." *JBL* 11 (1892): 206–210.

Barton, John. *Reading the Old Testament: Method in Biblical Study*. Louisville: Westminster John Knox Press, 1984.

Bauman, Eberhard. "ידע und seine Derivate." *ZAW* 28 (1908): 22–41.

———. "'Wissen um Gott' bei Hosea als Urform von Theologie." *EvT* 15 (1955): 416–425.

Baumann, Gerlinde. *Love and Violence: Marriage as a Metaphor for the Relationship between Yahweh and Israel in the Prophetic Books*. Translated by Linda M. Maloney. Stuttgart: Verlag Katholisches, 2000. Repr., Collegeville: Liturgical Press, 2003.

Beisner, E. Calvin. *Prosperity and Poverty: The Compassionate Use of Resource in a World of Scarcity*. Westchester: Crossway, 1988.

Ben Zvi, Ehud. "Observations on the Marital Metaphor of YHWH and Israel in its Ancient Israelite Context: General Considerations and Particular Images in Hosea." *JSOT* 28 (2004): 363–384.

———. *Hosea*. FOTL 31A1. Grand Rapids: Eerdmans, 2005.

Bendor, S. *The Social Structure of Ancient Israel*. Jerusalem: Simor, 1996.

Bentham, Jeremy. *An Introduction to the Principles of Morals and Legislation*. London: W. Pickering, 1823.

Berkovits, Eliezer. "Biblical Meaning of Justice." *Judaism* 18 (1969): 188–209.

Birch, Bruce C. *Hosea, Joel and Amos*. Westminster Bible Companion. Louisville: Westminster John Knox Press, 1997.

Bishops, U.S Catholic. *Economic Justice for All: Pastoral Letter on Catholic Social Teaching and the U.S. Economy*. Washington, DC: National Conference of Catholic Bishops, 1986.

Bjornard, Reider B. "Hosea 11:8–9, God's Word or Man's Insight." *BR* 27 (1982): 16–25.

Black, Max. *Models and Metaphors: Studies in Language and Philosophy*. Ithaca: Cornell University Press, 1962.

Blenkinsopp, Joseph. *A History of Prophecy in Israel*. Rev. ed. 1983. Louisville: Westminster John Knox Press, 1996.

Booth, Osborne. "The Semantic Development of the Term משפט in the Old Testament." *JBL* 61 (1942): 105–110.

Boshoff, W. "The Female Imagery in the Book of Hosea: Considering the Marriage Metaphor in Hosea 1–2 by Listening to Female Voices." *OTE* 15 (2002): 23–41.

Bosma, Carl J. "Creation in Jeopardy: A Warning to Priests (Hosea 4:1–3)." *CTJ* 34 (1999): 64–116.

Bovati, Pietro. *Re-Establishing Justice: Legal Terms, Concepts and Procedures in the Hebrew Bible*. Translated by Michal J. Smith. JSOTSup 105. Sheffield: JSOT Press, 1994.

Bowman, Craig D. "Reading the Twelve as One: Hosea 1–3 as an Introduction to the Book of the Twelve (the Minor Prophets)." *SCJ* 9 (2006): 41–59.

Braaten, Laurie J. "Earth Community in Hosea 2." In *The Earth Bible: The Earth Story in the Psalms and the Prophets,* edited by Norman C. Habel, 184–203. Sheffield: Sheffield Academic, 2001.

———. "God Sows: Hosea's Land Theme in the Book of the Twelve." In *Thematic Threads in the Book of the Twelve,* edited by Paul L. Redditt and Aaron Schart, 104–132. BZAW 325. Berlin: de Gruyter, 2003.

Braithwaite, John. *Crime, Shame, Reintegration.* 1989. Repr., Cambridge: Cambridge University Press, 1999.

———. "Restorative Justice as a Better Future." Paper presented at Dorothy J. Killam Memorial Lectures, Dalhousie University, 1996.

———. *Restorative Justice and Responsive Regulation.* Oxford: Oxford University Press, 2002.

Brekelmans, C. and J. Lust, eds. *Pentateuchal and Deuteronomistic studies: Papers Read at the 13th IOSOT Congress, Leuven, 1989.* BETL 94. Leuven: Leuven University Press, 1990.

Brenner, Athalya, ed. *A Feminist Companion to the Latter Prophets.* Sheffield: Sheffield Academic Press, 1995.

Bright, John. "The Prophets were Protestants: Fresh Result of valid Criticism." *Int* 2 (1947): 153–182.

Britt, Brian. "Unexpected Attachments: A Literary Approach to the term חסד in the Hebrew Bible." *JSOT* 27 (2003): 289–307.

Broshi, Margen and Israel Finkelstein. "The Population of Palestine in Iron Age II." *BASOR* 287 (1992): 47–60.

Browley, Robert L., ed. *Biblical Ethics & Homosexuality: Listening to Scripture.* Louisville: Westminster John Knox Press, 1996.

Brueggemann, Walter. "Amos 4:4–13 and Israel's Covenant Worship." *VT* 15 (1965): 1–15.

———. *Tradition in Crisis: A Study in Hosea.* Richmond: John Knox, 1966.

———. "The Uninflected Therefore of Hosea 4:1–3." In *Reading from this Place, vol 1: Social Location and Biblical Interpretation in the United States,* edited by Fernando F. Segovia and Mary A. Tolbert, 231–249. Minneapolis: Fortress Press, 1995.

———. *Theology of the Old Testament: Testimony, Dispute, Advocacy.* Minneapolis: Fortress Press, 1997.

Brunner, Emil. *Justice and the Social Order.* Translated by Mary Hottinger. London: Lutterworth Press, 1945.

Brunner, Hellmut. "Gerechtigkeit als Fundament des Thrones." *VT* 8 (1958): 426–428.

Buber, Martin. *The Prophetic Faith.* Translated by C. Witton-Davies. 1949. Repr., New York: Harper & Row, 1960.

Burch, M. "Justice." In *Evangelical Dictionary of Theology*, ed. Walter A. Elwell, 641–643. 2nd ed. Grand Rapids: Baker Academic, 2001.

Burns, Camilla. "Biblical Righteousness and Justice." *LM* 7 (1998): 153–161.

Burnside, Jonathan. "Retribution and Restoration in Biblical Context." In *Handbook of Restorative Justice,* edited by Gerry Johnstone and Daniel W. Van Ness, 132–148. Cullompton: Willan Publishing, 2007.

Burnside, Jonathan and Nicola Baker, eds. *Relational Justice: Repairing the Breach.* 1994. Repr., Winchester: Waterside Press, 2004.

Burrows, Millar. "Levirate Marriage in Israel." *JBL* 59 (1940): 23–33.

Buss, Martin J. *The Prophetic Word of Hosea: A Morphological Study.* BZAW 111. Berlin: Töpelmann, 1969.

Büchsel, Friedrich and Volkmar Herntrich. "κρίνω, κρίσις, κρίμα,..." *TDNT* 3, 921–954.

Calvin, John. *Institutes of the Christian Religion.* Translated by Henry Beveridge. Vol. 1. Edinburgh: Calvin Translation Society, 1845.

Cavadino, Michael and James Dignan. *The Penal System: An Introduction.* 4th ed. 1992. Repr., London: Sage Publication, 2007.

Childs, Brevard S. *Biblical Theology in Crisis.* Philadelphia: Fortress Press, 1970.

———. "The Canonical Shape of the Prophetic Literature." *Int* 32 (1978): 46–55.

———. *Introduction to the Old Testament as Scripture.* Philadelphia: Fortress Press, 1979.

Chisholm, Robert B. *Handbook on the Prophets.* Grand Rapids: Baker Academic, 2002.

Clark, Gordon R. *The Word Hesed in the Hebrew Bible.* JSOTSup 157. Sheffield: JSOT Press, 1993.

Clines, David J. A. "Beyond Synchronic/Diachronic." In *Synchronic or Diachronic?: A debate on Method in Old Testament Exegesis,* edited by Johannes C. de Moor, 53–67. OtSt 34. Leiden: E. J. Brill, 1995.

———, ed. *The Concise Dictionary of Classical Hebrew.* Sheffield: Sheffield Phoenix Press, 2009.

Cole, G. A. "Responsibility." In *New Dictionary of Christian Ethics and Pastoral Theology,* edited by David J. Akinson and David H. Field, 734–736. Leicester: Inter-Varsity Press, 1995.

Colwell, John E. *Living the Christian Story: The Distinctiveness of Christian Ethics.* Edinburgh: T. & T. Clark, 2001.

Conroy, C. "Reflections on the Exegetical Task: Apropos of Recent Studies on 2 Kings 22–23." In *Pentateuchal and Deuteronomistic studies: Papers Read at* the 13th IOSOT Congress, Leuven, 1989, edited by C. Brekelmans & J. Lust, 255–268. BETL 94. Leuven: Leuven University Press, 1990.

Coote, Robert B. "Hosea XII." *VT* 21 (1971): 389–402.

Cremer, Hermann. *Biblico-theological Lexicon of New Testament Greek*. Translated by William Urwick. 3rd English ed. Edinburgh: T & T Clark, 1883.

———. *Die paulinische Rechtfertigungslehre im Zusammenhange ihrer geschichtlichen Voraussetzungen*. Gütersloh: Bertelsmann, 1900.

Crenshaw, James L., ed. *Theodicy in the Old Testament*. London: SPCK, 1983.

Crüsemann, Frank. "Jahwes Gerechtigkeit (*ṣᵉdāqā/ṣādäq*) im Alten Testament." *EvT* 36 (1976): 427–450.

Daly, Kathleen and Russ Immarigeon. "The Past, Present, and Future of Restorative Justice: Some Critical Reflections." *CJR* 1 (1998): 21–45.

Danahue, John R. "Biblical Perspectives on Justice." In *The Faith That Does Justice: Examining the Christian Sources for Social Change*, edited by John C. Haughey, 68–112. New York: Paulist Press, 1977.

Daniels, Dwight R. "Is there a 'Prophetic Lawsuit' Genre?" *ZAW* 99 (1987): 339–360.

———. *Hosea and Salvation History: The Early Traditions of Israel in the Prophecy of Hosea*. BZAW 191. Berlin: Walter de Gruyter, 1990.

Dar, Shimon. "Samaria, Archaeological Survey of the Region." *ABD* 5, 920–930.

———. *Hosea*. OTG. Sheffield: Sheffield Academic Press, 1993.

Davies, Eryl W. "Inheritance Rights and the Hebrew Levirate Marriage." *VT* 31 (1981): 138–144.

———. "Inheritance Rights and the Hebrew Levirate Marriage." *VT* 31 (1981): 257–268.

Davies, Graham I. *Hosea*. NCBC. Grand Rapids: Eerdmans, 1992.

Day, John. "Pre-Deuteronomic Allusions to the Covenant in Hosea and Psalm 78." *VT* (1986): 1–12.

Dearman, J. Andrew. "Marriage in the Old Testament." In *Biblical Ethics & Homosexuality: Listening to Scripture*, edited by Robert L. Browley, 53–67. Louisville: Westminster John Knox Press, 1996.

———. "The Family in the Old Testament." *Int* 52 (1998): 117–129.

———. *Property Rights in the Eighth-Century Prophets*. SBLDS 106. Atlanta: Scholars Press, 1988.

———. "YHWH's House: Gender Roles and Metaphors for Israel in Hosea." *JNSL* 25 (1999): 97–108.

———. *The Book of Hosea*. NICOT. Grand Rapids: Eerdmans, 2010.

Dempsey, Carol J. *Justice: A Biblical Perspective*. St Louis: Chalice Press, 2008.

DeRoche, Michael. "The Reversal of Creation in Hosea." *VT* 31 (1981): 400–409.

Diestel, Ludwig. "Die Idee der Gerechtigkeit, vorzüglich im Alten Testament, biblisch-theologisch dargestellt." *JDTh* 5 (1860): 173–253.

Dietrich, Walter and Martin A. Klopfenstein, eds. *Ein Gott allein? JHWH-Verehrung und biblischer Monotheismus im Kontext der israelitischen und altorientalische Religionsgeschichte*. OBO 139. Göttingen: Vandenhoeck & Ruprecht, 1994.

Doorly, William. J. *Prophet of Love: Understanding the Book of Hosea*. New York: Paulist Press, 1991.

Duff, Antony and David Garland, eds. *A Reader on Punishment*. Oxford: Oxford University Press, 1994.

Eichrodt, Walter. *Theology of the Old Testament, I*. Translated by John Baker. 1959 [sixth German ed.]. Repr., London: SCM Press, 1961.

———. "'The Holy One in Your Midst': The Theology of Hosea." *Int* 15 (1961): 259–273.

Eidevall, Göran. *Grapes in the Desert: Metaphors, Models, and Themes in Hosea 4–14*. ConBOT 43. Stockholm: Almqvist & Wiksell, 1996.

Emmerson, Grace I. *Hosea: An Israelite Prophet in Judean Perspective*. JSOTSup. Sheffield: JSOT Press, 1984.

Enns, Peter. "משפט." *NIDOTTE* 2, 1142–1144.

Epsztein, Leon. *Social Justice in the Ancient Near East and the People of God*. London: SCM Press, 1986.

Erlandsson, Seth. "זנה, *zānāh*." *TDOT* 4, 99–104.

Eslinger, Lyle M. *Kingship of God in Crisis: A Close Reading of 1 Samuel 1–12*. BLS Series 10. Sheffield: Almond JSOT Press, 1985.

Fabry, H. J. "מַרְזֵחַ *marzēaḥ*." Pages 10–14 vol. 9 of *TDOT*.

Fahlgren, Karl H. *Ṣedāḳā, nahestehende und entgegengesetzte Begriffe im Alten Testament*. Uppsala: Almquist and Wiksells Boktryckeri-A-B, 1932.

Farr, George. "The Concept of Grace in the Book of Hosea." *ZAW* 70 (1958): 98–107.

Feinberg, Joel and Hyman Gross, eds. *Justice: Selected Readings*. Encino: Dickenson Publishing Company, 1977.

Fensham, F. C. "Widow, Orphan, and the Poor in ancient Near Eastern Legal and Wisdom Literature." *JNES* 21 (1962): 129–139.

———. "Father and Son as Terminology for Treaty and Covenant." In *Near Eastern Studies in Honor of William Foxwell Albright*, edited by Hans Goedicke, 121–135. Baltimore: Johns Hopkins Press, 1971.

———. "The Marriage Metaphor in Hosea for the Covenant Relationship between the Lord and his People (Hos 1:2–9)." *JNSL* 12 (1984): 71–78.

Ferguson, Henry. "The verb שפט," *JBL* 8 (1888): 130–136.

Fewell, Danna N., ed. *Reading between Texts: Intertextuality and the Hebrew Bible*. Louisville: Westminster/John Knox, 1992.

Fisch, Harold. *Poetry with a Purpose: Biblical Poetics and Interpretation*. Bloomington: Indiana University Press, 1988.

Fleischer, G. "ראֹשׁ *rōʾš* II." *TDOT* 13, 262–263.

Forrester, Duncan B. "Social Justice and Welfare." In *The Cambridge Companion to Christian Ethics*, edited by Robin Gill, 195–208. Cambridge: Cambridge University Press, 2001.

Freedman, D. N. and A. Welch. "שָׁדַד *šādad*; שֹׁד *šōd*." *TDOT*, 412–418.

Freedman, D. N. and B. E. Willoughby. "נָאַף *nāʾap*." *TDOT* 9, 113–118.

Fuhs, H. F. "נַעַר *naʿar*." *TDOT* 9, 474–484.

Galil, Gerson. "The Last Years of the Kingdom of Israel and the Fall of Samaria." *CBQ* 57 (1995): 52–65.

Garrett, A. Duane. *Hosea, Joel*. NAC 19A. Nashville: Broadman and Holman, 1997.

Gelston, Anthony. "Kingship in the Book of Hosea." In *Language and Meaning: Studies in Hebrew Language and Biblical Exegesis*, edited by James Barr, 71–85. OtSt 19. Leiden: E. J. Brill, 1974.

Gemser, B. "The Rib or Controversy-Pattern in Hebrew Mentality." In *Wisdom in Israel and in the Ancient Near East*, edited by M. Noth and D. W. Thomas, 120–137. Leiden: E. J. Brill, 1969.

Gerstenberger, Erhard. "Covenant and Commandment." *JBL* 84 (1965): 38–51.

Gill, Robin, ed. *The Cambridge Companion to Christian Ethics*. Cambridge: Cambridge University Press, 2001.

Ginsberg, Harold. L. "The Legend of King Keret." *ANET*, 142–149.

———. "Hosea's Ephraim, more Fool than Knave: a New Interpretation of Hosea 12:1–14." *JBL* 80 (1961): 339–347.

Gisin, Walter. *Hosea: Ein literarisches Netzwerk beweist seine Authentizistät*. BBB 139. Berlin: Philo, 2002.

Glueck, Nelson. *Ḥesed in the Bible*. Translated by Alfred Gottschalk. 1927 [German]. Repr., Cinncinnati: Hebrew Union College Press, 1967.

Goedicke, Hans, ed. *Near Eastern Studies in Honor of William Foxwell Albright*. Baltimore: Johns Hopkins Press, 1971.

Goldingay, John. "Justice and Salvation for Israel and Canaan." In *Reading the Hebrew Bible for a New Millennium: Form, Concept, and Theological*

Perspective, edited by Wonil Kim, et al., 169–187. Harrisburg: Trinity Press International, 2000.

Good, Edwin M. "Hosea 5:8–6:6: An Alternative to Alt." *JBL* 85 (1966): 273–286.

———. "Hosea and the Jacob Tradition." *VT* 16 (1966): 137–151.

———. "The Composition of Hosea." *SEÅ* 31 (1966): 21–63.

Gordis, Robert. "Hosea's Marriage and Message: A New Approach." *HUCA* 25 (1954): 9–35.

Gordon, Cyrus H. *Ugaritic Textbook: Grammar, Texts in Transliteration, Cuneiform Selections, Glossary, Indices*. AnOr 38. Rome: Pontificium Inst Biblicum, 1965.

Gossai, Hemchand. *Justice, Righteousness and the Social Critique of the Eighth-Century Prophets*. AUS 7: TR 141. New York: Peter Lang, 1993.

Gottwald, Norman K. *The Tribes of Yahweh: A Sociology of the Religion of Liberated Israel, 1250–1050 B.C.E.* Maryknoll: Orbis Books, 1979.

Gowan, Donald E. *Theology of the Prophetic Books: the Death and Resurrection of Israel*. Louisville: Westminster John Knox Press, 1998.

Graetz, Naomi. "God is to Israel as Husband is to Wife: The Metaphoric Battering of Hosea's Wife." In *A Feminist Companion to the Latter Prophets*, edited by Athalya Brenner, 126–145. Sheffield: Sheffield Academic Press, 1995.

Greenberg, Moshe. "Some Postulates of Biblical Criminal Law." *Yehezkel Kaufmann Jubilee Volume*. Jerusalem: 1960.

———. *Ezekiel 1–20*. AB 22. New York: Doubleday, 1983.

Greengus, Samuel. "Old Babylonian Marriage Contract." *JAOS* 89 (1969): 505–532.

Guenther, Allen R. *Hosea, Amos*. Believers Church Bible Commentary. Scottsdale: Herald Press, 1998.

Gutiérrez, Gustavo. *A Theology of Liberation: History, Politics, and Salvation*. Translated by Inda Caridad and John Eagleson. Maryknoll: Orbis Books, 1973.

Habermas, Jürgen. *The Theory of Communicative Action*. Vol. 1 of *Reason and the Rationalization of Society*. Boston: Beacon Press, 1984.

———. *Theory of Communicative Action*. Vol. 2 of *Lifeworld and System: A Critique of Functionalist Reason*. Boston: Beacon Press, 1987.

Haddox, Susan E. "Masculinity in Hosea's Political Rhetoric." In *Israel's Prophets and Israel's Past: Essays on the Relationship of Prophetic Texts and Israelite*

History in Honour of John H. Hayes, edited by Brad E. Kelle and Megan B. Moore, 174–200. London: T & T Clark, 2006.

Hamilton, V. P. "נַעַר." *NIDOTTE* 3, 124–127.

Hanson, K. C. "BTB Readers Guide: Kinship." *BTB* 24 (1994): 183–194.

Haran, Menahem. "The Rise and Decline of the Empire of Jeroboam Ben Joash." *VT* 17 (1967): 266–297.

Harper, William R. *A Critical and Exegetical Commentary on Amos and Hosea.* ICC. New York: Charles Scribner's Sons, 1905.

Harvey, Dorothea W. "Rejoice not, O Israel." In *Israel's Prophetic Heritage: essays in honour of James Muilenburg,* edited by Bernhard W. Anderson and Walter J. Harrelson, 116–127. London: SCM Press, 1962.

Haughey, John C., ed. *The Faith That Does Justice: Examining the Christian Sources for Social Change.* New York: Paulist Press, 1977.

Hayes, John H. *Amos the Eighth Century Prophet: His Time and His Preaching.* Nashville: Abingdon, 1988.

Hayes, John H. and Jeffrey H. Kuan. "The Final Years of Samaria." *Bib* 72 (1991): 153–181.

Hayes, John H. and Paul K. Hooker. *A New Chronology for the Kings of Israel and Judah: and its implications for Biblical History and Literature.* Atlanta: John Knox Press, 1988.

Hayes, Katherine M. *"The Earth Mourns": Prophetic Metaphor and Oral Aesthetic.* AcBib 8. Atlanta: Society of Biblical Literature, 2002.

Hayner, Priscilla B. *Unspeakable Truths: Transitional Justice and the Challenge of Truth Commissions.* 2nd ed. 2001. Repr., New York: Routledge, 2011.

Heflin, J. N. Boo. "The World of Hosea." *SwJT* 18 (1975): 6–21.

Helfmeyer, F. J. "הָלַךְ *hālakh.*" *TDOT* 3, 388–403.

Hertzberg, Hans Wilhelm. "Die Entwicklung des Begriffes משפט im AT." *ZAW* 40 (1922): 256–287.

Heschel, Abraham J. *The Prophets.* New York: Harper & Row, 1962.

Higginson, Richard. *Dilemmas: A Christian Approach to Moral Decision Making.* Louisville: John Knox Press, 1988.

Hill, David. *Greek Words and Hebrew Meanings: Studies in the Semantics of Soteriological Terms.* SNTSMS 5. Cambridge: Cambridge University Press, 1967.

Hillers, Delbert R. *Treaty-Curses and the Old Testament Prophets.* Rome: Pontifical Biblical Institute, 1964.

Hillers, Delbert R. *Covenant: The History of a Biblical Idea.* Seminars in the History of Ideas. Baltimore: Johns Hopkins Press, 1969.

Ho, Ahuva. *Ṣedeq and Ṣedaqah in the Hebrew Bible*. AUS 7: Theology and Religion, vol. 78. New York: Peter Lang, 1991.

Hoaas, Geir. "Passion and Compassion of God in the Old Testament: A Theological Survey of Hos 11, 8–9; Jer 31, 20 and Isa 63, 9+15." *SJOT* 11 (1987): 138–159.

Hoffmeyer, Jeffrey H. "Covenant and Creation: Hosea 4:1–3." *RevExp* 102 (2005): 143–151.

Holladay, John S. "Assyrian Statecraft and the Prophets of Israel." *HTR* 63 (1970): 29–51.

Holladay, William L. *The Root Šûbh in the Old Testament: With Particular Reference to Its Usages in Covenantal Contexts*. Leiden: E. J. Brill, 1958.

———. "Chiasmus, the Key to Hosea xii 3–6." *VT* 16 (1966): 53–64.

Hollenbach, David. "Modern Catholic Teachings Concerning Justice." In *The Faith That Does Justice: Examining the Christian Sources for Social Change*, edited by John C. Haughey, 207–231. New York: Paulist Press, 1977.

———. *The Common Good and Christian Ethics*. Cambridge: Cambridge University Press, 2002.

Hollinger, Dennis P. *Choosing the Good: Christian Ethics in a Complex World*. Grand Rapids: Baker Academic, 2002.

Holt, Else K. "דעת אלהים und חסד im Buche Hosea." *SJOT* 1 (1987): 87–103.

———. *Prophesying the Past: the use of Israel's History in the Book of Hosea*. JSOTSup 194. Sheffield: Sheffield Academic Press, 1995.

Hong, Seong-Hyuk. *The Metaphor of Illness and Healing in Hosea and Its Significance in the Socio-Economic Context of Eighth-Century Israel and Judah*. SBL 95. New York: Peter Lang, 2006.

Hornsby, Teresa J. "'Israel Has Become a Worthless Thing': Re-Reading Gomer in Hosea 1–3." *JSOT* 82 (1999): 115–128.

House, Paul R. *The Unity of the Twelve*. Bible and Literature 27. JSOTSup 97. Sheffield: Almond Press, 1990.

Hubbard, David A. *With Bands of Love: Lessons from the Book of Hosea*. Grand Rapids: Eerdmans Publishing, 1968.

———. *Hosea: An Introduction and Commentary*. TOTC 22a. Downers Grove: Inter-Varsity Press, 1989.

Huffmon, Herbert B. "The Covenant Lawsuit in the Prophets." *JBL* 78 (1959): 285–295.

———. "The Treaty Background of Hebrew yāda'." *BASOR* 181 (1966): 31–37.

Hugenberger, Gordon P. *Marriage as a Covenant: A Study of Biblical Law and Ethics governing Marriage developed from the Perspective of Malachi.* Leiden: E. J. Brill, 1994.

Hume, David. "Of Justice." In *Justice: Selected Readings,* edited by Joel Feinberg and Hyman Gross, 75–83. Encino: Dickenson Publishing, 1977.

Hunter, A. Vanlier. *Seek the Lord! A Study of the Meaning and Function of the Exhortations in Amos, Hosea, Isaiah, Micah, and Zephaniah.* Baltimore: St. Mary's Seminary, 1982.

Irvine, Stuart A. "Politics and Prophetic Commentary in Hosea 8:8–10." *JBL* 114 (1995): 292–294.

Jackson, Bernard S. *Essays in Jewish and Comparative Legal History.* SJLA 10. Leiden: E. J. Brill, 1975.

Jackson, Jared J. "Yahweh v. Cohen et al.: God's Lawsuit with Priest and People – Hosea 4." *PPer* 7 (1966): 28–32.

Jacob, Edmond. *Theology of the Old Testament.* Translated by Arthur W. Heathcote and Philip J. Allcock. New York: Harper, 1958.

Jacob, Edmond, Carl-A. Keller and Samuel Amsler. *Osée, Joël, Abdias, Jonas, Amos.* CAT 11a. Neuchatel: Delachaux & Niestlé, 1965.

Janzen, J. Gerald. "Metaphor and Reality in Hosea 11." *Semeia* 24 (1982): 7–44.

Jepsen, Alfred. "אָמַן, *'āman.*" *TDOT* 1, 292–323.

———. "Gnade und Barmherzigkeit im Alten Testament." *KD* 7 (1961): 261–271.

———. "Ṣdq & Ṣdqh." In *In Gottes Wort und Gottes Land,* edited by Henning G. Reventlow, 78–79. Göttingen: Vandenhoeck & Ruprecht, 1965.

Jeremias, Jörg. *Der Prophet Hosea: übersetzt und erklärt.* ATD 24/1. Gottingen: Vandenhoeck & Ruprecht, 1983.

———. "The Interrelationship Between Amos and Hosea." In *Forming Prophetic Literature: Essays on Isaiah and the Twelve in honor of J. W. Watts,* edited by James W. Watts and Paul R. House, 171–186. JSOTSup 235. Sheffield: Sheffield Academic Press, 1996.

Johnson, Aubrey R. "Hesed a Hāsîd." In *Interpretationes ad Vestus Testamentum Pertinentes,* edited by S. Mowinckel, 100–112. Oslo: Land og Kirke, 1955.

Johnson, B. "מִשְׁפָּט, judgment, Justice." *TDOT* 9, 86–98.

———. "צָדַק, *ṣādaq*" *TDOT* 12, 239–265.

Kaiser, Walter C. "Inner Biblical Exegesis as a Model for bridging the 'Then' and 'Now' gap: Hos 12:1–6." *JETS* 28 (1985): 33–46.

Kakkanattu, Joy Philip. *God's Enduring Love in the Book of Hosea.* FAT 2/14. Tübingen: Mohr Siebeck, 2006.

Kaminsky, Joel S. *Corporate Responsibility in the Hebrew Bible*. JSOTSup 196. Sheffield: Sheffield Academic Press, 1995.

Kamsler, Harold. "Hesed - Mercy or Loyalty." *JBQ* 27 (1999): 183–185.

Kautzsch, Emil F. *Über die Derivate des Stammes ṣdq im alttestamentlichen Sprachgebrauch*. Tübingen: Druck von Ludwig Friedrich Fues, 1881.

Keefe, Alice A. *Woman's Body and the Social Body in Hosea*. JSOTSup 338. Gender, Culture and Theory 10. Sheffield: Sheffield Academic Press, 2001.

Keil, Carl F. *The Twelve Minor Prophets, vol. 1*. Edited by C. F. Keil and F. Deitzsch. BCOT. Grand Rapids: Eerdmans, 1954.

Keita, Katrin. *Gottes Land: exegetische Studien zur Land-Thematik im Hoseabuch in kanonischer Perspektiv*. TTS 13. Hildesheim: Georg Olms Verlag, 2007.

Kelle, Brad E. "Hosea, Sargon, and the final Destruction of Samaria: A Response to M. Christine Tetley with a View toward Method." *SJOT* 17 (2003): 226–243.

———. *Hosea 2: Metaphor and Rhetoric in Historical Perspective*. SBLAB 20. Atlanta: Society of Biblical Literature, 2005.

———. "Hosea 1–3 in Twentieth-Century Scholarship." *CBR* 7 (2009): 179–216.

———. "Hosea 4–14 in Twentieth-Century Scholarship." *CBR* 8 (2010): 314–375.

Kerber, Guillermo. "Overcoming Violence and Pursuing Justice: an Introduction to Restorative Justice Procedures." *ER* 55 (2003): 151–157.

Kidner, Derek. *Love to the Loveless: The Message of Hosea*. The Bible Speaks Today. Downers Grove: InterVarsity, 1981.

King, Philip J. *Amos, Hosea, Micah: An Archaeological Commentary*. Philadelphia: Westminster Press, 1988.

———. "The Eighth, the Greatest of Centuries." *JBL* 108 (1989): 3–15.

Kittay, Eva F. *Metaphor: Its Cognitive Force and Linguistic Structure*. Oxford: Clarendon Press, 1987.

Kline, Meredith G. *By Oath Consigned: A Reinterpretation of the Covenant Signs of Circumcision and Baptism*. Grand Rapids: Eerdmans, 1968.

Knierim, Rolf P. *The Task of Old Testament Theology: Substance, Method, and Cases*. Grand Rapids: Eerdmans, 1995.

Knight, G.A. *Hosea: God's Love*. TBC. London: SCM Press, 1960.

Koch, Klaus. "Gibt es ein Vergeltungsdogma im Alten Testament." *ZTK* 52 (1955): 1–42.

———. *The Prophets*. Translated by Margaret Kohl. Vol. 1 of *The Assyrian Period*. London: SCM Press, 1978.

———. "Is There a Doctrine of Retribution in the Old Testament." In *Theodicy in the Old Testament*, edited by James L. Crenshaw, 57–87. London: SPCK, 1983.

———. "צָדֵק to be communally Faithful, Beneficial." *TLOT* 2, 1046–1062.

———. "צָדֵק." *THAT* 2, 501–502.

Köhler, Ludwig. *Hebrew Man: lectures delivered at the invitation of the University of Tübingen, December 1–16, 1956, with an appendix on Justice in the Gate.* Translated by Peter R. Ackroyd. London: SCM Press, 1956.

Kornfeld, W. "Adultère dans l'oriente antique." *RB* 57 (1950): 92–109.

Krause, Deborah. "A Blessing Cursed: The Prophet's Prayer for Barren Womb and Dry Breasts in Hosea 9." In *Reading between Texts: Intertextuality and the Hebrew Bible,* edited by Danna N. Fewell, 191–202. Louisville: Westminster/John Knox, 1992.

Kreuzer, Siegfried. "Gott als Mutter in Hosea 11." *TQ* 169 (1989): 123–132.

Kruger, Paul A. "Prophetic imagery: on Metaphors and Similes in the Book Hosea." *JNSL* 14 (1988): 143–151.

———. "Yahweh's Generous Love: Eschatological Expectations in Hosea 14:2–9." *OTE* 1 (1988): 27–48.

———. "The Divine Net in Hosea 7:12." *ETL* 68 (1992): 132–136.

———. "The Marriage Metaphor in Hosea 2:4–17 against its ancient Near Eastern Background." *OTE* 5 (1992): 7–25.

Kuhnigk, Willibald. *Nordwestsemitische Studien zum Hoseabuch*. BibOr 27. Rome: Biblical Institute Press, 1974.

Kwakkel, Gert. "Hosea, Prophet of God's Love." In *The Lion Has Roared: Theological Themes in the Prophetic Literature of the Old Testament*, edited by H. G. L. Peels and S. D. Snyman, 27–39. Eugene: Pickwick Publications, 2012.

Labuschagne, C. J. "קרא *qr'* to call." *TLOT* 3, 1158–1164.

Lofthouse, W. F. "Ḥen and Ḥesed in the Old Testament." *ZAW* 10 (1933): 29–35.

Landy, Francis. *Hosea*. Readings – A New Biblical Commentary. Sheffield: Sheffield Academic Press, 1995.

Lang, Bernhard. "The Social Organization of Peasant Poverty in Biblical Israel." *JSOT* 24 (1982): 47–63.

Lebacqz, Karen. *Six Theories of Justice: Perspectives from Philosophical and Theological Ethics*. Minneapolis: Augsburg Publishing House, 1986.

LeCureux, Jason T. *The Thematic Unity of the Book of the Twelve*. HBM 41. Sheffield: Sheffield Phoenix Press, 2012.

Lemche, Niels P. *Early Israel: Anthropological and Historical Studies on the Israelite Society Before the Monarchy.* VTSup 37. Leiden: E. J. Brill, 1985.

Lenski, Gerhard E. *Power and Privilege: A Theory of Social Stratification.* New York: McGraw-Hill Book Company, 1966.

Liedke, Gerhard. "שפט, to judge." *TLOT* 3, 1392–1399.

———. *Gestalt und Bezeichnung alttestamentlicher Rechtssatze.* WMANT 39. Neukirchen-Vluyn: Neukirchener Verlag, 1971.

Limburg, James. "Root *rîb* and the Prophetic Lawsuit Speeches." *JBL* 88 (1969): 291–304.

———. *Hosea–Micah.* Atlanta: Westminster John Knox Press, 1988.

Lindblom, J. *Prophecy in Ancient Israel.* Philadelphia: Muhlenberg, 1962.

Loewenstamm, Samuel E. "The Law of Adultery and the Law of Murder in Biblical and Mesopotamian Law." *AOAT* 204 (1980): 146–153.

Lohfink, Norbert. "Hate and love in Osee 9:15." *CBQ* 25 (1963): 417.

———. "Ich bin Jahwe, dein Arzt." In *"Ich will euer Gott werden": Beispiele biblischen Redens von Gott,* edited by Norbert Lohfink et al., 11–73. SBS 100. Stuttgart: Verlag Katholisches Bibelwerk, 1981.

Loya, Melissa T. "'Therefore the Earth Mourns': The Grievance of the Earth in Hosea 4:1–3." In *Exploring Ecological Hermeneutics,* edited by Norman C. Habel and Peter L. Trudinger, 53–62. SBLSymS 46. Atlanta: Society of Biblical Literature, 2008.

Lucas, J. R. *Responsibility.* 1993. Repr., Oxford: Clarendon Press, 1995.

Ludwig, Diestel. "Die Idee der Gerechtigkeit, vorzüglich im Alten Testament, biblisch-theologisch dargestellt." *JBTh* 5 (1860): 173–253.

Lundbom, Jack R. "Contentious Priests and Contentious People in Hosea IV 1–10." *VT* 36 (1986): 52–72.

Macintosh, A. A. *Critical and Exegetical Commentary on Hosea.* ICC. Edinburgh: T & T Clark, 1997.

MacRae, Allan and Howard Zehr. *The Little Book of Family Group Conferences: New Zealand Style.* Intercourse: Good Books, 2004.

Malchow, Bruce V. *Social Justice in the Hebrew Bible: What is New and What is Old.* Collegeville: Liturgical Press, 1996.

March, Eugene. "Prophecy." In *Old Testament Form Criticism,* edited by John H. Hayes, 141–178. San Antonio: Trinity University Press, 1974.

Marshall, Christopher D. *Beyond Retribution: A New Testament Vision for Justice, Crime, and Punishment.* Auckland: Lime Grove House Publishing, 2001.

———. "Offending, Restoration, and the Law-abiding Community: Restorative Justice in the New Testament and in the New Zealand Experience." *JSCE* 27 (2007): 3–30.

Marx, Karl. *Critique of the Gotha Programme: With Letters from Engels and the Gotha Programme.* Peking: Foreign Language Press, 1972.

Matthews, Victor H. *Manners and Customs in the Bible.* Peabody: Hendrickson Publishers, 1988.

May, Herbert G. "An Interpretation of the Names of Hosea's Children." *JBL* 55 (1936): 285–291.

Mays, James L. *Hosea.* OTL. Philadelphia: Westminster, 1969.

———. "Response to Janzen: 'Metaphor and Reality in Hosea 11'." *Semeia* 24 (1982): 42–51.

———. "Justice: Perspectives from the Prophetic Tradition." *Int* 37 (1983): 5–17.

McCarthy, Dennis J. *Treaty and Covenant: A Study in Form in the Ancient Oriental Documents and in the Old Testament.* Rome: Pontifical Biblical Institute, 1963.

———. "Hosea XII 2: Covenant by Oil," *VT* 14 (1964): 215–221

———. "Notes on the Love of God in Deuteronomy and on the Father-Son Relationship between Yahweh and Israel." *CBQ* 27 (1965): 144–145.

———. "*berit* in Old Testament History and Theology." *Bib* 53 (1972): 110–121.

McComiskey, Thomas E. "Hos 9:13 and the Integrity of the Masoretic Tradition in the Prophecy of Hosea." *JETS* 33 (1990): 155–160.

———. "Hosea." In *The Minor Prophets: An Exegetical and Expository Commentary, Vol. 1,* edited by Thomas E. McComiskey, 1–237. Grand Rapids: Baker Academic, 1992.

McFague, Sallie. *Metaphorical Theology.* Philadelphia: Fortress, 1982.

McIlroy, David. *Christian Perspectives: A Biblical View of Law and Justice.* Milton Keynes: Paternoster Press, 2004.

McKay, J. W. "Man's love for God in Deuteronomy and the Father/Teacher – Son/Pupil Relationship." *VT* 22 (1972): 426–435.

McKeating, Henry. "Sanctions against Adultery in Ancient Israelite Society, with some Reflections on Methodology in the Study of Old Testament Ethics." *JSOT* 11 (1979): 57–72.

McKenzie, Donald A. "Judicial Procedure at the Town Gate." *VT* 14 (1964): 100–104.

———. "Judge of Israel." *VT* 17 (1967): 118–121.

McKenzie, John L. "Knowledge of God in Hosea." *JBL* 74 (1955): 22–27.
McKenzie, Steven L. "The Jacob Tradition in Hosea 12:4–5." *VT* 36 (1986): 311–322.
McNutt, Paula. *Reconstructing the Society of Ancient Israel*. London: SPCK, 1999.
Mendenhall, George E. "Covenant Forms in Israelite Tradition." *BA* 17 (1954): 50–76.
———. "Covenant." *IDB* 1, 714–723.
Meyers, Carol. *Discovering Eve: Ancient Israelite Women in Context*. New York: Oxford University Press, 1991.
———. "The Family in Early Israel." In *Families in Ancient Israel*, edited by Leo G. Perdue et al., 1–47. Louisville: Westminster John Knox, 1997.
Milgrom, Jacob. *Cult and Conscience: The Asham and the Priestly Doctrine of Repentance*. Leiden: E. J. Brill, 1976.
Mill, John S. *On Liberty*. 2nd ed. London: John W. Parker & Son, 1859.
———. *Utilitarianism*. 11th ed. London: Longmans, Green & Co., 1891.
———. *Utilitarianism, Liberty & Representative Government*. Rockville: Wildside Press, 2007.
Miller, James M. and John H. Hayes. *A History of Ancient Israel and Judah*. Philadelphia: Westminster, 1986.
Miranda, J. Porfirio. *Marx and the Bible: A Critique of the Philosophy of Oppression*. Translated by John Eagleson. Maryknoll: Orbis Books, 1974. Repr., London: SCM Press, 1977.
Montgomery, James A. "Hebrew Hesed and Greek Charis." *HTR* 2 (1938): 97–102.
Moran, William L. "A Note on the Treaty Terminology of the Sefire Stelas." *JNES* 22 (1963): 173–176.
———. "The Ancient Near Eastern Background of the Love of God in Deuteronomy." *CBQ* 25 (1963): 77–87.
Morenz, Siegfried. *Egyptian Religion*. Translated by Ann E. Keep. Stuttgart: W. Kohlhammer GmbH, 1960. Repr., London: Methuen, 1973.
Morris, Gerald. *Prophecy, Poetry and Hosea*. JSOTSup 291. Sheffield: Sheffield Academic Press, 1996.
Moughtin-Mumby, Sharon. *Sexual and Marital Metaphors in Hosea, Jeremiah, Isaiah and Ezekiel*. OTM. Oxford: Oxford University Press, 2008.
Mowinckel, Sigmund. *Prophecy and Tradition: The Prophetic Books in the Light of the Study of the Growth and History of the Tradition*. Oslo: Jacob Dybward, 1946.
Muilenburg, James. "Form Criticism and Beyond." *JBL* 88 (1969): 1–18.

Murphy, Jeffrie. *Retribution, Justice, and Therapy: Essays in the Philosophy of Law*. London: D. Reidal Publishing, 1979.

Naʾaman, Nadav. "Historical and Chronological Notes on the Kingdoms of Israel and Judah in the Eighth Century B.C." *VT* 36 (1986): 91–92.

———. "Historical Background to the Conquest of Samaria (720 BC)." *Biblica* 71 (1990): 206–225.

———. "Azariah of Judah and Jeroboam II of Israel." *VT* 43 (1993): 227–234.

Nardoni, Enrique. *Rise Up, O Judge: A Study of Justice in the Biblical World*. Translated by Charles M. Sean. Peabody: Hendrickson, 2004.

Nash, Ronald H. *Social Justice and the Christian Church*. Milford: Mott Media, 1983.

Naudé, Piet. "Sola Gratia and Restorative Justice." *Scriptura* 83 (2003): 139–146.

Naumann, Thomas L. *Hoseas Erben: Strukturen der Nachinterpretation im Buch Hosea*. BWANT 131. Stuttgart: W Kohlhammer, 1991.

Neef, Heinz-Dieter. *Die Heilstraditionen Israels in der Verkündigung des Propheten Hosea*. BZAW 169. Berlin: Walter de Gruyter, 1987.

Nicholson, Ernest W. *God and His People: Covenant and Theology in the Old Testament*. Oxford: Clarendon Press, 1986.

Niebuhr, H. Richard. *The Responsible Self: An Essay in Christian Moral Philosophy*. 1963. Repr., Louisville: Westminster John Knox Press, 1999.

Niebuhr, Reinhold. *Moral Man and Immoral Society: A Study in Ethics and Politics*. London: SCM Press, 1932, 1963.

———. *An Interpretation of Christian Ethics*. 4th ed. London: Bradford & Dickens, 1936. Repr., London: SCM Press, 1948.

———. *The Nature and Destiny of Man: A Christian Interpretation*. Vol. 1 of *Human Nature*. 1941. Repr., London: Nisbet, 1949.

———. *The Nature and Destiny of Man: A Christian Interpretation*. Vol. 2 of *Human Destiny*. 1943. Repr., London: Nisbet, 1955.

Niehr, H. "שָׁפַט *šāpāṭ*, lead, rule; judge, ruler." Pages 411–430 in vol. 15 of *TDOT*.

Nissinen, Martti. *Prophetie, Redaktion, und Fortschreibung im Hoseabuch: Studien zum Werdegang eines Prophetenbuches im Lichte von Hos 4 und 11*. AOAT 231. Neukirchen-Vluyn: Neukirchener Verlag, 1991.

Nogalski, James D. *The Book of the Twelve: Hosea–Jonah*. Macon: Smyth & Helwys Publishing, 2011.

Nogalski, James D. and Marvin Sweeney, eds. *Reading and Hearing the Book of the Twelve*. SBLSymS 15. Atlanta: Society of Biblical Literature, 2000.

Noth, Martin and D. W. Thomas, eds. *Wisdom in Israel and in the Ancient Near East*. Leiden: E. J. Brill, 1969.

Noth, Martin. *The History of Israel*. Translated by P. R. Ackroyd. 2nd ed. New York: Harper & Row, 1960.

Nozick, Robert. *Anarchy, State, and Utopia*. New York: Basic Books, 1974.

———. "Distributive Justice." In *Justice: Selected Readings*, edited by Joel Feinberg and Hyman Gross, 120–128. Encino: Dickenson Publishing Company, 1977.

Nwaoru, Emmanuel O. *Imagery in Prophecy of Hosea*. ÄAT 41. Wiesbaden: Harrassowitz, 1999.

———. "The Role of Images in the Literary Structure of Hosea VII 8–VIII 14." *VT* 54 (2004): 216–222.

Nyberg, H. S. *Studien zum Hoseabuche*. UUÅ 6; Uppsala 1933.

O'Donovan, O. and R. J. Song. "Punishment." In *New Dictionary of Theology*, edited by Sinclair B. Ferguson et al., 458–459. Leicester: Inter-Varsity Press, 1988.

Östborn, Gunnar. *Tōrā in the Old Testament: A Semantic Study*. Translated by Cedric Hentschel. Lund: Håkan Ohlssons Boktryckeri, 1945.

O'Kennedy, D. F. "Healing as/or Forgiveness? The use of the term רפא in the Book of Hosea." *OTE* 14 (2001): 458–474.

Odell, Margaret S. "Who Were the Prophets in Hosea?" *HBT* 18 (1996): 78–95.

Ortlund, Raymond C. *Whoredom: God's Unfaithful Wife in Biblical Theology*. NSBT. Leicester: Inter-Varsity Press, 1996.

Palazzini, Pietro. "Justice." In *Dictionary of Moral Theology*, edited by Pietro Palazzini, 673–678. London: Burns Oates, 1962.

Patterson, Richard D. "The Widow, the Orphan, and the Poor in the Old Testament and Extra-biblical Literature." *BSac* 130 (1973): 223–234.

———. "An Overlooked Scriptural Paradox: The Pseudosorites." *JETS* 53 (2010): 19–36.

Paul, Shalom M. "The Image of Oven and the Cake in Hosea VII 4–10." *VT* 18 (1968): 114–120.

———. *Studies in the Book of the Covenant in Light of Cuneiform and Biblical Law*. VTSup 18. Leiden: E. J. Brill, 1970.

———. *Amos: A Commentary on the Book of Amos*. Hermeneia. Minneapolis: Fortress Press, 1991.

Pedersen, Johannes. *Israel: Its Life and Culture I–II*. Translated by Aslaug Møller. 1926. Repr., London: Oxford University Press, 1954.

―――. *Israel: Its Life and Culture III–IV*. Translated by Annie I. Fausbøll. 1940. Repr., London: Oxford University Press, 1954.

Pentiuc, Eugen J. *Long-suffering Love: A Commentary on Hosea with Patristic Annotations*. Brookline: Holy Cross Orthodox Press, 2002.

Perdue, Leo G. "The Israelite and Early Jewish Family." In *Families in Ancient Israel*, edited by Leo G. Perdue et al., 162–222. Louisville: Westminster John Knox, 1997.

Peritz, Ismar. "Women in the Ancient Hebrew Cult." *JBL* 17 (1898): 111–148.

Perlitt, Lothar. *Bundestheologie im Alten Testament*. WMANT 36. Neukirchen Vluyn: Neukirchener Verlag, 1969.

Petersen, David L. *The Roles of Israel's Prophets*. JSOTSup 17. Sheffield: JSOT Press, 1981.

Phillips, Anthony. *Ancient Israel's Criminal Law: A New Approach to the Decalogue*. Basil Blackwell: Oxford, 1970.

―――. "Another Look at Adultery." *JSOT* 20 (1981): 3–25.

Piper, John. "The Righteousness of God in Romans 3:1–8." *TZ* 36 (1980): 3–16.

Plato. *The Republic*. Translated by H. D. P. Lee. 1956. Repr., Harmondsworth: Penguin Books, 1967.

Ploeg, J. van der. "The social study of the Old Testament." *CBQ* 10 (1948): 72–80.

―――. "Studies in Hebrew Law." *CBQ* 12 (1950): 248–259.

Poobalan, Ivor. "The Period of Jeroboam II with Special Reference to Amos." *JCTS* 3 (2005): 43–74.

Premnath, Devadasan N. *Eighth Century Prophets: A Social Analysis*. St. Louis: Chalice Press, 2003.

―――. "Amos and Hosea: Sociohistorical Background and Prophetic Critique." *WW* 28 (2008): 125–132.

Pritchard, James B., ed. *The Ancient Near East: Supplementary Texts and Pictures Relating to the Old Testament*. Princeton: Princeton University Press, 1969.

Quell, Gottfried. "ἀλήθεια, ἀληθής, ἀληθινός, ἀληθεύω" *TDNT* 1, 232–237.

―――."δίκη, δίκαιος, δικαιοσύνη. . . ." *TDNT* 2, 174–178.

Rad, Gerhard von. *Old Testament Theology, I*. Translated by D. M. G. Stalker. Munich: Christian Kaiser Verlag,1957 [2nd German ed.]. Repr., London: Oliver and Boyd, 1962.

―――. *Old Testament Theology, II*. Translated by D. M. G Stalker. Munich: Christian Kaiser Verlag, 1960. Repr., London: SCM Press, 1965.

―――. *The Problem of Hexateuch and Other Essays*. Translated by E. Trueman Dicken. Edinburgh: Oliver & Boyd, 1966.

Raines, John C. "Toward a Relational Theory of Justice." *CC* 39 (1989): 129–160.

Rawls, John. *A Theory of Justice.* Cambridge: Harvard University Press, 1971.

———. "Justice as Fairness." In *Justice: Selected Readings,* edited by Joel and Hyman Gross Feinberg, 101–115. Encino: Dickenson Publishing Company, 1977.

Reimer, David J. "צדק" *NIDOTTE* 3, 744–769.

Reiterer, Friedrich V. *Gerechtigkeit als Heil: SDQ bei Deuterojesaja. Aussage und Vergleich mit der alttestamentlichen Tradition.* Graz: Akademische Druck, 1976.

Reventlow, Henning G., ed. *In Gottes Wort und Gottes Land.* Göttingen: Vandenhoeck & Ruprecht, 1965.

———. *Problems of Old Testament Theology in the Twentieth Century.* London: SCM Press, 1985.

Reventlow, Henning G. and Yair Hoffman, eds. *Justice and Righteousness: Biblical Themes and their Influence.* JSOTSup 137. Sheffield: JSOT Press, 1992.

Richards, I. A. *The Philosophy of Rhetoric.* 1936. Repr., New York: Oxford University Press, 1965.

Ricoeur, Paul. "Stellung und Funktion der Metapher in der biblischen Sprache." In *Metapher. Zur Hermeneutik religiöser Sprache,* edited by Paul Ricoeur and Eberhard Jüngel, 45–70. Munich: Kaiser, 1974.

Ringgren, Helmer. *Word and Wisdom: Studies in the Hypostatization of Divine Qualities and Functions in the Ancient Near East.* Lund: Hakan Ohlssons Boktryckeri, 1947.

Ripley, Jason J. "Covenantal Concepts of Justice and Righteousness, and Catholic-Protestant Reconciliation: Theological Implications and Explorations." *JES* 38 (2001): 95–108.

Ritschl, Dietrich. "God's Conversion." *Int* 15 (1961): 286–303.

Robinson, H. Wheeler. *Corporate Personality in Ancient Israel.* Rev. ed. Philadelphia: Fortress Press, 1980.

Roche, Declan. "Retribution and Restorative Justice." In *Handbook of Restorative Justice,* edited by Gerry Johnstone and Daniel W. Van Ness, 75–90. Cullompton: Willan Publishing, 2007.

Rodd, Cyril S. "Family in the Old Testament." *BT* 18 (1967): 19–26.

Rond, D. "Metaphor." *Journal Biblical Literature* 20 (1990): 33–37.

Rooy, H. F. van. "The Names of Israel, Ephraim and Jacob in the Book of Hosea." *OTE* 6 (1993): 135–149.

Rooy, Sydney. "Righteousness and Justice." *ERT* 6 (1982): 260–274.

Rosengren, Allan. "Knowledge of God according to Hosea the Ripper: the interlacing of theology and social ideology in Hosea 2." *SJOT* 23 (2009): 122–126.

Rosenthal, Franz. "Sedaka, Charity." *HUCA* 23 (1950–51): 411–430.

———. "Yehimilk of Byblos." *ANET,* page 653.

Routledge, Robin. "Hesed as Obligation: A Re-Examination." *TB* 46 (1995): 179–196.

———. *Old Testament Theology: A Thematic Approach.* Nottingham: Apollos, 2008.

Rowley, Harold Henry. *Men of God: Studies in Old Testament History and Prophecy.* Thomas Nelson: London, 1963.

Rudnig-Zelt, Susanne. *Hoseastudien: redaktionskritische Untersuchungen zur Genese des Hoseabuches.* FRLANT 213. Göttingen: Vandenhoeck & Ruprecht, 2006.

Rudolph, Wilhelm. *Hosea.* Gütersloh [West Germany]: Gerd Mohn, 1966.

Russell, L. M., ed. *Feminist Interpretation of the Bible.* Philadelphia: Westminster, 1985.

Sakenfeld, Katharine D. *The Meaning of Ḥesed in the Hebrew Bible.* Missoula: Scholars Press, 1978.

———. "Loyalty and Love: The Language of Human Interconnections in the Hebrew Bible." *MQR* 22 (1983): 190–204.

Schluter, Michael. *Christianity in a Changing World: Biblical Insight on Contemporary Issues.* London: Marshall Pickering, 2000.

———. "What is Relational Justice." In *Relational Justice: Repairing the Breach,* edited by Jonathan and Nicola Baker Burnside, 17–27. 1994. Repr., Winchester: Waterside Press, 2004.

Schmid, Hans H. *Gerechtigkeit als Weltordnung: Hintergrund und Geschichte der alttestamentlichen Gerechtigkeitsbegriffes.* BHT 40. Tübingen: J. C. B. Mohr, 1968.

Schmid, Konrad. *Genesis and the Moses story: Israel's Dual Origins in the Hebrew Bible.* Translated by James Nogalski. Siphrut 3. Winona Lake: Eisenbrauns, 2010.

Schmitt, John J. "The Gender of Ancient Israel." *JSOT* 26 (1983): 115–125.

———. "The Wife of God in Hosea 2." *BR* 34 (1989): 5–18.

———. "Yahweh's Divorce in Hosea 2 – Who is that Woman?" *SJOT* 9 (1995): 119–132.

Schottroff, Willy. "The Prophet Amos: A Socio-Historical Assessment of His Ministry." In *God of the Lowly: Socio-Historical Interpretations of the Bible,* edited by Willy Schottroff and Wolfgang Stegemann., 27–46 Translated by Matthew J. O'Connell. Maryknoll: Orbis Books, 1984.

Schreiner, J. "עָוֶל, עַלְוָה 'āwel, 'awlâ." *TDOT* 10, 552–530.

Schultz, Richard. "Justice." *NIDOTTE* 4, 837–846.

———. "שפט." *NIDOTTE* 4, 213–220.

Schüngel-Straumann, Helen. "God as Mother in Hosea in Hosea 11." In *A Feminist Companion to the Latter Prophets,* edited by Athalya Brenner, 194–218. Sheffield: Sheffield Academic Press, 1995.

Schütte, Wolfgang. *"Säet euch Gerechtigkeit!": Adressaten und Anliegen der Hoseaschrift.* BWANT 179. Stuttgart: W. Kohlhammer, 2008.

Seebass, Horst. "לָקַח *lāqaḥ.*" *TDOT* 8, 16–20.

———. "Righteousness, Justification." *NIDNTT* 3, 352–356.

Segovia, Fernando F. and Mary Ann Tolbert, eds. *Reading from this Place, vol 1: Social Location and Biblical Interpretation in the United States.* Minneapolis: Fortress Press, 1995.

Seifert, Brigitte. *Metaphorisches Reden von Gott im Hoseabuch.* FRLANT 166. Gottingen: Vandenhoeck & Ruprecht, 1996.

Seow, Choon L. "Hosea, Book of." *ABD* 3, 291–297.

———. "Hosea 14:10 and the Foolish People Motif." *CBQ* 44 (1982): 212–224.

Setel, T. Drorah. "Prophets and Pornography: Female Sexual Imagery in Hosea." In *Feminist Interpretation of the Bible,* edited by L. M. Russell, 86–95. Philadelphia: Westminster, 1985.

Sheppard, G. T. "The Last Words of Hosea." *Rev Exp* 90 (1993): 191–204.

Sherwood, Yvonne. *The Prostitute and the Prophets: Hosea's Marriage in Literary - Theoretical Perspective.* JSOTSup 212. Sheffield: Sheffield Academic Press, 1996.

Silva, Charles H. *A Literary Analysis of Hosea.* Ann Arbor: UMI Dissertation Services, 2006.

Silva, Moisés. *Biblical Words and their Meaning: An Introduction to Lexical Semantics.* Rev. and enl. ed. Grand Rapids: Zondervan, 1994.

Simundson, Daniel J. *Hosea, Joel, Amos, Obadiah, Jonah, Micah.* AOTC. Nashville: Abingdon, 2005.

Smith, Gary V. *Hosea, Amos, Micah.* The NIV Application Commentary. Grand Rapids: Zondervan, 2001.

Snaith, Norman H. *The Distinctive Ideas of the Old Testament.* London: Epworth Press, 1944.

Speake, Jennifer, ed. "Social Contract," in *A Dictionary of Philosophy.* London: Pan Books, 1979.

Steinberg, Naomi. *Kinship and Marriage in Genesis: A Household Economic Perspective*. Minneapolis: Fortress Press, 1993.

Stek, John H. "Salvation, Justice and Liberation in the Old Testament." *CTJ* 13 (1978): 133–165.

Stienstra, Nelly. *YHWH is the Husband of his People: Analysis of a Biblical Metaphor with Special Reference to Translation*. Kampen: Kok Pharos, 1993.

Stoebe, H. J. "Die Bedeutung des Wortes ḥäsäd im Alten Testament." *VT* 2 (1952): 244–254.

———. "חסד *ḥesed*, kindness." *TLOT* 2, 449–464.

Strang, Heather and John Braithwaite, ed. *Restorative Justice and Civil Society*. Cambridge: Cambridge University Press, 2001.

Stuart, Douglas. *Hosea–Jonah*. WBC 31. Nashville: Thomas Nelson, 1987.

Swaim, Gerald G. "Hosea the Statesman." In *Biblical and Near Eastern Studies,* edited by Gary A. Tuttle, 177–183. Grand Rapids: Eerdmans Publishing, 1978.

Swartley, Willard M. "The Relation of Justice/righteousness to Shalom/eirēnē." *Ex auditu* 22 (2006): 29–53.

Sweeney, Marvin A. *The Twelve Prophets: Hosea, Joel, Amos, Obadiah, Jonah*. Berit Olam 2. Collegeville: Liturgical Press, 2000.

Tångberg, K. Arvid. "'I am like an evergreen fir, from me comes your fruit': Notes on Meaning and Symbolism in Hosea 14:9b (MT)." *SJOT* 2 (1989): 81–93.

Tadmor, Hayim. "The Campaigns of Sargon II of Assur: A Chronological Historical Study." *JCS* 12 (1958): 22–40.

Tetley, M. Christine. "The Date of Samaria's Fall as a Reason for Rejecting the Hypothesis of Two Conquests." *CBQ* 64 (2002): 59–77.

Thiele, Edwin R. *The Mysterious Numbers of the Hebrew Kings*. Rev. ed. Grand Rapids: Kregel Publications, 1983.

Thomas, P. P. *Jeroboam II the King and Amos the Prophet: Asocial-Scientific Study on the Israelite Society during the 8th Century BCE*. Delhi: ISPCK, 2003.

Thompson, J. A. "Israel's 'Lovers'." *VT* 27 (1977): 475–481.

———. "The Significance of the verb *Love* in the David-Jonathan Narratives in 1 Samuel." *VT* 24 (1974): 334–338.

Törnkvist, Rut. *The Use and Abuse of Female Sexual Imagery in the Book of Hosea: A Feminist Critical Approach to Hos 1–3*. Uppsala Women's Studies A; Women in Religion 7. Uppsala: Uppsala University Library, 1998.

Turner, Claire. "Hosea: More than a Metaphor." *ExpTim* 121 (2010): 601–607.

Tuttle, Gary A., ed. *Biblical and Near Eastern Studies*. Grand Rapids: Eerdmans Publishing, 1978.

Tsukimoto, Akio. "Peace in the Book of Hosea: Hos. 2:20a in the Biblical Context." *AJBI* 30/31 (2004/5): 23–29.

Utzschneider, Helmut. *Hosea Prophet vor dem Ende: Zum Verhältnis von Geschichte und Institution in der alttestamentlichen Prophetie*. OBO 41. Göttingen: Vandenhoeck & Ruprecht, 1980.

Van Hecke, Pierre, ed. *Metaphor in the Hebrew Bible*. BETL 187. Leuven: Leuven University Press, 2005.

Vang, Carsten. "God's Love according to Hosea and Deuteronomy." *TB* 62 (2011): 173–194.

Vaux, Roland de. *Ancient Israel: Its life and Institutions*. Translated by John McHugh. London: Darton, Longman & Todd, 1961.

Vielhauer, Roman. *Das Werden des Buches Hosea: eine redaktionsgeschichtliche Untersuchung*. BZAW 349. Berlin: W. de Gruyter, 2007.

Voinov, Vitaly. "Observations on Old Testament Kinship Relations and Terminology." *BT* 55 (2004): 108–119.

Vollmer, Jochen. *Geschichtliche Rückblicke und Motive in der Prophetie des Amos, Hosea und Jesaja*. BZAW 119. Berlin: Walter de Gruyter, 1971.

Wacker, Marie-Theres. *Figurationen des Weiblichen im Hosea-Buch*. HBS 8. Freiburg: Herder, 1996.

Wadell, Paul J. *Happiness and the Christian Moral Life: An Introduction to Christian Ethics*. New York: Rowman & Littlefield Publishers, 2008.

Walsh, James P.M. *The Mighty from their Thrones: Power in the Biblical Tradition*. Philadelphia: Fortress Press, 1987.

Ward, James M. *Hosea: A Theological Commentary*. New York: Harper and Row, 1966.

Watts, James W. and Paul R. House, eds. *Forming Prophetic Literature: Essays on Isaiah and the Twelve in Honor of J. W. Watts*. JSOTSup 235. Sheffield: Sheffield Academic Press, 1996.

Weems, Renita J. "Gomer: Victim of Violence or Victim of Metaphor." *Semeia* 47 (1989): 87–104.

Weider, A. *Ehemetaphorik in prophetischer Verkündigung: Hos 1–3 und seine Wirkungsgeschichte im Jeremiabuch: Ein Beitrag zum alttestamentlichen Gottes-Bild*. FB 71. Wurzburg, Germany: Echter, 1993.

Weinfeld, Moshe. "כָּבוֹד *kābôd* II." *TDOT* 7, 22–37.

———. "The Covenant of Grant in the Old Testament and in the Ancient Near East." *JAOS* 90 (1970): 184–203.

———. *Social Justice in Ancient Israel and in the Ancient Near East*. Minneapolis: Fortress Press, 1995.

Wendland, Ernst R. *The Discourse Analysis of Hebrew Prophetic Literature: Determining the Larger Textual Units of Hosea and Joel*. MBPS 40. New York: Mellen Biblical Press, 1995.

Wenham, Gordon. "Law and the Legal System in the Old Testament." In *Law, Morality and the Bible: A Symposium,* edited by Bruce Kaye and Gordon Wenham, 24–52. Leicester: Inter-Varsity Press, 1978.

———. "Family in the Pentateuch." In *Family in the Bible,* edited by R. S. Hess and M. D. Carroll R., 17–31. Grand Rapids: Baker Academic, 2003.

Werblowsky, R. J. Zwi. "Judaism, or the Religion of Israel." In *The Concise Encyclopaedia of Living Faiths,* edited by R. C. Zaehner, 3–39. London: Hutchinson, 1971.

Westbrook, Raymond. "Adultery in Ancient Near Eastern Law." *RB* 97 (1990): 542–580.

Westermann, Claus. *Basic Forms of Prophetic Speech*. Translated by Hugh C. White. Philadelphia: Westminster Press, 1967.

———. *Prophetic Oracles of Salvation in the Old Testament*. Edinburgh: T&T Clark, 1991.

Wharton, James A. "Hosea 4:1–3, Exposition." *Int* 32 (1978): 78–83.

White, Ernest. "Biblical Principles for Modern Family Living." *RevExp* 75 (1978): 5–18.

White, R. E. O. "Vengeance." *EDT,* 1241–1242.

Whitelam, Keith W. *The Just King*. Sheffield: JSOT Press, 1979.

Whitt, R. Keith. "Righteousness and Characteristics of Yahweh." *JBPR* 3 (2011): 71–84.

Whitt, William D. "The Jacob Traditions in Hosea and their Relation to Genesis." *ZAW* 103 (1991): 18–43.

Wijngaards, Johannes. "Death and Resurrection in a Covenantal Context (Hos VI 2)." *VT* 17 (1967): 226–239.

Williamson, H. G. M. *He has Shown You What is Good: Old Testament Justice Then and Now*. Cambridge: Lutterworth Press, 2012.

Willi-Plein, Ina. *Vorformen der Schriftexegese innerhalb des Alten Testaments*. New York: Walter de Gruyter, 1971.

Wilson, Lindsay. *Joseph, Wise and Otherwise: The Intersection of Wisdom and Covenant in Genesis 37-50*. PBM. Carlisle: Paternoster Press, 2004.

Wilson, Robert R. "Israel's Judicial System in the Preexilic Period." *JQR* 74 (1983): 229–248.

Wilson, Robert R. "Enforcing the Covenant: The Mechanisms of Judicial authority in Early Israel." In *The Quest for the Kingdom of God*, edited by H. B. Huffmon, et al., 59–75. Winona Lake, Indiana: Eisenbrauns, 1983.

Winter, Urs. *Frau und Göttin: Studien zum weiblichen Gottesbild im Alten Israel und in dessen Umwelt*. 2nd ed. Göttingen: Vandenhoeck & Ruprecht, 1987.

Wolff, Hans W. "'Wissen um Gott' bei Hosea als Urform von Theologie." *EvT* 12 (1953): 533–554.

———. *Hosea*. Translated by Gary Stansell. Hermenia. BKAT 14.1. Neukirchner-Verlag: Neukirchen-Vluyn, 1965. Repr., Philadelphia: Fortress, 1974.

———. *Anthropology of the Old Testament*. London: SCM Press, 1974.

———. "Prophecy from the Eighth through the Fifth Century." *Int* 32 (1978): 17–30.

Woude, A. S. Van der. "Three Classical Prophets: Amos, Hosea and Micah." In *Israel Prophetic Tradition: Essays in Honour of Peter R. Ackroyd*, edited by Richard Coggins et al., 32–57. Cambridge: Cambridge University Press, 1982.

Wright, Christopher J. H. *God's People in God's Land: Family, Land, and Property in the Old Testament*. Grand Rapids: Eerdmans Publishing, 1990.

———. *Old Testament Ethics for the People of God*. Leicester: Inter-Varsity Press, 2004.

Wright, George E. *Biblical Archaeology*. Rev. ed. Philadelphia: Westminster, 1962.

Wyrtzen, David B. "The Theological Center of the Book of Hosea." *BSac* 141 (1984): 315–329.

Würthwein, Ernst. "Der Ursprung der prophetischen Gerichtsrede." *ZTK* 49 (1952): 1–16.

Yee, Gale A. *Composition and Tradition in the Book of Hosea: A Redaction Critical Investigation*. SBLDS 102. Atlanta: Scholars Press, 1987.

———. "Hosea." In *The Women's Bible Commentary*, edited by C. A. Newsom and S. H. Ringe, 195–204. Louisville: John Knox Press, 1992.

———. "The Book of Hosea." In *Introduction to Apocalyptic Literature, Daniel, the Twelve Prophets*, edited by Leander E. Keck, 197–297. 7 vols. The New Interpreter's Bible. Nashville: Abingdon, 1996.

———. *Poor Banished Children of Eve: Woman as Evil in the Hebrew Bible*. Minneapolis: Fortress Press, 2003.

Younger, K. Lawson. "The Fall of Samaria in Light of Recent Research." *CBQ* 61 (1999): 461–482.

Zaehner, R. C., ed. *The Concise Encyclopaedia of Living Faiths*. London: Hutchinson, 1971.

Zajda, Joseph et. al. "Education and Social Justice: Issues of Liberty and Equality in the Global Culture." In *Education and Social Justice*, edited by Joseph Zajda, 1–12. Dordrecht: Springer, 2006.

Zehr, Howard. *Changing Lenses*. 3rd ed. 1990. Repr., Scottsdale: Herald Press, 2005.

———. *The Little Book of Restorative Justice*. Intercourse: Good Books, 2002.

Zimmerli, Walther. "Das Gottesrecht bei den Propheten Amos, Hosea und Jesaja." In *Werden und Wirken des Alten Testaments: Festschrift für Claus Westermann zum 70 Geburtstag,* edited by Rainer Albertz, 216–235. Göttingen: Vandenhoeck & Ruprecht, 1980.

Zobel, H. J. "חֶסֶד ḥeseḏ." *TDOT* 5, 44–64.

———. "עֶלְיוֹן 'elyôn." *TDOT* 11, 121–138.

Zohary, M. *Plants of the Bible*. Cambridge: Cambridge University Press, 1982.

Langham Literature and its imprints are a ministry of Langham Partnership.

Langham Partnership is a global fellowship working in pursuit of the vision God entrusted to its founder John Stott –

> *to facilitate the growth of the church in maturity and Christ-likeness through raising the standards of biblical preaching and teaching.*

Our vision is to see churches in the majority world equipped for mission and growing to maturity in Christ through the ministry of pastors and leaders who believe, teach and live by the Word of God.

Our mission is to strengthen the ministry of the Word of God through:
- nurturing national movements for biblical preaching
- fostering the creation and distribution of evangelical literature
- enhancing evangelical theological education

especially in countries where churches are under-resourced.

Our ministry

Langham Preaching partners with national leaders to nurture indigenous biblical preaching movements for pastors and lay preachers all around the world. With the support of a team of trainers from many countries, a multi-level programme of seminars provides practical training, and is followed by a programme for training local facilitators. Local preachers' groups and national and regional networks ensure continuity and ongoing development, seeking to build vigorous movements committed to Bible exposition.

Langham Literature provides majority world pastors, scholars and seminary libraries with evangelical books and electronic resources through grants, discounts and distribution. The programme also fosters the creation of indigenous evangelical books for pastors in many languages, through training workshops for writers and editors, sponsored writing, translation, strengthening local evangelical publishing houses, and investment in major regional literature projects, such as one volume Bible commentaries like *The Africa Bible Commentary*.

Langham Scholars provides financial support for evangelical doctoral students from the majority world so that, when they return home, they may train pastors and other Christian leaders with sound, biblical and theological teaching. This programme equips those who equip others. Langham Scholars also works in partnership with majority world seminaries in strengthening evangelical theological education. A growing number of Langham Scholars study in high quality doctoral programmes in the majority world itself. As well as teaching the next generation of pastors, graduated Langham Scholars exercise significant influence through their writing and leadership.

To learn more about Langham Partnership and the work we do visit **langham.org**

www.ingramcontent.com/pod-product-compliance
Lightning Source LLC
Chambersburg PA
CBHW052012290426
44112CB00014B/2206